Following the Lamb

Following the Lamb

The Theme of Discipleship in the Book of Revelation

KEITH T. MARRINER

Foreword by David R. Beck

WIPF & STOCK · Eugene, Oregon

FOLLOWING THE LAMB
The Theme of Discipleship in the Book of Revelation

Copyright © 2016 Keith T. Marriner. All rights reserved. Except for brief quotations in critical publications or reviews, no part of this book may be reproduced in any manner without prior written permission from the publisher. Write: Permissions, Wipf and Stock Publishers, 199 W. 8th Ave., Suite 3, Eugene, OR 97401.

Wipf & Stock
An Imprint of Wipf and Stock Publishers
199 W. 8th Ave., Suite 3
Eugene, OR 97401

www.wipfandstock.com

PAPERBACK ISBN 13: 978-1-4982-3739-0
HARDCOVER ISBN 13: 978-1-4982-3741-3

Manufactured in the U.S.A.   01/11/2016

"Unless otherwise indicated, all Scripture quotations are from the ESV® Bible (The Holy Bible, English Standard Version®), copyright © 2001 by Crossway, a publishing ministry of Good News Publishers. Used by permission. All rights reserved."

"Scripture quotations taken from the New American Standard Bible®, Copyright © 1960, 1962, 1963, 1968, 1971, 1972, 1973, 1975, 1977, 1995 by The Lockman Foundation Used by permission." (www.Lockman.org)

Scripture quotations marked (NIV) are taken from the Holy Bible, New International Version®, NIV®. Copyright © 1973, 1978, 1984, 2011 by Biblica, Inc.™ Used by permission of Zondervan. All rights reserved worldwide. www.zondervan.com The "NIV" and "New International Version" are trademarks registered in the United States Patent and Trademark Office by Biblica, Inc.™

For my wife and daughters

Contents

List of Tables | viii
Foreword by David R. Beck | ix
Acknowledgments | xi
Abbreviations | xiii

1 Introduction | 1

2 Discipleship in the Ancient World | 17

3 Literature on Discipleship in the Gospel of John | 47

4 Discipleship in the Book of Revelation | 78

5 Conclusion | 222

Bibliography | 239
Author Index | 253
Scripture Index | 257

Tables

Table 1. Coding frame | 77

Foreword

It is an honor to be invited by Keith Marriner to provide this foreword for the publication of his exegetical analysis of the theme of discipleship in the book of Revelation, *Following the Lamb*. There is no topic more important for biblical research than the question of what it means to be a faithful disciple of Jesus Christ. When first approached by Keith about becoming involved in his research and writing in this area, I was very pleased with his interest to expand the scholarly research into this eminently practical topic by exploring a portion of the New Testament rarely probed for its insights into discipleship. When seeking relevant biblical passages to inform and instruct us in our own discipleship and the discipling of others, the book of Revelation rarely comes to mind. An examination of scholarly publications on the theme of discipleship further illustrates how neglected the final book of the New Testament has been in the discussion of this important topic. In *Following the Lamb*, Keith Marriner has helped to fill this gap in the careful exegetical examination of the biblical teaching on what it means to be a faithful follower of Jesus Christ.

One of the most significant contributions of this work is the development of a coding frame to identify the discipleship theme in Revelation through an analysis of discipleship motifs in the Johannine corpus and in recent Johannine scholarship. Utilizing the methodology of content analysis from social scientific research, Marriner develops a succinct coding frame for the recognition of the discipleship motif in Revelation. For many of us in biblical scholarship, this is a new approach. This work demonstrates the usefulness of this method for identifying the presence of themes not as textually explicit. This method is consistently followed, supported with careful and detailed exegetical research and analysis in the text of Revelation. The exegetical conclusions are cogently and convincingly presented.

Foreword

The resulting synthesis and identification of the discipleship motif in Revelation is sound and helpful.

Marriner's analysis leads to significant insights into what the author of the Apocalypse was communicating to his audience about the nature of faithful discipleship in the context of the persecution they were suffering. As believers today find themselves in greater conflict with the cultures around them, these insights are of inestimable value as the church strives to fulfill Jesus' mandate for us to be salt and light, faithfully following him and faithfully manifesting him in word and deed to a people and a culture to which the biblical revelation of the incarnate "Word made flesh" is increasingly unfamiliar and objectionable.

David R. Beck
Associate Dean of Biblical Studies
Professor of New Testament Greek
Southeastern Baptist Theological Seminary

Acknowledgments

THE ROAD FROM DISSERTATION to book is a long one. It could not have been completed were it not for the help and assistance of several individuals. First of all, there is my lovely wife and best friend, Jennifer. Her love, support, and constant encouragement motivated me to persevere in this study. There are also my two girls, Cora and Eleanor, whose invitations to play with them provided a much-needed respite from the rigors of study. I pray the sacrifice of time away from them has not proved too burdensome. I love you all very much.

To my father and mother I also owe a great deal of gratitude. They not only allowed me to use their home as a hotel when attending seminars in Wake Forest, but they also contributed financial support to me through the entire doctoral program. Words cannot express the heartfelt thanks I have for everything you have done for my family and me.

I also want to thank the Emmanuel College library staff for their diligence in tracking down resources for me. The speed at which they located articles and books enabled me to continue my research with little interruption. Thank you for your behind-the-scenes contribution to scholarship.

No book is complete without the assistance of a good copyeditor. I happen to know one of the best. Thank you Robyn Keeler for your time and skill to improve my sometimes awkward and crude efforts. This book is all the better for your keen eye and helpful suggestions.

There was also a group of individuals with whom I started this journey, my doctoral cohort. In particular, there are four men whom the Lord has used to sharpen my thinking, to be a source of encouragement, and perhaps most importantly, to be examples for me to follow of how one remains faithful to one's family and calling. Aaron, Mitch, Richard, and Steve, thank you, brothers.

Acknowledgments

Of course, I would never even have begun this study were it not for the encouragement of Dr. Ken Coley, the Director of EdD Studies at Southeastern Baptist Theological Seminary (SEBTS). When I approached him with the idea of doing a dissertation on the theme of discipleship in Revelation, he gave me latitude to pursue this topic, even though it is not the typical social science dissertation one finds in the field of education. Thank you for allowing me to pursue this topic and for what you have taught me about being a Christian educator.

Finally, I wish to acknowledge and thank Dr. David R. Beck, Associate Dean of Biblical Studies and Professor of New Testament and Greek at SEBTS. I have found it an honor and privilege to be your first Doctor of Education student. I hope I will not be the last. Thank you for your encouragement to continue in the work, as well as your sharp eye and thoughtful insights that I believe have only strengthened this work.

Abbreviations

Barn.	*Barnabas*
BDAG	Bauer, W., F. W. Danker, W. F. Arndt, and F. W. Gingrich. *Greek-English Lexicon of the New Testament and Other Early Christian Literature.* 3d ed. Chicago, 2000
BEB	*Baker Encyclopedia of the Bible.* Edited by W. A. Elwell. 2 vols. Grand Rapids, 1988
BECNT	Baker Exegetical Commentary on the New Testament
BSac	*Bibliotheca Sacra*
1 Clem.	*1 Clement*
DJG	*Dictionary of Jesus and the Gospels.* Edited by J. B. Green and S. McKnight. Downers Grove, 1992
DPL	*Dictionary of Paul and His Letters.* Edited by G. F. Hawthorne and R. P. Martin. Downers Grove, 1993
EBC	*Expositor's Bible Commentary*
GTJ	*Grace Theological Journal*
HTR	*Harvard Theological Review*
JBL	*Journal of Biblical Literature*
JETS	*Journal of the Evangelical Theological Society*
Jos. Asen.	*Joseph and Aseneth*
JSNT	*Journal for the Study of the New Testament*
JSNTSup	Journal for the Study of the New Testament: Supplement Series

Abbreviations

JSOTSup	Journal for the Study of the Old Testament: Supplement Series
LCL	Loeb Classical Library
LXX	The Septuagint
2 Macc	2 Maccabees
4 Macc	4 Maccabees
Mek. Ex.	*Mekilta Exodus*
NABPRSS	National Association of Baptist Professors of Religion Special Series
NAC	New American Commentary
NIBCNT	New International Biblical Commentary on the New Testament
NICNT	New International Commentary on the New Testament
NIDNTT	*New International Dictionary of New Testament Theology.* Edited by C. Brown. 4 vols. Grand Rapids, 1975–1985
NIDOTTE	*New International Dictionary of Old Testament Theology and Exegesis.* Edited by W. A. VanGemeren. 5 vols. Grand Rapids, 1997
NIGTC	New International Greek Testament Commentary
Pss. Sol.	*Psalms of Solomon*
Sir	Sirach
SNTSMS	Society for New Testament Studies Monograph Series
SPCK	Society for Promoting Christian Knowledge
T. Ash.	*Testament of Asher*
T. Benj.	*Testament of Benjamin*
TDNT	*Theological Dictionary of the New Testament.* Edited by G. Kittel and G. Friedrich. Translated by G. W. Bromiley. 10 vols. Grand Rapids, 1964–1976
TDOT	*Theological Dictionary of the Old Testament.* Edited by G. J. Botterweck and H. Ringgren. Translated by J. T. Willis, G. W. Bromiley, and D. E. Green. 8 vols. Grand Rapids, 1974–2006

ABBREVIATIONS

TLNT	*Theological Lexicon of the New Testament.* C. Spicq. Translated and edited by J. D. Ernest. 3 vols. Peabody, Mass., 1994
TLOT	*Theological Lexicon of the Old Testament.* Edited by E. Jenni, with assistance from C. Westermann. Translated by M. E. Biddle. 3 vols. Peabody, Mass., 1997
T. Mos.	*Testament of Moses*
TWOT	*Theological Wordbook of the Old Testament.* Edited by R. L. Harris, G. L. Archer Jr. 2 vols. Chicago, 1980
WUNT	Wissenschaftliche Untersuchungen zum Neuen Testament

1

Introduction

INTRODUCTION

THERE HAVE BEEN ONLY a handful of general studies on the theme of discipleship in the New Testament (NT), all of which have been written since 1950.[1] Only recently have scholars turned their attention to the motif of discipleship from the perspective of the Gospels.[2] Still, few other NT books have received much consideration regarding the theme of discipleship. Among those neglected NT books is the book of Revelation. Michael J. Wilkins in his biblical theology of discipleship, *Following the Master*, looks at the theme of discipleship in Revelation only tangentially.[3] Is this lack of interest due to the relative exclusion of the theme of discipleship in the Apocalypse? While it is true that the term "disciple" does not occur

---

1. The following are a few of the major studies written since 1950: Schweizer, *Lordship and Discipleship*; Rengstorf, "μαθητής," 415–461; Hengel, *Charismatic Leader*; Calenberg, "New Testament Doctrine of Discipleship"; Segovia, *Discipleship*; Michael J. Wilkins, *Following the Master*; and Longenecker, *Patterns of Discipleship*.

2. The following are some of the major studies from the Gospels: Luz, "Disciples in Matthew," 98–127; Wilkins, *Disciple in Matthew's Gospel*; Donaldson, "Discipleship in Mark," 67–77; Best, *Following Jesus*; Tannehill, "Disciples in Mark," 134–157; Martin, "Salvation and Discipleship," 366–380; Sweetland, *Journey with Jesus*; Longenecker, "Discipleship in Luke-Acts," 50–76; Siker-Gieseler, "Disciples and Discipleship," 199–227; Segovia, "Discipleship in the Fourth Gospel," 77–102; Beck, *Discipleship Paradigm*.

3. Wilkins, *Following the Master*.

outside of the Gospels and Acts, this does not mean the rest of the NT fails to contribute to what it means to be a disciple of Jesus Christ. Paul Helm and others have noted the idea of discipleship is neither "absent [nor] less dominant" outside of the Gospels and Acts.[4] According to Michael Wilkins, this includes the book of Revelation: "The consensus in the history of the church—ancient and modern—is that the concept of discipleship is apparent everywhere in the NT, from Matthew through Revelation."[5] In fact, there have been three brief studies on discipleship in the Apocalypse to date, the authors of which are Elisabeth Schüssler Fiorenza, David E. Aune, and Loren T. Stuckenbruck.[6] Each contribution to the idea of discipleship in Revelation is summarized in the following paragraphs.

Schüssler Fiorenza's essay briefly explores Rev 14:1–5 "to show how the rhetorical language of a text must be explored so that its symbolic-poetic images make 'sense' within its overall context and it has 'meaning' and the power of 'persuasion' in its own particular historical-social situation."[7] She proceeds to argue for Revelation's genre as "poetic language," which opens the text to a broader range of meanings, thus enabling the interpreter "to perceive the strength of the image with all its possible overtones of meaning for the writer as well as for the audience."[8] She goes on to discuss the author's rhetorical strategy of Revelation, which she defines as a "visionary rhetoric" that provides its audience with an "alternate world" in order to encourage believers to persevere in the face of the Domitian persecution of Christians.[9] Next, she describes how this "visionary rhetoric" functions in Rev 14:1–5. She concludes her chapter noting that the message of Revelation continues to resonate only with those Christians who experience a similar "rhetoric situation," namely Christian persecution.[10]

While Schüssler Fiorenza's essay does briefly explore the theme of discipleship in Revelation, it is limited largely to her interpretation of Rev 14:1–5, which is further interpreted in light of Revelation's "visionary rhetoric" and particular "rhetoric situation." This leaves the remainder of

---

4. Helm, "Disciple," 630. See also Luter Jr., "Discipleship," 267.

5. Wilkins, *Following the Master*, 293.

6. Schüssler Fiorenza, "Followers of the Lamb," 144–165; Aune, "Following the Lamb," 269–284; and Stuckenbruck, "Revelation," 1–5.

7. Schüssler Fiorenza, "Followers of the Lamb," 146.

8. Ibid., 149–150.

9. Ibid., 150, 156.

10. Ibid., 161.

Introduction

Revelation to be explored concerning the theme of discipleship. Further, her interpretation seems to limit the efficacy of Revelation to Christians undergoing religious persecution. This conclusion seems a bit too narrow. This argument would be similar to a Pentecostal or charismatic declaring that one must speak in tongues in order to truly identify with the guidelines for the *charisma* in 1 Cor 12–14. Contrary to Schüssler Fiorenza's conclusion, it appears equally as likely that Rev 14:1–5 and the book as a whole are useful to prepare Christians who have as yet not encountered persecution for what it truly means to follow Jesus "wherever he goes" (Rev 14:4).

David E. Aune's essay approaches the theme of discipleship in Revelation (a theme he believes was a central concern for John)[11] by addressing Rev 14:1–5, a group of passages that speak of "victory," and passages that look at having to be obedient to God's commands and "witnessing to the salvific significance of Jesus."[12] Regarding Rev 14:1–5 he notes several characteristics of discipleship, including: (1) Christians who have given their allegiance to God and Christ follow the Lord wherever he goes, which in the book of Revelation often means suffering and death, and (2) believers are those who persevere in remaining faithful to God and the Lamb.[13] Those passages that speak of victory do so paradoxically, for this victory is only won through suffering and death. Jesus' own death that results in victory serves as a paradigm for Christian discipleship.[14] Finally, Christians are those who keep God's commands and who testify to the "salvific significance of Jesus."[15]

While Aune does extend his study of discipleship in Revelation to include more than just an exegesis of Rev 14:1–5, he still does not provide an exhaustive study of the topic, which he admits is not the point of the essay.[16] What he does offer in brief is something of what John thought about discipleship "against the dark background of anti-Christian sentiment in the Roman province of Asia at the end of the first century AD."[17] However, he fails to provide a particular method by which he arrives at what John disclosed regarding discipleship in Revelation.

11. Aune, "Following the Lamb," 270.
12. Ibid., 270–271.
13. Ibid., 275–277.
14. Ibid., 278–279.
15. Ibid., 280–283. Aune believes the commands of God refer to the Decalogue.
16. Ibid., 270.
17. Ibid.

The final study is Loren T. Stuckenbruck's short article. The article is actually divided between the topics of discipleship in Revelation and the historical setting that prompted John to write. Regarding the historical situation, Stuckenbruck concludes that the Christians of first century Asia were not enduring widespread government persecution. Rather, he believes that John wrote to prepare believers for the persecution that was surely to come, since Christians were called to radical discipleship that would eventually lead to a "head-on collision between God's rule and the demonized Roman Empire."[18] Stuckenbruck concludes that Christian discipleship in the Apocalypse "involved living a life that was not only radically holy but also, as in the case of Jesus, was expected to result in death."[19] As with the studies of Schüssler Fiorenza and Aune, Stuckenbruck's study is far too brief and narrow of a focus to be considered a sufficient exploration of the theme of discipleship in Revelation.

DISCIPLESHIP, CHRISTIAN EDUCATION, AND SPIRITUAL FORMATION

Not only has the book of Revelation received little attention with regard to discipleship among biblical scholars, but it is also neglected in the literature of Christian education and spiritual formation. Perhaps, this is because Christian educators generally affirm the assessment of Kenneth O. Gangel, "The last two books of the NT [Jude and Revelation] do not add much to our understanding of educational ministry."[20] While the case was made previously that the book of Revelation does discuss discipleship, Gangel's comment leads one to wonder, "What does discipleship have to do with Christian education or even spiritual formation? Is there a relationship between them? Are they simply synonyms?"

First, it may be helpful to come to some understanding of what Christian education is, that is, how it is defined and what its goals or purposes are, from experts in the field of Christian education. The following three definitions provide an example of how Christian educators define *Christian education*.

---

18. Stuckenbruck, "Revelation," 4.
19. Ibid., 3.
20. Gangel, "What Christian Education Is," 28.

Introduction

1. Robert W. Pazmiño defines *Christian education* as "the process of sharing and gaining distinctives of the Christian story and truth (information) and Christian values, attitudes, and lifestyle (formation), and fostering the change of persons, communities, societies, and structures (transformation) by the power of the Holy Spirit to a fuller expression of God's reign in Jesus Christ."[21]

2. Elsewhere he defines it as "the deliberate, systematic, and sustained divine and human effort to share or appropriate the knowledge, values, attitudes, skills, sensitivities, and behaviors that comprise or are consistent with the Christian faith. It fosters the change, renewal, and reformation of persons, groups, and structures by the power of the Holy Spirit to conform to the revealed will of God as expressed in the Scriptures and preeminently in the person of Jesus Christ, as well as any outcomes of that effort."[22]

3. Werner C. Graendorf defines *Christian education* as "[a] bible-based, Holy Spirit-empowered (Christ-centered), teaching-learning process, that seeks to guide individuals at all levels of growth, through contemporary teaching means, toward knowing and experiencing God's purpose and plan, through Christ in every aspect of living, and to equip them for effective ministry, with the overall focus on Christ the Master Educator's Example and command to make mature disciples."[23]

Some themes common among each definition are: (1) Christian education is a holistic process of learning the Christian faith; (2) the goal is for the disciple of Jesus to mature and be conformed to the image of Christ; and (3) this is a Holy Spirit-empowered process of transformation.

Some of these same themes occur in definitions of *spiritual formation*:

1. *Spiritual formation* is "an intentional, multifaceted process which promotes the transformation by which Christ is formed in us so that we become His continually maturing disciples."[24]

2. "Christian spiritual formation refers to the intentional communal process of growing in our relationship with God and becoming conformed to Christ through the power of the Holy Spirit."[25]

---

21. Pazmiño, *Principles and Practices*, 44.
22. Pazmiño, *Foundational Issues*, 87.
23. Graendorf, "Challenge of Christian Education," 16.
24. Dettoni, "What Is Spiritual Formation?," 16.
25. Wilhoit, *Spiritual Formation*, 23.

3. "[S]piritual formation for the Christian basically refers to the Spirit-driven process of forming the inner world of the human self in such a way that it becomes like the inner being of Christ himself."[26]

Sophia R. G. Steibel has aptly described the similarities between Christian education and Christian spiritual formation. The similarities between the two largely include their goals in the life of the believer and the exploration of common themes. The differences between the two are largely a matter of methodology. Christian education focuses more on "teaching and learning," while spiritual formation relies more on the experiential.[27]

Given the similarities between Christian education and Christian spiritual formation, one is left to wonder if there may also be similarities between these two and discipleship. It may prove advantageous to look at the following definitions of *discipleship*.

1. According to Wilkins, *discipleship* "is the process of becoming like Jesus Christ. To be a disciple of Jesus Christ means living a fully human life in this world in union with Jesus Christ and growing in conformity to his image."[28]

2. Fernando F. Segovia understands *discipleship* in a narrow and a broader sense. Narrowly speaking, discipleship is "to be understood technically and exclusively in terms of the 'teacher/disciple' relationship with all its accompanying and derivative terminology."[29] With reference to its broader sense, discipleship is "[to] be understood more generally in terms of Christian existence—that is, the self-understanding of the early Christian believers as believers: what such a way of life requires, implies, and entails."[30]

3. Upon noting the holistic sense of discipleship, James G. Samra provides the following definition of *discipleship*: "Discipleship involves both becoming a disciple and being a disciple. At times the focus is on the entrance into the process (evangelism), but most often the focus is on growing in the process (maturity); it includes both teaching and life transformation. It is a general call for everyone and also an intense

---

26. Willard, *Renovation of the Heart*, 22.
27. Steibel, "Christian Education and Spiritual Formation," 342.
28. Wilkins, *Following the Master*, 342.
29. Segovia, "Introduction," 2.
30. Ibid.

Introduction

process for a select few. Therefore it is best to think of discipleship as the process of becoming like Christ."[31]

These three definitions repeat some of the same themes found in the definitions of Christian education and spiritual formation: (1) discipleship is a holistic process; (2) this process has as its goal greater conformity into the image of Christ; and (3) it includes a learning relationship, one that includes a teacher and student (disciple).

Several scholars from the disciplines of Christian education, spiritual formation, and biblical studies have recognized these similarities, particularly that discipleship is a holistic educational process. For instance, Gangel recognizes that "discipling becomes the centerpiece of the gospels, providing the link between teaching and learning."[32] Doug C. Bryan likewise recognizes the similar educational emphasis of each discipline: "Whether it is termed discipleship, Christian growth, or sanctification, Christian education/learning is a vital element of Christian growth."[33] In addition, Lucien Coleman notes that discipleship "implies lifelong enrollment in the school of Christian learning, for the essence of discipleship is leanership."[34] Eugene Peterson comes to similar conclusions regarding the educative elements of discipleship, "*Disciple (mathētēs)* says we are people who spend our lives apprenticed to our master, Jesus Christ. We are in a growing-learning relationship, always. A disciple is a learner."[35] Robert G. Hoerber succinctly states that discipleship "involves a process of learning—not merely the acquisition of knowledge, but the surrender of one's person to Christ in faith and service."[36]

All of this should be satisfactory to conclude that discipleship, although not exactly synonymous with either Christian education or Christian spiritual formation, does share a striking affinity with both disciplines, emphasis on the need for a holistic educative process for Christian growth and maturity into the image of Christ.[37]

---

31. Samra, "Biblical View of Discipleship," 220.
32. Gangel, "What Christian Education Is," 20.
33. Bryan, *Relationship Learning*, 13.
34. Coleman, *Why the Church Must Teach*, 30.
35. Peterson, *Long Obedience*, 17.
36. Hoerber, "Mathetes," 181.

37. For others who view discipleship as a holistic educative process see: Harder, "Concept of Discipleship," 347–358; Adams, *How to Change People*, 52–53; Eldridge, "Disciple," 75–88; and Parrett and Kang, *Teaching the Faith*, 259.

Given the brevity of previous studies on the topic of discipleship in Revelation, there is need for an in-depth analysis on the subject, one that should provide fruitful additions to the fields of both biblical and theological studies, as well as Christian education and spiritual formation.

STATEMENT OF THE PROBLEM

The purpose of this analysis is to develop the theme of discipleship in the book of Revelation through biblical and theological analysis. In order to accomplish this purpose, this study will consist of three areas of investigation: (1) an overview of the forms of discipleship in the ancient world, including the NT, (2) current research on the theme of discipleship in the Gospel of John, and (3) investigation of the theme of discipleship in the book of Revelation. The research questions are as follows:

1. What forms of discipleship existed in the ancient world?
2. How is the theme of discipleship developed in the Gospel of John according to current research?
3. How is the theme of discipleship developed in the book of Revelation?

DELIMITATIONS OF THIS STUDY

This study limits "current research" on the theme of discipleship in the NT and the Gospel of John to no earlier than 1950. It is also not in the interest of this study to present a comprehensive argument for one of the five historical approaches to interpreting Revelation (*historicist, preterist, idealist, futurist,* and *eclectic*).[38] Nor is it in the interest of this study to present

---

38. The following is a brief description of each of the five historical approaches to interpreting Revelation:
   1. The *historicist* interpretation views "the events of Revelation as unfolding in the course of history" (Pate, *Four Views,* 17).
   2. The *preterist* interpretation views "the events of Revelation in large part to have been fulfilled in the first centuries of the Christian era" (ibid.).
   3. The *futurist* interpretation proposes, "the events of Revelation are largely fulfilled, holding that chapters 4–22 await the end times for their realization" (ibid.).
   4. The *idealist* interpretation proposes, "Revelation sets forth timeless truths concerning the battle between good and evil that continues throughout the church age" (ibid., 18).
   5. The *eclectic* interpretation proposes the best way to interpret Revelation is to

Introduction

a complete argument for one of the predominant millennial perspectives (*amillennialism, historical/classical premillennialism, dispensational premillennialism,* and *postmillennialism*).[39]

RESEARCH ASSUMPTIONS

This research adopts the traditional belief regarding the authorship of the Apocalypse, that John the son of Zebedee, one of the Twelve, authored Revelation, as well as the Gospel of John and the Letters of John.[40] This is based on the following internal (#1–4) and external evidences (#5):

---

combine the strengths of several views, with the exclusion of the historicist (Osborne, *Revelation*, 21).

39. The following is a brief description of each of the millennial perspectives:

1. *Amillennialism*: According to this position the millennium, rather than being viewed as a literal thousand years that comes at the end of the age, is now present during the church age. Christ's millennial reign takes place now in heaven with the spirits of deceased believers. This position also believes in Christ's bodily return at the end of the age (Grudem, *Systematic Theology*, 1109–1110; Clouse, "Introduction," 9).

2. *Historical/Classical Premillennialism*: According to this position Christ's bodily return will take place prior to a literal thousand-year reign upon the earth. (Some proponents do not affirm a literal thousand-year reign.) It is distinguished from dispensational premillennialism by its single plan of redemption for both Israel and the Church (Grudem, *Systematic Theology*, 1111–1112; Lewis and Demarest, *Integrative Theology*, 377–378).

3. *Dispensational Premillennialism*: According to this position Christ's bodily return will take place prior to a literal thousand-year reign on the earth, and before the great tribulation period, resulting in two comings of Christ. This position also "maintains a clear distinction between the church and Israel." After the rapture of the Church great numbers of Jewish people will come to faith in Jesus, the Messiah. This position also maintains that God's promises to bless Israel that have yet to be fulfilled will one day be realized (Grudem, *Systematic Theology*, 1113–1114).

4. *Postmillennialism*: According to this position "the progress of the gospel and growth of the church will gradually increase ... As a result, there will be significant Christian influences on society, society will more and more function according to God's standards, and gradually a 'millennial age' of peace and righteousness will occur on the earth. This 'millennium' will last for a long period of time (not necessarily a literal one thousand years), and finally, *at the end of this period, Christ will return to earth*" [emphasis original] (ibid., 1111).

40. The author of this study recognizes that other persons have been considered for authorship of Revelation: John Mark, John the elder, John the Baptist and his followers, John the apostle, John as a pseudonym, another John, or Cerinthus (Mounce, *Revelation*,

9

1. The author of Revelation calls himself "John" on four occasions (1:1, 4, 9; 22:8). Since the author did not feel it necessary to provide further clarification as to who he was, it may indicate that he was well known by his audience, and perhaps was John the son of Zebedee who would have been extremely well known, not only by his audience, but also by Christians in general.[41]

2. The author, although referring to himself as a "prophet," "exercised an authority over the Asian churches [to whom the book was originally written] that went beyond that normally associated with NT prophets. This leads to the conclusion that although he wrote as a prophet, he functioned among his churches as an apostle."[42]

3. There is "strong evidence" to suggest that the author of Revelation was: (1) a Palestinian Jew, (2) who was very familiar with the Old Testament (OT), (3) who utilized a literary genre (apocalyptic) that was well known in "Palestinian Judaism," (4) who was acquainted with the temple cult in Jerusalem prior to AD 70, (5) who makes several explicit and implicit references to Jerusalem, (6) who wrote in a Greek style that would have been common for one whose native tongue was either Aramaic or Hebrew, and (7) who may have been among those who fled from Jerusalem following the Jewish revolt of AD 66–73.[43]

4. Critical scholars tend to believe that the linguistic and theological differences are so great between the Gospel of John and Revelation that they could not have been the work of a common author.[44] R. H. Charles has put forth several of these differences: grammatical differences, differences of repeated or emphasized terminology, different word forms to express the same idea, and differences in meaning of

---

10–15; Osborne, *Revelation*, 2).

41. Johnson, "Revelation," 580.

42. Mounce, *Revelation*, 26.

43. Aune, *Revelation 1–5*, l. The author of this research recognizes that Aune does not support the traditional authorship of Revelation. However, he provides evidence that while it may not affirm John the apostle as the book's author, it certainly does affirm that someone with John's background could have been the author.

44. Aune, *Revelation*, liv. Critical scholars in many ways affirm the view of Dionysius, bishop of Alexandria, who was the first to advance the notion that the differences between the Gospel of John, John's Letters, and Revelation were too great for the author who wrote the Gospel and the Letters (John the apostle) to also have written Revelation (Eusebius *Ecclesiastical History* 2.7.25).

Introduction

similar words and phrases.⁴⁵ However, the lack of similarities between the two books does not outright disqualify John the apostle from having written both books. Many of the differences may be attributed to the genres in which the Gospel and Revelation were written.

Although he notes several differences between the two books, Charles readily acknowledges that both the Gospel of John and Revelation are in some ways related to one another.⁴⁶ For instance, both authors attach "spiritual significance" to the terms ζωή ("life"), διψάω ("I thirst"), δόξα ("glory"), ποτίζω ("I drink"), νύξ ("night"), and ὁδηγέω ("I lead/guide"). There are also several terms shared in only the Gospel of John and Revelation, such as λόγος ("word"). The number "seven" occurs more frequently in the Gospel of John and Revelation than any other NT book.⁴⁷ Grant Osborne includes even more similarities.⁴⁸ While these considerations to do not absolutely affirm that John the apostle was the author, neither do they exclude him from consideration either.

5. The testimony of the Early Church widely accepted that John the apostle was the author of the Apocalypse. Osborne⁴⁹ notes several from the first two centuries who affirmed the apostle's authorship, including: Justin Martyr,⁵⁰ Irenaeus,⁵¹ the Muratorian Fragment,⁵² Clement of Alexandria,⁵³ Origen,⁵⁴ and Tertullian.⁵⁵

---

45. Charles, *Revelation*, 1.xxix–xxxii.
46. Ibid., 1.xxxii–xxxiv.
47. Ibid., 1.xxxii–xxxiii. Although he notes similarities between the two works, Charles does not believe John the apostle penned Revelation. Instead, he advances the notion that another John from Ephesus, John the elder, wrote the Apocalypse (ibid., 1.xl–xli, xlix–l).
48. Osborne, *Revelation*, 5.
49. Ibid., 2–3.
50. Justin Martyr *Dialogue* 81.4.
51. Irenaeus *Against Heresies* 4.20.11.
52. Patterson, *Revelation*, 21.
53. Clement of Alexandria *Instructor* 2.108.
54. Origen *De Principiis*. 1.2.10.
55. Tertullian *Against Marcion* 3.14.3.

METHOD

This study employs a qualitative content analysis to examine the theme of discipleship in the Apocalypse. Hesse-Biber and Leavy succinctly define content analysis as "[s]ystematically analyzing texts."[56] The following three definitions are provided as foundational for this researcher's approach to qualitative content analysis:

1. Leedy and Ormrod define content analysis as "a detailed and systematic examination of the contents of a particular body of material for the purpose of identifying patterns, themes, or biases."[57]

2. Margrit Schreier defines content analysis as "a method for describing the meaning of qualitative material in a systematic way. You do this by assigning successive parts of your material to the categories of your coding frame. This frame is at the heart of QCA [qualitative content analysis], and it covers all those meanings that feature in the description and interpretation of your material."[58]

3. Carol Grbich defines content analysis as "a systematic coding and categorising approach which you can use to unobtrusively explore large amounts of textual information in order to ascertain the trends and patterns of words used, their frequency, their relationship and the structures and discourses of communication."[59]

Each of these definitions highlights that content analysis is a systematic method. According to Schreier, central to this systematic methodology is the construction of a coding frame. Once a coding frame with its categories is established, one may proceed to analyze one's textual data in light of said categories.

Content analysis can be either quantitative or qualitative in its approach. In quantitative content analysis an emphasis is placed on recording *manifest content*.[60] Manifest content refers to "those elements that are physically present and countable."[61]

---

56. Hesse-Biber and Leavy, *Practice of Qualitative Research*, 310. Wallen and Fraenkel provided another simple definition of content analysis, "an analysis of the written or visual contents of a document" (*Educational Research*, 408).

57. Leedy and Ormrod, *Practical Research*, 144.

58. Schreier, *Qualitative Content Analysis*, 1.

59. Grbich, *Qualitative Data Analysis*, 112.

60. Schreier, *Qualitative Content Analysis*, 15.

61. Berg, *Qualitative Research Methods*, 242.

Introduction

This is often reduced to simply counting the recurrence of words in a given document. This results in easily quantifiable data, which is why it is a method used in quantitative content analysis. However, this method fails to account for how terms are used in a given context, or genre, or by a particular writer.[62] On the other hand, qualitative content analysis is not only concerned with manifest content, but also and primarily concerned with *latent content*. Latent content refers to looking at a text or other communication medium in order to "[interpret] the presence of a particular theme"[63] that "is not immediately obvious."[64] Besides the analysis of a document to observe repeated words or themes, content analysis may be used to identify syntax and semantics.[65] Thus, content analysis provides a systematic and focused method for various depths of textual analysis.

With regard to the flexibility of disciplines in which content analysis may be applied, Holsti has noted that content analysis "may be useful in various disciplines and for many classes of research problems."[66] Schreier has noted the usefulness of content analysis when applied to material that "requires some degree of interpretation."[67] It seems the application of content analysis to biblical data would be a natural fit.[68] However, such studies have been "relatively rare" in the field until quite recently.[69] Some examples of the use of content analysis in the field of biblical studies include:

---

62. McBurney, *Research Methods*, 227.
63. Ibid.
64. Schreier, *Qualitative Content Analysis*, 15.
65. Baird, "Content Analysis and the Computer," 256; Baird, "Content Analysis," 114. Berg notes, "Seven major elements in written messages [that] can be counted in content analysis: words or terms, themes, characters, paragraphs, items, concepts, and semantics" (*Qualitative Research Methods*, 246).
66. Holsti, *Content Analysis*, 3.
67. Schreier, *Qualitative Content Analysis*, 2.
68. William Paul Griffin gives three ways in which content analysis could be applied to the study of Scripture: (1) "it could illuminate characteristics of any given text, providing a list of what is or is not emphasized by a text"; (2) "it could be accessed by inputting the characteristics in which one is interested; the system would then provide a text or texts which approximate these characteristics"; and (3) "this system could be especially useful for comparing different texts, especially in terms of conceptual similarities and differences" (*God of the Prophets*, 22).
69. Griffin, *God of the Prophets*, 24.

1. Dan Lioy's study provides a content analysis of the Decalogue and the Sermon on the Mount in order to determine various relationships that exist, if any, between the two discourses.[70]
2. James L. Bazar's research utilizes content analysis to analyze the four canonical Gospels for instances of transformational and transactional language to determine to what extent Jesus exhibited either of these leadership styles.[71]
3. Daniel Lee Ray's study provides a content analysis of Jesus' teaching methods as found in the Gospels in order to determine to what extent he applied differentiated instruction.[72]
4. Thomas W. Hudgins's recently published dissertation utilizes content analysis to explore the theme of likeness education in the NT by way of an exegetical analysis of Luke 6:40.[73]

Content analysis methodology varies somewhat depending on the analyst. H. Russell Bernard lists six steps for content analysis: (1) begin with a theory one is interested in testing; (2) create a set of codes; (3) apply the codes to a text; (4) test coder reliability; (5) "creat[e] a unit-of-analysis-by-variable matrix from the texts and codes"; and (6) analyze the matrix.[74] Margrit Schreier provides an eight step process: (1) decide on a research question; (2) select the material to be analyzed; (3) build a coding frame; (4) divide the material into coding units; (5) try out the coding frame; (6) evaluate and modify the coding frame; (7) conduct the main analysis; and (8) interpret and present one's findings.[75] Richard E. Boyatzis offers three succinct steps: (1) elect a sample and design; (2) develop themes and code; and (3) apply the code.[76]

How does one go about finding coding themes with which to conduct a content analysis? Berg notes that categories for content analysis may be inductive, deductive, or both. The inductive method "begins with the researcher 'immersing' themselves in the documents . . . in order to identify the dimensions or *themes* that seem meaningful to the producers of each

---

70. Loiy, *Decalogue*.
71. Bazar, "Leadership within the Gospels."
72. Ray, "Jesus' Teaching Methods."
73. Hudgins, *Likeness Education*.
74. Bernard, *Research Methods*, 507.
75. Scheier, *Qualitative Content Analysis*, 6.
76. Boyatzis, *Transforming Qualitative Information*, 29.

Introduction

message" (emphasis original).[77] In a deductive approach "researchers use some categorical scheme suggested by a theoretical perspective, and the documents provide a means for assessing the hypothesis."[78] It is also possible to utilize a combination of the inductive and deductive approaches. This study utilizes a combination of both approaches.

The research proceeds as follows. Chapter two will provide an overview of the forms of discipleship in the ancient world, including the NT. This stage should answer the question, "What forms of discipleship existed in the ancient world?" This content may be utilized for comparative purposes.

Chapter three will provide a review and analysis of current literature on the theme of discipleship in the Gospel of John. This stage should answer the question, "How is the theme of discipleship developed in the Gospel of John according to current research?" Included in this chapter will be the development of a coding frame from the analysis of the theme of discipleship in the Gospel of John. An inductive method will be utilized to ascertain themes to be used in the development of a coding frame.[79]

Chapter four will be the application of the coding frame to the book of Revelation.[80] This is necessary because the book of Revelation lacks the traditional language of discipleship found in the Gospels and Acts. As noted previously, this, however, does not negate the presence of this topic in the rest of the NT corpus, which includes Revelation. This stage should answer the question, "How is the theme of discipleship developed in the book of Revelation?" In this case, a deductive method, one that utilizes previous research (the coding frame developed from studies of discipleship in the

---

77. Berg, *Qualitative Research Methods*, 245. See also Bernard, *Research Methods*, 493.

78. Berg, *Qualitative Research Methods*, 245–246. For more on the use of standard categories see Holsti, *Content Analysis*, 101–104.

79. Coffey and Atkinson define *coding* as "condensing the bulk of [one's] data sets into analyzable units by creating categories with and from [one's] data" (*Qualitative Data*, 26). Holsti offers another definition of coding, "the process whereby raw data are systematically transformed and aggregated into units which permit precise description of relevant content characteristics" (*Content Analysis*, 94).

80. With regard to data-driven [inductive] content analysis, Schreier notes, "it is usually *best* to build your coding frame using the same material that you want to analyse [sic.]" [emphasis added] (*Qualitative Content Analysis*, 91). While it is best, it is not entirely necessary. The reason for developing a coding frame from the Gospel of John to be applied to Revelation is primarily because of their shared authorship (see "Assumptions"). See also Wilkins, *Following the Master*, 294, 301–302.

Gospel of John), is used to analyze the Apocalypse for discipleship terminology and themes. This stage includes exegesis of the text of Revelation.

Chapter five will be a summary of the researcher's findings. The research concludes with some recommendations for future research.

2

Discipleship in the Ancient World

INTRODUCTION

The theme of discipleship has received little attention when considering the NT as a whole. All of the major works on the subject have been written since 1950. From the late 1960s to the present day, scholarly attention on discipleship shifted to the individual authors of the NT. This shift began with the Synoptic Gospels, and studies have continued to be focused largely on the Gospels and Acts.[1] The following survey addresses the topic of discipleship in the ancient world, including the NT (apart from the Gospel of John and Revelation).[2] The chapter charts the following order: (1) the historical background to NT discipleship, (2) the OT background to NT discipleship, and (3) the general characteristics of NT discipleship. The purpose of this chapter is to answer the question, "What forms of discipleship existed in the ancient world?"

---

1. Few studies have been undertaken on discipleship outside of the Gospels and Acts. Some of these can be found in Segovia, *Discipleship* and Longenecker, *Patterns of Discipleship*.

2. Johannine discipleship will be considered in chapter 3, per the outline provided at the conclusion of chapter 1. The pertinent literature on the theme of discipleship in the book of Revelation has already been reviewed in the introductory section of chapter 1. Chapter 4 is an analysis of the theme of discipleship in Revelation.

Following the Lamb

HISTORICAL BACKGROUND TO NEW TESTAMENT DISCIPLESHIP

This section is separated into two distinct units. The first section addresses the use of discipleship in the ancient Greco-Roman world largely through the use of its terminology, beginning with the term μαθητής ("disciple"). Finally, discipleship in Judaism is explored through its terminology, as well as certain relationships in the world of Judaism.

The Concept of Discipleship in the Greco-Roman World

The earliest use of μαθητής in the context of one who seeks to learn something is found in the work of the historian Herodotus.[3] The usage of the term μαθητής ("disciple") early on referred to someone who was an "apprentice" or "learner."[4] Eventually the term "disciple" came to be used as something of a technical term with reference to the "'institutional pupil' of the Sophists."[5] It would later be used in a "technical sense to refer to an 'adherent' of a great teacher, teaching, or master."[6] For there to be a "disciple" there must also be a "teacher" (διδάσκαλος).[7]

There were several master-disciple relationships in antiquity. One of some significance was the disciples of the Sophists. The Sophists' academic relationship raised the ire of Socrates and those who followed him (Plato, Xenophon, and Aristotle).[8] Rengstorf notes the difference between the Sophists and Socrates in this type of relationship. While the Sophists' relationship with their "pupils" was more or less based on a transaction, Socrates charged no fee for his services, but instead invited his students to

---

3. Herodotus *Histories* 4.77.1. Cf. Rengstorf, "μαθητής," 416.

4. Wilkins, *Following the Master*, 72. Cf. Rengstorf, "μαθητής," 416. Plato uses the term in this way with reference to one learning to play the flute (*Meno* 90.E). Physicians are also referred to as an "apprentice" (Plato *Republic* X.599.c).

5. Wilkins, *Disciple in Matthew's Gospel*, 41. Plato speaks of a disciple of Protagoras who "is taking the course professionally with a view to becoming a sophist" (*Protagoras* 315.A).

6. Wilkins, *Disciple in Matthew's Gospel*, 41. For instance, Euripides was highly esteemed because he was a disciple of Anaxagras (Diodorus Siculus *Library of History* 1.7.7; 1.38.4).

7. Rengstorf, "μαθητής," 416. So also Wilkins, *Disciple in Matthew's Gospel*, 41; Longenecker, "Introduction," 2–3. See also "μαθητής," BDAG, 609.

8. Wilkins, *Following the Master*, 74.

enter into a relationship with him.⁹ Socrates's relationship with his students was more of a mutual exploration of the truth, as opposed to Sophists, who were more formal educators.¹⁰ This may have been why Socrates so infrequently referred to his students as μαθηταί or to himself as a διδάσκαλος.¹¹

An additional form of the master-disciple relationship was the one found in the mystery religions. Here the disciple seeks to become a member of the society that has formed itself around a particular god. The master is necessary for this. The disciple follows the master until the goal of initiation has been achieved. Like the Sophists, this was an impersonal relationship.¹²

The death of one's teacher did not appear to completely sever the master-disciple relationship. After the death of their teacher the disciples continued to extol their teaching. In some cases the death of the teacher served to strengthen the resolve of the disciples to propagate their instruction. This desire to see their master's teaching live on led to the formation of communities of disciples for that expressed purpose.¹³

By the time of the late Hellenistic period, μαθητής continued to be used with reference to "learners" and "adherents." By the third century AD the term was used almost exclusively to refer to an "adherent" of a great teacher, one to whose teaching, and also to whose conduct, the disciple sought to adhere.¹⁴ The focus of the term on an "adherent" would make

---

9. Rengstorf, "μαθητής," 420.

10. Wilkins, *Following the Master*, 74.

11. Plato strongly opposed being grouped with the Sophists. For instance in *Apology* 33.A–33.B he stated, "But you will find that through all my life, both in public, if I engaged in any public activity, and in private, I have always been the same as now, and have never yielded to any one wrongly, whether it were any other person or any of those who are said by my traducers to be my pupils. But I was never any one's teacher. If any one, whether young or old, wishes to hear me speaking and pursuing my mission, I have never objected, nor do I converse only when I am paid and not otherwise, but I offer myself alike to rich and poor; I ask questions, and whoever wishes may answer and hear what I say." Cf. Rengstorf, "μαθητής," 418. Although Socrates and Plato rarely used the term μαθητής, they did use it when there was no danger of misinterpreting it with the Sophists' usage (Wilkins, *Disciple in Matthew's Gospel*, 42). For instance, Socrates used μαθητής with reference to "learners" (Plato *Republic* X.618.c), "disciples" (Plato *Symposium* 197.A), and "pupils" (Plato *Cratylus* 428.B).

12. Rengstorf, "μαθητής," 421.

13. Ibid., 423–424.

14. See Dio Chrysostom *Homer* 11.7.

an easy transition into the early church, where the focus was on being an "adherent" to a great master, namely, Christ.[15]

In addition to μαθητής, the verb μανθάνω is used in educational context, which included master-disciple relationships.[16] A student is one who learns, which is the common usage of the term μανθάνω ("I learn").[17] It is used with reference to the acquisition of knowledge, whether through the medium of teaching or an experience.[18] This knowledge may be "theoretical knowledge," that is, that which is unknown and speculative in nature.[19] The term was used in this way from the time of Socrates moving forward.[20]

Another term the Greeks used that carried religious or philosophical connotations, although with far less frequency than μαθητής, was ἀκολουθέω ("I follow"). The term may be used in either a literal or a figurative fashion, the latter referring to one who follows a teacher as a disciple.[21] In religious and philosophical use it may be used with God as the object one follows. The term more commonly used in antiquity is ἕπω (hepō), which is not found in the NT. In rare instances it means something akin to "becoming like God by acting as He does."[22] This comports with the Stoics' usage of the term, which suggested that one's goal for following a deity was to be incorporated into it.[23]

One additional term that could be used with reference to discipleship was μιμέομαι. The term is usually translated something like "imitate, emulate, follow."[24] When used, its context was the arts, education, and the

---

15. Wilkins, *Disciple in Matthew's Gospel*, 42.

16. In Plato *Euthydemus* 276.A one finds a close association between the terms μαθητής and μανθάνω. "Then Euthydemus asked: And are there persons whom you call teachers, or not? He agreed that there were. And the teachers of the learners [μανθανόντων] are teachers in the same way as your lute-master and your writing-master, I suppose, were teachers of you and the other boys, while you were pupils [μαθηταί]? He assented. Now, of course, when you were learning [ἐμανθάνετε], you did not yet know the things you were learning [ἐμανθάνετε]?"

17. "μανθάνω," BDAG, 615.

18. Müller, "μαθητής," 483.

19. Ibid.

20. Rengstorf, "μαθητής," 396.

21. See "ἀκολουθέω," BDAG, 36–37.

22. Kittel, "ἀκολουθέω," 210. One is able to become like God because all human beings come from him and "by means of reason conjoined with him" (Epictetus *Discourses* 1.9).

23. Blendinger, "ἀκολουθέω," 481.

24. "μιμέομαι," BDAG, 651.

family.²⁵ The term is often used in a negative sense in Greek usage, although not always. When it was used in a negative sense, the word referred "to quasi-dramatic 'aping' or [a] feeble copying with lack of originality."²⁶ It was also used with reference to Platonic cosmology.²⁷ In this instance, the visible world was viewed as the copy (μίμησις) of the "invisible archetype in the higher world."²⁸ Those philosophers who would give themselves to think of this ideal, higher world were said "to imitate God." The aim of the person in this case was to move "toward unity" with God.²⁹ Eventually the idea of imitating God would cross over into the ethical arena.³⁰

Whether the term "imitate" was actually used, the idea was reflected in the Greco-Roman culture. Students were encouraged to choose a teacher whose life they could see and imitate.³¹ For instance the Roman philosopher, Seneca, offers these words of advice to a potential disciple: "Choose a master whose life, conversation, and soul-expressing face have satisfied you; picture him always to yourself as your protector and pattern. For we must indeed have someone according to whom we may regulate our character."³² What Seneca expressed was the relational element of the discipleship relationship. The depth of the relationship was to be characterized by intimacy. Rengstorf recognizes this development in the Greco-Roman discipleship culture:

> The significant thing here is the way in which μαθητής is expounded in terms of μιμεῖσθαι. The center of gravity of μαθητὴν εἶναι is thus removed from the formal side of the relation between μαθητής and διδάσκαλος to the inner fellowship between the two and its practical effects, and this to such a degree that the latter is basic to the whole relationship. This is not without considerable

---

25. Michaelis, "μιμέομαι, μιμητής, κτλ.," 660–661. Euripedes speaks of the good in children imitating just parents (*Helen* 940). Xenophon speaks of how teachers attempt to make their students "copy" (imitate) their example (*Memorabilia* I.6.3).

26. Bauder, "μιμέομαι," 490.

27. Ibid., 491.

28. Ibid.

29. Morrison, *Mimetic Tradition*, 28–29.

30. Michaelis, "μιμέομαι, μιμητής, κτλ.," 662; Bauder, "μιμέομαι," 491. Plato states that to become like God is to take on his character, which he identifies as "righteous and holy and wise" (*Theaetetus* 176.B).

31. Calenberg, "New Testament Doctrine of Discipleship," 26–27.

32. Seneca *Epistles* 11.9–10.

significance in relation to the development of the Christian use of μαθητής.³³

Summary

The concept of discipleship in the Greco-Roman world is seen through the usage of its relevant terminology. The term μαθητής, which basically meant "learner," began to be used as a technical term for one who learned from a great master or teacher. What was actually learned (μανθάνω) varied depending on the teacher. The relationships that developed were initially more formal in nature, although in time became more informal, so that the student shared in the life of the master. In some cases, the passing of a great master meant the preservation and continuation of his teaching. Those who continued to study and appropriate his instruction would be considered his disciples. The idea of following (ἀκολουθέω, ἕπω) a teacher also figures prominently in Greek thought. The idea was that one not only literally followed one's teacher, but also figuratively followed his teaching and way of life (μιμέομαι).

The Concept of Discipleship in Judaism

What terminology existed that described the concept of discipleship in Judaism?³⁴ One term that proves prominent in this discussion is תַּלְמִיד (talmîdh). This term is similar to the Greek term μαθητής.³⁵ Rengstorf states, תַּלְמִיד "is used exclusively for the one who gives himself (as a learner) to Scripture and to the religious tradition of Judaism."³⁶ The role of teacher and learner was reserved only for men.³⁷ This learner was not alone in his quest for knowledge of the scriptures. He was to attach himself to a great teacher who determined what was to be learned.³⁸ One must have a rabbi

---

33. Rengstorf, "μαθητής," 417.

34. The emphasis here is on the time often referred to as second temple Judaism, although some mention is made to the Intertestamental Period.

35. Wilkins notes that both "μαθητής and תַּלְמִיד appear to be equivalent terms" (*Disciple in Matthew's Gospel*, 125). Cf. Rengstorf, "μαθητής," 442.

36. Rengstorf, "μαθητής," 431–432.

37. Ibid., 4.433.

38. Müller, "μαθητής," 485.

(i.e., teacher) if one was to be a תַּלְמִיד (i.e., student).³⁹ The student learned from his teacher by listening to his instruction and "appropriating what [was] heard."⁴⁰ The student would actually attach himself to a teacher and follow him "everywhere" he went, "learning from him and above all serving him."⁴¹ The method of instruction was lecture with the opportunity for questioning that led to open discussion, which included other students.⁴² The goal of the student was to become a teacher himself, so that he might garner the authority to teach his own students.⁴³ It was not until its use in the rabbinic literature that תַּלְמִיד began to take on the special meaning of one who studied Torah, both the written and the oral Torah. The oral and written Torah was the vehicle through which one followed the Lord.⁴⁴ This led to the view that Moses was the "absolute teacher."⁴⁵

Eventually schools formed around a rabbi. The two great rabbinical schools were Hillel and Shammai. Hillel's school had the greater impact of the two in terms of adherents and influence. The student followed the rabbi so closely that he would become a "representative of the tradition established by the rabbi."⁴⁶ This was true of disciples who studied *with* a particular rabbi and of those who studied *under the tradition* of a particular rabbi. Thus, one could study the tradition of a deceased rabbi under the instruction of a living rabbi and still be called a disciple of the deceased rabbi.⁴⁷ Rengstorf believes this pattern owes its genesis to Greek influences, rather than the OT, and provides several lines of evidence in its defense.⁴⁸ For instance, he notes their "lionizing of Moses," as well as the student-teacher relationship, which he believes was devoid in the OT.⁴⁹ He concludes "the

---

39. Rengstorf, "μαθητής," 434–435.
40. Ibid., 435.
41. Blendinger, "ἀκολουθέω," 481.
42. Ibid.
43. Müller, "μαθητής," 486.
44. Wilkins, *Disciple in Matthew's Gospel*, 125.
45. Rengstorf, "μαθητής," 437. Cf. Seift, *Education in Ancient Israel*, 100–101.
46. Rengstorf, "μαθητής," 436.
47. Ibid.
48. Ibid., 438–439.
49. Ibid., 438. Wilkins outright opposes Rengstorf on this latter point (*Disciple in Matthew's Gospel*, 218). With regard to the "lionizing of Moses" see, Sir 45:1. With regard to the student-teacher relationship, in particular, the custom of some rabbis to take fees, see Strack and Billerbeck, *Talmud and Midrash*, I.863.

[תַּלְמִיד] as such came into Judaism from the educative process of the Greek and Hellenistic philosophical schools."⁵⁰

While one might choose to follow a rabbi, one typically did not speak of following (ἀκολουθέω) God, since he could not be seen. Rather, one could and should "follow the qualities of God," that is, live consistent to his revealed character and actions.⁵¹ The rabbis believed this was possible by imitating (μιμέομαι) God "in the sense of developing the image of God" in people.⁵² This went a step further in the Pseudepigrapha that encouraged people to not only imitate God, but also to imitate persons of "outstanding character."⁵³ Philo also spoke of imitating righteous persons, either living or dead. He also called for the imitation of God, but tempered this, noting this exercise had its limitations. The thought of imitating God is altogether absent in the writings of Josephus.⁵⁴

---

50. Rengstorf, "μαθητής," 439.

51. Kittel, "ἀκολουθέω," 212. As God is gracious and merciful, so also should be his people Israel. This comes through imitating God's character (*Mek. Ex.* 15:2). See also *Soṭah*, 14a which, states, "What means the text: Ye shall walk after the Lord your God? Is it, then, possible for a human being to walk after the *Shechinah*; for has it not been said: For the Lord thy God is a devouring fire? But [the meaning is] to walk after the *attributes of the Holy One*, blessed be He. As He clothes the naked, for it is written: And the Lord God made for Adam and for his wife coats of skin, and clothed them, so do thou also clothe the naked. The Holy One, blessed be He, visited the sick, for it is written: And the Lord appeared unto him by the oaks of Mamre, so do thou also visit the sick. The Holy One, blessed be He, comforted mourners, for it is written: And it came to pass after the death of Abraham, that God blessed Isaac his son, so do thou also comfort mourners. The Holy one, blessed be He, buried the dead, for it is written: And He buried him in the valley, so do thou also bury the dead" (emphasis added).

However, some aspects of God's character were not to be imitated, including jealousy and anger (Cohen, *Everyman's Talmud*, 211-212).

52. Bauder, "μιμέομαι," 491.

53. Ibid. Cf. Michaelis, "μιμέομαι, μιμητής, κτλ.," 664. For example see 4 Macc 9:23, "'Imitate me, brothers,' he said. 'Do not leave your post in my struggle or renounce our courageous family ties.'" The idea of imitation occurs in other pseudepigraphical works. With regard to the imitation of good men, see *T. Benj.* 3:1; 4:1. With regard to the imitation of God see *T. Ash.* 4:3-4. The concept of imitation may also be found in the Jewish apocryphal work 2 Macc 6:27-28, "'Therefore, by bravely giving up my life now, I will show myself worthy of my old age and leave to the young a noble example of how to die a good death willingly and nobly for the revered and holy laws.' When he had said this, he went at once to the rack."

54. Michaelis, "μιμέομαι, μιμητής, κτλ.," 665-666. Philo refers to the imitation of physicians (*Sacrifices* 123), or Moses (*Moses* 158), and of fathers (*Sacrifices* 68).

Discipleship in the Ancient World

Summary

During the time of second temple Judaism rabbinical schools began to be developed. These were at first more informal, but eventually took a more recognized shape around the two great rabbinical schools of Hillel and Shammai. These schools were led by men who taught male students the Torah, both the oral and written Torah. A Rabbi did not so much gather disciples, as did disciples flock to them. A student chose his master. The rabbi taught his students not only by the words he spoke, but also by his example. The goal for the student was to become a master of the Torah, so that one could then teach one's own disciples. Although certainty is not possible, it is believed that the Greek model of discipleship played an influential role in the development of the concept of discipleship in Judaism.

While one might choose to follow a great teacher, one did not typically speak of following God, since unlike the teacher, he did not possess a physical body, and thus, could not be seen. However, in time, some of the religious writings of Judaism began to incorporate some aspect of people imitating God. The purpose was generally to aid in the development of the *imago Dei* in the individual.

OLD TESTAMENT BACKGROUND TO NEW TESTAMENT DISCIPLESHIP

This section concerns the possible OT historical background to NT discipleship. To do so, this section covers terminology usually associated with discipleship in the OT and with OT examples that appear to inform the later NT concept of discipleship.

Relevant Discipleship Terminology in the Old Testament

The apparent paucity of linguistic evidence for discipleship in the OT has led some scholars to conclude, chiefly Rengstorf, that it is completely absent in the OT.[55] Rengstorf notes that the term μαθητής does not appear in the

---

[55] "If the term is missing, so, too, is that which it serves to denote. Apart from the formal relation of teacher and pupil, the OT, unlike the classical Greek world and Hellenism, has no master-disciple relation. Whether among the prophets or the scribes we seek in vain for anything corresponding to it" (Rengstorf, "μαθητής," 427. Cf. Müller, "μαθητής," 485; Jenni, "למד," 648).

"established LXX tradition."⁵⁶ Furthermore, the term's Hebrew equivalent, תַּלְמִיד, occurs only once in the Hebrew Bible (1 Chr 25:8). Rengstorf believes the reason for the disuse of such terms is in part a matter of the Old Testament's emphasis on the community, rather than the individual.⁵⁷

Wilkins counters this conclusion, noting the master-disciple relationship is evidenced in the few uses of the OT terms תַּלְמִיד and לָמַד (*limmûdh*).⁵⁸ תַּלְמִיד is used of a pupil,⁵⁹ and of the disciple of a rabbi in rabbinical times.⁶⁰ לָמַד (*lāmad*, "to learn") carries the "idea of training as well as educating" (Hos 10:1; Deut 5:1; 2 Chr 17:7, 9).⁶¹ It is used with reference to observing the law, as well as for training animals (Hos 10:1; Judg 3:31) and military personnel (1 Chr 5:18; Isa 2:4; Mic 4:3), and "teaching and rehearsing songs" (Ps 60).⁶² לָמַד is a term that may be used of disciples of the Lord or of a human master.⁶³ Concerning the usage of both תַּלְמִיד and לָמַד Wilkins concludes, "Although the occurrences of these terms are scarce, they indicate that established master-disciple relationships are at least to be found among the musicians and writing prophets. The casual way in which the terms are used indicate an even broader usage behind these examples."⁶⁴

Of particular interest is the occurrence of לִמּוּדִם (*limmûdîm*) in Isa 8:16, "Bind up the testimony; seal the teaching among *my disciples*" (emphasis added). Israel W. Slotki believes the לִמּוּדִם are disciples of Isaiah who were instructed by him in the Torah.⁶⁵ Edward Young notes that the disciples in question are first and foremost God's disciples and Isaiah's in a secondary sense.⁶⁶ However, God uses means, Isaiah in this case, to medi-

---

56. Rengstorf, "μαθητής," 426.

57. Ibid., 427.

58. Wilkins, *Disciple in Matthew's Gospel*, 89–90. Calenberg adds that Rengstorf fails to acknowledge the usage of לָמַד, which would appear to "negate his conclusions" ("New Testament Doctrine of Discipleship," 42).

59. Merrill believes the proper translation of תַּלְמִיד in 1 Chr 25:8 is "pupil" based on its occurrence with מֵבִין (*mēbîn*, "teacher"), and its Aramaic cognate תַּלְמִידָא (*talmîda*) ("למד," 803).

60. Kaiser, "לָמַד," 480.

61. Ibid.

62. Jenni, "למד," 646–647.

63. Wilkins, *Disciple in Matthew's Gospel*, 89–90.

64. Ibid., 90.

65. Slotki, *Isaiah*, 41.

66. Kapelrud notes that the OT describes God as "the ultimate teacher" (לָמַד, 9). Cf. Merrill, "למד," 2.802. See also 2 Sam 22:35; Job 21:22; and Jer 32:33.

Discipleship in the Ancient World

ate his message and to teach it to his disciples. He concludes that one may, therefore, refer to them as disciples of Isaiah.[67]

An additional term that seems to be related to the concept of discipleship is הָלַךְ (hālakh), which occurs 1,547 times in the Hebrew OT.[68] The term is used either literally or figuratively. When used literally it expresses "the capacity for self-locomotion" (Gen 12:4; 13:5; 14:24; 33:12; Exod 14:29; Josh 14:10; 24:3; Judg 11:16, 18).[69] It may also be used metaphorically as a reference to one's life journey (Josh 8:35; 1 Sam 12:2),[70] the end of one's journey, meaning death (Gen 15:2; Josh 23:14),[71] or even following after a teacher. It is also used figuratively with relation to one's covenant relationship with God (Deut 26:17; 28:9; Josh 22:5).[72] Often, apostasy is referred to as going after or following false gods (Exod 32:1; Jer 5:23).[73] This usage is far more frequent than the handful of references to following God in covenant faithfulness. Sauer conjectures that "pagan cultic processions" may have been the reason for the largely one-sided usage of the expression.[74]

Summary

While linguistic evidence for the concept of discipleship is limited in the OT, it is not entirely absent. When it does occur, it appears to be used in a master-disciple relationship. Teaching the Torah and training persons to follow God's instructions were certainly important concepts in the OT, and these come through in the case of לָמַד. In addition, there appears to be sufficient evidence to conclude that Isa 8:16, a key text when determining the validity of discipleship in the OT, does in fact refer to the prophet Isaiah having a number of disciples. However, it must be recognized that these disciples are his only in a secondary sense, for the Lord God is one's teacher first and foremost.

---

67. Young, *Book of Isaiah*, 314. On the teaching function of prophets see Seift, *Education in Ancient Israel*, 37.
68. Sauer, "הלך," 366.
69. Ibid., 367. Cf. Helfmeyer, "הָלַךְ," 390–391; Coppes, "הָלַךְ," 216.
70. Helfmeyer, "הָלַךְ," 391–392.
71. Sauer, "הלך," 368.
72. Merrill, "הלך," 1033.
73. Sauer, "הלך," 369; Helfmeyer, "הָלַךְ," 395; Coppes, "הָלַךְ," 216.
74. Sauer, "הלך," 369.

Old Testament Examples of Discipleship

Were there any examples of the kind of relationship that might be identified with discipleship in the OT besides the one mentioned in Isa. 8:16? According to Rengstorf the answer must certainly be no. He notes that the relationship between Moses and Joshua, Elijah and Elisha, the prophets and their attendants, and Jeremiah and Baruch were not teacher-disciple relationships as is sometimes thought. Rather, Joshua, Elisha, Baruch, and others who followed the prophets were "servants" of those with whom they had a relationship.[75] In the end, Rengstorf reasons that the teacher-disciple relationship was absent in the OT because there was only one who was to be revered and whose word was to be followed, the Lord himself. The prophets spoke on God's behalf. Those to whom they spoke were God's people. God's word was not bound to only one prophet; rather, it was "continuous and dynamic."[76] Thus, there was no room for the kind of teacher-disciple relationship found among the Greeks, in which the human master's words were venerated, preserved, and transmitted to the next generation.[77]

On the other hand, there are those who argue contrary to Rengstorf's conclusion regarding the presence of examples of discipleship in the OT. Martin Hengel was one of the first to affirm the existence of discipleship relationships in the OT. Hengel notes how Josephus describes Elisha as a disciple of Elijah.[78] Josephus actually used the Greek word μαθητής.[79] In addition, Hengel sees the Elisha/Elijah call narrative as a clear analogy to Jesus' own calling of his disciples.[80] He further notes that Elijah and Elisha "are frequently used among the rabbis to exemplify the teacher-pupil relationship."[81]

Following Hengel is Richard Calenberg, who believed there were several OT pairs that provided evidence of a pattern of discipleship akin to the

---

75. Rengstorf, "μαθητής," 427–430.

76. Ibid., 431.

77. Ibid.

78. Martin Hengel, *Nachfolge und Charisma*. English translation: *Charismatic Leader*, 16. All references are to the English translation.

79. Josephus *Jewish Antiquities* 8.354, "he [Elisha] parted from them [his parents] and then went with the prophet [Elijah]; and so long as Elijah was alive he [Elisha] was his *disciple* and attendant" (emphasis added). The occurrence of μαθητής is absent in the LXX of 1 Kgs 19:21.

80. Hengel, *Charismatic Leader*, 16–17.

81. Ibid., 17.

Greeks and the rabbinical schools of Judaism.[82] In particular, he viewed the relationship between Elisha and Elijah as the definite master-disciple model in the OT.[83] This is due in part to the language used to describe Elisha following after Elijah. The Hebrew phrase includes the verb הָלַךְ, which may be used with reference to following after a teacher (cf. 1 Kgs 19:21).[84] Michael Wilkins comes to similar conclusions, noting the OT possesses examples of master-disciple relationships among the prophets (e.g., Samuel and Elisha), the scribal guild, and in the wisdom tradition.[85] His conclusion provides a corrective to Rengstorf, who believes the exclusion or limited occurrences of "disciple" terminology means the concept of discipleship did not exist in the OT.[86]

Summary

As noted in the previous section, there is one ultimate teacher in Israel, and all are his disciples. That being said, there does appear to be strong evidence for the existence of disciple-teacher relationships of a secondary nature in the OT. The God of Israel used human means to instruct and lead his people. He called and commissioned men to lead the nation (i.e., Moses) and to speak his word to them (i.e., Elijah). In order to perpetuate the continuation of these ministries, it was necessary to enlist others and prepare them to carry on the work in the absence of the current leader. Discipleship was the process by which this reality was realized.

---

82. Calenberg, "New Testament Doctrine of Discipleship," 51–63.
83. Ibid., 60.
84. Ibid., 50. Cf. Sauer, "הלך," 368, 370.
85. Wilkins, *Disciple in Matthew's Gospel*, 90–91.
86. Ibid., 218. Elsewhere Wilkins highlights the Old Testament's understanding of discipleship as the basis of discipleship in the NT: "the one master-disciple relationship that is analogous to the Old Testament's is the relationship between Jesus and his disciples. The God of the Old Testament who calls his people to a covenantal relationship is the same God of the New Testament who, in Jesus, calls his people to the new covenantal relationship" (*Following the Master*, 54).

Following the Lamb

CHARACTERISTICS OF NEW TESTAMENT DISCIPLESHIP

This section begins with a summary of discipleship terminology used throughout the NT, with specific emphasis on the Synoptic Gospels and the Epistles. This is followed by a look at Jesus' distinct form of discipleship, and closes with the apparent emphases on discipleship as articulated in the Epistles.

Relevant Discipleship Terminology in the New Testament

There are several key terms used in the NT that relate to the concept of discipleship. This section reviews several of the most prominent, beginning with "disciple" (μαθητής).

Μαθητής ("Disciple")

Richard Longenecker notes that although believers are occasionally referred to as people of "the Way" and "Christians," the most common designation for followers of Christ in the Gospels and Acts is "disciple" (μαθητής).[87] Μαθητής occurs at least 250 times and only in the Gospels and Acts.[88] Apart from a few exceptions, a μαθητής is one who is a disciple of Jesus.[89] According to Rengstorf, when it does occur, the term refers to "the existence of a personal attachment which shapes the whole life of the one described as μαθητής."[90] Wilkins adds, "a 'disciple' of Jesus . . . was one who adhered to his master, and the type of adherence was determined by the master himself."[91] In the book of Acts, the term is used "to designate the person who has placed faith in Jesus Christ."[92] The term "disciple" becomes synonymous with one who is a genuine believer in Jesus Christ.[93]

---

87. Longenecker, "Introduction," 2.

88. Rengstorf numbers its occurrence at 250 times ("μαθητής," 441), while Müller has its occurrence at 264 times ("μαθητής," 484).

89. Rengstorf, "μαθητής," 442, 457. Cf. Müller, "μαθητής," 486. The few exceptions include references to disciples of John the Baptizer, Moses, and the Pharisees.

90. Rengstorf, "μαθητής," 441.

91. Wilkins, *Disciple in Matthew's Gospel*, 42.

92. Wilkins, "Disciples," 181. Cf. Freyne, *Twelve*, 217.

93. Wilkins, "Disciples," 181.

It is not always easy to distinguish who the disciples are in the Gospel accounts. For instance, at times, in the Gospels, large crowds (λαός, ὄχλος) followed Jesus. He even taught these groups. Were they disciples, or is it best to categorize them in some other way? Wilkins notes some of the distinct groups of persons who followed Jesus, beginning with the disciples and the crowds. The difference between the disciples and the crowd was their respective responses to Jesus and his call. Those who were genuine disciples of Jesus exhibited "the twin prerequisites of discipleship: paying the cost and committing themselves to the cause."[94]

Another necessary distinction is between "the Twelve" (ὁ δώδεκα) and other "disciples." "The Twelve" were typically mentioned as a group, and only rarely were individual members mentioned.[95] While some of the Gospel writers essentially view the two groups as synonymous for literary and theological reasons (i.e. Matthew and Mark), it would appear that Jesus called out "the Twelve" specifically from among a larger number of "disciples" (cf. Luke 6:13, 17).[96] "The Twelve" are presented as the "nucleus of the community of Jesus" and as the guardians of Jesus' message that would be taught to the future community of believers.[97] "The Twelve" were distinctly called to be co-workers of Jesus in proclaiming the message of the Kingdom and were to prepare for their future role as leaders in the early church.[98]

It is also necessary to note the relationship between "the Twelve" and the "apostles" (ἀπόστολοι). Although the term "apostle" predominantly occurs in the Pauline corpus, it is not without a witness in the Gospels and Acts.[99] Wilkins notes that "the Twelve" were a distinct group of Jesus' disciples, who were also called to be apostles.[100] One must also make a distinction between the occurrence of the referent, apostles in the Gospels and Paul's usage of the referent. In order to come to an understanding of the distinction, Freyne believes one would be well advised to go to Luke-Acts. He notes that for Luke "an apostle is so closely linked to that of witness to the

---

94. Ibid., 177. See also Müller who notes that the disciples "would have been a circle of immediate followers who were commissioned to particular service" ("μαθητής," 489).

95. Wilkins, *Following the Master*, 152. For a brief description of the individual disciples see Wilkins, "Disciples," 179–181. For slightly longer descriptions see Wilkins, *Following the Master*, 152–167.

96. Wilkins, "Disciples," 178.

97. Freyne, *Twelve*, 47–48.

98. Wilkins, "Disciples," 178.

99. Freyne, *Twelve*, 49.

100. Wilkins, *Following the Master*, 149.

life of Jesus that of all the apostolic men who helped to spread the church the Twelve alone fully deserved that title."[101] Luke was also aware of Paul and used the term "apostle" in Paul's case to refer to his "preeminent position in the missionary achievement of the apostolic church."[102] For Freyne, the similarity between the use of the term "apostle" with reference to "the Twelve" and to Paul is their missionary activity. That both have elevated positions in the church seems for the most part to be inconsequential to the term "apostle."[103]

Ἀκολουθέω ("I follow")

In addition to the use of the noun "disciple," the verb "I follow" (ἀκολουθέω) is "also used in the Gospels to identify the 'disciples' as those committed to Jesus."[104] The term ἀκολουθέω occurs almost exclusively in the Gospels, with reference to following the earthly Jesus.[105] Scholars limit its usage outside of the Gospels with reference to the discipleship of Jesus to Rev 14:4, where the 144,000 follow the exalted Lamb.[106] While all disciples "followed" Jesus, only some physically followed him by abandoning their former way of life to walk with him. Other disciples followed Jesus in a "figurative" sense.[107] Women were included among those who followed Jesus in this figurative sense, since they too exhibited the twin characteristics of discipleship.[108]

---

101. Freyne, *Twelve*, 254–255.

102. Ibid., 255.

103. Ibid.

104. Longenecker, "Introduction," 2. Kittel notes all other uses of the verb "speak of a following which has no religious significance" ("ἀκολουθέω," 213 n. 28).

105. Blendinger, "ἀκολουθέω," 481.

106. Schweizer, *Lordship and Discipleship*, 12. Cf. Blendinger, "ἀκολουθέω," 1.482. Donaldson addresses the reality that post-Easter disciples can be said to follow Jesus as his disciples. He does so from the literary purpose of Mark's Gospel. Mark's audience, those who were disciples of the risen and ascended Lord, were called to follow Jesus. "Thus, 'following' becomes an enduring characteristic of the church for all time and not just a possibility for the twelve" ("Discipleship in Mark," 75).

Kittel believes the occurrence of the term in Rev 14:4 is an *obvious* application of Matt 10:38 to a specific group of Christians, those to whom John was writing ("ἀκολουθέω," 214). Rev 19:14 may also use ἀκολουθέω with some relevance to discipleship. This will be explored in chapter 4.

107. Wilkins, "Disciples," 178. Cf. Kittel, "ἀκολουθέω," 213. On the literal and figurative sense of ἀκολουθέω see also Kingsbury, "Following Jesus," 46.

108. Wilkins, "Disciples," 178.

Discipleship in the Ancient World

When used with reference to individuals in the Gospels, ἀκολουθέω "is always the call to decisive and intimate discipleship of the earthly Jesus."[109] The term ἀκολουθέω "is essentially restricted to the gospels."[110] According to Donaldson, disciples of Jesus were not the only ones to follow Jesus. The crowds literally followed him, although not as disciples.[111] Kittel notes the disciples' following Christ was evidence of his divine nature.[112] Blendinger does not deem the usage of the term in Acts and Paul's letters "theologically significant."[113] The disuse of the discipleship nuance of the term in the rest of the NT is likely related to the departure of the physical presence of Jesus. However, other terms are used to convey similar ideas.[114]

One such term is μιμέομαι ("I imitate"). The word group is found almost exclusively in the Pauline Epistles, with additional occurrences in Hebrews and 3 John.[115] Bauder notes that the verb and its cognates only occur 11 times in the NT. In each case, the specific term used is "linked with obligation to a specific kind of conduct."[116] This conduct cannot be divorced from following God's will.[117] One is to imitate the example of another.

An additional term is ὀπίσω ("behind, after"). With reference to ὀπίσω Bauder notes, "passages where the genitive *opisō mou* ["follow after me"] refers to Jesus . . . are particularly significant theologically. *Opisō* here takes on the meaning of *akoloutheō*, follow, go 'behind' someone."[118] The phrase is used in Mark 1:17 in the context of Jesus calling disciples to be fishers of men. Thus, this usage chiefly relates to Jesus' discipleship.[119] Finally, one may briefly note the verb μανθάνω ("I learn"), which occurs mostly outside

---

109. Blendinger, "ἀκολουθέω," 482.

110. Ibid., 483.

111. Donaldson, "Discipleship in Mark," 75.

112. Kittel, "ἀκολουθέω," 213. He believes this is related to the Hellenistic "religious and philosophical notion of following God."

113. Blendinger, "ἀκολουθέω," 482.

114. Kittel, "ἀκολουθέω," 214. Several terms could be presented in this section, such as πορεύομαι ("I go, walk"), which may be used in a figurative sense to refer to conducting one's life according to God's will. This is similar to the way הָלַךְ is used in the OT. However, only a few key terms are presented to provide a general overview of the terminology that is often applied to the concept of discipleship in the NT.

115. Michaelis, "μιμέομαι, μιμητής, κτλ.," 666.

116. Bauder, "μιμέομαι," 491.

117. Michaelis, "μιμέομαι, μιμητής, κτλ.," 672–673.

118. Bauder, "ὀπίσω," 493.

119. Ibid.

of the Gospels. When μανθάνω does occur it usually refers to learning "the will of God."[120]

Summary

Of the several terms related to the concept of discipleship in the NT, two in particular stand out with reference to the Gospels and Acts, μαθητής and ἀκολουθέω. Μαθητής is found exclusively in the Gospels and Acts, and apart from a few instances refers to one who is a disciple of Jesus Christ. Given its occurrence in Acts it would appear that one could be a disciple of the resurrected and ascended Christ. It refers to someone who is in a teacher-disciple relationship.

The other term found almost exclusively in the Gospels is ἀκολουθέω. Like μαθητής, it is used to identify those who are committed to Jesus. It may be used in a literal and figurative sense. The literal sense refers to actually following around the historical Jesus. It may also be used in a figurative sense of those disciples who followed Jesus, although they may not have been included among those who severed all ties to literally walk with him. Just as one may be a disciple of the risen and exalted Christ, so also one may be said to follow him. That being said, the term is not found in the NT Epistles in a discipleship context. The reason for this is almost certainly related to the first century practice of a teacher's disciples literally following him around. This way of following Jesus ceased with his ascension. The remainder of the NT employs different terminology to convey how a disciple of Jesus Christ continues to follow after him (i.e., μιμέομαι).

Jesus' Form of Discipleship

While there are a few similarities between Jesus and Jewish rabbis of his day (Jesus was called "teacher," as were they), scholars tend to emphasize the differences between Jesus' form of discipleship and that of his Jewish contemporaries.[121] Perhaps the first to popularize the uniqueness of Jesus' form of discipleship was C. G. Montefiore. According to Montefiore, "[d]iscipleship such as Jesus demanded and inspired (a following, not for study but for service—to help the Master in his mission, to carry out his

---

120. Müller, "μαθητής," 486.
121. Donaldson, "Discipleship in Mark," 68.

instructions and so on) was apparently a *new thing*, at all events, something which did not fit in, or was not on all-fours, with usual Rabbinic customs or with customary Rabbinic phenomena" (emphasis added).[122] Years later, Hengel sought to provide justification "both exegetically and in terms of Religionsgeschichte [history of religions]" of Montefiore's thesis, which rested heavily on Matt 8:21ff (//Luke 9:59f).[123] In the final analysis, Hengel concludes that Montefiore was correct in his assessment regarding Jesus' distinctive form of discipleship. Nevertheless, in at least a couple of places he tempers the certainty of Montefiore's conclusions.[124] For instance, Hengel believes the Religionsgeschichte with which Jesus' form of discipleship seems to have the most similarities is "the apocalyptic prophets and popular Zealot leaders in Palestine and in the Cynic philosophers of the Hellenistic-Roman World."[125] In another instance, he surprisingly and strikingly believes there is but one "genuine analogy" of Jesus' form of discipleship with the OT. Hengel notes, "[a]s to the call of the disciples, in the last analysis only the call of the Old Testament prophets by the God of Israel himself is a genuine analogy."[126] It would seem then, for Hengel, that Jesus' form of discipleship, while differing from how Jesus' Jewish contemporaries made disciples, did in fact have a historical precedent, one that was in keeping with the God of Israel's interactions with certain people of God in the OT.[127]

Although one may find an OT analogy to Jesus' form of discipleship, it is also widely recognized that there are differences between Jesus' form of discipleship and that of first century Jewish rabbis. The following is a summary of the distinctive features of Jesus' form of discipleship as found in the Gospels.

First, unlike other Jewish rabbis, Jesus issues a call for his disciples to follow him.[128] This was uncharacteristic of the teacher-disciple relationships of Jesus' day. A would-be disciple would attach himself to a master, in order to learn from him the way of the Lord, by way of his instruction

---

122. Montefiore, *Gospel Teachings*, 218.

123. Hengel, *Charismatic Leader*, 2.

124. Ibid., 87.

125. Ibid., 34.

126. Ibid., 87.

127. Elijah's call of Elisha and subsequent relationship may also be a valid OT analogy to Jesus' form of discipleship (cf. 1 Kgs 19:21).

128. Schweizer, *Lordship and Discipleship*, 20; Rengstorf, "μαθητής," 444; Blendinger, "ἀκολουθέω," 482; Wilkins, "Discipleship," 187; Kingsbury, "Following Jesus," 49; Sweetland, *Journey with Jesus*, 43–44, 83–84.

and lifestyle. However, Jesus initiated the teacher-disciple relationship by calling certain men to be his followers, to be in a relationship with him.[129]

Second, as has been previously stated, Jesus' form of discipleship was unique in that it was both broad and narrow. The scope of those called could be narrowly defined as "the Twelve" or other men who left everything in order to physically follow him. However, it could be broadly conceived to include those who were not asked to bear this cost.[130]

Third, Jesus broke significant social and religious barriers of his day with his call of discipleship to those who may be deemed unclean, social outcasts, or on the lower end of the social scale. Jesus called the poor and sinners not only to repentance, but also to be his disciples.[131] Jesus also gathered women to be his disciples, something that was unthinkable during his time.[132]

Fourth, while other disciples sought to supplant their master, or to become teachers leading their own band of disciples, Jesus' discipleship forbade such a thing. Jesus' disciples came to follow him and recognize him as the long awaited Messiah. Since he was understood as such, there was no aspiration on the part of his disciples to part with his instruction and gather their own disciples.[133] Those who became Jesus' disciples were required to be so for life. He would always be their master, and they would always be in the position of his disciples.[134]

Fifth, this did not mean Jesus' disciples were not expected to mature in their discipleship. However, unlike their rabbinical counterparts, they did not seek to become masters of the Torah, nor did he "call men to acquire and master traditional models of conduct";[135] rather, they were "stamped and fashioned" by Jesus, in order to become like him, but not greater than

---

129. Müller, "μαθητής," 488.

130. Wilkins, "Discipleship," 187.

131. Dunn, *Jesus and Discipleship*, 59. Cf. Müller, "μαθητής," 488.

132. Wilkins, "Discipleship," 187.

133. Rengstorf, "μαθητής," 448.

134. Wilkins, "Discipleship," 188. Cf. Donaldson, "Discipleship in Mark," 68. While it is true that in the rabbinic tradition "the student was bound to his teacher for the rest of his life," what made this different from Jesus' form of discipleship was that a student could after enough time and study graduate to become a rabbi and admit disciples into his instruction, and even surpass his teacher [Lohse, "ῥαββι," 962]. This was not so with Jesus' disciples.

135. Blendinger, "ἀκολουθέω," 482.

him.[136] This meant that Jesus' own pattern for ministry and his relationship with his heavenly Father were to be the pattern of life for his disciples.[137]

Sixth, Jesus' form of discipleship also meant that his disciples were "with Jesus" and they served him.[138] To be "with Jesus" meant his disciples were made to share in his teaching,[139] participate in his mission and authority,[140] witness to his person and work, and also to join in his sufferings, sometimes even to the point of death.[141]

Seventh, Jesus demanded nothing but total allegiance to his person. This required of his disciples to relinquish all old ties on their lives, in order to fully pursue Jesus' discipleship.[142] Hengel limits this requirement "to individuals [Jesus] invited to 'follow' him in specific situations."[143] However, Freyne believe this call was necessary of all disciples of Jesus, whether of those who first followed him or of future disciples.[144] Wilkins notes that while all were called to absolute allegiance to Jesus, this did not mean that all must leave "family, profession and property" to follow after Jesus.[145] It would seem that the cost to follow Jesus was in part situational, although no less absolute in its requirement for his disciples to give their entire lives, every aspect of them, in service to him.[146]

---

136. Rengstorf, "μαθητής," 448–449.

137. Donaldson, "Discipleship in Mark," 68. One example of how Jesus' pattern for ministry was to provide a pattern for his disciples (both past and present) is found in his application of the Messianic phrase "Son of Man." For a general overview of the background of the "Son of Man" and its usage in Mark's Gospel see Longenecker, "'Son of Man' Imagery," 222–243.

138. Schweizer, *Lordship and Discipleship*, 20. Cf. Müller, "μαθητής," 488–489.

139. Wilkins, "Discipleship," 188.

140. Hengel, *Charismatic Leader*, 73; Müller, "μαθητής," 489; Freyne, *Twelve*, 23; Sweetland, *Journey with Jesus*, 43–44, 83–84.

141. Donaldson, "Discipleship in Mark," 76; Müller, "μαθητής," 489; Blendinger, "ἀκολουθέω," 482; Hengel, *Charismatic Leader*, 72; Wilkins, "Discipleship," 188.

142. Schweizer, *Lordship and Discipleship*, 20. Cf. Blendinger, "ἀκολουθέω," 482.

143. Hengel, *Charismatic Leader*, 61.

144. Freyne, *Twelve*, 108.

145. Wilkins, "Discipleship," 187. Related to the cost of discipleship, see also Green, "Cross-Bearing," 117–133. Green concludes that the requirement for a disciple of Jesus to bear one's cross means "to submit to the rule against which [one] was formerly in rebellion" (ibid., 127).

146. Müller, "μαθητής," 488.

Finally, Jesus' form of discipleship cannot be separated from God's gift of salvation.[147] Wilkins expresses that in Luke-Acts both salvation and discipleship are entered through faith in Christ alone.[148] Like salvation, following Jesus as his disciple is a "decisive act," which calls for a response.[149] Wilkins also draws together Matt 28:19–20 and the command to disciple "all nations," and Luke 24:47 and the promise that "repentance for the forgiveness of sins will be preached in his [Jesus'] name to *all nations*, beginning in Jerusalem" (emphasis added) to show that "Jesus' ministry to Israel was to be the beginning point of what would be later a universal offer of salvation to all the peoples of the earth."[150] It is difficult to separate Jesus' call to be his disciple from his call to forgiveness of one's sins.[151] This aspect of Jesus' form of discipleship was certainly beyond the pale of Jewish discipleship in the first century.

Summary

Jesus' form of discipleship differed significantly from those of his Jewish contemporaries. While it was quite different, it was not without precedent, most notably God's own calling of OT prophets. Jesus' form of discipleship according to the Synoptic Gospels and Acts emphasizes such areas as: lifelong discipleship with Jesus; servanthood; participating with Jesus in his teaching, mission, authority, and sufferings; and the unique bond between salvation and discipleship.

---

147. Schweizer seems to allude to this when he states, "His [Jesus'] calling is the beginning of something new, changing all things. It takes place in sovereign liberty and can at once assume the character of an act of divine grace" (*Lordship and Discipleship*, 20).

148. Wilkins, *Following the Master*, 210.

149. Schweizer, *Lordship and Discipleship*, 20.

150. Wilkins, *Following the Master*, 188–189.

151. Segovia succinctly notes the inseparable nature of discipleship and salvation with respect to the entirety of the NT when he states, "belief in Jesus the Christ emerges as the very ground of discipleship: it is faith that constitutes the basic presupposition and point of departure for all Christian disciples" ("Introduction," 17). He further notes, "belief implies and entails a very definitive style of life on the part of the believer. Furthermore, . . . such a way of life is, quite often, distinctly patterned on or modeled after the life and ministry of Jesus" (ibid.,18).

Discipleship in the Ancient World

Discipleship in the New Testament Epistles

Having surveyed discipleship in the Greco-Roman world, second temple Judaism, the OT context, and the Synoptic Gospels and Acts, it may prove useful to provide a brief overview of the ways in which discipleship is conveyed in the NT Epistles. It is undeniable that key terminology used to convey the concept of discipleship from the Gospels and Acts is missing in the rest of the NT. However, this does not mean that the topic of discipleship is non-existent. As was seen in the section covering the concept of discipleship in the OT, to merely rely on lexemes to fully investigate a topic like discipleship is tenuous. While lexemes are helpful in telling part of the story, they are unable to describe all of it. So too with one's investigation of discipleship in the NT Epistles.

Wilkins notes that although the term "disciple" is not found outside of the Gospels and Acts, there is other terminology used to designate "disciples" that is found in the Gospels, Acts, and the rest of the NT. Some of the terms found in the Gospels and the rest of the NT include: "*believers, brothers/sisters, servants,* and *church.*"[152] Some of the designations for believers that occur both in Acts and the rest of the NT include: "*saints* and *Christians.*"[153] He finds that these two groups of terms "provide a link between those who are called disciples in the Gospels and Acts and those who are called other terms in the Acts and Epistles."[154]

One may also investigate the concept of discipleship in the NT Epistles by looking for evidence of discipleship themes located in the Gospels and Acts. This may be done by searching for specific occurrences of those themes or by allusions to said themes.[155] One theme in particular that stands out in the NT Epistles and the scholarly literature is the concept of imitation.[156] Several terms are used throughout the NT and in the ancient

152. Wilkins, *Following the Master*, 294.

153. Ibid.

154. Ibid. For a fuller explanation of these terms usage in the NT see Wilkins, *Following the Master*, 294–301.

155. Wilkins (*Following the Master*) does the first on pages 301–304 and the latter on pages 305–308. Segovia notes many of the same methods for investigating the concept of discipleship in the NT along with the usage of source critical methods of investigation ("Introduction," 4–5). In the work on discipleship edited by Longenecker it is essentially assumed that discipleship is addressed throughout the NT ("Introduction," 5–6).

156. Although the terms occur infrequently, one can find the idea of imitation throughout the NT Epistles. Hernando refers to this as "implicit imitation language" ("Imitation Language in Paul," 2).

world with reference to the concept of imitation. The word group that is directly related to the concept of imitation includes the nouns μιμητής, συμμιμητής (only in Phil 3:17), and the verb μιμέομαι.[157] The ancient Greek usage of the word group often had a negative connotation, although when used positively it referred to relationships between parents and their children, teachers and their pupils, and even God and human beings.[158] What is of interest in these relationships is the "transfer of character or personality from one person to another."[159]

It appears that Paul in particular picks up on the relationship between a parent and child with his employment of the terms μιμητής and μιμέομαι. Paul speaks to the churches he founded as a father to his children. Thus, Paul serves as a spiritual father to these churches.[160] What Paul calls for is not so much for his audience to imitate his particular way of living the Christian life, one that, although common to all Christians, would also have characteristics unique to Paul's example;[161] rather, Paul ultimately calls for believers to imitate Christ, whom Paul seeks to imitate and follow.[162] The imitation of Paul is akin to the disciple-teacher relationships in the OT. They were discipleship relationships of a secondary nature. The ultimate

---

157. Both Michaelis ("μιμέομαι, μιμητής, κτλ.," 673) and Furnish (*Ethics in Paul*, 219) believe μιμητής replaces μαθητής in the NT Epistles. Hays arriving at a similar conclusion states, "Jesus' death is consistently interpreted in the New Testament as an act of self-giving love, and the community is consistently called to take up the cross and follow in the way that his death defines. (When 'imitation of Christ' is understood in these terms, the often-proposed distinction between discipleship and imitation disappears. To be Jesus' disciple is to obey his call to bear the cross, thus to be like him.)" (*Moral Vision*, 197.)

Additional terms are used in the NT that may carry the idea of imitation or an example to follow. They include: ὑπόδειγμα (in John, Hebrews, James, and 2 Peter), ὑπογραμμος (only in 1 Pet 2:21), and in some cases τύπος and ὑποτύπωσις.

158. DeBoer, *Imitation*, 15-16. Cf. Michaelis, "μιμέομαι, μιμητής, κτλ.," 660-661.

159. Sanders, "Imitating Paul," 358.

160. Weaver, "Paul's Call to Imitation," 197. See also DeBoer, *Imitation*, 213-214.

161. Stanley, "Become Imitators of Me," 877. Stanley believes Paul's teaching was essentially the same as that of the other apostles, but that he was "also aware that, . . . his personal testimony to Christ, his preaching and way of life [had] their own characteristic modalities" (ibid.). However, DeBoer, in refuting the claim of Stanley, argues, "Paul's call to imitation is not in order to secure certain Pauline characteristics in the Christianity that is coming to expression in his readers. The characteristics which must come to expression are those basic to Christianity itself. Paul is not making special pleas for his version of Christianity and his manner of [the] Christian life" (*Imitation*, 209).

162. Bauder, "μιμέομαι," 491.

and first discipleship relationship was between God and his people. So also is the case in the NT. One is a disciple of Jesus first and foremost.

Paul is not the only NT writer to urge his audience to imitate Christ, himself, or other examples. The idea of imitation is found throughout the NT corpus, even when specific imitation language is absent, as in Hebrews 11, where several examples are given of those whose faith in God endured, leaving an example for others to follow (cf. Heb 12:1).[163]

What precisely is one to imitate? The most common characteristic held out for believers to follow is self-denial or selflessness. Linda L. Belleville, in addressing the concept of discipleship in 1 and 2 Corinthians, looks at several models that illuminate the characteristic of selflessness.[164] Jesus is to be an exemplar for the church at Corinth as one who (1) denies self in the service of others (cf. 2 Cor 8:9);[165] (2) exhibits forbearance and gentleness towards those who need correction (10:1);[166] and suffers as one serves others (1:5; 4:10; and 13:4).[167] Paul was an example of one who led by serving, which included serving alongside those he was entrusted to lead (1:24; 4:5).[168] The final example Paul presents to the Corinthian church is the Macedonian churches that served as a model of joyous living and generosity in the midst of persecution (8:1–5).[169] Imitation is not limited only to Christ, but extended to those who rightly follow his example.[170]

This idea of imitating selflessness, particularly the example of Christ's self-denial, is heightened in Paul's letter to the church at Philippi, so much so that Gerald F. Hawthorne believes that discipleship in Philippians is centrally located in the theme of imitation of Christ.[171] For Hawthorne

---

163. For instance, Hudgins believes that Paul's words to Timothy in 2 Tim 3:10–11a are provided as an example for Timothy to follow. The list represents the education Timothy received under Paul's tutelage (*Likeness Education*, 85). While Paul does not use μιμέομαι or one of its cognates, he does use the term "παρηκολούθησάς from παρακολουθέω ['follow closely'], [which] is a cognate of one of the words (ἀκολουθέω) semantically related to μαθητής" (ibid., 70).

164. Belleville, "'Discipleship in the Corinthian Correspondence,'" 120–142.

165. Ibid., 127–130.

166. Ibid., 131–133.

167. Ibid., 133–137.

168. Ibid., 137–139.

169. Ibid., 139.

170. Spicq includes the endurance and patience exhibited by the prophets who spoke on behalf of God as an exemplar for believers to follow ("ὑπόδειγμα," 404).

171. Hawthorne, "Discipleship in Philippians," 163–179.

Christ's example in Phil 2:5–11 serves as *the* pattern for discipleship in the letter.[172] William S. Kurz also identifies Paul as an exemplar for the Philippian Christians to follow.[173] He believes that both Paul and Christ provide an example to imitate of those who set aside their rights or self-interest, which may have resulted in their safety, for the good of others, an act which also results in their own personal suffering. They endured such suffering by putting their hope or trust in God to vindicate them, and exalt and reward them.[174] This striving to be like Christ or even Paul is not to be done by sheer will power, but "is made possible by the power of the living, exalted Christ, who is present and at work within the lives of believers through the work of the Holy Spirit (cf. 1:11, 19, 2:12b–13)."[175]

The idea of imitating the suffering of Christ found in Paul's letters is also prominent in the letter to the Hebrews. William L. Lane argues that Jesus is presented as the "ultimate paradigm of heroic discipleship" in the letter.[176] Because of this, those who are committed to following Christ will also experience shame, reproach, and suffering.[177] The imitation of suffering is also evident in 1 Peter. The picture Peter provides is one of discipleship that views the Christian as following Christ on his or her journey to heaven. Following Christ includes imitating his example of one who suffered unjustly and who did not retaliate against those who persecuted him, but instead continued to do what was good.[178] John H. Elliott sees this theme prominently on display in 1 Pet 2:18–25 in the apostle's instruction to slaves.[179]

---

172. Ibid., 167, 169, 177. Hawthorne readily recognizes that some object to an imitation of Christ interpretation of Phil 2:5–11. For a sample of those against such an interpretation see Michaelis, "μιμέομαι, μιμητής, κτλ.," 672 and Bauder, "μιμέομαι," 491–492. For one who believes Phil 2:5–11 presents a pattern for Christians to follow see Hurtado, "Jesus as Lordly Example," 113–126.

173. Kurz, "Kenotic Imitation," 103–126.

174. Ibid., 122.

175. Hawthorne, "Discipleship in Philippians," 178. Wild focuses on the believer's union with Christ as the ability to actually follow Christ's example of being obedient to God ("Discipleship in Ephesians," 135–136). Elliott believes 1 Pet 2:18–25 emphasizes that Jesus is not just an example to follow, but the one who has paid the price to secure salvation and the ability to follow him faithfully ("Backward and Forward," 187, 203). He writes that Jesus is "both an enabler and an exemplar" (ibid., 187).

176. Lane, "Discipleship in Hebrews," 208, 213.

177. Ibid., 223.

178. Michaels, "Going to Heaven with Jesus," 253.

179. Elliott, "Backward and Forward," 188–189. Elliott believes the slaves mentioned in this text serve "an illustrative and paradigmatic function" of what is expected of all

Slaves were to do what was right even if suffering unjustly because: (1) they had been called to do so, and (2) Christ suffered for them, leaving them an example to follow.[180] This calling to patiently endure unjust suffering was not something that believers were to do alone, but it was something one was to do with fellow travelers on their journey heavenward. Together the church encourages its members to continue on in the face of obstacles to enter into their eternal home.[181]

In addition to these characteristic, Robert L. Plummer, who focuses his attention on 1 Cor 11:1, believes Paul's missionary example is set forth as an model for the church to follow.[182] While Paul is to be an exemplar for the church as a whole, the scope of his example is limited in the case of the individual believer based on "an individual believer's giftedness and life situation [to] determine the manifestation of that obligation [to evangelize] (1 Cor 12:12–30)."[183]

Lest one fall into the perspective that discipleship in the epistles is strictly about doing what is right, Michael P. Knowles notes that discipleship is more than right ethical living; it must first and foremost be grounded in a correct understanding of the person and work of Jesus Christ. Only after understanding rightly who Jesus is, what he taught, and what he came to do is one prepared to live in light of that reality.[184] The extent to which one is

---

believers (ibid., 188–189).

180. Ibid., 193.
181. Michaels, "Going to Heaven," 267.
182. Plummer, "Imitation of Paul," 219–235.
183. Ibid., 235.
184. Knowles, "Discipleship in Colossians," 201. On the other hand, Jervis appears to place greater emphasis on the ethical dimension of discipleship. In her essay on discipleship in Romans she concludes, "The gospel, for Paul, is the manifestation of the 'righteousness of God,' that is, the manifestation of God's own character. God's revelation of his own character in the gospel (1:17) is an invitation and opportunity for human beings to become as God is. This is not possible through human endeavor, for righteousness is not a property of humanity but of God. Humans may become righteous only by recognizing that righteousness is not a property of humanity, but only of God, and submitting to the 'righteousness of God' (10:3)" ("Discipleship in Romans," 161). It is possible that this greater emphasis on the ethical dimension is simply due to the limitations of what Romans attributes to the concept of discipleship, rather than Jervis's own notions of NT discipleship.

Davids notes how James draws heavily on the teaching of Jesus in his letter, so much so that Davids concludes, "the 'system of meaning and values' that he [James] wants his readers to adopt appears in the teaching of Jesus" ("Discipleship in James," 227).

to live in light of this reality is all-inclusive. One's whole life and being is to be lived in this world with respect to God.[185]

Summary

Although lacking the discipleship terminology that is dominantly portrayed in the Gospels and Acts, the NT Epistles are not devoid of the concept of discipleship. A key idea utilized throughout the epistles is the idea of imitation, in particular the imitation of religious exemplars.[186] The example *par excellence* for believers to follow is that of Jesus Christ. Perhaps no passage better illustrates what is required of followers of Christ than his example in Phil 2:5–11. There Jesus is given as one who selflessly sets asides his rights and prerogatives for the good of others. Jesus is also set forth as an example of one who patiently endures unjust suffering, knowing full well that God would vindicate him. Not only does Christ provide an example to follow, but he is also the one who enables Christians to emulate him through the power of the indwelling Holy Spirit.

CONCLUSION

The concept of discipleship in the Greco-Roman world is seen through the usage of its relevant terminology. The term μαθητής, which broadly referred to a "learner" or "pupil," was also used as a technical term for one who learned from a great master or teacher. The idea of following (ἀκολουθέω) a teacher also figures prominently in Greek thought. The idea was that one not only literally followed one's teacher around, but also figuratively followed his teaching and way of life (μιμέομαι).

During the time of second temple Judaism rabbinical schools began to be developed. These schools were led by men who taught male students both the oral and written Torah. The rabbi taught his students not only by the words he spoke, but also by his example. The goal for the student was to become a master of the Torah, so that one could then teach one's own disciples.

---

185. Johnson, "Discipleship in James," 177.

186. For a more detailed discussion of the theme of imitation in the NT see Hood, *Imitating God in Christ*.

While one might choose to follow a great teacher, one did not typically speak of following God, since unlike the teacher, he did not possess a physical body, and thus, could not be seen. However, in time, some of the religious writings of Judaism began to incorporate some aspect of people imitating God. The purpose was generally to aid in the development of the *imago Dei* in the individual.

While linguistic evidence for the concept of discipleship is limited in the OT, it is not entirely absent. When it does occur, it appears to be used in a master-disciple relationship. There appears to be sufficient evidence to conclude that Isa 8:16, a key text when determining the validity of discipleship in the OT, does in fact refer to the prophet Isaiah having a number of disciples. However, it must be recognized that these disciples are his only in a secondary sense, for the Lord God is one's teacher first and foremost. In addition to these few instances, one may include several examples found throughout the OT of what could be characterized as teacher-student relationships (e.g., Moses and Joshua, and Elijah and Elisha).

Of the several terms related to the concept of discipleship in the NT, two in particular stand out with reference to the Gospels and Acts, μαθητής and ἀκολουθέω. Μαθητής is found exclusively in the Gospels and Acts, and apart from a few instances refers to one who is a disciple of Jesus Christ. Like μαθητής, ἀκολουθέω is used to identify those who are committed to Jesus. It may be used in a literal and figurative sense. The literal sense refers to actually following the historical Jesus. It may also be used in a figurative sense of those disciples who followed Jesus, although they may not have been included among those who severed all ties to literally walk with him. Just as one may be a disciple of the risen and exalted Christ, so also one may be said to follow him.

It appears that by and large Jesus' form of discipleship differed significantly from his Jewish contemporaries. While it was quite different, it was not without precedent, most notably God's own calling of OT prophets. Jesus' form of discipleship according to the Synoptic Gospels and Acts emphasizes such areas as: lifelong discipleship with Jesus; servanthood; participating with Jesus in his teaching, mission, authority, and sufferings; and the unique bond between salvation and discipleship.

Although lacking the discipleship terminology that is dominantly portrayed in the Gospels and Acts, the NT Epistles are not devoid of the concept of discipleship. A key idea utilized throughout the epistles is the idea of imitation, in particular the imitation of religious exemplars. The example *par excellence* for believers to follow is that of Jesus Christ. Not only does Christ provide an example to follow, but he is also the one who enables Christians to emulate him through the power of the indwelling Holy Spirit.

3

Literature on Discipleship in the Gospel of John

INTRODUCTION

HAVING DISCUSSED THE CONCEPT of discipleship as it is broadly portrayed in the NT (with the exclusion of the Gospel of John and Revelation), this chapter shifts the focus to one particular book of the NT, the Gospel according to John and its particular contribution to the theme of discipleship. This is developed by reviewing the recent and relevant scholarly literature written on the topic of discipleship from the perspective of the Fourth Gospel. In addition to this, the review will be used to develop a coding frame by which to analyze the theme of discipleship in the book of Revelation. So, the present chapter is divided into two main sections: (1) review of the recent literature on discipleship in John and (2) the development of a coding frame to be used for analysis of the Apocalypse.

JOHANNINE DISCIPLESHIP IN RECENT SCHOLARSHIP

In the early to mid 1980s, both R. Alan Culpepper[1] and Fernando Segovia[2] commented on the lack of scholarly activity on the theme of discipleship in

1. Culpepper, *Anatomy*, 115.
2. Segovia, "Discipleship," 77.

John's Gospel. This is particularly surprising given that the term "disciple" (μαθητής) occurs with greater frequency in the Fourth Gospel than in any other NT book.[3] While scholarly work on discipleship in John may have been scarce in the past, this is not the case today. Since the 1970s several works have been produced addressing the topic of discipleship in John. The following survey presents chronologically the major contributions to discipleship in the Gospel of John from 1970 to the present day.

The Period from 1970 to 1979

Three particular studies are worthy of note, those produced by Ramon Moreno Jiménez, Rudolf Schnackenburg, and Marinus de Jonge.

Ramon Moreno Jiménez[4]

Ramon Moreno Jiménez provides the first significant treatment of the usage of the term μαθητής in the Fourth Gospel. His work is divided into three sections, although only section two is briefed here. In this section he discusses the use of μαθητής in key texts: 8:31; 13:35; and 15:8. Each of these texts indicates something about the nature of discipleship in John's Gospel.[5] First, the true disciple of Jesus must abide in his word (8:31).[6] Abiding in Jesus' word is linked to recognition of who Jesus truly is, namely, the Son of God.[7] This comes through a deepening knowledge of who Jesus is.[8] Second, the true disciple of Jesus displays love for other disciples (13:35).[9] The origin of the mutual love that was to exist between the disciples is Jesus' own love.[10] Finally, the genuine disciple is in union with Christ, which is expressed in the vine and the branches metaphor (15:8).[11] Jiménez sees in the vine and the branches motif a word from Jesus to all believers for all

---

3. Ibid.
4. Jiménez, "Discípulo," 269–311.
5. See also Wilkins, *Following the Master*, 230–235.
6. Jiménez, "Discípulo," 276.
7. Ibid., 278.
8. Ibid., 277.
9. Ibid., 279.
10. Ibid., 280.
11. Ibid., 280–283.

times. This is because the bond between Jesus and his disciples is not based on physical proximity, but faith and love.[12]

Following his analysis of these texts, Jiménez focuses his attention on the Beloved Disciple, whom he believes stands as a paradigm of discipleship.[13] He notes the following characteristics of this disciple: (1) he is in union with Christ; (2) he believes in Jesus' resurrection without seeing evidence of Jesus' resurrected body; and (3) he recognizes Jesus as Lord.[14]

Jiménez concludes this section by discussing how it was possible for disciples to follow the ascended Christ. He recognizes that the characteristics of Jesus' disciples during his earthly ministry still characterize post-resurrection disciples. Jesus' discipleship is about communion with Jesus, something that is still possible. Like his disciples during his first advent, Jesus' disciples are those who believe that he is both Christ and God, and they express love for one another.[15]

Rudolf Schnackenburg[16]

In an excursus in his commentary on the Gospel of John, Rudolf Schnackenburg briefly discusses "the circle of the disciples and the concept of discipleship in the Gospel of John."[17] He begins by noting the emphasis the author placed on "discipleship and the circle of the disciples."[18] After briefly describing how the disciples function in the narrative of the Gospels, and their participation with Jesus in his public ministry, Schnackenburg provides three characteristics of the disciples in John's Gospel. The disciples represent: (1) "those who are made believers by Jesus through his word and his signs," (2) "the later community in contrast to the unbelieving Jews," and (3) "the later believers in that they are challenged and tempted and their faith is inadequate."[19] In addition to the disciples' representative roles,

---

12. Ibid., 283.
13. Ibid., 286.
14. Ibid., 285–286.
15. Ibid., 287–288.
16. Schnackenburg, "The Disciples," 203–217.
17. Ibid., 205.
18. Ibid.
19. Ibid., 206–207.

Schnackenburg notes that the distinguishing "mark of discipleship" is "reciprocal love," according to John 13:35.[20]

Marinus de Jonge[21]

Marinus de Jonge refers to the Fourth Gospel as "the book of the disciples."[22] The disciples, in this case, refer not only to those included in the pages of the Gospel, but also to the primary audience, which he determines to be "the (Johannine) church" based on the words of John 20:30–31.[23] Next, he views the mission of the disciples according to selected texts in John 20. He essentially concludes that the disciples' mission is to "act as Jesus' representatives and thus as God's representatives, on earth."[24] He adds, the disciples were only able to fully represent Jesus after his return to the Father, for it was only then that they "were able to grasp the full meaning of what they had heard and seen" from Jesus.[25]

He follows this with a discussion of the role of the disciples and the Holy Spirit in chapters 13–17 in particular, as well as related passages. He concludes, it is only through the enabling of the Spirit, who is himself a witness to Jesus, that the disciples are able to teach effectively about Jesus and witness to him.[26]

De Jonge concludes the chapter with two further areas of inquiry: (1) the true nature of discipleship and (2) God's initiative in a positive response to the message about Jesus. Looking primarily at 1:35–51, de Jonge notes that the recurrence of the word "to follow" throughout this section (and even elsewhere) is used to denote discipleship. Further, "to follow" after Jesus "implies a complete trust in Jesus, perseverance, and martyrdom."[27] He draws the conclusion that true disciples of Jesus exhibit certain qualities: they "listen, see, believe, overcome offence, remain with Jesus, and follow him."[28] In addition, Jesus exhorts his disciples to evidence

---

20. Ibid., 208.
21. De Jonge, *Jesus*, 1–27.
22. Ibid., 1.
23. Ibid., 2.
24. Ibid., 5.
25. Ibid., 7.
26. Ibid., 12.
27. Ibid., 13.
28. Ibid., 14.

their discipleship through mutual affection for one another and by bearing much fruit.[29] The chapter comes to a close with a discussion of why some respond positively to the gospel while others do not. De Jonge concludes that for John, the reason some respond positively to Jesus and others do not is based solely on God's initiative.[30]

The Period from 1980 to 1989

The relevant studies from the period include: Mathew Vellanickal, Jeffrey S. Siker-Gieseler, R. Alan Culpepper, and Fernando F. Segovia.

Mathew Vellanickal[31]

In his article, Mathew Vellanickal takes as his overarching premise that in John's Gospel Jesus is described as both revealer of the Father and master teacher, and that the response to him is described in terms of discipleship.[32] Discipleship is a response in which one recognizes "in the teaching of Jesus the words of eternal life," that he is "the Holy one of God," and as a result attaches oneself to him, to become his disciple.[33] Being a disciple of Jesus is something that "becomes in Johannine theology the response of all the believers to the word of salvation."[34]

Following this introduction to discipleship in John's Gospel, Vellanickal describes the way in which John presented the essential call to discipleship. Vellanickal believes John recorded historical accounts largely to express his theology.[35] This is the case with discipleship in John 1:35–42, from which Vellanickal derives nine essential characteristics of a genuine call to discipleship.[36] These nine characteristics are: election and call, human testimony, hearing, following, seeking, finding, coming and seeing,

---

29. Ibid.
30. Ibid., 20.
31. Vellanickal, "Discipleship," 131–147.
32. Ibid., 131–132, 147.
33. Ibid., 132.
34. Ibid., 133.
35. Ibid., 134.
36. Collins, likewise, focuses his analysis of discipleship in John's Gospel on 1:35–39 ("Discipleship," 248–255). This article also appears in his book, *These Things*, 46–55. This study will always refer to this book.

remaining with Jesus, and missionary sharing. They are essential parts of the disciple's process of experiencing and knowing Jesus.[37]

The nine essentials of the call are described briefly in the following paragraph. First is election and call. By this, Vellanickal means that God takes the initiative in calling persons to be his disciples.[38] Second, God uses means to call persons to be his disciples. Thus, the second essential of human testimony is mentioned.[39] Third, the one who hears Jesus is the one who become "attuned to the voice of Jesus or God through a constant union with him in prayer."[40] Fourth, Vellanickal describes following Jesus as the "characteristic of the call to discipleship."[41] The verb ἀκολουθέω is used in the Gospels with reference to Jesus in discipleship context. In John's Gospel, to follow Jesus as his disciple means serving him, dying to self, and potentially following him in his death.[42] Fifth, seeking Jesus touches on an intrinsic and basic human need to find something greater than oneself, to find something "lasting, surpassing temporality, change and death, namely, to find God himself."[43] Sixth is finding Jesus. To find Jesus for Vellanickal means that one should desire to search for him, to be with him, and "expect to find fulfillment in being with Jesus alone."[44] It speaks to Jesus being all-sufficient for the disciple. Seventh, coming to Jesus means believing in Jesus or placing faith in Jesus.[45] Eighth, remaining with Jesus speaks to the "permanency of the relationship between the Father and the Son (14:10) and between the Son and the Christian (15:4–7)."[46] In addition, it refers to the "mutual indwelling presence of the Father, Son, and the believer."[47] It refers to a life lived in communion with Jesus. Ninth, and finally, those who are called to be Jesus' disciples, to experience life with him, become those who share their experience with others. This is what Vellanickal refers to as missionary sharing. The goal is that others will respond positively to Jesus'

37. Vellanickal, "Discipleship," 141.
38. Ibid., 135.
39. Ibid.
40. Ibid., 136.
41. Ibid.
42. Ibid.
43. Ibid., 137.
44. Ibid., 138.
45. Ibid.
46. Ibid., 139.
47. Ibid.

call to discipleship and in turn will also tell others of their experience with Jesus.[48]

Vellanickal follows this analysis with a discussion of the conditions of and keynote of discipleship. He notes three conditions of becoming a disciple of Jesus: remaining in Jesus' word (8:31–32), hating one's life (12:25), and serving Jesus (12:26).[49] He concludes with the "distinguishing mark" of Jesus' disciples, which is "brotherly love."[50]

In the final analysis, Vellanickal understands Jesus' form of discipleship as "an advanced stage of the life of faith resulting from a constant and dynamic indwelling presence of Jesus' words in us."[51] This suggests that discipleship is something reserved for mature Christians or for those who are firmly committed to Jesus, perhaps like the Twelve who left everything to follow him.

Jeffrey S. Siker-Gieseler[52]

In his article, Siker-Gieseler notes that although disciples and discipleship comprise a singular theme in John's Gospel, there are differences. *Disciples* refer to those who historically followed Jesus, while *discipleship* is on display in particular individuals.[53] In addition, "disciples function primarily on a surface level in John, denoting the historical group of disciples," while "discipleship . . . has a deeper dimension that transcends a strict historical understanding although it includes it."[54] Discipleship is largely relegated to

---

48. Ibid., 140.

49. Ibid., 141–145. "Conditions" may not be the best way to frame this section, although Vellanickal believes it is. It is true that 8:31 and 12:16 are conditional sentences, third class conditional sentences according to Wallace, *Greek Grammar*, 699. However, it is probably not best to view these as Jesus laying down conditions of discipleship. Commenting on 8:31, Morris notes that this verse is "telling them [Jesus' audience] in what discipleship consists. When anyone abides in Christ's word, then that person is a true disciple" (*John*, 405). Perhaps, it would be better to view these as evidences of genuine Christian discipleship.

50. Vellanickal, "Discipleship," 145.

51. Ibid., 147.

52. Siker-Gieseler, "Disciples and Discipleship," 199–227.

53. Ibid., 199.

54. Ibid., 207.

chapters 1–12, while the disciples are the focus in 13–21. Both of these lines come together in the Beloved Disciple.[55]

Following a review of the relevant literature on disciples and discipleship, Siker-Gieseler turns his attentions to his analysis of the disciples and discipleship in John's Gospel. In order to determine how the disciples are characterized in John, Siker-Gieseler looks first at what they say and do, and secondly, what is said and done to them.[56] The sayings of the disciples include: various questions, particularly questions about the disciples' relationship with Jesus (e.g., 1:38; 13:25; 13:6, 37); their misunderstandings (e.g., 4:33; 6:7–9); their objections to Jesus, which are primarily among the wider group of disciples (e.g., 6:60; 8:33; 12:4; 13:14; 20:25); their testimony about Jesus (e.g., 1:41–46; 6:68); and their confessions about who Jesus is (e.g., 1:49; 6:69).[57] The disciples are also shown doing many things, most often "following (1:37; 10:4, 27; 18:15), seeing (1:39; 6:19; 20:25; 21:9), believing (2:11, 22; 17:8; 20:3), knowing (10:4; 17:7, 25), remembering (2:17, 22; 12:16; 16:4, 21), hearing (1:37; 21:7), and keeping (17:6)."[58]

Next, Siker-Gieseler addresses what is said about the disciples and what is done to them. He chiefly focuses on what Jesus says about them, beginning with how he addresses them (e.g., "the twelve," "my brothers," and "friends"). Siker-Gieseler believes this reveals the nature of the relationship between Jesus and his disciples, which is "a family relationship . . . similar to Jesus' relationship to the Father."[59] One also finds in the Fourth Gospel Jesus asking questions of the disciples, commanding and reprimanding them, exhorting them, providing explanations that lead to greater belief, making promises to them, making predictions of what will happen to them as a group and to certain individuals within the group, and several conditional statements related to what it means to be one of his disciples.[60]

Next, Siker-Gieseler provides several ways in which the disciples are acted upon. For instance, the disciples are "chosen and called" (e.g., 1:42–43; 6:70), they have been "given several things," including eternal life

---

55. Ibid., 199.
56. Ibid., 208.
57. Ibid., 208–210.
58. Ibid., 210.
59. Ibid., 211.
60. Ibid., 211–214.

Literature on Discipleship in the Gospel of John

(e.g., 10:28), and they "are loved by the Father and the Son" (13:1; 17:23, 26; 19:26).[61]

From here, Siker-Gieseler focuses on several individuals in John's Gospel whom the author uses "to communicate the meaning of discipleship."[62] Four individuals are discussed apart from the Beloved Disciple at the close of the article. The four persons addressed in this section are the Samaritan woman (4:7–30), the Capernaum official (4:46–54), the man born blind (9:1–41), and Mary, the sibling of Martha and Lazarus (11:1–44). These four individuals reveal that discipleship means "testifying to Jesus, ordering all of one's concerns to faith in Jesus," coming to greater understanding of one's beliefs, "signified in part by testifying and confessing about Jesus," and coming to a fuller comprehension and belief in Jesus as the Son of God "and the meaning of this for the person in discipleship."[63] These individuals characterize what it means for future believers, those who will not physically follow Jesus, to be a disciple of Jesus, since they, like future believers, did not "accompany Jesus at all, rather they believe[d] on the basis of his word . . . (cf. 20:29–31)."[64] On the whole, Siker-Gieseler views the examples of discipleship portrayed in the Gospel of John favorably, over against the example of the disciples that are regularly portrayed negatively.[65]

With regard to the place of the Beloved Disciple in John's Gospel, Siker-Gieseler believes he "functions as discipleship among the disciples. He personifies the [positive aspects of] discipleship seen in chapters 1–12 and manifests it among the disciples in chapters 13–21."[66]

Although Siker-Gieseler offers several insights into Johannine discipleship as it is revealed in the Fourth Gospel, he rather strangely separates disciples from discipleship. For him, the disciples of Jesus, namely the Twelve, do not appear to experience discipleship, apart from the Beloved Disciple. This is because discipleship is framed as those who believe in Jesus on account of his word and are not those who physically follow after him. Nothing in the Gospel of John itself uses these words in this manner. In fact, the term *discipleship* does not occur anywhere in Scripture. It would be

---

61. Ibid., 214.
62. Ibid., 215.
63. Ibid., 219.
64. Ibid., 220.
65. Ibid., 221.
66. Ibid., 222.

far more helpful to simply understand discipleship as the process by which a disciple of Jesus becomes more like Jesus.[67]

R. Alan Culpepper[68]

Culpepper devotes ten pages to the discussion of the characterization of the disciples in John's Gospel. He begins his analysis by stating that the disciples in the Gospel of John are presented as imperfect models with whom the readers may identify.[69] The disciples' literary contribution is to help move the plot along and to function as "surrogates for the church and the reader . . . and often ask question that may naturally occur to the reader along the way."[70] Culpepper then takes the reader through John's narrative, highlighting along the way what the disciples contribute to discipleship. For instance, Culpepper looks at the opening call narrative (1:35ff) and finds the "pattern for the role of the disciples in bringing faith to others."[71] He also declares that real faith leads to following Jesus (1:37, 38, 40).[72] Not only this, but genuine disciples receive and accept Jesus' words (8:31).[73] This does not imply that the disciples understand everything that Jesus says. However, their lack of understanding of who Jesus is and what he has done does not necessarily remove them from being one of his disciples.[74]

Culpepper shifts his focus from the disciples as a group to individually named disciples, in order to ascertain their representative purpose in the narrative.[75] Andrew becomes the "model of the disciple who bears much fruit (15:8)."[76] Peter stands in for the process of discipleship.[77] The Beloved

---

67. One may also consult any one of the three definitions provided for discipleship in chapter 1 ("Discipleship, Christian Education, and Spiritual Formation").

68. Culpepper, *Anatomy*, 115–125.

69. Ibid., 115.

70. Ibid.

71. Ibid.

72. Ibid., 116.

73. Ibid., 117.

74. Ibid., 117–118.

75. Culpepper is not alone in seeing individuals in John's Gospel as representative figures. See also Collins, *These Things*, 1–45. Similarly see Whitters, "Discipleship in John," 422–427; Palatty, "Discipleship," 285–306.

76. Culpepper, *Anatomy*, 120.

77. Ibid., 121.

Disciple represents "the ideal disciple, the paradigm of discipleship."[78] Nathanael is representative of "true Israel."[79] Thomas is representative of "all who ... embrace the earthly Jesus but have not yet to recognize the risen Christ."[80] Finally, Judas stands in as the "representative defector."[81] While Culpepper's work emphasizes the literary importance of the disciples in the flow of the narrative, he tends to disregard the historical context of the disciples.[82]

Fernando F. Segovia[83]

In his contribution to *Discipleship in the New Testament*, Fernando Segovia proposes to study discipleship in John's Gospel by analyzing the characterization of Jesus' disciples in the narrative.[84] While other scholars have treated the Gospel as a whole, or selected small portions to illuminate truths contained in the entirety of the work, Segovia limits himself to only those sections that he believes constitute the earliest version of the Fourth Gospel. Therefore, this leads him to exclude large sections of the book (e.g., 13:1b–3, 12–20, 34–35; 15–17; 21).[85]

Segovia sees the characterization of the disciples unfolding in four stages:

1. The gathering of the elect and the initial incomprehension of "the world" (John 1–3)

2. The elect on "the way" and the growing rejection of "the world" (John 4–12)

3. The farewell to the elect and the exclusion of "the world" (John 13–14)

---

78. Ibid. See also Siker-Gieseler, "Disciples and Discipleship," 222; Beck, "Anonymity," 153. None of this requires one to dismiss the historicity of the Beloved Disciple. As Raymond Brown aptly puts things, "the Beloved Disciple was no less a real human being than was Simon Peter, but the Fourth Gospel used each of them in a paradigmatic capacity" (*Community*, 83).

79. Culpepper, *Anatomy*, 123.

80. Ibid., 124.

81. Ibid., 125.

82. Ibid., 105.

83. Segovia, "Discipleship," 76–102.

84. Ibid., 79.

85. Ibid.

4. The vindication of the elect and the judgment of "the world" (John 18–20).[86]

The characterization of the disciples is then used to shed light on the community situation to which the author of the Fourth Gospel was writing.[87] He concludes that there are three main aspects of discipleship that are interrelated to the historical situation of the Gospel's audience, which he believes was a dispute between "a Christian community and a parent synagogue(s) from which most of the former's present members have been forced to separate because of their belief in Jesus."[88] First, "the narrative presents and develops a thorough and systematic contrast between the disciples as believers and all those who reject Jesus' claims."[89] Second, but related to the first, "belief in Jesus' claims constitutes the sole basis for [the disciples'] separation [from the world]," the world being anyone who rejects Jesus' claims, including unbelieving Jews.[90] Finally, "belief [in Jesus' claims] itself is presented as requiring and undergoing a process of gradual understanding and perception."[91]

While it may be a noble pursuit to ascertain the community to which the Gospel was directed, Segovia does so at the expense of the narrative in its canonical form, as well as the historical relationship between Jesus and his disciples, and what it contributes to a well-formed vision of Christian discipleship. In addition, his praise of the works of Martyn[92] and Brown[93] (and one would assume their conclusions regarding the Johannine community) appear to result in something of a self-fulfilling prophecy as his conclusions affirm their own.[94]

The Period from 1990 to 1999

Since the 1990s, seven studies on discipleship in John are worthy of closer attention. They are those written by Raymond F. Collins, J. A. du Rand,

86. Ibid., 79–80.
87. Ibid., 78, 90.
88. Ibid., 92. So also Brown, *Community*, 58–91.
89. Segovia, "Discipleship," 90.
90. Ibid., 92. Cf. 91.
91. Ibid., 92.
92. Martyn, *Gospel of John*.
93. Brown, *Community*.
94. Segovia, "Discipleship," 90 n. 64, 92 n. 68.

Literature on Discipleship in the Gospel of John

W. Hulitt Gloer, David R. Beck, Andreas J. Köstenberger, Melvyn R. Hillmer, and Paul Palatty.

Raymond F. Collins[95]

Collins begins his discussion of discipleship in the Fourth Gospel by recounting the differences between Jesus' initial call of his disciples in John with that of the Synoptics, after which, he sets out to describe what discipleship means from John's perspective, the portrayal of which he finds in 1:35–39.[96] Collins notes that this passage is found in the context of the Baptizer's testimony about Jesus. Only after hearing that Jesus is "the Lamb of God, who takes away the sin of the world" (1:29; cf. 1:35) are the soon-to-be disciples ready to become followers of Jesus. This sets up an emphasis in the Fourth Gospel that "one becomes a follower of Jesus because someone has witnessed to Jesus. In [the evangelist's] perspective discipleship is a consequence of witness having been borne to Jesus."[97]

Before his analysis of John 1:35–39, Collins notes that John's Gospel must be read on two levels: (1) as a "narrative tale" and (2) as a "symbolic tale."[98] As a "narrative tale," the Gospel recounts historical events of historical persons. As a "symbolic tale," the Gospel reports "the story of the Johannine community, its faith and its struggles."[99] It is this symbolic narrative that is the focus of Collins's study.

In John 1:35–39 Collins finds four key terms related to discipleship: "to follow," "to seek," "to stay," and "to see."[100] His symbolic reading of the text leads him to conclude that the author of John intended to present 1:35–39 as a paradigm of discipleship. Alongside this aim, the author deftly utilizes different narrative strategies in order to "invite the readers to participate in the drama that is unfolding before them."[101] Regarding John's use of "to follow," Collins states that John uses the term in a sense similar to that of the Synoptics, who use the term metaphorically to refer to one

---

95. Collins, *These Things*, 46–55.
96. Ibid., 46–47. He delineates about seven differences in total.
97. Ibid., 49.
98. Ibid.
99. Ibid.
100. Ibid.
101. Ibid., 50.

who is a disciple of Jesus.[102] The symbolic use of "to see" indicates that Jesus invites his disciples to experience a relationship with him, one which Collins describes in terms of "greater intimacy" with Jesus.[103] A disciple is also someone who "seeks" Jesus; that is, he or she seeks to understand who he or she is by rightly interpreting the scriptures that testify to Jesus' being the Messiah.[104] The symbolic use of "to stay" means to continually abide or remain with Jesus.[105] Finally, Collins states that the second occurrence of "to see" in the narrative places an emphasis on the disciples' understanding of who Jesus is, an understanding that results in their staying with Jesus, and thus becoming his disciples.[106]

Collins closes his study of discipleship in John's Gospel with an additional word of how the reader is brought into the narrative. One of the initial pair of disciples is left unnamed. This is likely the Beloved Disciple, but on a symbolic level he is the reader of the Gospel, "for the story of the first encounter is the story of anyone who is truly a disciple of Jesus."[107] Collins's reading of the text on two levels is unfortunate and unnecessary. He hardly provides sufficient evidence for determining his "symbolic" reading as the method for ascertaining the identity of and conditions facing the Johannine community.

J. A. du Rand[108]

Following a brief survey of Johannine discipleship, du Rand looks at the usage of μαθητής ("disciple") and related terms in John's Gospel such as ἀδελφός ("brother"), υἱός ("son"), τεκνίον ("child"), and φίλος ("friend").[109] Next, he addresses some distinctive characteristics of discipleship according to the Farewell Discourse (John 13–17), which he views as a key theme.[110]

---

102. Ibid., 51.
103. Ibid.
104. Ibid., 52.
105. Ibid., 53.
106. Ibid., 53–54.
107. Ibid., 55.
108. Du Rand, "Perspectives," 311–325.
109. Ibid., 315–316.

110. Ibid., 320–321. Commenting on the emphasis on discipleship in the Farewell Discourse du Rand states, "[t]he repetitiveness of the theme of discipleship and the reciprocal relationship between Jesus' relation to the Father and his relation to the disciples

The first is the basis for discipleship, which is believing in Jesus. Belief in Jesus means to follow him "no matter what the cost."[111] Following Jesus is worked out in keeping Jesus' words and loving one another (cf. 13:35). Second, discipleship included knowing Jesus. Only those who are Jesus' own know him. To know Jesus is to perceive or have an understanding of his person and work.[112] The final characteristic of Johannine discipleship that du Rand comments on is love. According to du Rand, "[d]iscipleship is based on faith actualized by love."[113] Abiding in Jesus and obeying his love command enables the disciples to love one another, which is the mark of their discipleship with Jesus.[114] Related to obedience is John's usage of "to follow." Following Jesus for du Rand means "to participate in the salvation He brought (cf. 8:12)."[115] The ability to fully follow Jesus was possible only after Jesus' resurrection.[116]

W. Hulitt Gloer[117]

In a rather lengthy article, Gloer studies discipleship in John from two perspectives: (1) the disciples as a group and (2) individual portrayals of some of the disciples, including the Twelve and other characters. He focuses his study here because he believes it is in line with the purpose of the author of the Fourth Gospel, which is "to challenge the readers to continuing growth in discipleship" through viewing the disciples in the narrative and thereby identifying with them.[118]

First, Gloer addresses the disciples as a group. He believes the disciples as a group function as a singular character whom the reader may observe and whose maturation as disciples of Jesus the reader may see.[119] The group is almost always referred to as "disciples," over against "the Twelve,"

---

are dominant features in the narrative" (ibid., 320).

111. Ibid., 317.
112. Ibid.
113. Ibid.
114. Ibid., 318.
115. Ibid.
116. Ibid.
117. Gloer, "Come and See," 269–301.
118. Ibid., 276. Cf. 277, 291.
119. Ibid., 277.

and never "apostles." This enables the readers, whom Gloer believes to be disciples of Jesus, to identify with this group of Jesus' followers.[120]

Next, Gloer leads the reader through the Gospel of John, noting how the disciples as a group contribute to one's understanding of discipleship. He places particular emphasis on 1:35–51; 6:1–71; and 13:21—21:25. The contribution of 1:35–51 to one's understanding of discipleship is to show how the narrative "establishes the pattern and the goal for all who would be disciples of Jesus."[121] The disciples in this passage follow[122] Jesus, abide with him, hear and obey his words,[123] testify to others about him, and are promised to see "greater things," "things that will lead to deeper insights into Jesus' unique relationship to the Father."[124] The contribution of John 6 to one's understanding of discipleship is to present the question of whether or not one is prepared to accept the words of Jesus and thus believe in him.[125] The final lengthy passage of 13:21—21:25 contributes several characteristics of true discipleship. True discipleship includes: (1) obedience to Jesus' words; (2) believing that Jesus is the eternal Word sent from the Father; (3) recognizing that Jesus came to serve and ultimately give his life for sinners; (4) following Jesus in his suffering; (5) a process of increased, but gradual understanding of who Jesus is; and (6) abiding with him.[126]

Gloer's article concludes with his portrayal of individual disciples and what one can learn about discipleship from their example. From them one learns that a genuine disciple of Jesus is one who: (1) accepts the words of Jesus; (2) obeys Jesus' commands; (3) grows in one's understanding Jesus' person and work, "and the implication of Jesus' identity for the disciple"; and (4) testifies about Jesus no matter what the consequences.[127]

---

120. Ibid., 278.

121. Ibid., 279. Elsewhere in the article, Gloer concludes that 1:35—2:11 "is paradigmatic of the nature of a positive response to Jesus. The disciples have responded to the word of Jesus. They have followed him, and as a result they have seen" (ibid., 280).

122. Ibid. The verb ἀκολουθέω ("I follow") becomes a technical term in John for discipleship.

123. Ibid., 284. Accepting and obeying Jesus' words is a hallmark of an authentic disciple.

124. Ibid., 279–280.

125. Ibid., 284, 287.

126. Ibid., 289–290.

127. Ibid., 301.

Literature on Discipleship in the Gospel of John

Melvyn R. Hillmer[128]

In his contribution to *Patterns of Discipleship in the New Testament*, Melvyn Hillmer presents his understanding of discipleship in John's Gospel by first identifying the disciples and then speaking of discipleship in terms of relationship and action. He believes there are three groups who are identified with the "disciples" in John's Gospel: (1) those who followed the earthly Jesus, (2) those who comprised the Johannine community, and (3) genuine believers in Jesus throughout time.[129] He concludes this first section by noting that true disciples are those who have saving faith in Jesus and who openly bear witness about him.[130]

Next, Hillmer investigates discipleship from its relational aspect. Key to his development of discipleship as relational is his understanding of the place belief in and knowledge of Jesus play in the Fourth Gospel. Belief in Jesus "characterizes the true disciple throughout" the Gospel.[131] It is through belief in Jesus that one enters into a relationship with him and maintains it. Further, it results in eternal life.[132] To know Jesus, likewise, means to be in relationship with him. Knowledge of Jesus' identity and mission is necessary to believe in him. The one disciple in the Fourth Gospel who epitomizes this kind of relational discipleship is the Beloved Disciple.[133]

As important as the relational aspect is to John's presentation of discipleship in the Fourth Gospel, it must also include action on the part of the disciple. The term the evangelist uses most frequently with reference to discipleship as action is "follow." The verb (ἀκολουθέω) often refers to following Jesus as his disciple. Thus, Hillmer concludes, "[t]o be a disciple of Jesus, therefore, is to accept him as the Messiah, to live in accordance with his teachings, and to pattern one's life after him."[134]

---

128. Hillmer, "They Believed," 77–97.
129. Ibid., 78–79.
130. Ibid., 84.
131. Ibid.
132. Ibid., 85.
133. Ibid., 88.
134. Ibid., 89.

Following the Lamb

David R. Beck[135]

David R. Beck contends that the anonymity of certain characters in John's Gospel enhances the reader's ability to identify with them and participate in the narrative, which inclines "readers to identify with the disciple Jesus loved and participate in his discipleship paradigm."[136] This level of reader identification and participation is possible because "[t]he lack of a name removes the nomination barrier that distinguishes the character from other characters and from the reader."[137] An additional reason for focusing on the unnamed characters in John is their positive response to Jesus. This likewise, predisposes the reader to identify with them.[138]

Beck identifies the following anonymous characters with narrative significance that respond positively to Jesus: Jesus' mother (2:1–5; 19:25–27), the Samaritan woman (4:4–42), the royal official (4:46–53), the lame man (5:2–16),[139] the woman caught in adultery (7:53—8:11),[140] the man born blind (9:1–41), and after chapter 9 the anonymous disciple known as the Beloved Disciple.[141]

Through his study of anonymous characters, Beck concludes that genuine discipleship in John consists of three characteristics. The first is an "active faith response to Jesus' word." Second, and related to the first, is that faith in Jesus is not sign faith; that is, it is not based on "any visible demonstration" of Jesus' power. Finally, the one who expresses faith in Jesus becomes a "witness to the power of Jesus' word and what it accomplishes."[142]

---

135. Beck, *Discipleship Paradigm*. See also his article, "Anonymity," 143–158.

136. Beck, *Discipleship Paradigm*, 2.

137. Ibid., 1.

138. Ibid., 5.

139. It is difficult to see how the lame man can be viewed as providing a positive response to Jesus. Several scholars have noted the lame man's less than pure motives in telling the Jewish authorities about Jesus healing him on the Sabbath. Some of these scholars include: Carson, *John*, 245–246; Morris, *John*, 271–273; Ridderbos, *John*, 188–190; and Köstenberger, *John*, 181–183; 183 n. 41.

140. The textual evidence for the inclusion of this text in John's Gospel is anything but certain. For a brief synopsis of the textual evidence see Metzger, *Textual Commentary*, 187–189. Beck recognizes this, but still includes the text in his analysis because "it fits the narrative pattern of anonymous characters given significant textual space and a challenge to respond in faith to Jesus' word" ("Anonymity," 152).

141. Beck, *Discipleship Paradigm*, 51–136.

142. Ibid., 137.

Literature on Discipleship in the Gospel of John

Andreas J. Köstenberger[143]

Although not a work on discipleship per se, Köstenberger's work does provide a portrait of the disciples, their task, and mission. The purpose of his work appears to be concerned with investigating the mission of Jesus in the Fourth Gospel and to what extent the disciples continue his mission. The disciples' mission is described in terms of "harvesting," "fruitbearing," and "witnessing."[144]

Regarding the place of the disciples in John's Gospel, Köstenberger concludes that the author of the Gospel is concerned with both their "historical role" and their "representative function for later believers."[145] With regard to the characterization of individual disciples, the Beloved Disciple serves "as a figure of identification for the reader."[146] Köstenberger believes the most significant conclusion to be drawn from his investigation of the characterization of the disciples in John "is that of the priority of salvation history over literary strategy."[147] While some understand the disciples to be the fulfillment of the OT covenant community, Köstenberger notes that the author of the Fourth Gospel proclaims that Jesus is the one who replaces Israel (cf. 15:1). According to John's eschatology, Jesus continues his work of harvesting souls and bearing fruit through his disciples (cf. chapter 15; 12:24–26).[148]

From here, Köstenberger turns to the task of the disciples. In the Fourth Gospel the disciples are sent out into the harvest (4:38), bear fruit (15:16), testify about Jesus (15:27), and forgive the sins of others (20:23).[149] The disciples' mission is described in terms of "following" and "being sent." However, before the disciples can follow Jesus, they must first "come" to him. John associates "spiritual overtones" to the description of the disciples and others coming to Jesus. Coming to Jesus may be equated to believing in him.[150]

---

143. Köstenberger, *Mission of Jesus*, 141–198. Much of this content has been replicated, reformatted, and summarized in his book, *Theology of John*, 481–508.
144. Köstenberger, *Mission of Jesus*, 141.
145. Ibid., 167.
146. Ibid.
147. Ibid., 168.
148. Ibid., 169.
149. Ibid.
150. Ibid., 177.

Based on his study of "follow" in the Fourth Gospel, Köstenberger concludes the following points. First, in the course of the Gospel there is a move from literal following of Jesus to figuratively following him (cf. 1:37, 40, 43; 8:12).[151] Second, the scope of those who follow Jesus is widened from the original disciples to include all who believe in him (cf. 1:37–43; 8:12; chapter 10).[152] Third, following Jesus means dying to self (cf. 12:26; 21:15–23).[153] Fourth, following Jesus means following him in his death, which includes a life of "self-sacrifice, albeit not of atoning value and service (cf. 13:1–15; 15:13)."[154] Fifth, following Jesus is a "prerequisite" for being sent out on mission (cf. 17:18; 20:21).[155] Finally, John 21:15–23 shows that there are different ways for believers to follow Jesus; not everyone will follow him in physical death.[156]

Köstenberger plainly states that Jesus sends the disciples as the Father sent him. This leads Köstenberger to conclude that Jesus' mission is the disciples' mission, however, this does not diminish the uniqueness and once-for-all character of Jesus' work.[157] In fact, Köstenberger goes so far as to state that Jesus' mission does not conclude with his ascension, but it continues as he ministers through the Spirit and his disciples.[158] Nevertheless, he does provide several reasons for which Jesus sends the disciples: to bring glory to him and to do his will (cf. 4:3; 5:30, 38), to witness to Jesus (cf. 12:44, 45; 13:20), to know him (cf. 15:15; 17:7, 8, 25), and to follow Jesus' example (cf. 13:12–17).[159]

Paul Palatty[160]

Paul Palatty's article focuses on the characterization of the disciples in the Gospel of John to develop the Johannine theme of discipleship.[161] He bases

---

151. Ibid., 178.
152. Ibid.
153. Ibid.
154. Ibid., 179.
155. Ibid.
156. Ibid., 180.
157. Ibid., 195.
158. Ibid., 196.
159. Ibid., 195.
160. Palatty, "Discipleship," 285–306.
161. Ibid., 288.

this method on previous studies that have understood the disciples as not only historical figures, but also persons of "symbolic significance" that may serve as representative characters to emulate.[162] Beginning with the call narrative (1:35–50), Palatty mines what can be gathered about discipleship from Jesus' interaction with several of the disciples. In particular, he covers Jesus' relationship with Andrew, Peter, Philip, Nathanael, and the unnamed disciple, whom he identifies with the Beloved Disciple.[163] His analysis of the Beloved Disciple takes him beyond the call narrative to address other passages (13:23–26; 19:25–27; 20:2–10; 21:7, 24). Finally, he discusses the relationship between Jesus and Judas, and Jesus and Thomas.[164]

This leads him to several discoveries; those germane to the topic of discipleship in John are listed below.

1. The evangelist of the Fourth Gospel does not deal with the theme of discipleship as a subject to be studied, but as a relationship to be experienced.

2. This relationship is a process of coming, seeing, believing, and remaining with Jesus. Remaining with Jesus enables one to live like him. The "keynote" of Jesus' discipleship relationship is love, love for one's fellow disciples.

3. The disciples in John function as models of what it means to be a disciple of Jesus.

4. Jesus extends his call of discipleship to all persons. The aim or goal of the Fourth Gospel is to see all persons enter into Jesus' discipleship.[165]

The Period from 2000 to Present

Since 2000, there have been only two book-length treatments on discipleship in the Gospel of John. Those written by Rekha M. Chennattu and Marianus Pale Hera are presented in this section.

---

162. Ibid.
163. Ibid., 292–298.
164. Ibid., 298–302.
165. Ibid., 305–306.

Following the Lamb

Rekha M. Chennattu[166]

Chennattu identifies John 1, 13–17, and 20–21 as the discipleship narratives and discourses that are "entirely dedicated" to discipleship in the Fourth Gospel.[167] She also seeks to analyze 13–17 and 20–21 since previous studies have not provided a detailed analysis of these texts with respect to the theme of discipleship in John.[168] What makes her study of discipleship in John stand out from others is her belief that OT covenantal motifs lie behind John's presentation of discipleship, and that this results in a definition of Johannine discipleship that views discipleship in terms of an covenantal relationship.[169] The portions of her work that are summarized here are her exegesis of John 1, 13–17, and 20–21 and the OT covenantal motifs that lie behind John's presentation of discipleship.

Chennattu understands the inclusion of 1:35–51 at the beginning of John as paradigmatic of discipleship for the entire Gospel.[170] Accordingly, Chennattu believes the Fourth Gospel presents the call narrative in 1:35–51, not only as part of the ongoing introduction to the Gospel, but also as a "hermeneutical frame that will influence and shape the interpretation of the rest of the story."[171] Since it is a paradigm, it appears elsewhere in the Gospel.

There are several key terms contained in the call narrative that take on greater meaning in the course of the Gospel. The first is "I follow" (ἀκολουθέω), which is indicative of one's commitment to Jesus.[172] Second is "I remain/abide" (μένω), which the disciples desire to do because of the revelation about Jesus.[173] It is also used of the disciples' remaining/abiding with Jesus, which only hints at what it means to have an abiding relationship with Jesus (cf. 15:1–17).[174] Third are the terms "I come" (ἔρχομαι) and "I see" (ὁράω), both of which are used to describe Jesus' invitation "to enter

---

166. Chennattu, *Johannine Discipleship*.
167. Ibid., 23.
168. Ibid., 19.
169. Ibid., 180.
170. Ibid., 49.
171. Ibid., 23.
172. Ibid., 29.
173. Ibid., 32.
174. Ibid.

into a *personal relationship with Jesus* and to be open to the ongoing revelation of God in Jesus."[175]

In addition to exploring key discipleship terminology in 1:35–51, Chennattu discovers the following OT covenant motifs at play in the narrative. The first is abiding in God's commands and in himself. This is displayed through the idea of abiding in Jesus' words and himself. Second is knowledge of the Messiah. The disciples' knowledge that Jesus is the Messiah progresses throughout the course of the Fourth Gospel, although one sees hints of it in Nathanael's acknowledgement of Jesus as rabbi, the Son of God, and the King of Israel (cf. 1:49). Third, one's knowledge of God in the OT implies a covenant relationship with him. Nathanael's own knowledge of Jesus is interpreted by Jesus as acknowledgement of his belief in him, and thus, the beginning of a covenant relationship (cf. 1:49–50). Fourth, old covenant members were to pass on their faith to the next generation. Here, one sees both Andrew and Philip telling others that they had found the long-awaited Messiah, who was Jesus (cf. 1:40–41, 45). Fifth, name changes were linked to the covenant motif in the OT, as in the case of Abraham (cf. Gen 17:1–22). One sees this similarly on display in the example of Simon, whom Jesus renames Cephas (cf. John 1:42). Finally, in the OT, the Lord makes several promises as part of his covenant with Israel (cf. Exod 25:8; 29:45–46). In John 1:50–51, Jesus is the one who makes promises to those who will follow him as his disciples.[176]

Next, Chennattu sets out to analyze John 13–17 for how it reflects discipleship as a covenant relationship. For starters, Chennattu views chapters 13–17 as similar to the OT covenant renewal ceremonies.[177] For instance, the consequences of discipleship articulated in 15:18—16:24, namely, persecution (cf. 15:18–20; 16:2) and the gift of the Holy Spirit (15:26–27; 16:4–24), are similar to the warnings presented in Josh 24:19–20, prior to the Israelites' covenant renewal ceremony. In addition, the disciples are afforded an opportunity to respond to what Jesus has just taught them (cf. John 16:25–33). This is like the opportunity the Israelites had to respond to the Lord's declaration of his covenant with them in Josh 24:25–28.[178]

There are several old covenant themes that recur in John 15–17: "election [15:16], intimate abiding relationship [15:1–17], indwelling presence

---

175. Ibid., 31.
176. Ibid., 43–49.
177. Ibid., 88.
178. Ibid., 134.

[17:20–23], keeping God's commandments [15:9–17], and mutual knowledge [17:6–8, 25–26]."[179] Within chapters 15–17 Chennattu finds the greatest concentration of the Johannine paradigm of discipleship. In 15:1–17 she identifies the following discipleship themes: "to abide in Jesus' love, to glorify the Father by means of bearing much fruit, to keep the covenant commandments of love, and to be the chosen people of God."[180]

When she turns to her analysis of John 20–21, Chennattu draws special attention to the promise-fulfillment motif common in covenant material of the OT, which she sees throughout this passage. For instance, Jesus promised he would return to the Father (13:33; 14:28), the fulfillment of which is his resurrection.[181] In addition, some of the earlier themes of the discipleship paradigm resurface in John 20–21, such as bearing witness (cf. 20:23) and the importance of the disciples abiding with Jesus if they are to bear fruit (cf. 15:5); a truth she sees displayed in the miraculous catch of fish (cf. 21:1–6).

Her study on discipleship as covenant relationship is aimed at understanding the relevance of it for the Johannine community and describing their identity.[182] Chennattu's findings lead her to conclude, "the paradigm of discipleship as a covenant relationship redefines the community as the chosen people of God and consolidates the group as a distinct social and religious community."[183] She characterizes this community as a "perceived . . . deviant group within synagogue Judaism of post-70 CE."[184] While Chennattu's work contributes to a fuller understanding of Johannine discipleship, it unconvincingly attempts to draw conclusions about the Gospel's original audience.

Marianus Pale Hera[185]

Following a presentation of the relevant literature on discipleship, Hera turns his attention to advancing his argument that John 17 presents discipleship flowing out of John's presentation of Christology. Hera believes

179. Ibid., 139.
180. Ibid., 138.
181. Ibid., 177.
182. Ibid., 22.
183. Ibid., 211.
184. Ibid.
185. Hera, *Christology and Discipleship*.

Literature on Discipleship in the Gospel of John

Jesus' prayer in John 17 is primarily Christological in nature. At the same time, the prayer took place in the presence of Jesus' disciples. Although a prayer, John 17 "functions as an address and admonition to the disciples, like the rest of Jesus' farewell discourse. It portrays how John views the true identity of the disciples of Jesus. John 17 therefore exhibits not only a christological teaching but a teaching about discipleship."[186]

However, before proceeding to John 17, Hera surveys John 1–12 for instances of Christology and discipleship. What he finds are five elements that identify a relationship between Christology and discipleship. First, there is a movement from Christology to discipleship. Christological teaching leads to teaching about the true nature of discipleship.[187] For instance, Jesus' first "sign" (σημεῖον) at Cana of Galilee through which Jesus' glory is revealed is so that the disciples believe in him (2:11; cf. 20:31). Also, the narrative of the man born blind is presented as an argument about who Jesus is and results in the man placing faith in Jesus (9:38).[188] Second, there is an emphasis on the significance of knowing Jesus. Essentially, knowledge about Jesus leads to discipleship. This is seen in several places, but first in the call narrative. The first two disciples follow Jesus and remain with him on account of first hearing John the Baptizer's testimony that Jesus was the Lamb of God (1:35–37). According to Hera, "[i]n the Johannine context, to know Jesus means to believe in him and become his disciple."[189] Further, to not know Jesus is to reject him (cf. 1:10–11; 15:21–25).[190] Third, Jesus is the model for the disciples. According to Hera, "John develops his portrait of a true disciple on the pattern of Jesus' own identity in his unique Father-Son relationship with God."[191] This is seen most clearly through Jesus' use of καθώς ("just as"). One particular occurrence, John 10, displays that Jesus knows his sheep and his sheep know him "just as" the Father knows him and he knows the Father (10:14–15).[192] Fourth, there is a balance between divine sovereignty and human responsibility. John portrays discipleship as

---

186. Ibid., 36.

187. Ibid., 85–86. Hera makes this perfectly clear, "In the Fourth Gospel the christological content of the narrative leads to discipleship, and the teaching about discipleship flows from the Gospel's Christology, which is the heartbeat and the center of the Johannine thought" (ibid., 85–86).

188. Ibid., 85

189. Ibid., 86.

190. Ibid.

191. Ibid., 87.

192. Ibid.

a result of divine initiative and at the same time something for which human beings are responsible. God's children are those who are "born . . . of God" (1:13). And yet, this same group is those who "believed in his name" (1:12).[193] The final element of relationship between Christology and discipleship is the central role of Jesus. Hera believes that for John "Jesus is the ultimate goal of discipleship."[194] In the end, it is about solely following Jesus and being his disciple.[195]

Following his analysis of the relationship between Christology and discipleship in John 1–12 Hera turns his attention to the literary context, text critical questions, and structure of John 17. With regard to the structure, Hera believes the prayer is one of moving from Christology to discipleship. He sees in these two themes "the unifying thread that holds the prayer in John 17 as a coherent unity."[196]

Finally, in chapter four, Hera presents his analysis of John 17. He believes John 17 is clearly a presentation of Christology in the form of a prayer.[197] In addition, John 17 presents a positive picture of the disciples, rather than portraying them as a group who are fraught with misunderstandings of Jesus' person and work.[198] The following positive presentation of the disciples occurs in John 17: they keep Jesus' words; they know who Jesus is; they believe in him; they are given to Jesus by the Father; Jesus is glorified in them; Jesus desires for them to be protected, consecrated, united, and abide in him.[199] Further, in John 17 the same elements that identify a relationship between Christology and discipleship in John 1–12 are on display.[200]

In addition, Hera finds two supplemental sets of qualities and characteristics of Jesus' disciples in John 17. One set of qualities is seen in the ἵνα clauses (except in 17:1, 4, 12). In these instances, the disciples are shown to have the following qualities: "having eternal life, knowledge, unity, joy,

---

193. Ibid.
194. Ibid., 88.
195. Ibid.
196. Ibid., 122.
197. Ibid., 167.
198. Ibid.
199. Ibid.
200. Ibid., 168–169. These elements are: (1) the movement from Christology to discipleship, (2) an emphasis on the significance of knowing Jesus, (3) Jesus as the model for the disciples, (4) the balance between divine sovereignty and human responsibility, and (5) the central role of Jesus.

Literature on Discipleship in the Gospel of John

being consecrated, being with Jesus, and seeing his glory."[201] Another set of characteristics is seen through the use of καθώς (except in 17:2) with respect to Jesus' position as a model for his disciples. Here the following qualities his disciples should have include: "unity, separation from the world, being sent into the world, and being loved by the Father."[202] Although Jesus serves as a model, this does not negate his unique person and work.[203]

CODING FRAME BASED ON ANALYSIS OF RELEVANT LITERATURE

Having covered the relevant literature on discipleship in the Gospel of John, one is left with determining what method of analysis presented in the literature will lead to developing an effective coding frame. Hera has pointed out that various methods have proven useful in analyzing the theme of discipleship in John's Gospel, including studies that mainly focus on key terms (such as seeking, following, abiding, etc.), those which emphasize the characterization of the disciples in an effort to determine a paradigm of discipleship, and his own method that looks at the relationship between Christology and discipleship.[204] Therefore, no one presentation will be used, but each of the works surveyed will be analyzed in the development of a coding frame.

The call narrative of John 1:35–51 proved to be an important text with respect to John's portrayal of discipleship. Several of the works reviewed relied heavily on this text in their assessment of the nature of discipleship in the Gospel of John.[205] Some even viewed this passage as paradigmatic of discipleship for the whole of John's Gospel.[206] Therefore, this "paradigm of discipleship" is primary for the development of the coding frame. Not only key terms but also discipleship themes, which flow out of 1:35–51 and are further developed in John's Gospel, are noted.

201. Ibid., 174.
202. Ibid.
203. Ibid.
204. Ibid., 176.
205. Those scholars include: de Jonge, *Jesus*, 12–14; Vellanickal, "Discipleship," 134–140; Collins, *These Things*, 47–55; Gloer, "Come and See," 276–280; and Chennattu, *Johannine Discipleship*, 22–49.
206. Collins, *These Things*, 50; Gloer, "Come and See," 279–280; and Chennattu, *Johannine Discipleship*, 49.

1. *The uses of ἀκολουθέω and similar terms that are used with reference to being a disciple or follower of Jesus (e.g. ὀπίσω).* "Follow" is used throughout John's Gospel to denote discipleship (1:43; 8:12; 10:4–5, 15, 27; 12:26; 21:19, 22). Following Jesus includes a life of sacrificial service, which may mean suffering as Jesus did (12:24–26; 13:1–15; 15:20). The call of Jesus to "come and see" (ἔρχομαι and ὁράω) is a reminder of God's initiative in calling disciples (1:39). At times, the call to come to Jesus is synonymous with a call to believe in him (6:35). Following Jesus is a result of being called by him.

2. *Union with Christ.* To "remain" or "abide" (μένω) with Jesus in the course of the Gospel means to permanently commune with Jesus (1:39; cf. 6:56; 15:1–17). "Remain" is also used with reference to keeping Jesus' teachings and commands (8:31). Those who do so are identified as his disciples.

3. *The uses of γινώσκω, ὁράω, and similar terms that are used to articulate coming to an understanding of Jesus' person and work.* Knowledge of Jesus is indicative of a relationship with him. Jesus interprets Nathanael's knowledge of who he is as acknowledgement of Nathanael's belief in him (1:49–50; cf. 10:4; 17:3). In addition, both ἔρχομαι and ὁράω may be used to call the disciple to arrive at a greater understanding of Jesus' person and work as is seen in the responses of the first disciples (1:39, 41, 45, 49).

4. *Believe (πιστεύειν) in Jesus Christ for salvation.* "Belief" in Jesus as God's Son and Messiah is necessary for salvation, which in John's Gospel is often referred to as "eternal life" (3:16–17; 20:31).

5. *Membership and election of the people of God.* Jesus calls his first disciples to follow him. While some may interpret Jesus' walking by the disciples as an instance of his call or choosing his disciples,[207] it is probably better to refer to his call of Philip (1:43) as an indication of Jesus' choosing of his disciples, something that is expressed elsewhere in the Gospel (6:70). It is also possible to see in the renaming of Peter (1:42) and affirmation of Nathanael (1:47) a reflection of the election motif of the OT. Those with whom God initiated a covenant would often receive a new name (e.g., Abraham and Israel), which indicated

---

207. Vellanickal, "'Discipleship,'" 135.

a change in their character, role, or status. Something similar may be at play in the renaming of Peter.[208]

6. *Bear witness to Jesus.* Those who follow Jesus call others to follow him (1:41, 45–46). Disciples are expected to be witnesses to Jesus (cf. 15:27). Jesus' disciples are those who publicly testify to his person and work regardless of the consequences (1:40–41, 45; cf. 4:7–45; 15:27; 17:20–21).

7. *Witness to "greater things."* Jesus promises the disciples that they will witness "greater things" (1:51), which refer to "revelations of God's glory in Christ."[209] As the Gospel unfolds, the disciples encounter displays of God's glory in his Son (cf. 2:11; 11:4, 40; 12:23–24; 13:31).

8. *Keep and obey Jesus'/God's commands.* On several occasions Jesus issues commands to his disciples (1:43; 6:10–12; 12:7; 13:34; 15:9). These commands, these words of Jesus they are to keep and obey. Further, they serve as evidence of one's love for Jesus (14:15, 21, 23; 15:10).

In addition to these eight that are mentioned in 1:35–51 and expanded upon elsewhere, there are additional discipleship themes emphasized in the relevant literature. These include the following:

9. *Consequences of following Jesus.* Jesus makes clear that there is a cost to following him as one of his disciples. Since Jesus suffered for his commitment to his Father, Jesus' disciples can also expect to suffer loss for their commitment to him (12:24–26; 13:1–15; 15:20).

10. *Marks of discipleship.* On three distinct occasions, Jesus articulates what marks someone as one of his disciples. Jesus' disciples are those who: (1) keep his teaching, that is, hold to it and obey it[210] (8:31–32); (2) have love for other disciples (13:34–35); and (3) bear much fruit (15:8) on account of their union with Christ (15:4).

11. *Distinction between Jesus' disciples and non-disciples.* There are several ways in which John distinguishes the disciples, those who believe in Jesus and follow him, from the world, those who are opposed to him and reject him as God's sent Son and Messiah. From the onset of the Gospel, the world is characterized as those who do not recognize

---

208. Morris, *John*, 140–141.
209. Köstenberger, *John*, 87.
210. Carson, *John*, 348.

Jesus, while God's children are those who receive him by believing in Jesus' name (1:10–13). Jesus even prays for the Father to "sanctify," or consecrate, his disciples (17:17). They are to be distinct from the world and yet remain in it (17:15–16).

12. *Jesus as the model for his disciples.* Jesus' relationship with his Father serves as an example of the kind of relationship Jesus' disciples are to have with him. This may be seen in some of the "just as" (καθώς) statements (6:56–57; 10:14–15).

SUMMARY

To date, several works have been written on discipleship in the Gospel of John. Those surveyed in this chapter happen to be the relevant scholarly works. These works have utilized various methods to study the concept of discipleship in John. Some have emphasized the characterization of the disciples and other characters (Culpepper, Beck, Palatty); others have focused on key terminology located in significant texts (Vellanickal, du Rand, Gloer); others have used some mixture of the two methods (Schnackenburg, Collins); and still others have addressed discipleship as it relates to some other Johannine theme (Köstenberger, Hera) or some additional motif (Chennattu).

In spite of these differences, these works have focused on many of the same pericopae and have arrived at similar conclusions regarding discipleship in John's Gospel. The themes most often represented have been utilized in the construction of the coding frame that will be employed to conduct a content analysis of the theme of discipleship in the book of Revelation.

Coding frame
1. The uses of ἀκολουθέω and similar terms that are used with reference to being a disciple or follower of Jesus (e.g., ὀπίσω).
2. Union with Christ.
3. The uses of γινώσκω, ὁράω, and similar terms that are used to articulate coming to an understanding of Jesus' person and work.
4. Believe (πιστεύειν) in Jesus for salvation.
5. Membership and election of the people of God.
6. Bear witness to Jesus.
7. Witness to "greater things."
8. Keep and obey Jesus'/God's commands.
9. Consequences of following Jesus.
10. Marks of discipleship.
11. Distinction between Jesus' disciples and non-disciples.
12. Jesus as the model for his disciples.

Table 1. Coding frame.

4

Discipleship in the Book of Revelation

INTRODUCTION

IN THE PREVIOUS CHAPTER, a coding frame was developed in which a content analysis on the theme of discipleship in Revelation could be conducted. This chapter, then, is the application of that coding frame to the Apocalypse. The analysis of Revelation utilizes the structure proposed by Carson, Moo, and Morris[1] with slight modification:

1. Prologue (1:1–20)
2. Messages to the Seven Churches (2:1—3:22)
3. A Vision of Heaven (4:1—5:14)
4. The Seven Seals (6:1—8:5)
5. The Seven Trumpets (8:6—11:19)
6. Seven Significant Signs (12:1—14:20)
7. The Seven Bowls (15:1—16:21)
8. The Fall of Babylon (17:1—19:5)

---

1. Carson et al., *Introduction*, 466-467. The slight modification refers to sections eight and nine, which Carson et al. combine (Rev 17:1—20:15) (467). Instead, Mounce's outline and headings are followed for sections eight and nine (Mounce, *Revelation*, 35).

9. The Final Victory (19:6—20:15)

10. A New Heaven and a New Earth (21:1—22:5)

11. Epilogue (22:6-21)

AN ANALYSIS OF REVELATION 1:1-20

Discipleship Language[2]

In Rev 1:1 the intended audience of the "revelation" is referred to as "his servants" (τοῖς δούλοις αὐτοῦ). The term δοῦλος ("servant, slave") occurs fourteen times in Revelation. In three occurrences it is used literally (cf. 6:15; 13:16; 19:18), and the remaining eleven carry a metaphorical meaning.[3] The antecedent of "his," in the phrase "his servants," may be Jesus Christ or God. The immediate antecedent appears to be Jesus, since it is Jesus who receives from God "the revelation."[4]

Later in the same verse John, the author of the book, is also called "his servant" (δούλῳ αὐτοῦ). One encounters the same difficulties in locating the antecedent of the possessive pronoun. It probably matters little whether one affirms that John is God's servant or Jesus' servant.[5]

It is still necessary to identify who the "servants" are, regardless of whether the servants in question are servants of God or of Jesus. Aune believes "servant" is used here as a general term for Christians, which is one of the ways it is used elsewhere in the book (cf. 2:20; 7:3; 19:2, 5; 22:3, 6).[6] In an earlier article, he argued that "servant" in 1:1 may be a reference

---

2. This aspect of the coding frame was formally articulated as "The uses of ἀκολουθέω and similar terms that are used with reference to being a disciple or follower of Jesus (e.g., ὀπίσω)" at the conclusion of chapter 3.

3. Aune, *Revelation 1-5*, 13. Aune breaks down the eleven metaphorical uses into the following categories: Moses (15:3); John (1:1), prophets (10:7; 11:18), and most frequently Christians (1:1; 2:20; 7:3; 19:2, 5; 22:3, 6).

4. This seems to be the conclusion of Patterson, *Revelation*, 53. Aune believes the antecedent of the possessive pronoun is God, since the verse closely parallels Rev 22:6, where the servants are clearly God's (Aune, *Revelation 1-5*, 13. So also Beale, *Revelation*, 1125; Kistemaker, *Revelation*, 77). The distinction may not be necessary, since elsewhere in the book others are referred to as Jesus' servants (cf. 2:20).

5. Aune appears to favor the antecedent as God (*Revelation 1-5*, 17), while Mounce seems to favor it as Jesus (*Revelation*, 42).

6. Aune, *Revelation 1-5*, 13. So also Koester, *Revelation*, 211; Osborne, *Revelation*, 54 n. 5.

to a circle of prophets. His reasoning led him to the conclusion that John himself is to be viewed among the circle of prophets, since he designates himself a "servant" also (cf. 1:1).[7] While Bauckham is uncertain that one can conclude with any certitude that the "servants" in 1:1 are this circle of prophets, he does not outright dismiss the interpretation that John's designation of himself as a "servant" refers to his prophetic role.[8] However, it is far more likely that the use of the term "servant" in both instances refers to Christians in general, since the word "prophet" does not occur in the immediate context. Only in Rev 10:7 and 11:18 are the "servants" explicitly referred to as "prophets," and in 11:18 the "servants" are also identified as "saints," that is, Christians in general.[9]

If these "servants" are Christians, then might this be an example of discipleship language in the book of Revelation? Michael Wilkins seems to think so. He notes several terms used in place of "disciple" (μαθητής) in the NT Epistles and Revelation. Among these terms is "servant" (δοῦλος, διάκονος). This is actually a term Jesus used not only with reference to his own mission, but also with respect to how his disciples were to relate to him and one another for the sake of the Kingdom (cf. Mark 10:42–45; Luke 22:24–27).[10] In addition, the Christians in the early chapters of Acts bear the same designation (cf. Acts 2:18; 4:29).[11] John in the Fourth Gospel actually uses the term three times with direct reference to Jesus' disciples (cf. John 13:16; 15:15; 20). The use of "servant" with reference to Jesus' disciples in the Gospels and Acts, and its use in Revelation with reference to Christians appears to provide a link that suggests "servants" in Rev 1:1 and elsewhere in the book (cf. 2:20; 7:3; 19:2, 5; 22:3, 6) is in fact discipleship language.

---

7. Aune, "Prophetic Circle," 110. R. H. Charles comes to a similar view apparently based on Amos 3:7 and Jer 23:18, and the use of "servant" for "prophets" in Rev 10:7; 11:18; 19:2 (*Revelation*, 1.6). So also Smalley, *Revelation*, 27.

8. Bauckham, *Climax of Prophecy*, 86.

9. The phrase "for rewarding your servants, the prophets and saints" is an example of a dative in simple apposition. In this grammatical construction, the second dative, of which both "prophets and saints" (τοῖς προφήταις καὶ τοῖς ἁγίοις) are, serves to clarify the first dative, which is "servants" (τοῖς δούλοις). Thus, the kinds of servants the Lord God Almighty will reward are prophets and saints. For a fuller explanation of the dative of simple apposition see: Wallace, *Greek Grammar*, 152–153.

10. Wilkins, *Following the Master*, 298. Mark Wilson provides a table with a host of designations ascribed to Christians in the book of Revelation, including "servants" (*Charts on Revelation*, 35).

11. Thomas, *Revelation 1–7*, 53.

Discipleship in the Book of Revelation

In the NT, δοῦλος ("servant, slave") may be used of the Christian who obediently serves the command of the κύριος ("Lord") (cf. Rom 12:11; 14:18; Col 3:24).[12] Similarly to John in Rev 1:1, the apostle Paul frequently referred to himself in the opening of his letters as a δοῦλος Χριστοῦ Ἰησοῦ ("servant of Christ Jesus") (cf. Rom 1:1; Phil 1:1; Gal 1:10).[13] The "servants'" relationship to the "Lord" is one of exclusive subordination to his rule (Eph 6:9).[14] Christians are the possession of the one who has purchased them; all allegiance is owed to Christ their master.[15] Christ is *the* Lord of the Christian because he is the one who has freed him or her from the bondage of sin (Rom 6:17). The means of manumission, Jesus' own death, is the payment that transfers ownership of the individual from being a "slave [servant] to sin" to being a "slave [servant] of God" and his Son, Jesus Christ (1 Cor 6:20; 7:23; Gal 3:13; 4:4–5; Rev 5:9; 14:3; Rom 6:22).[16]

As a servant of Jesus, John lived to serve him. In the context of Rev 1, John serves as the one who will record in a book what he will be shown and will then send that message to the seven churches of Asia Minor.[17] Jesus initially commissions John for this task in 1:11 and reaffirms this in 1:19.[18]

---

12. Tuente, "δοῦλος," 596.
13. Ibid.
14. Ibid.
15. Spicq, "δοῦλος, οἰκέτης, κτλ.," 382.
16. Tuente, "δοῦλος," 3.597; Spicq, "δοῦλος, οἰκέτης, κτλ.," 381.
17. Osborne, *Revelation*, 56.
18. There is debate as to the relationship between the command to write in Rev 1:11 and 1:19 and what John is to write down in 1:19. Osborne believes that according to 1:19, what John is to write down concerns the entirety of the vision. He believes the three relative clauses, introduced by ἅ ("what," NIV; "that," ESV), provide an outline for the entire book: (1) "that you have seen" = 1:12–16; (2) "that are [now]" = chapters 2–3; and (3) "that are to take place after this" = chapters 4–22. Thus, he believes the command in 1:11 "most likely introduces the visions of the whole book and is expanded in verse 19" (*Revelation*, 84). However, the difficulty with such chronological approaches is the fact that chapters 4–22 deal with the past, present, and future (Aune, *Revelation 1–5*, 105).

So, if the relative clauses do not necessarily refer to the chronology of the book, then to what might they refer? Beale argues that John had Dan 2:28–29, 45 in mind when he used these three relative clauses, particularly his use of μετὰ ταῦτα ("after this") in the third clause, "that are to take place *after this*" (emphasis added, Rev 1:19c). The phrase "after this," then, is used by John "as an eschatological reference, particularly to the general period of the latter days, which had begun, was presently ongoing, and would continue in the future until the consummation" (Beale, *Revelation*, 155). He admits that if John did not have Dan 2 in mind, then one of the chronological approaches would be preferable (ibid., 216).

The use of the term "servant" for both John and his audience serves to show that both are servants of the Lord Jesus Christ. John does see himself as greater than his fellow Christians with whom he suffers (cf. Rev 1:9).[19] All Christians are servants of Christ, which "becomes a beautiful title of honor for God's people."[20]

Bear Witness to Jesus

In Rev 1:2 one is introduced to the first occurrence of the μαρτυρία ("witness") word group. Here, John, the author of the book, is identified as one "who bore witness to the word of God and to the testimony of Jesus Christ." In this verse alone one finds both the verbal form of "witness" (μαρτυρέω) and the noun (μαρτυρία). The verb μαρτυρέω occurs four times in Revelation. The noun μαρτυρία occurs nine times in the book. The usage of the noun (μαρτυρία) is found almost exclusively in the Johannine literature. It is used sparingly with reference to one who is a witness of someone or something (John 8:17; 1 John 5:9; 3 John 12). Most of its occurrences refer to one who witnesses to Jesus' person and work, so that those who hear the testimony may come to faith in Christ. Of the nine occurrences of μαρτυρία in Revelation, six of them are part of the genitive phrase "testimony of Jesus [Christ]," which may refer to "Christian revelation in general."[21]

The verb μαρτυρέω refers to what a "witness" actually does. One is a "witness" because one offers a testimony of what one has seen. One is an eyewitness to someone's actions or words, or to an event. This is what the entire Apocalypse is: John's testimony about "everything he saw" (NIV), which for him is defined as "the word of God and the testimony of Jesus Christ" (Rev 1:2, NIV). Of its four occurrences in Revelation, μαρτυρέω refers to the content of the vision John saw and recorded, save 22:18, where either Jesus or John testifies to a warning to everyone who may add or detract from the content of the book.[22]

---

19. Keener, *Revelation*, 55; Osborn, *Revelation*, 55.

20. Johnson, "Revelation," 595. Aune provides extensive evidence that δοῦλος was a title of honor in the ancient world (*Revelation 1–5*, 16–17).

21. Strathmann, "μάρτυς, μαρτυρέω, κτλ.," 499–501. Bauckham notes that of the fourteen occurrences of "Jesus," seven are connected with μαρτυρία or μαρτύρων (1:2, 9; 12:17; 17:6; 19:10 [twice]; 20:4) (*Climax of Prophecy*, 34; Bauckham, *Theology of Revelation*, 66).

22. Both the NIV and ESV translate μαρτυρέω "I warn," which is the point of the verse. Revelation 22:18–19 serve as a warning to not add to or take away from the content

Discipleship in the Book of Revelation

John bears witness to "the word of God and to the testimony of Jesus Christ."[23] These two genitive phrases are closely linked. The "testimony of Jesus Christ" serves to explain the "word of God" to which John was a witness.[24] What John bore witness to was then recorded as the content of the entire book.[25]

The two genitive phrases ("the word of God and the testimony of Jesus Christ," NIV) are usually taken as objective[26] or subjective genitives,[27] but may also be an instance of a plenary genitive, a genitive that is both objective and subjective in nature.[28] If this is the case, then what John bore witness to was the word *about* God that was also *from* God and the testimony *about* Jesus that was also *from* Jesus. The ambiguous nature of this genitive construction allows for both a subjective and objective feel to the genitive phrases.[29]

---

of the book, in order not to suffer the consequences. The NASB favors a translation closely tied to the lexical meaning of μαρτυρέω, "I testify."

23. The phrase "word of God" occurs seven times (cf. Rev 1:2, 9; 6:9; 17:17; 19:19, 13; 20:4) and the phrase "testimony of Jesus [Christ]" occurs six times (cf. 1:2, 9; 12:17; 19:10 [twice]; 20:4) (Osborne, *Revelation*, 56–57).

24. Beale, *Revelation*, 184; Mounce, *Revelation*, 42–43. Thomas believes the καὶ ("and") separating the two phrases is "epexegetical" (*Revelation 1–7*, 59). So also Aune, *Revelation 1–5*, 19 and Blount, *Revelation*, 28. For an explanation of the epexegetical use of καὶ see: Robertson, *Grammar*, 1181.

25. The aorist form of the verb ὁράω (translated "he saw" in 1:2) is likely an example of an epistolary aorist. Wallace defines an epistolary aorist as "the use of the aorist indicative . . . in which the author self-consciously describes his letter from the time frame of the audience" (*Greek Grammar*, 562).

26. Osborne, *Revelation*, 57. He also notes a "subjective sense" to the phrase (*Revelation*, 57). Curiously, Osborne mentions that the phrase "word of God" is a possessive genitive or genitive of source, but makes no attempt to ascertain whether or not it is objective or subjective (*Revelation*, 56).

27. Aune, *Revelation 1–5*, 19; Charles, *Revelation*, 1.7; Johnson, "Revelation," 595; Kistemaker, *Revelation*, 78; Koester, *Revelation*, 213; Ladd, *Revelation*, 23; Mounce, *Revelation*, 42 n. 18; Smalley, *Revelation*, 30.

28. Beale, *Revelation*, 183–184; Wallace, *Greek Grammar*, 119–121. Keener merely notes the phrases could either be an objective or subjective genitive (*Revelation*, 56). Perhaps his own ambiguity concerning an ambiguous genitive construction is intended to allow room for both aspects to inform the meaning of the two phrases, thus, leading one to conclude that "the word of God and the testimony of Jesus Christ" (NIV) are plenary genitives.

29. Beale believes similar genitive phrases throughout Revelation (cf. 1:1; 1:9; 6:9; 20:4) are ambiguous and thus should likely be understood as plenary genitives (*Revelation*, 184). Koester notes the difficulty in distinguishing whether the author has an

Following a blessing to those who read the book, hear it, and "keep what is written" (1:3), John greets the seven churches to whom Revelation will be sent (1:4–5a) and gives praise to the one "who loves us and has freed us from our sins by his blood" (1:5b–8). In Rev 1:9 John states his comradery with other Christians in suffering for the Kingdom and speaks of his exile to the isle of Patmos because of "the word of God and the testimony of Jesus" (NIV). Here one encounters a third term from the μαρτυρία word group, the noun μάρτυς ("testimony"). The term μάρτυς may be used simply to refer to one who bears witness to the facts. This may take place as part of legal proceedings. Often these proceedings required two to three witnesses, as was the case for a capital offense (cf. Deut 17:6). The necessity of two or three witnesses is also affirmed in the case of confronting an erring church member (cf. Matt 18:16). In Luke, especially, one finds the term used with reference to one who publicly testifies to the life, death, burial, and bodily resurrection of Jesus, as well as the significance of these events (cf. Luke 24:45–48). Jesus' disciples were qualified to be "witnesses [μάρτυρες] of these things" because they had actually been eyewitnesses to Jesus' ministry. Since they were eyewitnesses and shared in Jesus' ministry, they would likewise be sent out to bear witness to the gospel of Jesus Christ.[30] Similarly, in Revelation, three of the five occurrences of μάρτυς refer to those who remain faithful to Jesus, in part by proclaiming God's word (cf. Rev 2:13; 11:3; 17:6). In these instances, those who are Jesus' witnesses suffer death as a result.[31]

On the whole, the μαρτυρία word group in Revelation refers "to verbal witness to the truth of God ... along with living obedience to the commands of God. . . . [and the implication] that faithful witness will incur opposition and [may even] lead to death (2:13; 11:7; 12:17)."[32] A "witness,"

---

objective or subjective genitive in mind regarding the phrase "testimony of Jesus Christ," since those who are witness to Jesus' testimony (subjective genitive) are to bear witness to him (objective genitive). His understanding of the genitive phrase "word of God," which he believes is clearly a subjective genitive, leads him to draw the same conclusion regarding the parallel phrase "testimony of Jesus Christ" (*Revelation*, 213). So also Kistemaker, *Revelation*, 78.

30. Strathmann, "μάρτυς, μαρτυρέω, κτλ.," 492.

31. Ibid., 495.

32. Bauckham, *Theology of Revelation*, 72. See also Osborne's summation of the "witness" word groups usage in Revelation: "In Revelation 'witness' refers to fearless public proclamation and authentication, usually in the face of tremendous opposition, of divine realities in word and life" (*Revelation*, 56).

then, is one who faithfully follows Christ[33] by bearing witness to his life and teaching and the salvific significance of it for sinful humanity, counting the cost of such a lifestyle along the way.[34]

Marks of Discipleship (Keep Jesus' Teaching)

After introducing himself to his audience and briefly explaining the content of the book, John adds a blessing addressed to the reader and to those who heed the words of the book (Rev 1:3). John has just stated that the content of the "prophecy" is not of his own creation, but is "the word of God and the testimony of Jesus Christ" (1:2b, NIV). Thus, the ultimate author of this work is God the Father and his Son, Jesus Christ.

The blessing (or beatitude) is the first of seven recorded in Revelation (1:3; 14:13; 16:15; 19:9; 20:6; 22:7, 14) and functions similarly to the beatitudes of Matt 5 and Luke 6.[35] As was previously noted, the revelation is recorded for "servants," that is, for Christians. Here, one finds two groups in particular that make up part of the larger group of Christians. First, there is "the one who reads aloud the words of this prophecy" (1:3a). Revelation was not the only NT book written to be read aloud (cf. 1 Thess 5:27; Col 4:16; Eph 3:4). The book was likely to be read when all of the Christians in a particular community would have gathered together for instruction in the Scripture, most likely the Lord's Day (Sunday).[36] This was a common practice in Jewish and early Christian worship services.[37]

The audience of this revelation is described as "those who hear, and who keep what is written in it" (Rev 1:3b).[38] These are not two groups,

---

33. In Revelation bearing witness to Christ is not something reserved only for prophets, but is intended of all Christians in general (Bauckham, *Climax of Prophecy*, 161–162).

34. Spicq notes that a biblical "witness" is not one who merely waits to be called on to give an account, but one who actively proclaims what one has seen and heard ("μάρτυς," 448).

35. Several scholars have observed that this is one of several allusions to Jesus' words in the Gospels, possible Luke 11:28. The most extensive work is that by Vos, *Synoptic Traditions*. See also the helpful summary and discussion of this and other works by Aune (*Revelation 1–5*, 264–265).

36. Barr, "Oral Enactment," 253; Johnson, "Revelation," 596. It appears that the reader may have been an official position in the church at the time of Tertullian (*Prescription* 41).

37. Koester, *Revelation*, 213.

38. A lone plural article governs both participles οἱ ἀκούοντες ... καὶ τηροῦντες

but one. The ones who hear and keep the words of the prophecy are those who receive a blessing. It is not enough merely to hear the words of Christ; one must also respond positively to his words (cf. Jas 1:22). The response in Rev 1:3b is that of taking the prophecy to heart. The phrase "take to heart" (NIV) or "keep" (ESV) is a translation of the participle τηροῦντες (tērountes) from the verb τηρέω (tēreō). Τηρέω occurs several times in Revelation with reference to Jesus' words (1:3; 3:3, 8, 10; 22:7, 9) and God's commands (12:7; 14:12). Taken with the participle ἀκούοντες ("who hear"), the pair may form an *hendiadys*, two words joined by a copulative that are used to convey one idea. The intended idea is probably obedience to Jesus' and the Father's words.[39]

The ground of the exhortation to obey the words of the Father and the Son is "for the time is near" (1:3c). This phrase occurs one other time in Revelation at the end of the book (cf. 22:10).[40] The term καιρὸς ("time") with the definite article may refer to the end times,[41] present trials,[42] or both.[43] While there may be a lack of certainty concerning the referent of "time," most scholars are in agreement that the phrase "the time is near" expresses the idea of imminence.[44] This idea is bolstered by the context (cf. 1:1).

The final phrase, "the time is near," serves as both an encouragement and a warning to those who listen to the book's content. It is an encouragement to Christians who currently suffer for the faith in this present world, something the early church knew all too well. They must only suffer for a little while longer "for the time is near." It also may be taken as a warning to nominal Christians or unbelievers to truly respond in faith to Christ, or

---

("those who hear ... and keep"). Thus, these are not two groups of people, but one. For an explanation of this grammatical construction see Wallace, *Greek Grammar*, 281–283.

39. Beale, *Revelation*, 184; Keener, *Revelation*, 57; Mounce, *Revelation*, 43; Osborne, *Revelation*, 58.

40. The only differences in the Greek text are the word order and the inclusion of the verb "to be" (εἰμί) in Rev 22:10. However, both the meaning and translation are identical.

41. Aune, *Revelation 1–5*, 21; Thomas, *Revelation 1–7*, 61.

42. Beale, *Revelation*, 185.

43. Beale states, "But as will be seen (below, on v. 7), the repeated statements in the following chapters that Christ will 'come quickly' likely do not allude primarily to his apocalyptic appearance at the end of the age but to all his unseen comings in judgment throughout the age and climaxing with the final parousia" (ibid.).

44. Aune, *Revelation 1–5*, 21; Beale, *Revelation*, 185; Osborne, *Revelation*, 59; Thomas, *Revelation 1–7*, 61.

even faithful Christians to persevere in their walk with Christ because the end of this present world is hastening.[45]

Come to an Understanding of Jesus' Person and/or Work

There are several terms used throughout the NT that may be used in terms of coming to an understanding of who Jesus is. These words may refer to cognitive knowledge of some kind (γινώσκω) or even to sensory words by which one comes to an understanding of some thing (ὁράω, ἀκούω). These same terms may be used in the context of coming to understand something about Jesus' person and work. While the occurrence of terms clearly related to knowledge are infrequent in the book of Revelation, sensory terms abound.[46] The regularity of these terms seems to stem from the nature of the revelation John receives, which is highly visual and auditory. Because of this these two terms are generally unhelpful in tracking the theme of discipleship in Revelation.[47] However, this does not mean that all record of visual and auditory markers prove unhelpful. Ἰδού ("Behold!" "See!" "Listen!") in particular is used "to highlight critical prophetic oracles."[48] Of its 26 occurrences, 12 of them are related to understanding something about Jesus' person and work (1:7, 18; 3:20; 5:5; 14:1, 14; 16:15; 19:11; 21:3, 5; 22:7, 12). Twice in Rev 1 ἰδού occurs in the context of a revelation concerning Jesus (1:7, 18).

What, then, might Rev 1:7, 18 teach one about the person and work of Jesus? Revelation 1:7 concerns Jesus' coming in blessing and judgment, as well as his second coming, while 1:18 is about his eternality, his overcoming death, and his authority and power over death and Hades. But first, it may prove helpful to discuss the details of these passages to appreciate more fully the truths they provide about Jesus' person and work.

Revelation 1:7 appears to be based on two OT texts, Dan 7:13 and Zech 12:10. The verse also seems to be related to sayings of Jesus found in the Gospels, both Matt 24:30 and John 19:37. Daniel 7:13 contains a

---

45. Smalley, *Revelation*, 31.

46. For instance, ὁράω ("I see") and ἀκούω ("I hear") saturate the book. Ὁράω occurs 63 times and ἀκούω occurs 46 times in Revelation.

47. That being said, the verb ἀκούω is prominent in the repeated phrase, "let him *hear* what the Spirit says to the churches" (emphasis added, Rev 2:7, 11, 17, 29; 3:6, 13, 22), which is discussed later in this chapter.

48. Osborne, *Revelation*, 69.

vision of "one like a son of man" to whom God ("the Ancient of Days") gave authority over all people and whose kingdom was an everlasting kingdom (7:13–14).[49] The context of Zech 12:10 describes the future eschatological repentance of Israel, who will "mourn" over "him whom they have pierced."

How, then, does this apply to Rev 1:7? First, it must be recognized that the verse is primarily concerned with Jesus proclaiming his "coming." To what this coming refers is a matter of debate. It could refer to his warning to several churches in Rev 2–3 (cf. 2:5, 16; 3:11) to come in judgment,[50] or more likely to his second coming, since he comes "with the clouds," which is a "common apocalyptic image used of Christ's return" (cf. Mark 13:26; 14:62; 1 Thess 4:17).[51]

Second, "every eye" that sees him "coming with the clouds" are "all the peoples on earth" (1:7). The phrases "every eye" and "of the earth" are actually alterations or additions to Zech 12:10, upon which this part of Rev 1:7 is based. Thus, those who see Jesus coming and "wail on account of him" are not limited to Israel alone, but include both Jewish and Gentile persons from "all tribes of the earth."[52]

Third, what does it mean that "all tribes of the earth will wail on account of him"? Does the mourning refer to that which is indicative of genuine repentance, or does it have to do with despair of imminent judgment?[53] Several modern commentators tend to believe this refers to genuine repentance of "those who pierced him," with "those who pierced him" referring to all of sinful humanity.[54] However, most believe the mourning envisioned is of the unrepentant at the second coming of Christ (cf. Matt 24:30; Rev 18:9).[55]

49. As will be seen, Dan 7 is one of the primary OT texts alluded to in Revelation (Osborne, *Revelation*, 68).

50. Beale, *Revelation*, 198.

51. Osborne, *Revelation*, 70. Johnson believes this is a "clear reference to the return of Christ" ("Revelation," 601).

52. Beale, *Revelation*, 196–197; Koester, *Revelation*, 219.

53. The idea of genuine repentance appears to be conveyed in the NASB rendering of the phrase, "all the tribes of the earth will mourn over Him," while the idea of despair over impending judgment seems to be the way the translators of the NIV understood it, "all peoples will mourn because of him."

54. Bauckham, *Climax of Prophecy*, 322; Beale, *Revelation*, 197; Beasley-Murray, *Revelation*, 58–59; Caird, *Revelation*, 18.

55. Aune, *Revelation 1–5*, 59; Johnson, "Revelation," 601; Keener, *Revelation*, 73; Kistemaker, *Revelation*, 86–87; Ladd, *Revelation*, 29; Mounce, *Revelation*, 51; Thomas, *Revelation 1–7*, 79.

Perhaps it is best to see something of both ideas at play. If the "coming" of Jesus refers primarily to his second coming, which almost all commentators affirm, then his appearance will be met with mixed reactions. Those who are repentant will gaze on him with joy and welcome him, while others, the unrepentant, will dread his appearing. Both the conversion of the nations and the judgment of the nations occur side by side throughout the book of Revelation.[56] What this teaches the reader about Jesus is that he is coming again, and that those who repented over their sin will see him, as will those whose time for repentance has run out.[57]

The second occurrence of ἰδού in Rev 1 is found in verse 18. As noted previously, this text is concerned with Jesus' eternality, his overcoming death, and his authority and power over death and Hades. It may prove helpful though to include 1:17b, since it contains what Jesus revealed to John about his person and work. The vision of Christ described in 1:12–16 resulted in John falling "at [Jesus'] feet as though dead" (1:17a). Jesus places his "right hand" on John and gently encourages him to "stop being afraid" (author's translation).[58] Besides placing his hand on John, Jesus offers comfort to his servant by relaying to John something of who Jesus is: "I am the first and the last" (1:17b).

The phrase "I am" (ἐγώ εἰμι) is a familiar one in both the OT and NT. God uses it as he reveals himself to Moses (cf. Exod 3:14). It is found throughout John's Gospel in Jesus' seven "I am" sayings (cf. John 6:35; 8:12; 10:7, 11; 11:25; 14:6; 15:1). In addition, in Revelation the Lord God is recorded saying, "I am [ἐγώ εἰμι] the Alpha and the Omega" (Rev 1:8), a phrase strikingly similar to how Jesus refers to himself in 1:17b.[59] All of this probably points to the fact that Jesus is not just another angel sent to relay God's message to his servant, but fully God himself with the same divine nature, although distinct in his person.[60]

---

56. After laying out the case for each position, Osborne appears to take this mediating position (*Revelation*, 68–71).

57. Osborne states that "see" likely has a double meaning: "'see' at the moment of conviction of sin and also 'see' at the parousia, when the time for repentance is over" (*Revelation*, 70).

58. The present tense imperative φοβοῦ with μή (a form of negation) is frequently used for the cessation of an activity already in progress (Wallace, *Greek Grammar*, 724).

59. Bauckham believes the phrases should be considered equivalents (*Theology of Revelation*, 26). Similar phrases occur of God (Rev 21:6) and Jesus (22:13) at the close of Revelation.

60. Ibid., 54–58.

According to Bauckham, the title "the first and the last" is derived from Isa 41:4; 44:6; 48:12, where the text identifies "the God of Israel as the sole Creator of all things and sovereign Lord of history."[61] This understanding of God's person is thus applied to Christ in Rev 1:17b and elsewhere (cf. 22:13).

As Jesus continues to identify himself to John, he places an emphasis on his eternality: "I am . . . the living one" (Rev 1:18a). God refers to himself as the "living one" commonly (cf. Josh 3:10; Ps 42:2; Hos 1:10; Acts 14:15; Rom 9:26). In Revelation he is the one "who lives for ever and ever" (cf. Rev 4:9, 10; 10:6).[62] So, Jesus also is eternal God.

Jesus' eternality is highlighted by the reality of his bodily resurrection from the dead (1:18b). He "was dead" (NIV), but is no longer in that state.[63] He now continues to be alive.[64] In order to drive home his eternal state Jesus announces he is alive "forevermore" (1:18b). There would have been no doubt in John's mind that this Jesus standing before him was the living and eternal Son of God.

This one who has overcome death "[has] the keys of Death and Hades" (1:18c).[65] In Revelation, Hades is where the dead are kept, save the martyrs (6:9–11), until the resurrection on the last day (20:13–14). Hades is to be distinguished from the "bottomless pit" ("Abyss," NIV), which is the realm

---

61. Ibid., 27.

62. Osborne, *Revelation*, 95.

63. The tense of the verb γίνομαι is aorist and is certainly a consummative aorist (Wallace, *Greek Grammar*, 559).

64. The tenses of the verb and participle in the phrase ζῶν εἰμι are present and should be taken as progressive presents that express continuous action (Wallace, *Greek Grammar*, 518). The combination of the anarthrous present participle with a verb of being is a periphrastic participle (ibid., 647).

65. There is some question among commentators as to whether the genitive phrases "the keys of death and of Hades" (NASB) should be understood as possessive or objective genitives. If the phrase is possessive, then death and Hades would be personified, and one would understand the phrase "the keys *belonging* to death and Hades" (Roloff, *Revelation*, 37). However, if the phrase is taken as an objective genitive, then death and Hades are to be understood spatially, as a place, and one would understand the phrase "the keys *to* death and Hades" (Aune, *Revelation 1–5*, 103). Most scholars believe it is best to understand the genitives as objective, since Hades in particular is largely described as a place in Scripture (the realm of the dead) and Greco-Roman literature (Caird, *Revelation*, 26; Johnson, "Revelation," 607; Koester, *Revelation*, 247; Mounce, *Revelation*, 61; Smalley, *Revelation*, 56; Thomas, *Revelation 1–7*, 119–120). A few commentators believe both grammatical constructions, the possessive and objective genitive, may be in mind (Beale, *Revelation*, 214–215; Kistemaker, *Revelation*, 100–101; Osborne, *Revelation*, 96).

for demons, the beasts, and Satan (9:1, 11; 11:7; 17:8; 20:1–3). Hades is not depicted as a fiery place of torment as it is in Luke 16:23. That designation is reserved for the lake of fire, the second death, where the wicked are sent after being brought from Hades for the judgment (Rev 19:20; 20:10, 14–15; 21:8). Both death and Hades are thrown into the lake of fire, thus ushering in an eternal existence where death is no more (20:13–14).[66]

What John and his audience gather from this description of Jesus is, first of all, his eternality, a state in which he continues since he has overcome death through his bodily resurrection. He also has full power over the resurrection.[67] As the resurrected Christ who has "conquered death and has himself come out of Hades, he alone can determine who will enter death and Hades and who will come out of these. He has the 'keys.' For the Christian, death can only be seen as the servant of Christ."[68] Christ has power and authority that declare his divine status as a member of the Godhead.

Consequences of Following Jesus

John speaks of himself and his audience as being "fellow partakers" (NASB) "in the tribulation and the kingdom and the patient endurance . . . in Jesus" (1:9a). It would appear that grammatically and contextually the three datives should be taken together and viewed as a single unit.[69] If this is the case, then what does this single unit convey to one about the partnership of John and his audience?

First, John and his fellow brothers and sisters in Jesus share "in the tribulation" (ἐν τῇ θλίψει). The term θλῖψις is understood by some to refer to all suffering Christians undergo, since they live in the last days.[70] Others extend this suffering to the period of the great tribulation that precedes the millennial reign of Christ.[71] Still others believe the "tribulation" John and his readers suffer is specifically Jewish and Roman persecution.[72] Although one cannot totally rule it out, it is at least unnecessary to understand

---

66. Koester, *Revelation*, 248.

67. Ford, *Revelation*, 383.

68. Johnson, "Revelation," 607.

69. Beale, *Revelation*, 200–201; Thomas, *Revelation 1–7*, 86. Against see Aune, *Revelation 1–5*, 75–76.

70. Beasley-Murray, *Revelation*, 63–64.

71. Mounce, *Revelation*, 54.

72. Patterson, *Revelation*, 65.

"tribulation" here as a reference to the great tribulation, since the adjective "great" does not accompany "tribulation." Neither is there sufficient evidence to assume the suffering which John and his readers now share is merely persecution of the Jewish or Roman variety, although John may certainly be experiencing such himself (cf. Rev 1:9b). It appears that John simply desires to convey to his audience that what he and they share is something all Christians have been promised, the opportunity to suffer and be counted worthy to suffer "dishonor for the name" (Acts 5:41) because of their commitment to follow Christ.

Second, they also share "in . . . the kingdom" (ἐν . . . βασιλείᾳ). The term βασιλεία refers to the kingdom of God. The rule and reign of God in his kingdom is something that John and his readers (and all Christians) experience now in the present world. They too are currently reigning with Christ (cf. Rev 1:6). However, although inaugurated, the fullness or consummation of God's kingdom is something that is not yet (cf. 21:1—22:5), thus the need for "patient endurance."[73]

Finally, John and his audience are to share "in . . . patient endurance" (ἐν . . . ὑπομονῇ). Ὑπομονή is something that is necessary because the church faces hostility in this present age (cf. 3:9–10; 13:10; 14:12), as well as false teaching that seeks to undermine the faithful teaching of God's word (cf. 2:2–3).[74] Beale aptly summarizes how these three datives form one unit: "faithful endurance through tribulation is the means by which one reigns in the present with Jesus."[75]

That John and his fellow Christians are "in Jesus" speaks to the identity and union they share with Christ.[76] Beale goes so far as to argue, "the threefold self-description in v. 9a is modeled on the description of Christ in v. 5a."[77] Whether one can affirm the certainty of this claim, it does serve to emphasize the consequences of following Christ, and even being in union with him, namely, suffering for one's commitment to him. This is certainly evident in the case of John, since he notes that he was exiled to Patmos "on

---

73. Osborne, *Revelation*, 80–81.
74. Koester, *Revelation*, 250.
75. Beale, *Revelation*, 201.
76. Thomas understands the preposition ἐν ("in") as clarifying "the realm of John's joint participation" (*Revelation 1–7*, 87).
77. Beale, *Revelation*, 201. See also Caird, who likewise sees the believers reigning through suffering as modeled on Christ reigning "from the Cross" (*Revelation*, 19–20).

account of the word of God and the testimony of Jesus" (1:9b).⁷⁸ The "word of God" in the NT typically refers to "the gospel tradition of Jesus' words and acts: e.g., Luke 5:1; 8:11, 21; 11:28; Acts 4:31; 6:2, 7; 8:14, 25; 11:1; 12:24; 13:5, 44, 48–49; 15:35–36; 17:13; 18:11; 19:10, 20; 1 Cor 14:36; 2 Cor 2:17; 4:2; 1 Thess 1:8; 4:15."⁷⁹ John was banished to Patmos for proclaiming the word about and from God, and for preaching the testimony by and to Jesus.⁸⁰ The entirety of the phrase appears to be a general reference to John's preaching.⁸¹ Here, then, one finds an example of the possible consequences Christians face for following Jesus: (1) either general suffering for following him or (2) government persecution for preaching the word of God.

Keep and Obey Jesus' Commands

Twice in chapter one Jesus commands John to write down what he sees (Rev 1:11, 19). He is also commanded to write in 2:1, 8, 12, 18; 3:1, 7, 14; 14:13; 19:9; and 21:5. Of these occurrences all but three come from Christ (14:13, an unidentified voice from heaven; 19:9, an angel; 21:5, God the Father). In the other instances, John can be said to obey Jesus' commands. And so, what John sets out to write down is disclosed in the pages of the book of Revelation.⁸²

---

78. Aune notes three reasons that have been put forth as to why John was on Patmos. (1) The Roman authorities exiled him to the island. It is possible that John went to Patmos voluntarily, either for (2) the purpose of preaching the gospel or (3) so he might seclude himself in order to receive the revelation. Aune believes the first is more likely, since elsewhere the phrase "word of God and the testimony of Jesus" occurs in the context of persecution (cf. Rev 6:9; 20:4), although there is no grammatical reason for excluding the other two possibilities (*Revelation 1–5*, 81–82).

79. Beale, *Revelation*, 202.

80. As earlier, the genitive phrases "word of God and the testimony of Jesus" may be understood as plenary genitives.

81. Mounce, *Revelation*, 55. This differs from Rev 1:2 where the phrase refers to the content of the book of Revelation.

82. One particular term used of keeping and obeying God's commands (cf. Rev 12:7; 14:12) and Jesus' teaching (cf. 1:3; 3:3, 3:8, 10; 22:7, 9) is τηρέω ("I keep"). The uses of τηρέω with regard to Jesus' teaching are discussed in this study under the heading, "Marks of Discipleship (Keep Jesus' Teaching)."

Witness to "Greater Things"

In John 1:50 Jesus promised the disciples that they would be witnesses to "greater things," which refer to "revelations of God's glory in Christ."[83] What one finds in Rev 1:12–16 may be one instance of John encountering "revelations of God's glory in Christ"; an additional experience of the greatness of the Son of Man.[84]

Before John sees the greatness of the Son of Man, he first hears a "loud voice" (1:10) that instructs him to write down what he sees and send it to the seven churches of Asia Minor (1:11). Next, he proceeds to turn around to see who it was that spoke to him. The first thing he witnessed was "seven golden lampstands" (1:12b). As 1:20 makes clear, these lampstands represent the seven churches, presumably the seven churches to which John is to send the vision (cf. 1:11; 2–3).

The remainder of the vision is fixed on one individual in particular, whom John identifies as "one like a son of man" (1:13).[85] The descriptor "one like a son of man" is drawn primarily from Dan 7:13.[86] The title is applied to

---

83. Köstenberger, *John*, 87. Both John 1:51 and Rev 1:13 apply the title "son of man" to Jesus, which adds to the connection between the two texts.

84. Beale believes the vision encompasses Rev 1:12–20. He bases this on the understanding that 1:12–20 fits the typical pattern of visions in the Old Testament (*Revelation*, 205), and in particular this specific vision of the exalted Christ seems to have its background in a vision recorded in Zech 4:2, 10 (Beale and McDonough, "Revelation," 1091). The typical pattern is as follows:

   1. The initial vision: vision of Christ portrayed as the end time priest, king, and judge (1:12–16).
   2. The seer's response: John falls prostrate before Christ (1:17a).
   3. The interpretation of the vision: Jesus is priest, king, and judge because he has overcome death (1:17b–18). His kingly role is primarily as king over the church (1:19–20) (Beale, *Revelation*, 205–206).

85. Although the article is missing before "son of man," Thomas chooses to translate it with the definite article (*Revelation 1–7*, 97), as does the NRSV. They may understand the phrase "son of man" as a monadic noun, a one-of-a-kind noun, which does not need the article to be definite (Wallace, *Greek Grammar*, 248). Thomas is also convinced of the Messianic connotations of the Dan 7:13 passage on which the Rev 1:13 usage is based. This leads him to translate the phrase with the definite article (*Revelation 1–7*, 98).

86. This connection is made all the stronger when one considers the case in which "one like a man" occurs. Normally in Revelation ὅμοιος ("one like") is followed by the dative case (cf. 1:15; 2:18; 4:3, 6, 7; 9:10, 19; 11:1; 13:2, 4, 11; 18:18; 21:11, 18), but here and in 14:14 it occurs in the accusative, which it also does in Dan 7:13 LXX (Osborne, *Revelation*, 87 n. 8; Thomas, *Revelation 1–7*, 98).

Jesus in the Gospels (cf. Mark 13:26) and Acts (7:56).[87] At first, John does not clearly identify who this "one like a son of man" is. The expression could be used of an angelic being, as could aspects of the individual's appearance in Rev. 1:13–15.[88] However, as the vision unfolds, it becomes clear that this individual is Christ (cf. 1:18).

The glorified Christ is seen "in the midst of the lampstands... clothed with a long robe and with a golden sash around his chest" (1:13). The depiction is of Jesus as the high priest tending to the lampstands, which are representative of churches.[89]

Christ is also described as one with a head of white hair, so white that it is likened to wool from a sheep and to snow (1:14a). Once again, Dan 7 provides the background to this descriptor of Christ. In Dan 7:9 the "Ancient of Days," that is, God himself, is described as having clothes "white as snow" and a head of hair that was "like pure wool."[90] What one finds here is a clear instance in which the OT descriptions for God are applied to Jesus, "thereby stressing the unity between the Father and the Son."[91] Such brilliant white denotes "purity (Rev 3:4; 19:14), honor (3:18; 4:4), and victory

---

87. In both of these passages the definite article precedes the phrase "son of man."

88. Koester, *Revelation*, 252–253.

89. Beale succinctly draws the parallels between OT priest and Jesus' priestly role in Rev 1:13: "Part of Christ's priestly role is to tend the lampstands. The OT priest would trim the lamps, remove the wick and old oil, refill the lamps with fresh oil, and relight those that had gone out. Likewise, Christ tends the ecclesial lampstands by commending, correcting, exhorting, and warning (see chapter 2–3) in order to secure the churches' fitness for service as lightbearers in a dark world" (*Revelation*, 208–209). Other scholars, however, believe one cannot definitively find an allusion to the OT high priest, since angels, rulers, and even dignitaries are described as wearing similar raiment (Aune, *Revelation 1-5*, 93–94; Charles, *Revelation*, 1.27–28; Koester, *Revelation*, 245–246; Osborne, *Revelation*, 89; Thomas, *Revelation 1–7*, 99–100).

90. The phrase ἡ δὲ κεφαλὴ αὐτοῦ καὶ αἱ τρίχες λευκαὶ ὡς ἔριον λευκὸν ὡς χιών, which is rendered "His head and His hair were white like wool, like snow" (NASB) should not be taken to mean his head was also white. This is likely a use of an epexegetical or explanatory καὶ (Aune, *Revelation 1-5*, 95). This is how the translators of both the ESV and NIV understand the phrase.

91. Osborne, *Revelation*, 90. Kistemaker believes the fact that Jesus' hair is referred to as white as wool and snow, while the clothes of the Ancient of Days is likened to show, should indicate that John did not have a copy of Daniel in front of him, but, rather, he was alluding to it from memory (*Revelation*, 96).

(3:5; 6:2; 7:9; 19:11)."⁹² In addition, white hair conveyed wisdom and dignity, due to years of experience (cf. Lev 19:32; Prov 16:31).⁹³

Next, John notes the character of Christ's eyes, which "were like a flame of fire" (Rev 1:14b). This imagery is apparently drawn from Dan 10:6 and the appearance of "a man clothed in linen" whose "eyes [were] like flaming torches."⁹⁴ The image "may portray either [Christ's] penetrating scrutiny or fierce judgment."⁹⁵

John's eyes fix onto the feet of Christ's body, which were "like burnished bronze, refined in a furnace" (1:15a).⁹⁶ Similar imagery is found in Ezek 1:13, 27; 8:2 and Dan 10:6. Several commentators note that the image "emphasizes the glory and strength of Christ."⁹⁷ Not to be overlooked is the concept of purity in the image of "bronze, refined in a furnace."⁹⁸ The image is of molten metal glowing as it is exposed to the intense heat of a furnace, so that any impurities residing in the metal may be eliminated. This does

---

92. Koester, *Revelation*, 246.

93. Mounce, *Revelation*, 58; Osborne, *Revelation*, 90. One ancient commentator of Revelation believed the description of white hair referred to the eternal existence of Christ (Andrew of Caesarea, *Apocalypse*, 61). Apparently, so does Thomas, *Revelation 1-7*, 101.

94. The "man clothed in linen" is typically taken as either the angel Gabriel or a theophany. Norman W. Porteous believes the man is "Gabriel in view of his manner of addressing Daniel (cf. vv. 11 and 19)" (*Daniel*, 151; so also Montgomery, *Daniel*, 154). Stephen R. Miller believes the man in linen is God, "probably in the person of the divine Messiah" (*Daniel*, 281; so also Lacocque, *Daniel*, 206).

95. Johnson, "Revelation," 606. The aspect of judgment is accentuated by Beale (*Revelation*, 209) and Beasley-Murray (*Revelation*, 67). Mounce focuses on the image's portrayal of "penetrating insight" (*Revelation*, 59).

96. The noun χαλκολίβανον in the phrase "like burnished bronze" is rare, occurring only in Rev 1:15 and 2:18 in all of the extant ancient Greek literature, and thus, difficult to ascertain what precisely it means. Colin J. Hemer after suggesting four aspects of the term concludes that χαλκολίβανον was an alloy of copper and zinc made in Thyatira for coinage and possible armor (*Seven Churches of Asia*, 116–117). Koester dismisses outright the suggestion that the term had anything to do with the local bronze-workers in Thyatira (*Revelation*, 246).

97. Osborne, *Revelation*, 91. So also Mounce, *Revelation*, 59. Both Johnson ("Revelation," 606) and Kistemaker (*Revelation*, 96) emphasize the aspect of glory, while Patterson emphasizes Christ's "irresistible strength" (*Revelation*, 68).

98. Beale, *Revelation*, 210; Thomas, *Revelation 1-7*, 102. The author of this study recognizes the text-critical issue presented in the phrase ὡς ἐν καμίνῳ πεπυρωμένης (and elsewhere), however; such a discussion is beyond the scope of this work. For a brief discussion of the textual evidence see: Metzger, *Textual Commentary*, 663–664. Osborne, *Revelation*, 91; Thomas, *Revelation 1-7*, 102.

not mean that Jesus needs to have any impurities of his own character removed. Rather, it sets out to emphasize his moral purity. The fact that he is found walking among his churches may indicate that they too are to reflect his holiness.[99]

The next detail John draws attention to is the intensity of Jesus' voice: "his voice was like the roar of many waters" (Rev 1:15b). In the OT God's voice is likened to "many waters" (cf. Ezek 1:24; 43:2). The context of Ezek 43:2 has God positioned in the eschatological temple. Beale believes this parallels Rev 1:12, 16, where Christ is found in the heavenly temple. This serves to highlight Christ's divine attributes, which he shares with God the Father.[100] Jesus' voice has already been described as "loud" and "like a trumpet." It would appear that the mention of his voice "like the roar of many waters" carries this image forward. The Lord's voice "connotes awe-inspiring power and majesty."[101]

The next image John witnesses is the highly symbolic "seven stars" being held in Jesus' "right hand" (1:16a). That Christ holds these stars in his "right hand" speaks to his power and protection over that which he holds.[102] He is sovereign over the "seven stars."[103] What the "seven stars" represent is expressed in 1:20; "the seven stars are the angels of the seven churches."[104]

The next image of Christ is of "a sharp two-edged sword"[105] coming from "his mouth" (1:16b). The "sword" coming out of his mouth represents Jesus' role as judge and his dispensing judgment. If the sword represents the act of judgment, then Christ's "mouth" represents the manner in which his

---

99. Beale, *Revelation*, 210; Thomas, *Revelation 1–7*, 102.

100. Beale, *Revelation*, 210.

101. Beasley-Murray, *Revelation*, 67.

102. Kistemaker, *Revelation*, 97; Koester, *Revelation*, 246; Smalley, *Revelation*, 55.

103. Koester states that an imperial coin during the time of Domitian had an image of the emperor's son on one side surrounded by seven stars. The coin's inscription read, "divine Caesar, son of the emperor Domitian." The image of his son surrounded by seven stars along with the coin's inscription was meant to display the divinity and power of the son. However, in Revelation it is Jesus, who is seen as the one true ruler (cf. Rev 1:5) and the divine Son of power and authority (1:16a) (*Revelation*, 253).

104. Bruce J. Malina believes the seven stars may be an allusion to the constellation Pleiades (*Star Visions and Sky Journeys*, 70). Adela Yarbro Collins believes the seven stars refer to the seven planets of the Hellenistic world (*Cosmology and Eschatology*, 121). So also Charles, *Revelation*, 1.30. Aune mentions the constellation Ursa Major has been put forth as a possible source for the seven stars (*Revelation 1–5*, 97–98).

105. The ῥομφαία δίστομος ("two-edged sword") "was a large, broad Thracian sword used often in cavalry charges" (Osborne, *Revelation*, 92).

judgment will be realized; it will be proclaimed.[106] In summing up the purpose of the description, Thomas writes, "the description is upon the judicial authority of Christ. It combines the force of a warrior defeating his enemies in battle and the pronouncement of his sentence of judgment upon them."[107]

The final depiction of Christ's person in Rev 1:12–16 is of his face, which "was like the sun shining in full strength" (1:16c). Certain commentators believe this description has Judg 5:31 (LXX) as its background.[108] In Judges the metaphor is used with reference to Israelite warriors being "like the sun as he rises in his might." Daniel 10:6 may also be in view, since the face of the man dressed in linen is described as being like "lightning."[109] In either case, the appearance of the persons depicted in the OT texts is that of warriors. A possible NT allusion might be to Jesus' transfiguration when his "face shone like the sun, and his clothes became as white as light" (Matt 17:2).[110] If this is the case, then the apostle is the only witness "to be given a second foreview of that glory."[111] While the OT texts seem to articulate the theme of judgment, both of the NT texts articulate the theme of God's glory. It is difficult to determine precisely what John intended as the likely background to Rev 1:16c. Perhaps, one should simply draw on both understandings. Christ reveals himself as the glorified Messianic judge.[112]

SUMMARY

What preliminary observations may be drawn on the concept of discipleship in Revelation according to chapter one? First, one of the terms used of Jesus' disciples in the NT is "servant." One's call from God (whether as an apostle, pastor, or whomever), does not exempt one from servant status. In fact, all Christians are to view themselves as God's servants, those who have been bought with the blood of Christ. The ground is level at the foot of the

---

106. Aune notes that the sword is a "metaphor for the tongue" (*Revelation 1–5*, 98).

107. Thomas, *Revelation 1–7*, 104.

108. Beale, *Revelation*, 212; Charles, *Revelation*, 1.30.

109. Beale, *Revelation*, 212; Koester, *Revelation*, 247.

110. Osborne, *Revelation*, 93. This may be a closer parallel, since the term used in Rev 1:16c for "face" (ὄψις) can also be understood as referring to one's outward appearance, as in John 7:24 (Mounce, *Revelation*, 60).

111. Thomas, *Revelation 1–7*, 105.

112. Osborne believes both themes are in view, although the "predominant" theme is that of glory (*Revelation*, 93).

cross. That a Christian is Christ's servant means that the believer owes total allegiance to Christ. He is their Lord.

Second, while John, the apostle and author of the Apocalypse, is identified as a witness in Rev 1:2, he is not alone. Jesus is one who testifies (1:5; 3:14; 22:20), as does Antipas (2:13), the "two witnesses" (11:3), those who suffered and died because of their testimony about Jesus (1:9; 6:9; 11:7; 12:17; 17:6; 20:4), and Christians in general (12:11, 17; 19:10). Thus, bearing witness to Jesus' life and teaching and the salvific significance of it is the ministry of all Christians. Bearing witness to Jesus is not without its costs. The cost in Revelation is depicted as suffering, as John suffers as an exile, but the primary cost for testifying of Jesus in Revelation is death. In spite of this, Jesus' disciples are not to shrink away from maintaining a faithful witness to Jesus Christ.

Third, Jesus' teaching is the word of God. He is divine, and according to Heb 1:1–3 Jesus is "the exact imprint of [God's] nature," the pinnacle of divine revelation, the ultimate disclosure of God. Faithfully following Christ brings with it blessing, the full measure of which eludes the Christian in the present world. This blessing is closely tied to hearing and doing Jesus' teaching. It is the result of obedience to Christ's words.

Fourth, each of the twelve occurrences of ἰδού related to understanding something about Jesus' person and work are directed to Christians, and primarily John as the one who received the revelation. Believers are those who can truly see Jesus and gain insight concerning him. This is likely due to the Spirit's indwelling presence that leads Christians to all truth, namely, truth pertaining exclusively to Jesus (cf. John 14:16–17, 26). What is unveiled about Jesus' person and work in Rev 1 relates to his coming in blessing and judgment, now and in the future (1:7), as well as his divinity, his role as the agent of creation, his eternality, his overcoming death, and his authority and power over Hades and the resurrection (1:18). It may be that for the Christian, understanding something of Jesus' person and work is intended to encourage and compel one to serve him faithfully, as indicated in the example of John (1:17, 19).

Fifth, all Christians are promised the opportunity to suffer because of their commitment to follow Christ. In addition, all Christians live in the Kingdom and are subject to Christ's rule. This does not mean they fully experience all of the benefits of being persons in God's kingdom; they still experience hardships and trials. Since this is the case, there is a need for disciples of Jesus to endure patiently the suffering they may face in this present broken world. The motivation to endure with patience any suffering for following Christ is the truth that one is "in Jesus," that is, securely in union with him, even now, present with him, and reigning with him in glory.

Sixth, Jesus is still in a discipling relationship with his followers. Even as the ascended and exalted Christ, he clearly has authority over them and demonstrates leadership over his earthly disciples. Although not physically present with his disciples, he still has charge over them, and they are still to obediently follow his commands.

Finally, John is given a vision of the exalted and risen Christ walking amongst his churches. Jesus' symbol-laden appearance identifies him as high priest, the caretaker and intercessor for his people. His appearance is also strikingly white, which denotes his absolute holiness. His eyes ablaze like fire point to his omniscience, his penetrating and exhaustive insight, which enables him to pronounce just judgments (cf. 1:16b). His feet of pure bronze walking in the midst of his churches recall the command of God to his people, "You shall be holy, for I am holy" (1 Pet 1:16; cf. Lev 20:26). Jesus' voice is awesome and powerful. It spoke the worlds into existence, commanded the dead to be raised, and as John will soon witness, would announce a revelation of "what [John had] seen, what is now and what will take place later" (Rev 1:19, NIV). What John sees is the glory of Christ, a glory beyond that on display through his death, resurrection, and ascension. This is the exalted and sovereign Lord, in command and in control of all things. It is this vision of Jesus Christ that his followers may hold on to as a source of hope in this fallen world.

AN ANALYSIS OF REVELATION 2:1—3:22

Witness to "Greater Things"

As noted previously, Rev 1:12–16, and perhaps even 1:12–20, provides John with a witness to the greatness of the Son of Man, the risen and exalted Jesus Christ. In his introductory remarks to each of the seven churches of Asia Minor, Jesus utilizes certain aspects of this vision to address each church's particular situation.[113] Beginning with the church at Ephesus, he is the one "who holds the seven stars in his right hand, [and] who walks among the

---

113. Beale, *Revelation*, 229; Homcy, "To Him Who Overcomes," 194–196, esp. 196; Osborne, *Revelation*, 111.

Discipleship in the Book of Revelation

seven golden lampstands" (2:1b; cf. 1:13, 16).[114] Jesus is the sovereign, omniscient, and omnipotent Lord of his church, who continually protects it and watches it.[115] Christ knows the difficulty the church has faced and has enabled them to persevere through the hardships they had endured (2:3). But he was also keenly aware of their sin of forsaking "the love [they] had at first" (2:4). So, he would judge them if they failed to repent and change their ways (2:5).

To the church at Smyrna he is the one who is "the first and the last, who died and came to life" (2:8b; cf. 1:17b, 18b). Jesus is the eternal Creator and sovereign Lord of history. This would indeed be of comfort to a suffering church such as Smyrna, who may wonder where the Lord is in all of their suffering.[116] Jesus is also the one who has conquered death and is raised to life forevermore. As such, those who may die for their faith (2:10d) can rest assured that the one triumphant over death has the ability to raise them up on the last day to resurrection life (cf. John 11:25–26).[117]

---

114. The term translated "holds" (κρατῶν) in Rev 2:1b differs from 1:16 (ἔχων). There are some scholars who believe the present participle κρατῶν in 2:1b is more emphatic than the present participle ἔχων in 1:16, and therefore means to "hold tightly" or "hold fast." These scholars include: Ladd, *Revelation*, 38; Osborne, *Revelation*, 112; Thomas, *Revelation 1–7*, 131–132. However, reading any deeper meaning into the word change is not necessary. John is known for his use of synonymous terms, which he may use for the sake of variety (see the famous example in John 21:15–19).

Another difference is that of the description of Jesus as one who "walks among" (περιπατῶν ἐν μέσῳ) the seven churches in Rev 2:1b and is simply "in the midst" (ἐν μέσῳ) of them in 1:13. Some scholars view the addition of the present participle περιπατῶν as more emphatic than its absence in 1:13. These scholars include: Osborne, *Revelation*, 112 and possibly Kistemaker, *Revelation*, 111–112. It would seem the inclusion of the present participle might be to emphasize Jesus' *continual* presence (progressive present) among the churches, watching over them and protecting them, whereas in 1:13 this emphasis is not explicit.

115. Osborne believes the image of Jesus walking among the churches portrays him as caring for the churches and attending to their needs, as well as watching over them in the sense of one who judges their actions (*Revelation*, 112; so also Beasley-Murray, *Revelation*, 73; Johnson, "Revelation," 612; Smalley, *Revelation*, 60). Ladd appears to emphasize the aspect of caring for the churches (*Revelation*, 38). Thomas sees the emphasis on Jesus' control over the churches, rather his protection (*Revelation 1–7*, 132; so also Mounce, *Revelation*, 68).

116. Beale believes the suffering the church endured was "economic hardship because of Jewish slander" (*Revelation*, 239, cf. 240–241). Hemer notes that it may have been due to Jewish and pagan mobs that destroyed the property of Christians (*Seven Churches of Asia*, 68).

117. Hemer states that the letter's recipients may have found the description of Jesus as the one "who died and came to life" as analogous to the history of the city, which

To the church at Pergamum Jesus is the one who "has the sharp two-edged sword" (Rev 2:12b; cf. 1:16b). He is truly the one who pronounces and executes judgment ultimately.[118] If the church at Pergamum fails to repent, then Christ will come and "war against them with the sword of [his] mouth" (2:16b).[119]

To the church at Thyatira he is "the Son of God, who has eyes like a flame of fire, and whose feet are like burnished bronze" (2:18b; cf. 1:14b, 15a).[120] Similarly to the church at Pergamum, Jesus is portrayed as the holy omniscient judge with the strength of a warrior to execute his judgments. He is able to see through the false teaching being perpetrated by "Jezebel" and judge her and her offspring (2:20–23).

To the church at Sardis, Jesus identifies himself as the one "who has the seven spirits of God and the seven stars" (3:1a; cf. 1:16a). First, he "has the seven spirits of God." The fact that Jesus "has" or "holds" (NIV) the seven spirits shows his control and power. Osborne and others[121] believe the "seven spirits" is likely a reference to the "seven-fold Spirit" in Zech 4:1–14 (cf Rev. 1:4; 4:5; 5:6), and thus, it is believed to be a "symbol for the

---

experienced something of its own death in 600 BC and its resurrection in 290 BC (*Seven Churches of Asia*, 63–65).

118. Osborne believes this depiction of Christ may have been due to the fact that the "Roman proconsul in charge of the province resided in Pergamum, and the symbol of his total sovereignty over every area of life . . . was the sword. This tells the church that it is the exalted Christ . . . who is the true judge" (*Revelation*, 140).

119. Charles sees a clear connection between Christ's depiction in Rev 2:13b and its application to the situation of the church (*Revelation*, 1.26). Against see Hemer, *Seven Churches of Asia*, 85.

120. The title "Son of God" occurs 46 times in the NT, but is found only here in Revelation. It is used of the risen exalted Christ sparingly: Acts 13:33; Rom 1:3; Col 1:13; 1 Thess 1:9–10; Heb 1:5; 5:5; Rev 2:13 (Aune, *Revelation 1–5*, 201). The reason for its occurrence in a letter to the church at Thyatira may have been due to the presence of the cult of Apollo and the deification of the Roman emperor (both were prominent in Thyatira), both of which were identified as the sons of god, that being Zeus (Beale, *Revelation*, 259; Mounce, *Revelation*, 85). Koester identifies the title more with emperor worship (*Revelation*, 298, 304–305), while Osborne identifies the title with the worship of the Greek god (*Revelation*, 153).

121. Osborne, *Revelation*, 173; Beale, *Revelation*, 189; Johnson, "Revelation," 599; Kistemaker, *Revelation*, 82; Ladd, *Revelation*, 25; Patterson, *Revelation*, 59–60; Smalley, *Revelation*, 33; Thomas, *Revelation 1–7*, 68, 244. Koester believes the "seven spirits" refers to "angelic beings that serve as attendants of God" that are to be distinguished from the angels associated with each church (*Revelation*, 312). Similarly see Aune, *Revelation 1–5*, 219; Charles, *Revelation*, 1.13; Mounce, *Revelation*, 93.

divine Spirit," the Holy Spirit.[122] The church in Sardis was dead and in need of new life. The Holy Spirit is the one who can take what is dead and bring it back to life. It is Christ who has the power to send the Spirit to do this work. Second, Jesus "has ... the seven stars." Christ is also sovereign over the churches. Nothing the church at Sardis would face, or any of the other churches for that matter, was beyond the scope or control of Jesus.

To the church at Philadelphia, Jesus identifies himself as "the holy one, the true one, who has the key of David, who opens and no one will shut, who shuts and no one opens" (3:7b). At first blush, it appears that in this letter Jesus fails to allude to the earlier revelation of himself in 1:12–20.[123] However, although the connections are not as clear, they do seem to be there, nonetheless. For instance, his white hair (cf. 1:14) and possession of features that dazzled brightly (cf. 1:15a, 16b) suggest the theme of Christ's holiness.[124] Jesus also identifies himself as "true," which may be an allusion, not to 1:12–20, but to 1:5a and his identity as the "faithful witness."[125] In addition, 1:18b makes mention of Jesus being in the possession of "the keys of death and Hades." Here in 3:7b he also holds a key (singular), the "key of David.[126]

The combination "the holy one, the true one" is found only one other place in Revelation (6:10), where it is attributed to God the Father. The adjective "holy" (ἅγιος) is used often of God in the OT (cf Ps 16:10; Hab 3:3; Isa 1:4; 37:23; 40:25)[127] and is a common title for Christ in the NT (cf. Mark 1:24; Luke 1:35; 4:34; John 6:69; Acts 3:14; 4:27, 30; 1 John 2:20).[128] In calling himself "the holy one," Jesus identifies himself with the one true God, having a divine nature. That Jesus is "holy" speaks not only to his purity, but also to his utter transcendence, his holy otherness from the rest of creation.[129]

---

122. Bauckham, *Climax of Prophecy*, 162; *Theology of Revelation*, 110.
123. Mounce brings attention to this (*Revelation*, 99), as does Smalley, *Revelation*, 88.
124. Koester, *Revelation*, 328.
125. Beale, *Revelation*, 283; Koester, *Revelation*, 328.
126. Ibid., Beasley-Murray, *Revelation*, 99–100; Charles, *Revelation*, 1.86. Kistemaker does not see a connection between Rev 3:7b and 1:18b (*Revelation*, 158).
127. Koester, *Revelation*, 323; Osborne, *Revelation*, 186–187.
128. Koester, *Revelation*, 323; Thomas, *Revelation 1–7*, 273.
129. Johnson, "Revelation," 631; Osborne, *Revelation*, 187.

The adjective "true" (ἀληθινός) identifies Jesus as the genuine Messiah and the faithful one.[130] His faithfulness is contrasted with those "who say they are Jews and are not, but lie" (Rev 3:9a). As the faithful one, his promise that he is "coming soon" (3:11) could be trusted by the faithful in Philadelphia to continue to endure suffering for a little while longer (3:10).

To the church at Laodicea Jesus is the "Amen, the faithful and true witness, the beginning of God's creation" (3:14b; cf. 1:5). Osborne notes that this is the only letter that does not allude to the previous vision of Christ in 1:12–20.[131] Jesus introduces himself to the church at Laodicea with three titles. First, Jesus is the "amen." This is believed to have been an allusion to Isa 65:16, where God is twice called "the God of truth." The term translated "true" in this instance is the Hebrew word אָמֵן ('āmēn).[132] In Rev 3:14b, Jesus is concerned with relaying to the church at Laodicea the truthfulness of his divine word, which is indeed lacking in the church (3:17).[133]

Second, Jesus is "the faithful and true witness," which offers further clarity to his introduction as the "amen." In 19:11 Jesus is also described as "faithful and true." "True" is attributed to God the Father in 6:10; 15:3; 16:7; 19:2, 9. Coupled with "witness," Jesus is a faithful witness to all that the Father has seen fit to reveal through him, and all of his divine disclosure is true; it is accurate and truthful, as opposed to the Laodicean congregation, which appears to be neither.[134]

Finally, Jesus identifies himself as "the beginning of God's creation." The term ἀρχή may be translated "ruler" (NIV) or "origin/source," and either makes sense in this instance. Both ideas may be in mind.[135] If this is

---

130. Thomas believes the term ἀληθινός should be translated "genuine," in order to emphasize Jesus' genuineness as the real Messiah. As the real Messiah he is faithful and can be trusted (*Revelation 1–7*, 273–275). This is in opposition to those who believe ἀληθινός functions here as a synonym for ἀληθής ("true"). Charles believes this is how ἀληθινός should be understood in Rev 3:7, which is similar to its usage elsewhere, when it is found together with other terms: πιστός ("faithfulness"; 3:14; 19:11; 21:5; 22:6) and δίκαιος ("righteous"; 15:3; 16:7; 19:2). Ἀληθινός is also used for God in the LXX to draw attention to his faithfulness (Exod 34:6; Isa 65:16; Ps 86:15), while ἀληθής is never used (*Revelation*, 1.87–88; so also Hemer, *Seven Churches of Asia*, 161). Both Osborne (*Revelation*, 187) and Beale (*Revelation*, 283) believe both aspects of the term are likely at play, and one should consider both in understanding what it means for Jesus to be "true."

131. Osborne, *Revelation*, 203 n. 3; so also Aune, *Revelation 1–5*, 263.

132. Aune, *Revelation 1–5*, 255; Beale and McDonough, "Revelation," 1097–1098.

133. Johnson, "Revelation," 636.

134. Beale, *Revelation*, 302–303; Beasley-Murray, *Revelation*, 104.

135. Osborne, *Revelation*, 204–205.

the case, then Jesus is the "ruler" of creation, in the sense that he has the supremacy over all things (Col 1:18).[136] He is the one who stands sovereignly over all creation and has authority over it (cf. Rev 1:5). He is also the "source" or "beginning" of creation, in the sense that "all things were made through him, and without him was not any thing made that was made" (John 1:3; cf. Col 1:15–17).[137] The church at Laodicea believed it was rich and powerful, able to take care of itself, but it was wrong. Therefore, Christ, as the all sufficient, omnipotent one, urges them to "buy from [him] gold refined by fire, so that [they] may be rich, and white garments so that [they] may clothe [themselves] and the shame of [their] nakedness may not be seen, and salve to anoint [their] eyes, so that [they] may see" (Rev 3:18).

Marks of Discipleship

In John's Gospel Jesus notes three marks of his discipleship. They are keeping his teaching (8:31–32), having love for one another (13:34–35), and bearing much fruit (15:8). All three are found in the letters to the seven churches. In several places, Jesus mentions the "deeds" (NIV) or "works" of the churches (cf. Rev 2:2, 19; 3:1, 8). In all but one instance (3:1) the deeds are positive expressions of the faithfulness of the churches' relationship with Christ. They are evidence of the fruit they bear as disciples of Jesus Christ. In 2:19 this is particularly clear, as the deeds of the church at Thyatira are greater than when they first began: "I know your works, your love and faith and service and patient endurance, and *that your latter works exceed the first*" (emphasis added).

The particular works expressed by this church are: love (ἀγάπη), faith (πίστις), service (διακονία), and perseverance (ὑπομονή).[138] The deeds of the church at Thyatira "exceeded" (πλείονα) their previous works. How the

---

136. Koester believes the emphasis is on Christ as "ruler" (*Revelation*, 336). So also Patterson, *Revelation*, 138.

137. Bauckham believes the emphasis is on Christ as "source" or "origin." He also believes this depiction of Jesus as "source" expresses his eternality with God the Father (*Theology of Revelation*, 56–57). So also Caird, *Revelation*, 57; Ladd, *Revelation*, 65; Mounce, *Revelation*, 108–109; Smalley, *Revelation*, 97; Thomas, *Revelation 1–7*, 303–304.

138. The repetition of σου ("your") at the end of the four accusatives ("love and faith and service and patient endurance") show that they make up the "works" (σου τὰ ἔργα, "your works") the Lord refers to (Mounce, *Revelation*, 85 n. 8; Osborne, *Revelation*, 154; Smalley, *Revelation*, 73; Thomas, *Revelation 1–7*, 211). For a fuller explanation of this grammatical construction see Abbott, *Johannine Grammar*, 606.

works were greater is not clearly expressed. It may be that they did even more works than in the beginning. The quantity of good deeds had increased, which is in keeping with the NIV. However, it is also possible that the quality of the works is in view, so that the works may show greater evidence of the spiritual maturity of the church, which is in keeping with the NLT.[139] But it is also possible that the church's deeds were not only greater in number, but also of greater quality.[140] And so these works, which were progressing in number and in quality, were the fruit they bore as a result of their union with Jesus Christ.

One of the fruit born by the believers in Thyatira was "love." There is nothing in the context per se that helps one identify the recipient of this love as God, other believers, or other persons in general. In discussing the referent for "love" in 2:4 scholars are divided over the one for whom the love of the church at Ephesus had waned.[141] Had they abandoned their love for God[142] or for one another?[143] Several scholars recognize the difficulty in separating the love Christians are to have for one another from the love they are to have for God, based in part on the "Greatest Commandment" (Mark 12:29–31; Matt 22:37–39; Luke 10:27).[144]

If the referent for "love" in Rev 2:4 could include God and other persons, including believers, then it is also possible that in 2:19 the love exemplified by the church at Thyatira was also love not only for God, but also for one another. The disciples of the church at Thyatira are not only fruit bearing, but also evidence love for one another.

---

139. Charles is of this opinion (*Revelation*, 1.69).

140. Osborne, *Revelation*, 155; Thomas, *Revelation 1–7*, 212–213.

141. Revelation 2:4 is the only other occurrence of the noun ἀγάπη ("love") in the letters to the seven churches. This may suggests that a contrast was intended between the churches of Ephesus and Thyatira.

142. Walvoord, *Revelation*, 55.

143. Beasley-Murray, *Revelation*, 75; Charles, *Revelation*, 1.51; Mounce, *Revelation*, 69–70; Roloff, *Revelation*, 45.

144. Johnson, "Revelation," 613; Keener, *Revelation*, 106; Kistemaker, *Revelation*, 114–115; Osborne, *Revelation*, 115–116; Thomas, *Revelation 1–7*, 140. Even Beasley-Murray (*Revelation*, 75) and Mounce (*Revelation*, 69), who believe the love that was lost was primarily that directed toward believers, note that love for God and Christ should also be included.

Beale interestingly argues that the love lost in Ephesus was not for God or others, but failure to provide a faithful witness to the gospel (*Revelation*, 230–231).

In addition to these two marks of discipleship, there is evidence of Christians keeping Jesus' teaching in 2:13, 25–26; 3:3, 8, 10.[145] In the case of the church at Philadelphia this is especially clear. The verb τηρέω ("I keep") occurs twice in the letter addressed to them with respect to keeping and obeying Jesus' word (3:8, 10). While neither 3:8 nor 10 may be a specific teaching from Jesus, what the church held to was teaching that at one time came from Jesus. He clearly taught his disciples about his mission, which is the core of the gospel message (3:8). Further, his own example of perseverance in the face of suffering is one of the ways in which he would have taught his disciples how to endure when they faced any kind of trial (3:10). It would appear, then, that the believers at the church of Philadelphia evidenced this third mark of those who follow Jesus: they keep, that is, they guard and obey his teaching,[146] whether it is teaching directly from him or merely about him.

Come to an Understanding of Jesus' Person and/or Work

Earlier it was noted that ἀκούω ("I hear") occurs often in Revelation. Most of these are due to the nature of the revelation to which John bore witness. However, there is the repeated phrase to each of the seven churches, which requires special attention. The conclusion to each of the letters to the seven churches one finds the repeated phrase, "He who has an ear, let him *hear* what the Spirit says to the churches" (emphasis added, 2:7, 11, 17, 29; 3:6, 13, 22). What is one to make of this saying?

First, it appears similar to other sayings found in both the Gospels and the OT that indicate some will hear the message, while others may not (cf. Mark 4:10–12; Isa 6:9–10).[147] Second, this is a command (ἀκουσάτω) for those who can hear to hear what the Spirit has to say. Third, while the letter is addressed to each church, the command to hear requires the individual disciple to respond.[148] Fourth, to hear the message means more than merely to listen to the words. To hear in the biblical sense means not only to listen, but also to do what one has heard. It is likened to a call to be obedient to

---

145. One also finds evidence of keeping/obeying Jesus' commands, specifically his command to John to write to each of the seven churches (Rev 2:1, 8, 12, 18; 3:1, 7, 14).

146. Osborne, *Revelation*, 189–190.

147. For an extended discussion on this see Beale, *Revelation*, 236–239.

148. The verb ἀκουσάτω is a third person singular aorist active imperative.

God's word.[149] Fifth, almost all commentators identify Jesus as the apparent source of the messages, since it seems that he is the one commanding John to write each letter (cf. 2:1, 8, 12, 18; 3:1, 7, 14). However, the saying emphasizes that it is the Spirit who speaks to the churches. The apparent difficulty may be alleviated by viewing the Spirit as relaying the words of Christ to the churches through the means of a prophet (John).[150]

Finally, the message of Christ is given "to the churches." Although seven churches are individually addressed, each letter closes with an invitation for "churches" (plural) to hear and obey the messages. This leads several commentators to conclude that each letter is an invitation to all churches for all times to consider whether Christ's words speak to their particular context.[151] Thus, the seven churches of Asia Minor serve as representatives to churches throughout the ages.[152]

Believe in Jesus Christ

The book of Revelation does not include a single occurrence of the verb πιστεύω ("I believe").[153] Nor are there any instances of people experiencing initial salvation, going from unbelievers to believers. Some scholars even deny the concept of saving faith in Revelation.[154] However, that does not mean the idea of belief in Jesus for salvation is not present. The verb νικάω

---

149. Kistemaker, *Revelation*, 118; Koester, *Revelation*, 270; Osborne, *Revelation*, 122; Thomas, *Revelation 1–7*, 151.

150. Bauckham, *Climax of Prophecy*, 160; *Theology of Revelation*, 118. Others attempt to alleviate the difficulty, noting the Spirit is the Spirit of Christ (Thomas, *Revelation 1–7*, 151) or Christ is the one speaking to the churches through the Spirit (Beale, *Revelation*, 234; Beasley-Murray, *Revelation*, 76; Kistemaker, *Revelation*, 118) or it is simply the Spirit himself (Osborne, *Revelation*, 122).

151. Homcy, "To Him Who Overcomes," 194; Osborn, *Revelation*, 122; Smalley, *Revelation*, 63–64; Thomas, *Revelation 1–7*, 150. Smalley even notes that the verb "says" (λέγει) occurs in the present tense, indicating that the Spirit continually speaks these words to churches (*Revelation*, 63). This may be an instance of either a progressive or customary present (Wallace, *Greek Grammar*, 518, 521–522).

152. Beasley-Murray, *Revelation*, 76.

153. It does include instances of the terms πίστις ["faith"] (Rev 2:13, 19; 13:10; 14:12), πιστός ["faithful"] (1:5; 2:10, 13; 3:14; 17:14; 19:11; 21:5; 22:6), and ἄπιστος ["faithless"] (21:8).

154. Boring, *Revelation*, 95. Boring states, "the whole word-group for faith and believing . . . never has the Pauline meaning of 'obedience in personal trust that mediates our relationship to God.'"

("I overcome") that is found repeatedly in the letters to the seven churches (cf. 2:7, 11, 17, 26–28; 3:5, 12, 21) may have salvific undertones. According to A. T. Robertson, "faith is dominant in Paul, victory is dominant in John, faith is victory (1 John 5:4)."[155] Osborne believes that the theme of overcoming in Revelation is "analogous to πιστεύω (*pisteuō*, believe) in Paul, referring to an active trust in God that leads to faithfulness in the difficult situations of life lived for Christ."[156]

In addition, there are promises attached to those who overcome in each of the letters to the seven churches (2:7, 10, 17, 26–28; 3:5, 12, 21). These promises "relate to participation in the kingdom of God, as described in the closing vision of the Revelation."[157] Those who are participants in God's kingdom are certainly Christians, that is, those who have trusted Christ alone for salvation. One of the promises, "the right to eat from the tree of life" (2:7b, NIV), recalls images of the Garden of Eden from Genesis 2–3. Life, even eternal life, was connected to the tree of life. Here, John reintroduces the image of the tree of life to convey "symbolically the truth of eternal life . . . the gift of eternal life that [Christ] alone gives."[158] Eternal life that Christ offers is something Christians alone may experience by faith.

Further, there are the instances of πίστις ("faith") used in both Rev 2:13, 19. In 2:13 Christ affirms that the church in Pergamum "did not renounce [their] faith in [him]" (NIV). The genitive in the construction τὴν πίστιν μου may be taken as either an objective ("faith in me") or a possessive genitive ("my faith"). The first would refer to one's faith in Christ for salvation, while the possessive genitive would refer to the Christian faith as a body of teaching. Osborne believes the former is in view, given that "πίστιν always refers to an active and persevering trust in Christ . . . and is equivalent to πιστός."[159] So the faith the believers of Pergamum expressed

---

155. Robertson, *Word Pictures*, 300.

156. Osborne, *Revelation*, 123; see also Beasley-Murray, *Revelation*, 77–79; Kistemaker, *Revelation*, 118–119; Rosscup, "The Overcomer of the Apocalypse," 261–286; Thomas, *Revelation 1–7*, 152–153.

157. Beasley-Murray, *Revelation*, 78.

158. Johnson, "Revelation," 615. See also Aune (*Revelation 1–5*, 152–153) and Keener (*Revelation*, 107–108) who recognize the tradition in Judaism that viewed the tree of life as a metaphor for eternal life. Aune also notes an additional Jewish tradition that understood the tree of life as a metaphor for election into the people of God (ibid., 153).

159. Osborne, *Revelation*, 142. So also Beale, *Revelation*, 246; Charles, *Revelation*, 61; Robertson, *Word Pictures*, 6.304; Thomas, *Revelation 1–7*, 186; Wallace, *Greek Grammar*, 116. Blount believes the genitive is subjective, meaning Christ's own faith is in view, "the faith in his own lordship, to which he testified and for which he died on the cross"

at the martyrdom of their brother in Christ, Antipas, may very well be a continuation of the faith they had initially expressed in Christ when they first came to believe in him. Those who have saving faith in Christ remain faithful to him.

In 2:19 the same term occurs in a list of deeds the believers in Thyatira were known for. Thomas argues for πίστις meaning faith in Christ, noting the idea of faithfulness would be redundant since it is "so close to the meaning of endurance," which also makes the list.[160] Those who have faith in Christ for salvation show evidence of it through their faithfulness to him in the midst of conflict.[161]

One final passage that may contribute to the theme of belief in Christ for salvation is 3:20. Here, Jesus promises to come and fellowship with the one who opens the door in response to Jesus' knocking. The two most compelling interpretations of 3:20 are: "(1) that it represents a call to the individual for present fellowship, and (2) that it is eschatological and speaks of the imminent return of Christ."[162] In the first instance, the call of Christ, represented by knocking, was either to believers or unbelievers. If believers, then it was a call for them "to renew themselves in a relationship with Christ that has already begun."[163] Verse 19 may indicate that those being addressed are in fact Christians, since Christ disciplines those he loves. It may also be possible for unbelievers to be in view. Johnson takes this position, arguing that those addressed in the letter to the church at Laodicea were Christians in name only and thus in need of genuine repentance.[164]

Others believe 3:20 is essentially eschatological in nature and thus a call to be prepared for Christ's second coming by repenting. Thomas argues strongly for this position, basing it on, among other things, the use of the "door" metaphor, one used elsewhere of Christ's imminent coming (cf. Matt 24:33; Mark 13:29; Luke 12:36; Jas 5:9); the occurrence of ἰδού, an

---

(*Revelation*, 57).

160. Thomas, *Revelation 1–7*, 212; so also Aune, *Revelation 1–5*, 202.

161. Koester, *Revelation*, 298; Osborne, *Revelation*, 154.

162. Mounce, *Revelation*, 113. Some commentators believe the verse refers to partaking of the Lord's Supper (Blount, *Revelation*, 83–84; Caird, *Revelation*, 58; Roloff, *Revelation*, 65).

163. Beale, *Revelation*, 308. So also Beasley-Murray, *Revelation*, 107; Osborne, *Revelation*, 212–213.

164. Johnson, "Revelation," 638. So also Kistermaker, *Revelation*, 174–175. Beale allows for the possibility of nominal Christians hearing this message (*Revelation*, 308).

eschatological marker of sorts; and the reference to the future messianic banquet in Rev 3:20.[165]

Koester perhaps provides the most attractive position. He believes the text primarily is about the readers' renewal of their relationship with Christ, and secondarily intended to anticipate his *parousia*.[166] While not definitive, 3:20 may allude to unbelievers coming to Christ for the first time. If so, this would be the lone occurrence of this in the book of Revelation. This passage aside, there is sufficient evidence in the letters to the seven churches of belief in Christ for salvation in Revelation.

Consequences of Following Jesus

As in Rev 1 the consequences for following Jesus as one of his disciples is to undergo suffering. In the letters to the church in Smyrna and Pergamum one finds instances of Christians suffering on account of their devotion to Christ. In 2:9 Jesus declares his awareness of the believers in Smyrna facing "tribulation," "poverty," and "slander." The term for "tribulation" θλῖψις also occurred in 1:9. There, as here, it refers to the suffering Christians endure, since they live in the last days. Some scholars believe "poverty" and "slander" explain the kind of "tribulation" the Smyrnaean Christians were enduring.[167]

While one cannot be certain as to the cause of their "poverty" (πτωχεία),[168] several scholars attribute it to persecution the Smyrnaean

---

165. Thomas, *Revelation 1–7*, 321–322. Aune has argued that the passage may have its genesis in the pagan magical practice of inviting a god or lesser god for the purposes of divination. Here, though, the tables are turned, so to speak, and Christ is the one who makes the invitation, rather than the worshiper (*Revelation 1–5*, 250–254, 264). However, one cannot be certain of any apparent historical connections between Rev 3:20 and ancient Greco-Roman cultic practices. Neither does this view adequately help one to interpret the meaning of 3:20.

166. Koester, *Revelation*, 349.

167. Osborne, *Revelation*, 129; Thomas, *Revelation 1–7*, 162.

168. Thomas believes πτωχεία refers to abject poverty, as opposed to πενία, which was the word for ordinary poverty (*Revelation 1–7*, 163; so also Smalley, *Revelation*, 65). In other words, the Christians in Smyrna were reduced to nothing and would have likely resorted to begging. Osborne, on the other hand, while affirming that the two terms may have carried this nuance in secular Greek, notes that there is no indication this was the case in the NT. He believes the two terms function merely as synonyms for one another (*Revelation*, 129 n. 2).

Christians encountered on account of their fidelity to Christ.[169] In spite of their material poverty, this church was "rich" in Christ. This was the converse of the situation in Laodicea, where that church claimed to be "rich" in spiritual blessings, but whom the Lord declared were in fact "wretched, pitiable, poor, blind, and naked" (3:17).

Not only did they suffer poverty, but they also suffered "slander" (βλασφημία) from a "synagogue of Satan" (2:9b). While the term here for "slander" is often used with respect to blaspheming God, it is clearly used with respect to the Smyrnaean Christians.[170] It would appear that Jewish persons brought false charges against the Christians in Smyrna in order to get them into trouble with the Roman authorities.[171] Although these Jewish persons were genetically descendants of Abraham, they were not his spiritual children, thus the reason for their description as "those who say that they are Jews and are not" (2:9b). Rather than being children of Abraham, they were children of their father the devil (cf. John 8:31–47). Just as he was a false accuser and slanderer of the people of God, so the Jewish persons of Smyrna followed in his footsteps, falsely accusing the Christians of wrongdoing.

The Smyrnaean church was to be prepared for further suffering that would occur shortly (Rev 2:10). The one who would inflict misery on them would be the devil himself through the means of Jewish and Roman instruments, who would put some of them in prison for ten days.[172] The purpose of this imprisonment was to "test" the Christian church, both those thrown into prison and those who escaped this aspect of persecution (cf.

---

169. Aune, *Revelation 1–5*, 161; Johnson, "Revelation," 617; Mounce, *Revelation*, 74; Osborne, *Revelation*, 129–130; Thomas, *Revelation 1–7*, 163.

170. Koester believes John used this term here to show the close relationship between God and his followers. To denounce a Christian is to denounce God as well (*Revelation*, 275). See also the depiction of Paul and Jesus' words to him in Acts 9:1, 5.

171. Mounce, *Revelation*, 75; Thomas, *Revelation 1–7*, 164. Polycarp in the mid second century decried the Jewish persecution of Christians in Smyrna, particularly the persecution he personally faced (*Martyrdom* 12.2; 13.1). Paul and others also suffered Jewish instigated persecution for the cause of Christ in the earliest years of the NT church (cf. Acts 13:50; 14:2, 5, 19; 17:5).

172. Beale believes the "ten days" is an allusion to Dan 1:12–15 where the Hebrew young men were tested for a period of ten days (*Revelation*, 242). However, it is difficult to equate what Daniel and his friends endured, a testing of the benefit of their Hebrew diet as opposed to the Babylonian king's, and what some in the church at Smyrna would face, imprisonment with the possibility of death.

Discipleship in the Book of Revelation

Heb 10:33–34).[173] However, Jesus reassured them that the time of affliction would be limited to around ten days.[174] This did not necessarily mean that some of them would not suffer the greatest penalty (death), since the Lord encouraged them to remain faithful "unto death" (Rev 2:10c; cf. 2:13). Those who endured to the end could be assured that they would experience eternal life as their "victor's crown" (NIV) (cf. Jas 1:12).[175]

An additional passage that may address the suffering of Christians is Rev 3:10: "Because you have kept my word about patient endurance, I will keep you from the hour of trial that is coming on the whole world, to try those who dwell on the earth." This may refer to escaping the "hour of trial"[176] or being brought through it, so that one must endure the hardship.[177] The trial may refer to God's wrath against unbelievers.[178] While Christians

---

173. The verb πειράζω ("I test, tempt") is in the passive voice, which has led some scholars to conclude that God is the unnamed subject of the verb, given John's affinity with the divine passive in Revelation (Osborne, *Revelation*, 133). Others believe the unnamed subject of the verb is Satan, since if John had intended God testing Christians in order to prove their faith, he would have used a different verb entirely, δοκιμάζω ("I examine [in order to approve]") (Thomas, *Revelation 1–7*, 168). While the majority of occurrences of πειράζω appear to speak of testing in a negative light, this is not the case in every context. 2 Corinthians 13:5 states that believers are to test themselves to see if their faith is genuine, and in Heb 11:15 God is actually the one who tests Abraham. Further, the nouns πεῖρα and πειρασμός, which are cognates of πειράζω, also may be used of God testing to prove someone, or of the enemy trying to lead someone to commit a sin. In the end, it may be best to take the position of Osborne, who siding with Beckwith (*Apocalypse*, 454), believes the verb in Rev 2:10 may have a double meaning. While Satan desired to tempt the Smyrnaean Christians to apostatize because of persecution, God would use this as an opportunity to test the genuineness of their faith in him (Osborne, *Revelation*, 133).

174. The "ten days" may be actual or simply be an expression meaning a brief period of time (Aune, *Revelation 1–5*, 166; Johnson, "Revelation," 618).

175. Beale, *Revelation*, 243; Ladd, *Revelation*, 45; Thomas, *Revelation 1–7*, 173. The award to be treasured was not the "wreath" awarded to the one who won an athletic contest (Mounce, *Revelation*, 76), but what it represented. It is the "crown that is life" (genitive of apposition).

176. Thomas, *Revelation 1–7*, 283–290.

177. Beale, *Revelation*, 289–292.

178. Beasley-Murray (*Revelation*, 101), Koester (*Revelation*, 326, 331), and Osborne (*Revelation*, 193–194) believe what is described in Rev 3:10 is the wrath of God, which believers will be kept from enduring, but not by removal. They also believe the book of Revelation shows that Christians will continue to endure persecution until Christ returns, persecution at the hand of the enemy. See also Johnson, who affirms removal from experiencing God's wrath, but who likewise recognizes the possibility that one could remain present with unbelievers and yet not experience God's wrath directed at them

would be free from experiencing God's wrath, they would remain targets of persecution for following Christ. It appears that 3:10 refers to a time of suffering under which Christians may be tested to prove their faith in Christ.

The disciple of Jesus is one who suffers because of his or her relationship with him. The world does not praise those who follow him, but persecute them. The kind of suffering believers may be called to endure is defamation of character or even death. Even though Jesus' disciples may suffer, they may do so assured of their present state and future hope. Presently, they are rich in the spiritual blessings Jesus has bestowed on them, and they have a sure hope of victory in the end, should they continue to remain faithful to Christ.

Jesus as a Model for His Disciples

In a letter to the church in Pergamum, Jesus announces to the Christians there that he is aware of how they did not shrink back from following him, "even in the days of Antipas my faithful witness, who was killed among you" (2:13c). The phase "faithful witness" (ὁ μάρτυς ὁ πιστός) occurs only two other times in Revelation, and both are used to describe Christ (cf. 1:5; 3:14).[179] The parallels between 1:5 and 2:13 are even more striking. In 1:5 Jesus is a "faithful witness" in his testimony about God, which in his case leads him to the cross (notice "his blood"). Likewise, Antipas' faithfulness as a witness to Christ would culminate in his death.[180] These connections

---

("Revelation," 633).

179. Beale points out that the awkward nominative in apposition to oblique cases (ὁ μάρτυς ὁ πιστός) strengthens the connections between Rev 2:13 and 1:5 where the same construction occurs (*Revelation*, 247; Blount, *Revelation*, 58 n. 3). John's "audience would certainly take note of such a construction" (Wallace, *Greek Grammar*, 62). Osborne believes the repetition of μου ("my") with both ὁ μάρτυς and ὁ πιστός means one should understand them as separate characteristics. Antipas is "my witness, my faithful one" (*Revelation*, 142).

The only difference in 2:13, and 1:5 and 3:14 is the inclusion of the possessive genitive pronoun μου, indicating that Antipas is Jesus' faithful witness. Hemer believes the genitive pronouns should be taken as objective genitives. Even still, this does not dissuade him from seeing the title of Jesus in 1:5 and 3:14 as being applied to Antipas in 2:13 (*Seven Churches of Asia*, 86). Revelation 3:14 also includes καὶ ἀληθινός ("and true") rendering the phrase "the faithful and true witness."

Thomas following Charles (*Revelation*, 1.62) believes the use of μάρτυς in 2:13 may refer to martyr in the technical sense of the word, "though the clear-cut use of it in the sense of martyr was not yet in evidence elsewhere" (Thomas, *Revelation 1-7*, 187).

180. Koester believes Antipas's death was not the result of mob violence, but an

indicate that Antipas followed the "pattern Jesus set" as one who remained a faithful witness even to the point of death (cf. 6:9; 11:3–10; 12:11; 17:6).[181] So too, all of Christ's disciples are to be prepared to follow him to the end, even if that end is death as a faithful witness.

Membership and Election of the People of God

There are only a handful of well-defined occurrences of this theme in the course of Revelation, three of which clearly occur in chapters 2–3. All three occurrences are located as part of the promises to those who overcome in Pergamum, Sardis, and Philadelphia. To the churches in Pergamum and Philadelphia, there is the promise of a "new name" (2:17; 3:12).[182] The "new name" given to the believers at Pergamum is the name of God, Christ, both God and Christ, or a personal name given to the individual Christian. Those scholars who believe the name of a member of the Godhead is given differ as to the meaning of the "new name." Some believe it refers to God's possession of the believer, similar to the seal they receive elsewhere in the book (cf. 7:2, 3, 4, 5, 8; 9:4; 14:1; 22:4),[183] while others believe it is indicative of an intimate relationship with Christ/God,[184] or members of the new covenant community,[185] or even recognition of Christ's lordship over the believer.[186] Proponents of this view also see a close connection between 2:17; 3:12; and 19:12. However, in 3:12 the name is not one name,

---

officially sanctioned death at the hand of the Romans (*Revelation*, 292). So also Ladd, *Revelation*, 46. Ford believes Antipas was issued the death sentence as a result of his refusal to acknowledge the "power of Caesar" (*Revelation*, 399). So also Mounce, *Revelation*, 80.

181. Koester, *Revelation*, 288. So also Keener, *Revelation*, 123; Roloff, *Revelation*, 51.

182. The church in Pergamum is also promised "hidden manna" and a "white stone" that has a "new name written on the stone." For a full discussion on these items see Hemer, *Seven Churches of Asia*, 96–102.

183. Ford, *Revelation*, 400–401; Kistemaker, *Revelation*, 134.

184. Beasley-Murray, *Revelation*, 88; Patterson, *Revelation*, 111. Beasley-Murray believes the "new name" may also be a new name given to the individual believer. He believes both positions have merit, and so does not argue in favor of one particular view.

185. Beale, *Revelation*, 255.

186. Koester, *Revelation*, 290.

but three.[187] Also, in 19:12 the name that is hidden is known only to Christ, while in 2:17 the name is known by the one who receives it.[188]

Other commentators argue in favor of the "new name" being a personal name given to the individual Christian. The background for Christ giving a "new name" to the believer is rooted in the OT (cf. Gen 32:28; Isa 62:2; 65:15). What is promised in Rev 2:17 may be similar to what occurred in the OT as God at times gave a new name to those with whom he had entered into a covenant relationship (e.g., Abraham and Israel).[189] Revelation 2:17, though, is a promise to Christians in general, for the one who perseveres to the end will receive a new name. Some have argued that Christians are already in a covenant relationship, and thus 2:17 cannot refer to something reserved for the last day.[190] However, there is no need to reject the reality that Christians experience a new relationship with God through Christ in the present. What is promised in 2:17 is simply the fullness or perfecting of what God has begun through his Son. The new covenant relationship is experienced now, but will be more fully realized in the *eschaton*.[191] Regardless of the specific referent of the "new name" that will be given, it is plausible that it is an allusion to the old covenant election motif.

Similar ideas occur in both 3:5, 12. In 3:5 those in Sardis who persevere to the end are promised that their names will not be blotted out of the "book of life" (cf. 13:8; 17:8; 20:12, 15; 21:27; see also Luke 10:20; Phil 4:3; Heb 12:23). The names of those included in the book are in covenant relationship with God through Christ, "who was slain from the creation of the world" (Rev 13:8, NIV). The names of those in the book of life are "believers whose salvific destiny has been determined because their names

---

187. Thomas, *Revelation 1–7*, 202.

188. Hemer, *Seven Churches of Asia*, 102–103; Smalley, *Revelation*, 71.

189. Beasley-Murray, *Revelation*, 88; Hemer, *Seven Churches of Asia*, 102–103; Thomas, *Revelation 1–7*, 202. Beale does not reject this aspect of the giving of a "new name," although he still believes the name given is that of God/Christ (*Revelation*, 255). Others who believe the name is a personal "new name" given to the Christian differ in their meaning. Mounce believes the name is new in quality and "appropriate to the New Age" (*Revelation*, 83). Smalley hints at the covenantal aspect, but comes short of clearly speaking in favor of it. He believes the giving of a "new name" symbolizes "entrance into new life and status" (*Revelation*, 71).

190. Charles, *Revelation*, 1.67.

191. Hemer, *Seven Churches of Asia*, 103; Smalley, *Revelation*, 71.

Discipleship in the Book of Revelation

have already been written in the book before the foundation of the world."[192] They are the elect people of God.[193]

In Rev 3:12 Jesus first promises to the believers in Philadelphia to make the one who is victorious into "a pillar in the temple of my God. Never shall he go out of it." Elsewhere in the NT, Christians are identified as the temple of God, the dwelling place of his Holy Spirit (cf. 1 Cor 3:16–17; 2 Cor 6:16; Eph 2:19–22). The promise is of permanently being in God's presence.[194] Jesus also promises to those who overcome to write on them "the name of my God, and the name of the city of my God" and "my own new name." The three names written on the faithful Christian "show that the faithful belong to God, hold citizenship in the New Jerusalem, and are in a special way related to Christ."[195] These three truths appear to be another way of identifying one as a member of God's people.

Jesus' earlier promises to the one who perseveres to the end receiving the crown of life, the promise of suffering for his name, or even giving himself as an example for his disciples to follow may be grounded in the truth of election. For the disciples who have accepted the reality that they

---

192. Beale, *Revelation*, 279.

193. Osborne (*Revelation*, 183 n. 3:5) does not believe Rev 3:5 teaches divine election, but instead that one may lose one's salvation. He makes a distinction between 3:5 and the occurrence of the phrase "book of life" in 13:8; 17:8; and 20:15, noting that those whose names were not written in the book of life were "earth-dwellers who worship the beast and have always rejected the gospel." On the other hand, 3:5 refers to those Christians in the church at Sardis who "failed to remain true to Christ." He sees further evidence of "losing one's place in the kingdom" elsewhere in the book (cf. 2:5; 21:7–8; 22:17–18) and the NT (cf. John 15:1–6; Heb 6:4–6; 10:26–31; 2 Pet 2:20–22).

In response to such claims, Beale argues that Rev 3:5 does not indicate the possibility of believers having their names erased from the book of life. He provides the following points as evidence. First, he believes the negative expression is intended to be understood as a positive guarantee that those whose names have been written down will not be removed (*Revelation*, 279–280). Thomas refers to this as an example of *litotes*, "a figure of speech in which an affirmative is expressed by the negative of a contrary statement" (*Revelation 1–7*, 261). Second, nowhere in the book of Revelation are unbelievers' names "associated positively with the 'book of life,' but only the 'books' of judgment" (Beale, *Revelation*, 280). Therefore, it would be impossible for the reprobate to be excluded from a book to which they never actually belonged. Third, the repeated use of ὄνομα ("name") in 3:1, 4, 5 [2x] is "related by a common theme that contrasts genuine believers with false Christians" (ibid.). Some claim a name for themselves (3:1), one that on closer inspection will be shown to be false (3:5), while others do indeed bear a name and prove faithful to Christ (3:4).

194. Koester, *Revelation*, 326.

195. Mounce, *Revelation*, 105.

are God's elect, this leads to assurance that he will grant them the strength to follow Christ faithfully, even while suffering for him. God's election does not give one a reason to be idle, but it energizes the disciple to live for Christ, confident that what he has begun he will also bring to completion. The emphasis is not on what the disciples can do in their own power, but ultimately on what God has done.

Discipleship Language

Discipleship language is sparse in the letters to the seven churches. One that has previously been discussed at length, δοῦλος ("servant") occurs in Rev 2:20. The second occurrence of discipleship language is found in Rev 3:4: "Yet you have still a few names in Sardis, people who have not soiled their garments, and they will *walk* with me in white, for they are worthy" (emphasis added). While some in the church at Sardis had become lax in their devotion to Christ in the midst of an hostile culture, there were some who had remained faithful to him.[196] Those who remained faithful are promised the blessing of walking with Jesus in the future. In the NT the verb περιπατέω ("I walk") may refer to physically walking, but it is used just as often in a figurative manner. Whether the walking envisioned in 3:4 is literal or not, or perhaps even both, cannot be known with certainty. Mounce sees its usage as an allusion to both Enoch walking with God (cf. Gen 5:22, 24), a sign of his intimacy with God, as well as Jesus' Galilean ministry (cf. John 6:66).[197] That Mounce understands the term as discipleship language is fairly clear, since he links Rev 3:4 to additional passages of Jesus leading Christians (7:9–10) and to disciples of Jesus following him (14:4).[198] Smalley similarly notes that in the NT "'walking' often becomes a synonym for Christian discipleship."[199] The future tense of the verb περιπατήσουσιν ("they will walk") looks to indicate that the time when Jesus' disciples will walk with him clothed in white garments is at the time of the new heaven

---

196. Koester, *Revelation*, 319.

197. Mounce, *Revelation*, 95. Similarly Kistemaker, *Revelation*, 153.

198. Ibid. The verb ἀκολουθέω ("I follow") used in Rev 14:4 is something of a technical term in the Gospels (and John in particular) for discipleship.

199. Smalley, *Revelation*, 84. So also Aune, *Revelation 1–5*, 222. Osborne believes the walking is more likely an allusion to "triumphal procession imagery," in which citizens would don white robes and accompany the military following a victory (*Revelation*, 179; so also Hemer, *Seven Churches of Asia*, 147).

and new earth.[200] This indicates that Jesus' disciples will continue to be his disciples, following him into eternity. One never graduates from being his disciple.

SUMMARY

There are several preliminary observations concerning discipleship in the Apocalypse that 2:1—3:22 sheds light on. First, the recurrence of the image of the exalted Christ revealed in 1:12–20 is referred to either explicitly or implicitly as Jesus addresses each of the seven churches of Asia Minor. In doing so, Jesus shows how he is the remedy to what each church needs in their particular situation. Since the churches may be representative of all churches for all time, Christ's particular disclosure of himself to each church continues to speak to churches today. He is still the solution or answer for all of the problems and challenges disciples of Jesus presently face.

Second, the three marks of discipleship included in the Fourth Gospel appear in Rev 2:1—3:22. Jesus knows the works of each church. He has complete understanding of the strengths and weaknesses of his disciples. He draws attention to their growth in bearing fruit, loving one another, and obeying his teaching. The fruit they bore evidenced their growth as followers of Jesus Christ and their faithfulness to him. The love they shared for one another interconnected to the love they expressed toward God. The church at Philadelphia exemplified keeping Jesus' teaching, namely, the message of the gospel, as well as Jesus' own teaching (including his example) about his endurance to fulfill his mission. Jesus' disciples keep his teaching by obeying it.

Third, each of the letters to the seven churches closes with the phrase, "He who has an ear, let him hear what the Spirit says to the churches" (2:7, 11, 17, 29; 3:6, 13, 22). In each of these instances, it would seem that the Holy Spirit relays the words of Christ to the churches through the means of a prophet, in this case the apostle John. Jesus continues to speak to his disciples through the Holy Spirit, not necessarily through prophetic gifts (although he may), but he speaks authoritatively through his Spirit-inspired

---

200. Beasley-Murray, *Revelation*, 97. Charles argues that the white robes are actually "spiritual" or glorified bodies (*Revelation*, 1.82–83). Thomas concurs with Charles that spiritual bodies are referred to in this way several times in Revelation (cf. 6:11; 7:9, 13–14; 19:8); however, in Rev 19:8b the white garments are not spiritual bodies, but the righteous deeds of the saints (*Revelation 1–7*, 258).

word, the Bible. The ability to hear, that is, listen to the teaching of Scripture and obey it, is something that distinguishes Jesus' disciples from non-disciples. Only those who are in a discipling relationship with him hear his voice and follow him (cf. John 10:4–5).

Fourth, although the verb πιστεύω ("I believe") does not occur in the book of Revelation, that does not mean the idea is excluded entirely from the book's content. The theme of "overcoming" is closely tied to "belief" in Jesus. The one who overcomes is the one who believes in Jesus Christ (cf. 1 John 5:4–5). In addition, there are allusions to "eternal life," something one experiences only by faith in Christ alone for salvation. Those who have faith in Christ for salvation show evidence of their relationship to him by faithfully following him. This does not mean that a disciple of Jesus is never in a place to strengthen his weakening faith, as may be evidenced by the church in Laodicea (cf. Rev 3:14–22, esp. v. 20). Remembrance of the gospel and one's acceptance of it may be one of the means the Lord uses to increase a disciple's faith in him. This reaffirmation of the truth and reality of the gospel in one's life may lead one to commit oneself to depending wholly on Christ, not only for salvation, but also for everything else (cf. 3:17–18).

Fifth, the book of Revelation makes it painfully clear that following Christ is not without consequences. In the letters to the churches in Smyrna and Pergamum one finds mention of their suffering for Christ. The disciples in Smyrna faced poverty and slander for their fidelity to Christ. Although Christians may suffer material loss, that does not mean they are not "rich" in Christ's blessings (2:9; cf. Eph 1:3–14), although suffering does not necessarily mean one is experiencing the riches of being in Christ. The Smyrnaean Christians also suffered "slander," which may have also attributed to their poverty. The Lord also made them aware that they would continue to suffer. Their suffering, though, was not without purpose. It would be a means of testing their faith in Christ (cf. Rev 3:10), which would one day be rewarded with the "crown of life" (2:10). The suffering Christians face may lead to death (2:10; cf. 2:13). Disciples of Jesus today should expect no less.

Sixth, Christian preachers and teachers often hold up Jesus as a model whose example disciples of Jesus are to follow. This is nothing new, since the Apocalypse presents Jesus in this manner for this reason. Jesus is described as the "faithful witness" (1:5; 3:14), as is Antipas (2:13), a disciple of Jesus who suffered death for his faithful witness to Christ. To what extent and in what way disciples of Jesus are to pattern their lives after his is not fully expressed in this passage. The example of Antipas is limited to his faithfulness as a witness and his faithful witness that eventually resulted in his death. In this way he pattered his life after Christ. So, disciples of Jesus may follow Jesus' example as a faithful witness to his testimony about God and may even follow Jesus in the consequences for such a testimony.

Seventh, there is sufficient evidence to indicate that the early chapters of Revelation contribute to the idea of membership and election of the people of God. For instance, the believers in Pergamum and Philadelphia are promised a "new name" (2:17; 3:12), which may be an allusion to the old covenant election motif. In 3:12 the three names written on the Christians in Philadelphia indicate they "belong to God, hold citizenship in the New Jerusalem, and are in a special way related to Christ."[201] These three truths appear to be another way of identifying one as a member of God's people. The same can be intimated for all disciples of Jesus Christ. If they are followers of Christ, then they are also the elect people of God and members of his covenant community, the church.

Finally, one finds additional discipleship language in the letters to the seven churches. The recurrence of δοῦλος ("servant") is found in 2:20. An additional term, περιπατέω ("I walk"), occurs in 3:4. The idea of walking is often used in the NT as a "synonym for Christian discipleship."[202] The future tense of the verb is used here, which may indicate that believers are always disciples of Jesus Christ, even in the new heaven and new earth. A disciple of Jesus never graduates from his school.

AN ANALYSIS OF REVELATION 4:1—5:14

Following the seven letters to the churches of Asia Minor, John is called up to heaven to pay witness to God and the Lamb in God's throne room (4:1–2). What he saw next was a Holy Spirit-inspired vision of God, the creator and sovereign over all creation, and his Christ, the crucified and victorious Lamb, whose death redeemed sinners and who alone was worthy to loose the scrolls containing all of God's plan for human history (4:3—5:14). Each vision of God and Christ is punctuated by heavenly worship, worship from the twenty-four elders (4:10–11; 5:8–14), as well as others ("four living creatures," 4:8; "angels" and "four living creatures," 5:11–14). This section contains but a few brief depictions of the theme of discipleship.

---

201. Mounce, *Revelation*, 105.
202. Smalley, *Revelation*, 84.

Discipleship Language

There are two ways in which disciples are referred to in this section of Revelation. The first is found repeatedly in chapters 4 and 5, that being the designation "twenty-four elders" (4:4, 10; 5:5, 6, 8, 11, 14). The second is the referent "saints" that occurs in 5:8. In Rev 4–5 one finds various descriptions of the "twenty-four elders." First, they are seated on twenty-four thrones that encircled God's throne, at the center of which the Lamb is found standing (4:4a; 5:6). Second, they are dressed in white and wearing golden crowns (4:4b). Third, they participate in worshiping both God (4:10–11) and the Lamb (5:8–14). Fourth, one of the elders comforts John, who feared God's will for his creation would not come to fruition (5:5). Finally, they play harps and hold bowls of incense, which represent the prayers of the "saints" (5:8).

The question remains, who are the "twenty-four elders"? Various answers have been proposed. Most scholars believe the "twenty-four elders" are either heavenly (i.e., angels)[203] or earthly figures (i.e., human beings).[204] Those who favor a view that the "twenty-four elders" are angelic beings in general note: (1) these elders perform functions attributed to angels elsewhere in the book; (2) they are described as being clothed in white, which is similar to angels elsewhere; and (3) Isa 24:23 may be an instance in which angels are called "elders."[205] On the other hand, Ford, recounting the work of André Feuillet, notes four arguments against assigning the identity of the "twenty-four elders" to angelic beings.[206] In addition, human beings are called "elders" in both testaments (cf. Heb 11:2). There may also be a connection to Rev 21:12–14, where the gates are named for the twelve tribes and the foundations are named for the twelve apostles, so that the number twenty-four may represent both groups.[207] Perhaps Beale's view is to be favored since it combines the best features of each position. If it is possible that the "twenty-four elders" represent the people of God in some fashion,

---

203. Beasley-Murray, *Revelation*, 114; Hurtado, "Jewish Apocalyptic Analogies," 114; Krodel, *Revelation*, 155; Ladd, *Revelation*, 75; Mounce, *Revelation*, 121–122; Osborne, *Revelation*, 230; Roloff, *Revelation*, 70; Thomas, *Revelation 1–7*, 348.

204. Aune, *Revelation 1–5*, 314; Ford, *Revelation*, 80.

205. For these and additional lines of support see Osborne, *Revelation*, 229 and Thomas, *Revelation 1–7*, 328.

206. Ford, *Revelation*, 72. For Feuillet's entire argument see: "Twenty-Four Elders," 183–214.

207. Beale, *Revelation*, 326; Koester, *Revelation*, 360.

Discipleship in the Book of Revelation

then this may indeed be another instance of discipleship language in the book of Revelation.

If the "twenty-four elders" represent the people of God, then what might be said about them? Since they are in heaven and not on earth, it would appear that they are those saints who have died and now rest in God's presence. They have persevered and received in part their reward, rewards that are promised to all believers who persevere in their faith (cf. 2:10; 3:5, 21).[208] The first aspect of their reward is kingship, which is represented by the twenty-four thrones on which they are seated (4:4a) and the golden crowns (στεφάνους χρυσοῦς) they wear (4:4b; cf. 5:10).[209] This kingship, of course, must be viewed as that which is under the absolute sovereignty of Christ, as he is depicted as *the* king (cf. 14:14).[210] They are also robed in white garments (ἱματίοις λευκοῖς), which may "denote spiritual purity and righteousness."[211] They participate in worshiping both God (4:10-11) and the Lamb (5:8-14) with harps (5:8; cf. 11:16-18; 19:4). One offers comfort and instruction to John (5:5; cf. 7:13-14).[212] They also appear to have a priestly function as they present the prayers of the saints before Christ (5:8; cf. 5:10).

The other term found in the section that refers to disciples of Jesus Christ is "saints" (ἁγίων) in 5:8. The term ἅγιος ("holy," "saint") occurs 25 times in Revelation; second only to the book of Acts (53 times). The term is used several times with reference to Christians (cf. Rev 5:8; 8:3, 4; 11:18; 13:7, 10; 14:12; 16:6; 18:20, 24; 19:8; 20:9).[213] Here in 5:8 the "saints" are characterized as those who pray to God. What they pray is not specified, although many commentators believe their prayers likely consist of the prayers of 6:9-11 and 8:3-4. In 6:9-11 the prayers are of the martyred saints calling out to God for justice and vindication, while in 8:3-4 the petition of the saints is closely followed by God's judgment of the wicked.[214]

---

208. Koester, *Revelation*, 362.
209. Mounce, *Revelation*, 122.
210. Smalley, *Revelation*, 118.
211. Ibid.
212. Koester, *Revelation*, 375; Osborne, *Revelation*, 252.
213. Aune, *Revelation 1-5*, 359; Koester, *Revelation*, 379; Ladd, *Revelation*, 89.
214. Beale, *Revelation*, 357; Osborne, *Revelation*, 259; Thomas, *Revelation 1-7*, 397-398. Ladd believes the prayers were for the coming of God's kingdom in its fullness (*Revelation*, 89), which of course would have been preceded by his judgment. Johnson believes all three referents may be in mind ("Revelation," 648).

If this is the case, then prayer is something that God's people may engage in whether in heaven or on earth.[215]

What might this teach one about the theme of discipleship in Revelation? First, Jesus' disciples are not from one particular people group. They are the people of God from both testaments, which include various people groups. This should encourage disciples to make disciples of all nations. The gospel is freely offered to all peoples. Second, disciples of Jesus Christ are "holy." That is what it means for them to be a "saint." This does not mean one will no longer struggle with temptation or succumb to it. Being "holy" does not necessarily mean being perfect. However, it does serve to remind the disciples of who they are in Christ and that one day the full reality of what it means for them to be "saints" will be realized.

Jesus as the Model for His Disciples

One passage in particular appears to refer to this discipleship theme. In Rev 5:5 Jesus, described as "the Lion of the tribe of Judah, the Root of David," is said to have "conquered." The verb used here (νικάω) is the same that recurs in the letters to the seven churches (2:7, 11, 17, 26; 3:5, 12, 21). Beale and others believe this connection means the basis of the believers' victory is Christ's own victory.[216] The text goes on to answer how he "conquered," which was through suffering death (5:6, 9, 12). This is similar to what was promised to the church in Smyrna (2:10–11). It would appear that even the manner in which Jesus has overcome might prove to be an example for his disciples to follow.

Come to an Understanding of Jesus' Person and/or Work

Revelation 5:5 is one of several occurrences of ἰδού ("Behold!" "See!" "Listen!") related to understanding something about Jesus' person and work. In 5:5–14 one finds an elongated description of who Jesus is and what he has done. First, he is described as "the Lion of the tribe of Judah, the Root of David" who has "conquered" (5:5b).[217] The term that occurs first in this de-

---

215. Smalley, *Revelation*, 135.

216. Beale, *Revelation*, 350; Osborne, *Revelation*, 253.

217. This is the only place where these two titles are linked together in Scripture (Johnson, "Revelation," 647).

scription is actually the verb νικάω, translated "conquered."²¹⁸ This is likely for emphasis. What Jesus has triumphed over is left unnamed; however, given the repeated emphasis on his death (5:6, 9, 12), the triumph envisioned here is that which took place through the cross (cf. Isa 25:8; John 16:33; 1 Cor 15:54).²¹⁹

Next, Jesus is called "the Lion of the tribe of Judah, the root of David." God was often depicted as a lion (Job 10:16; Isa 31:4; Jer 50:44; Hos 5:14; Amos 3:8); a mantle Jesus now dons himself "as divine warrior."²²⁰ The background to the phrase, "the Lion of the tribe of Judah," is Gen 49:9–10, where Jacob blesses Judah, comparing him to a lion's cub growing until it can overcome its prey and return with it to its lair. Jewish interpreters understood the phrase to refer to the Messiah, since the promise will be fulfilled when the "scepter" and the "ruler's staff" is found between the feet "to whom it belongs" (NIV).²²¹ The might and the strength of the Messiah is the emphasis in the first part of Jesus' depiction in Rev 5:5b.²²²

He is also given the title "the Root of David," a designation taken from Isa 11:1–5, and in particular 11:1.²²³ This title for the Messiah, the Davidic king, also carries militaristic overtones, since in 11:4 "the Root of David" is said to "strike the earth with the rod of his mouth, and with the breath

---

218. The exact form is ἐνίκησεν an aorist active indicative third person singular verb. Osborne believes the aorist in this case functions as either a global or punctiliar aorist (*Revelation*, 253). Wallace believes this is an instance of a consummative aorist (*Greek Grammar*, 559–560). Mounce (*Revelation*, 132) and Thomas (*Revelation 1–7*, 387 n. 46) appear to understand the aorist similarly.

219. Aune, *Revelation 1–5*, 349; Beasley-Murray, *Revelation*, 124; Koester, *Revelation*, 376.

220. Osborne, *Revelation*, 253. Koester notes that the image of a lion may also indicate kingship or royalty given the context of Gen 49:10 (the mention of a "scepter" and "ruler's staff"), 1 Kgs 10:19–20, where the image of a lion was on the king's throne, and Prov 19:12, where kings were compared to lions (*Revelation*, 375).

221. Bauckham notes that both titles for the Davidic Messiah, drawn from Gen 49:9 and Isa 11:1–5, were "classic texts for Jewish messianic hopes in the first century." The emphasis was on God's Messiah as "conqueror of the nations, destroying the enemies of God's people" (*Climax of Prophecy*, 214).

222. This is the only place in the NT where the Messiah is referred to as "the Lion of the tribe of Judah" (Ladd, *Revelation*, 83).

223. The writers of the NT identified Jesus as a descendent of David (Matt 1:1, 6; Mark 10:47; Luke 2:4; 3:31; Rom 1:3; 2 Tim 2:8), and thus, the rightful Davidic king (Koester, *Revelation*, 376).
This title occurs one other time in Revelation (22:16) in the phrase "I am the root and the descendant of David" (Aune, *Revelation 1–5*, 350).

of his lips he shall kill the wicked."[224] However, as already noted, Jesus does not conquer as one might anticipate, through military might, but through his sacrificial death (Rev 5:6, 9, 12).[225]

Next, Jesus is described as one who "can open the scroll and its seven seals" (5:5c; cf. 5:9). Since[226] he has overcome his enemies, Christ is able "to effect the divine plan of redemption and judgment, as symbolized by the opening of the book and its seals."[227]

John then sees "between the throne and the four living creatures and among the elders . . . a Lamb standing, as though it had been slain" (5:6a).[228] Throughout Scripture the "lamb" (ἀρνίον) is associated with sacrifice and particularly substitutionary sacrifice.[229] The Passover lambs of Exod 12 were slain, so that when the death angel swept through Egypt, those who resided in the houses sprinkled with lamb's blood would be spared. The lamb died instead of the Israelites. In Isa 53 the "suffering servant" is depicted as a lamb that silently goes to be slaughtered on behalf of the sins of others, so that they might be pardoned (53:4, 5, 7, 12).[230] In John 1 Jesus is identified

---

224. Osborne, *Revelation*, 254.

225. Ladd identifies the enemies that Christ has conquered as Satan, sin, and death (*Revelation*, 84–85). Smalley includes all those who are the enemies of God (*Revelation*, 131).

226. Thomas believes the aorist infinitive ἀνοῖξαι ("can open") is best understood as purpose, rather than result (*Revelation 1–7*, 388). Smalley, on the other hand, believes the infinitive expresses result (*Revelation*, 131). So also Patterson, *Revelation*, 165. Wallace admits it can be "difficult to distinguish [purpose] from result" (*Greek Grammar*, 590). However, result seems to fit here, since the emphasis is on Jesus' ability to open the scrolls, an ability he immediately possesses as a result of overcoming.

227. Beale, *Revelation*, 350; so also Mounce, *Revelation*, 132; Thomas, *Revelation 1–7*, 388.

228. Koester notes, "the word 'as' (*hōs*) does not suggest that the Lamb merely appeared to have been slain; it refers to what has actually happened" (*Revelation*, 375). So also Aune, *Revelation 1–5*, 353; Smalley, *Revelation*, 132.

229. Koester states that the slaying of the lamb in Rev 5:6 has several layers or "dimensions of meaning" (*Revelation*, 376). He lists three: vulnerability, sacrifice of deliverance, and atonement for sin (ibid., 376–377). He is persuaded, as are most scholars, that the theme of deliverance is prominently on display, while atonement for sin is likely a "subtheme" (ibid., 377). Aune similar combines the two themes (*Revelation 1–5*, 353), as does Osborn (*Revelation*, 256), because of the allusion to the "suffering servant" of Isa 53. Thomas appears to emphasize the atonement for sin meaning (*Revelation 1–7*, 390–391). Beale believes the background of the "slain Lamb" is both Exod 12 and Isa 53 (*Revelation*, 351).

230. Ladd notes that Judaism did not identify the "suffering servant" with the Messiah, since the Messiah was a figure who conquered, rather than suffered (*Revelation*, 86).

as "the Lamb of God, who takes away the sin of the world" (1:29; cf. 35).[231] This theme of Jesus as God's Lamb, sent to redeem sinful humanity through his substitutionary death, tracks through the entire Fourth Gospel right up to the end, where Jesus' crucifixion coincides with the sacrifice of the Passover lambs (19:14, 31–36).[232]

The Lamb depicted in Rev 5 has not only died at the hands of others, but now lives, since he is found standing.[233] Revelation 5:6a provides a visual representation of Christ's declaration in 1:18, "I am the Living One; I was dead, and now look, I am alive for ever and ever!" (NIV) He is also found near the throne of God,[234] which may point to his role as mediator of the people of God.[235]

The Lamb also has "seven horns and seven eyes, which are the seven spirits of God sent out into all the earth" (5:6b, NIV). One of the

231. The word typically used for "lamb" in John's Gospel (ἀμνός) differs from that which is used in Revelation (ἀρνίον). Norman Hillyer has made much of this difference, noting that the use of ἀρνίον in the LXX and 1 Enoch 90 convey the idea of a triumphant warrior, rather than, the idea of a sacrificial lamb ("'The Lamb' in the Apocalypse," 229). However, he also readily recognizes that Rev 5:6 shows Jesus as one who redeems through his sacrificial death (ibid., 232). Johnson argues that 1 Enoch 90 is not a likely link, since it bears little resemblance to the image of the Messianic Lamb in Revelation ("Revelation," 648). Bauckham, likewise, sees "no evidence that the Lamb was already established as a symbol of the messianic conqueror in pre-Christian Judaism," which would include both the LXX and 1 Enoch references (Climax of Prophecy, 183).

232. Carson, John, 603. See also Hoskins, "Deliverance from Death," 285–299. Hoskins insists that while the first Passover sanctified or set apart firstborn sons and animals to God (cf. Num 3:13), it still retained an element of atonement and substitution (ibid., 288, 292–293).

233. The term ἀρνίον ("lamb") occurs 29 times in Revelation, where it refers to Jesus in all but one instance (Rev 13:11).

234. Aune discusses three ways in which the phrase ἐν μέσῳ may be understood: (1) in the middle, and so in the center of everything described as in Rev 7:17; (2) between two things, in this case the throne, and the four living creatures and the elders; or (3) in a position near the throne, in close proximity to it (Revelation 1–5, 351–352). Aune and others (Beale, Revelation, 350) prefer the last view, since the Lamb approaches the throne in 5:7. Osborne combines both (2) and (3), so that the Lamb is near the throne, encircled by others (Revelation, 255). Christ's nearness to the throne, perhaps sitting at the Father's right hand, would not preclude him from accepting worship, as appears to be the case in 5:9–14 (Beale, Revelation, 350). Thomas, who also mentions Christ's sitting at the right hand of God, favors the first view, that the Lamb is at the center of everything, which he believes is in keeping with 3:21 and 7:17 (Revelation 1–7, 389–390).

235. Charles, "Apocalyptic Tribute," 466. The depiction of Christ as king and priest may allude to Zech 6:9–15, especially vv. 12–13 where "the Branch," a messianic figure is both a king and a priest.

characteristics of apocalyptic literature is the mixing of metaphors with a single referent, something that is equally characteristic of John's writing.[236] The image thus far of Christ is as the lion who is the resurrected lamb with the horns of a ram. A horn was a standard image for strength, honor, and authority (Deut 33:17; Ps 112:9; Rev 12:3; 13:1, 11; 17:3, 7, 12, 16)[237] and may even included the power to save (Ps 18:2).[238] Here the number seven refers to fullness and shows that Christ's strength and authority is absolute.[239] The "seven eyes" are identified as "the seven spirits of God sent out into all the earth."[240] Bauckham believes the "seven spirits of God" are "sent out" (ἀπεσταλμένοι)[241] to declare to the nations what God has done in Christ to provide salvation (cf. Rev 5:9).[242] Others believe the image conveys the complete omniscience of Christ.[243]

The Lamb then "went and took the scroll from" God the Father,[244] and "when he had taken the scroll, the four living creatures and the twenty-four

---

236. Bauckham, *Climax of Prophecy*, 179.

237. Ford, *Revelation*, 86; Ladd, *Revelation*, 87; Mounce, *Revelation*, 133; Osborne, *Revelation*, 257; Smalley, *Revelation*, 132–133.

238. Koester, *Revelation*, 377.

239. Beale, *Revelation*, 351; Thomas, *Revelation 1-7*, 392. Koester believes the number "seven" refers to "Jesus' messianic identity" (*Revelation*, 377).

240. Beale believes the OT background to this phrase is Zech 3:9; 4:2, 10 (*Revelation*, 355).

241. This is only one of three occurrences of the verb ἀποστέλλω in Revelation (1:1; 22:6). The sending motif is emphasized in the Gospel of John. Jesus is sent from the Father (John 5:24, 30; 8:42; 11:42), he and the Father send the Holy Spirit (14:26; 15:26; 16:7), and Jesus sends his disciples as the Father sent him (20:21). The mission to declare God's salvation began with Jesus' mission and according to Rev 5:6 continued to be a part of Jesus' mission, no doubt through his Spirit-enabled disciples (see Johnson, "Revelation," 647; Smalley, *Revelation*, 133).

Charles believes it is probably not the Spirit that is sent, but the eyes due to the agreement in gender (masculine) of ἀπεσταλμένοι and ὀφθαλμοὺς, as well as the relationship of the terms in the background to this text, Zech 4:10 (*Revelation*, 1.142). Thomas, on the other hand, believes the agreement with the participle ἀπεσταλμένοι should be "according to sense," rather than relying on a "strictly grammatical" reading (*Revelation 1-7*, 393). Thus, Thomas believes the one who is sent is the "seven spirits of God." So also Smalley, *Revelation*, 133.

242. Bauckham, *Climax of Prophecy*, 336–337; so also Kistemaker, *Revelation*, 207; Osborne, *Revelation*, 257.

243. Koester, *Revelation*, 377; Osborne, *Revelation*, 257; Thomas, *Revelation 1-7*, 392. Beale believes it refers to carrying out "the sovereign plan of the Lord" (*Revelation*, 355).

244. Beale, *Revelation*, 356; Koester, *Revelation*, 377; Ladd, *Revelation*, 89; Smalley, *Revelation*, 133; Thomas, *Revelation 1-7*, 394.

elders fell down before the Lamb" and worshiped him (5:7–8a, 14).[245] The songs of worship sung about and in the presence of the Lamb in 5:9–10, 12–13 provide further reflections on who Christ is and what he has accomplished.[246] In 5:9–10 he is found to be worthy to take the scroll and open its seals because (ὅτι) of his substitutionary atoning death.[247] The cross is the avenue Jesus had to tread in order to enter into his glory, his exaltation by the Father, which included his position of authority (cf. Phil 2:8–11). His cross work[248] resulted in those "ransomed" from[249] every people group[250] to

---

245. Christ takes the scroll and keeps it; "hence [he] reigns over the events of human history" (Keener, *Revelation*, 188).

246. The song of Rev 5:9–10 is called a "new song." Beale notes that a "'new song' is always an expression of praise for God's victory over the enemy.... In this case, the 'new song' celebrates the defeat of the powers of evil and sin" (*Revelation*, 358; so also Beasley-Murray, *Revelation*, 126–127; Blount, *Revelation*, 114). Smalley adds that the newness of the song speaks to the "new creation" brought about by the Lamb, "new creatures" as a result of Christ's redemption, and "new life" received by all in Christ (*Revelation*, 136). The "new song" also brings to light allusions to the OT (Pss 33:3; 40:3; 96:1; Isa 42:10) (Mounce, *Revelation*, 135; Koester, *Revelation*, 379).

247. Koester (*Revelation*, 379) notes that the verb σφάζω ("I slaughter, murder") could be used of either violent death by the sword (1 Sam 15:33; 2 Kgs 25:7; 1 John 3:12) or the slaughter of the Passover lambs (Exod 12:6; Ezra 6:20), as well as other animal sacrifices (Lev 14:13, 25; cf. 16:11, 15; Ezek 40:41–42). Jesus' death draws on both of these images: he was violently killed (crucifixion) and he died as a sacrificial lamb. Blount limits the scope of σφάζω to Jesus' violent death (*Revelation*, 110).

Osborne believes the OT background to σφάζω is likely Isa 53:7: "he was led like a lamb to the slaughter" (NIV) (*Revelation*, 260). So also Charles, "Apocalyptic Tribute," 470; Mounce, *Revelation*, 135 n. 31; Smalley, *Revelation*, 136.

The two verbs "slain" and "ransomed" (ἐσφάγης καὶ ἠγόρασας) should be taken together as the cause for or basis of the Lamb's authority (Beale, *Revelation*, 359). Beale believes the Lamb's making the saints into a kingdom and priesthood adds to the basis of his authority (ibid., 362). So also Aune, *Revelation 1–5*, 361; Mounce, *Revelation*, 135; Smalley, *Revelation*, 136; Wall, *Revelation*, 103–104.

248. The preposition ἐν is likely the instrumental use of the preposition. Beale seems to arrive at this conclusion, although he does so by noting the instrumental use of the dative case ("instrumental dative of price") in prepositional phrase ἐν τῷ αἵματί σου (*Revelation*, 359). Similarly Ladd, *Revelation*, 91; Mounce, *Revelation*, 136; Smalley, *Revelation*, 136.

249. Christ's substitutionary death does not purchase all people, but certain ones out from [ἐκ] (Thomas, *Revelation 1–7*, 401), "every tribe and language and people and nation." The parallel passage Rev 14:3–4 makes this clear (Aune, *Revelation 6–16*, 814; Beale, *Revelation*, 359).

For a brief description of the ancient practice of redemption, which may be the background of the usage of ἀγοράζω ("I ransom, redeem") in 5:9 see Ladd, *Revelation*, 91.

250. The four terms φυλῆς καὶ γλώσσης καὶ λαοῦ καὶ ἔθνους ("[from every] tribe and

be made "a kingdom and priests to our God" and to "reign on the earth" (Rev 5:10; cf. Exod 19:6). Christians are those who have access to the presence of God, and who share in Christ's reign over the earth. The Lamb was "worthy" not only to take the scroll and open its seals, but also "to receive power and wealth and wisdom and might and honor and glory and blessing ... forever and ever" (Rev 5:12–13).[251] His worthiness to receive praise is based on his substitutionary death.[252] Christ shares this praise with his Father, which points to Jesus' divinity (5:13–14).[253]

SUMMARY

There are a handful of observations on the topic of discipleship that arise out of Rev 4:1—5:14. First, the people of God are made up of all saints from all times, including both old covenant believers (prior to Jesus' first advent) and new covenant believers. While old covenant saints did not follow Christ in the same way new covenant saints did and do, they do so presently in their current state in heaven. In heaven, believers from both testaments together worship God and the Lamb.

Second, Jesus' disciples, even in heaven, serve him by serving God's people. The example presented in Rev 5:8 is of believers presenting the

---

language and people and nation") are meant to stress the "universal nature of the church" (Mounce, *Revelation*, 136). So also Aune, *Revelation 1–5*, 361; Kistemaker, *Revelation*, 221; Thomas, *Revelation 1–7*, 401. For more on this fourfold expression see Bauckham, *Climax of Prophecy*, 326–333.

251. Christ receives this praise from everyone, including Christians and non-Christians, and every creature. Beale believes Christ receives this praise in the future, since elsewhere in Revelation it is stated that people "will be judged because they do not submit to and praise the sovereignty of Christ while they live on earth (cf. Rev 14:7–11; 16:4–11, 21)" (*Revelation*, 365). So also Ladd, *Revelation*, 93; Patterson, *Revelation*, 175; Thomas, *Revelation 1–7*, 407–408. Beale sees the worship in 5:9–12 and 5:13 as an example of the New Testament's "already-and-not-yet" framework (*Revelation*, 365).

Aune notes "each of the seven prerogatives" attributed to Christ are also attributed elsewhere to God, and some may even be "bestowed on [earthly] kings by God" (*Revelation 1–5*, 365). For his discussion on these "seven prerogatives" see pages 365–366.

252. Osborne, *Revelation*, 262.

253. Bauckham notes the Trinitarian nature of this worship: "John does not wish to represent Jesus as an alternative object of worship alongside God, but as one who shares in the glory due to God. He is worthy of divine worship because his worship can be included in the worship of the one God" (*Theology of Revelation*, 60).

Beale discusses how even Rev 5:9–12 emphasize Jesus' deity, since he is addressed in the same way God the Father is in 4:11 and 5:13 (*Revelation*, 358, 365).

prayers of the saints to Christ. If the content of the prayers in 5:8 are those described in 6:9–11 and 8:3–4, then all disciples of Christ, including those presently with him in heaven, continue to engage in prayer. Such prayer reinforces the Christians' absolute dependence on Christ for everything. There is nothing they can do that is of any sustaining value apart from him.

Third, Jesus provides an example for how believers may overcome, that is, through suffering for God. This does not mean Jesus' disciples overcome sin and death through their own suffering. The sole basis for the Christians' victory over sin and death is Christ's own victory gained through the cross.

Fourth, the vision of Christ leads his disciples to worship him. He is not just their teacher, but also their Messiah, Savior, King, high priest, and God, and as such is worthy of worship. Dwelling on Christ and all he has done for his people enables his disciples to grow in their love and adoration for him, which may be expressed through worship.

Finally, disciples of Jesus will be made up of "persons from every tribe and language and people and nation" (5:9). And these people are made to be like Christ as he makes them "a kingdom and priests to our God" and to "reign on the earth" (5:10).

AN ANALYSIS OF REVELATION 6:1—8:5

This section of Revelation covers the "seven seals" that the Lamb breaks in order for "the divine plan of redemption and judgment" to unfurl.[254] The greatest concentration of the theme of discipleship occurs in chapter 7. That is not to say that the theme of discipleship is absent in the rest of the section. In 6:9 mention is made of the souls of those who had been killed "for the word of God and for the witness they had borne" (bearing witness to Jesus). These martyred saints cry out to God, wondering how long before his judgment would fall on those who slew them. They were to wait until more of their brothers and sisters suffered a similar end (6:10–11) (consequences of following Jesus). Also, in 8:3–4 one finds another prayer, one offered by the "saints" (ἁγίων), whose prayers are likened to "incense" rising before the presence of God (discipleship language). The ideas found in these texts have been discussed in greater detail elsewhere. Therefore, the remainder of this analysis focuses on 7:1–17.

Chapter 7 falls between the opening of the first six seals and the seventh seal. The first six seals depict conquest, violence, economic hardship,

254. Beale, *Revelation*, 350.

death, the cries of the saints for vindication and the judgment of those who killed them, as well as cataclysmic disasters (6:1–14). Sinful humankind, both great and small, interpreted these earth-shattering events as God's judgment against them (6:15–17). But before God's judgment is meted out, John hears of "144,000 . . . from every tribe of the sons of Israel" who receive God's seal on their foreheads (7:1–8). After this John witnesses a "great multitude that no one could number, from every nation, from all tribes and peoples and languages" worshiping God and the Lamb (7:9–17). Immediately after this the seventh and final seal is opened, revealing not the destruction of the wicked anticipated at the end of chapter 6, but instead, the prayers of the saints (8:1–5).[255]

The 144,000 and the Great Multitude

Before getting to the analysis of discipleship themes in the chapter, it is perhaps helpful to first discuss who the groups described in chapter 7 are. Who are the 144,000 and who is the "great multitude" John sees?

The 144,000 is generally understood in one of two ways. It is either taken literally of a particular group of persons, or figuratively of some group.

---

255. This brief synopsis is not intended to convey a particular chronology of events unfolded in Rev 6–8. Several scholars have provided ample reasons for not holding to a strict chronological reading of these chapters. For instance, Keener notes that "after this" (Μετὰ τοῦτο) in 7:1 does not necessarily express chronology any more than the "after these" (Μετὰ ταῦτα) in 7:9. This phrase simply marks the next thing John "saw" (εἶδον). The "servants of God" are sealed before the harming of the earth (7:2), the destruction of which is described in 6:12–16. Keener concludes, "the point is simply that those who can withstand the day of God's wrath (6:17) are those whom God has empowered to withstand the previous plagues (7:2–3)" (*Revelation*, 229–230). Others, such as Thomas, believe the use of "after this" is used to indicate the unfolding of a new vision, but still maintain the placement of the vision in 7:1–8 is chronologically after the events of 6:12–16 (*Revelation 1–7*, 463–464). Thomas acknowledges the apparent problems with this approach, since the earth and its inhabitants are harmed in the first six weeks, while chapter 7 begins with neither apparently harmed, including the people of God. He conjectures, "perhaps the indirect nature of the wrath's early manifestation does not require [God's seal]" (ibid., 464). However, Duvall and Hays have argued rather convincingly that one should not be mainly concerned with developing a "strict chronological map of future events" when reading Revelation (*Grasping God's Word*, 290). In making their case they reference the relationship between 6:12–16 and 7:3, as well as 6:12–16 to the rest of the book, particularly the repeated and unfolding visions of the end of the age (6:12–16; 11:15–19; 19–22). Regarding the relationship between 6:12–16 and 7:3, they conclude, "to force a strict chronological sequence of this [set of events] wouldn't make sense" (ibid., 291; so also Beale, *Revelation*, 406–407, 408; Keener, *Revelation*, 414–415).

Discipleship in the Book of Revelation

For instance, Thomas understands the number to refer to redeemed Jewish persons who will witness to Christ during the great tribulation (7:1–8).[256] Further, he takes the "great multitude" to refer to Gentile and Jewish believers who died during the period of the opening of the first six seals and those who have come out of the great tribulation (7:9–17).[257] On the other hand, Beale argues the number 144,000 should be understood figuratively of the entirety of God's people who are sealed to protect them from faltering in their faith (7:1–8).[258] The depiction of the "great multitude" is understood to be the same group, only now enjoying eternal blessedness (7:9–17).[259]

Both the position advocated by Thomas and that of Beale have their difficulties. However, the greatest number of difficulties seems to surround Thomas's position and others who see two distinct groups.[260] If Beale is essentially correct, then the picture presented in 7:1–8 is of the sealing of all believers for their protection, and the second image is of Christians enjoying eternal blessedness (7:9–17). Regardless of the position, though, both recognize that the groups identified (whether one or two) are made up of followers of Christ, those whom Christ has bought with his own blood.

---

256. Thomas, *Revelation 1–7*, 474–475, 478. See also Walvoord, *Revelation*, 140–141. Gundry likewise identifies the 144,000 as a distinct group of Jewish Christians. However, he argues against their specific role as witnesses during the great tribulation (*Tribulation*, 81–82). Interestingly, Beale, who identifies the 144,000 as representative of all Christians, believes they "perform the witnessing role intended for true Israel" (*Revelation*, 411).

257. Thomas, *Revelation 1–7*, 485. In support of two distinct groups, Gundry notes the two groups are contrasted with one another in two ways. First, one group is given a specific number (144,000), while the other is unnumbered. Second, one group is identified with a specific nationality/ethnicity, while the other is made up of peoples from all ethnicities (*Tribulation*, 81).

258. Beale, *Revelation*, 416–418. Aune notes that most modern scholars take this position (*Revelation 6–16*, 447). This position in no way denies the possibility that a Jewish remnant will be saved (Ladd, *Revelation*, 112–113).

259. Beale, *Revelation*, 424–426; see also Bauckham, *Climax of Prophecy*, 215–216, 225–226.

260. A few of the greater difficulties with Thomas's position include: (1) the difficulty in understanding why one group would be sealed (the 144,000) and not the other (the great multitude). (2) If the 144,000 are Jewish believers, then this would be the only time in the NT when Jewish Christians received preferential treatment, as opposed to the Gentile believers. (3) The Greek term δοῦλος ("servant") is always used of believers in general throughout the book of Revelation, but Thomas's position calls for a different understanding of its usage in this one instance (Beale, *Revelation*, 413–414).

Distinction between Jesus' Disciples and Non-Disciples

Throughout the book of Revelation John records several descriptors used to differentiate Jesus' disciples from non-disciples. Some of these include the inclusion (cf. 3:5; 21:27) or exclusion (13:8; 17:8; 20:12, 15) of one's name from the book of life, worship of the true Trinity (4:10; 5:14; 7:11; 11:1, 16; 13:15; 14:7; 15:4; 19:4, 10; 20:4; 22:8–9) or worship of a false trinity (9:20; 13:4, 8, 12; 14:9, 11; 16:2; 19:20), and having unsoiled, white clothing (7:9, 13, 14; 22:14) or soiled, unclean clothing (22:11, 15). Here in Rev 7 one encounters perhaps the most pervasive characteristic used throughout the book to note one who is a follower of Christ and one who is not a disciple of his, that being a mark or seal (7:2, 3, 4, 5, 8).[261] In the course of the book, one either receives God's seal or the mark of the beast.

In Rev 7 the 144,000 are those who receive "the seal of the living God" (7:2).[262] The purpose for such a seal was to express "ownership, protection, and privilege,"[263] and it gave authority to the one who bore the document. One delivered a message in the name of the one's whose impression sealed the document.[264] The difference with the seal mentioned in Rev 7 and throughout the book is that it was a seal placed on a person, not a document.

Next, one must consider the reason for the sealing of the 144,000. Koester lists two general possibilities, while Beale notes three more precise options. Koester notes both protection and belonging as the reasons for sealing of the 144,000.[265] The 144,000 are protected from God's judgment against the ungodly (9:4), but not from the threats of God's enemies

---

261. Occurrences of bearing God's/Jesus' "seal" (noun: σφραγίς, verb: σφραγίζω) include: Rev 7:2, 3, 4, 5, 8; 9:4; 14:1; cf. 22:4. Occurrences of receiving the "mark" (χάραγμα) of the beast include: 13:16, 17; 14:9, 11; 16:2; 19:20. An occurrence of rejecting the beast's mark is found in 20:4.

262. In the ancient world a seal was typically made from a "gemstone or metal that bore an image and was often set in a ring" (Koester, *Revelation*, 415). Common images inscribed on the seal were "deities, people, and animals" (ibid.). The seal, in its ring form, when pressed into wax, perhaps on an important document, "left a distinct impression that served as the owner's signature" (ibid.).

263. Osborne, *Revelation*, 307.

264. Koester, *Revelation*, 415; Osborne, *Revelation*, 307.

265. Koester, *Revelation*, 425. See also Aune, *Revelation 6–16*, 455, 457–459; Beale, *Revelation*, 409–412; Johnson, "Revelation," 658; Kistemaker, *Revelation*, 248; Osborne, *Revelation*, 308; Smalley, *Revelation*, 183; Thomas, *Revelation 1–7*, 471–472.

directed against his people (13:8–10).²⁶⁶ With regard to belonging, those who bear God's seal belong to him. It is his "servants" who receive God's seal (7:3).²⁶⁷

Although agreeing with Koester's conclusions in general, Beale notes three specific possibilities for why the 144,000 are sealed. First, they are protected from physical harm, namely, that which God brings about on the earth and its inhabitants. This is the position of Koester. Second, they are protected from demons or the Antichrist.²⁶⁸ Finally, there is the position of Beale, which is protection from losing one's salvation.²⁶⁹ Under this position, both believers and unbelievers may experience physical affliction from the hand of God. While the unbeliever experiences this affliction as a manifestation of God's wrath, the Christian endures such suffering in order to strengthen one's faith in God and resolve to persevere to the end. The point of enduring suffering is to refine the follower of Christ, while it serves to harden unbelievers against God (cf. 9:19–21).²⁷⁰ Thus, the protection believers experience is "spiritual protection," not physical protection.²⁷¹

God's seal also marks one as a member of his people and thus may be viewed as a metaphor for salvation.²⁷² Beale draws on parallels found in 7:4 and 14:1, and 7:3 and 22:3–4. In 7:4 the 144,000 receive God's seal on their foreheads. In 14:1 the seal on their foreheads is revealed to be the names of Jesus and the Father. In 7:3 the 144,000 are called God's servants. In 22:3–4 the servants who will serve Christ for eternity bear his name on their foreheads. The "name" of God and Christ marks one as his, one belongs to him, since he possesses his servants/slaves, as opposed to those who bear the name of the beast on their foreheads (13:17; 14:9–11).²⁷³

When it comes to the OT background for the idea of God using a seal to protect his people and to indicate they belong to him, most scholars turn to Ezek 9 and Exod 28:36–38. In Ezek 9:4 the Lord instructs "the

266. Koester, *Revelation*, 416; so also Ladd, *Revelation*, 117; Mounce, *Revelation*, 157; Patterson, *Revelation*, 191–192; Thomas, *Revelation 1-7*, 469.

267. Koester, *Revelation*, 416.

268. Charles supports this position (*Revelation*, 1.205).

269. Beale, *Revelation*, 409.

270. Ibid., 409–410.

271. Ibid., 410.

272. So also Johnson, "Revelation," 658–659; Smalley, *Revelation*, 182.

273. Beale, *Revelation*, 410–411. This discussion may also contribute to the theme of "membership and election of the people of God," which was discussed more fully in the analysis of Rev 2:17; 3:12.

man clothed in linen" to go throughout the city of Jerusalem marking the foreheads of the faithful, so as to preserve them from the coming destruction that the ungodly will endure.[274] In both Ezek 9 and Rev 7 physical protection appears to be at the fore, while the idea of spiritual protection is implicit at best.

With respect to the idea of the seal used to indicate those who are the Lord's, the likely background is Exod 28:36–38.[275] This text describes the plate of pure gold that was to be placed on the turban of the high priest. The "seal" was to read "Holy to the Lord" (28:36). Koester makes the connection between Exod 28:36–38 and Rev 7, noting that Christians in the book of Revelation are identified as "priestly people (1:6; 5:10), and those bearing the name of God come before his throne and see his face (14:1; 22:4)."[276] This is similar to the function of the high priest in the OT, who also bore God's name on his forehead as a seal as he performed his priestly duties.

All in all, the idea presented in Rev 7:1–8 is that God's people, his servants, those who follow Christ, receive God's seal, his promise to keep his own and to protect his people from the coming wrath. They also bear his name, which is symbolic of belonging wholly to him, as opposed to the ungodly throughout the book of Revelation who bear the seal/name of the beast and who will feel the full fury of God's righteous anger against sin. The disciple of Jesus is reminded that there are things far worse to experience than death. One may have to endure the wrath of God.

Discipleship Language

In Rev 7 both the noun "servant" (7:3) and the verb "serve" (7:15) occur. The noun was discussed in greater detail earlier in this chapter. By way

---

274. A partial list of commentators who view Ezek 9 as the likely background to Rev 7 include: Aune, *Revelation 6–16*, 452; Beale, *Revelation*, 409; Beasley-Murray, *Revelation*, 142–143; Boring, *Revelation*, 128; Mounce, *Revelation*, 157; Osborne, *Revelation*, 310; Roloff, *Revelation*, 97.

Additional texts discussed as the possible background to Rev 7 include: Gen 4:15, God's mark of protection on Cain (Aune, *Revelation 6–16*, 452; Koester, *Revelation*, 416) and Exod 12:7, 13, 22–28, the protection of the Hebrews during the first Passover (Aune, *Revelation 6–16*, 456, 480; Beale, *Revelation*, 409; Patterson, *Revelation*, 193; Smalley, *Revelation*, 182).

275. So is the view of Beale, *Revelation*, 412; Ford, *Revelation*, 117; Koester, *Revelation*, 416.

276. Koester, *Revelation*, 416.

Discipleship in the Book of Revelation

of reminder, the noun δοῦλος ("servant") is usually used in Revelation as a general term for Christians.[277] And so here in Rev 7, John witnesses the servants of God, both Jewish and Gentile believers from every ethnic group,[278] wearing white robes and bearing palm branches[279] as they exalt God and the Lamb (7:9–10). Later, those dressed in white are identified as those "coming out of the great tribulation. They have washed their robes and made them white in the blood of the Lamb" (7:14).[280]

---

277. Aune, *Revelation 1–5*, 13; Koester, *Revelation*, 211; Osborne, *Revelation*, 54 n. 5; Smalley, *Revelation*, 188.

278. This "great multitude" may be the fulfillment of the Abrahamic promise that all the nations would be blessed through Abraham's seed (Gen 13:16; 15:5; 22:17–18; 26:3–4).

279. Both J. A. Draper ("Heavenly Feast," 133–147) and Edwin Reynolds ("Feast of Tabernacles," 245–268) have illustrated the connection between this Jewish festival and Rev 7 although through different avenues. Draper shows the connection by way of exploring Zech 14 as the likely background of Rev 7, while Reynolds draws on the Pentateuch for his background. Ford is not as certain of the connection to Tabernacles (*Revelation*, 126). The Feast of Dedication has also been proposed (Sweet, *Revelation*, 152).

280. When precisely τῆς θλίψεως τῆς μεγάλης ("the great tribulation") takes place is a matter of debate. Space and time only allow for a brief list of the most frequently offered interpretations.

First, "the great tribulation" may refer to a future tribulation, one that has yet to begin (Osborne, *Revelation*, 324–325). A great deal of weight is placed on the article with θλῖψις ("tribulation"). Typically, θλῖψις is used throughout Revelation to refer to the suffering of Christians (1:9; 2:9, 10); however, here, so the argument goes, the article means the suffering envisioned is a particular suffering and "most likely refers to that final war against the saints waged by the dragon (chapter 12) and his followers, the earth-dwellers" (Osborne, *Revelation*, 324; so also Keener, *Revelation*, 244; Mounce, *Revelation*, 164; Thomas, *Revelation 1–7*, 496). The OT prophet Daniel appears to allude to a time of intense persecution of God's people (12:1), as does Jesus (Matt 24:21) and Paul (2 Thess 2:3) (Johnson, "Revelation," 664). It is something that takes place prior to the return of Christ (Beasley-Murray, *Revelation*, 147; Mounce, *Revelation*, 164; Thomas, *Revelation 1–7*, 496) and perhaps, during the seven-year tribulation period (Thomas, *Revelation 1–7*, 486). Against this understanding of the phrase "great tribulation" see D. A. Carson's explanation of the phrase used for the general persecution of Christians in an eschatological context, namely, Matthew 24 and especially v. 21 ("Matthew," 502–504).

Second, "the great tribulation" may refer to the persecution Christians endure throughout the church age (cf. John 16:33; Acts 14:22; Rom 5:3; 2 Tim 2:11–12; 1 Pet 4:12; Rev 1:9; 2:10). This view largely focuses on the lack of time mentioned in the text. Caird notes the ambiguity of the time, but offers no definitive stance (*Revelation*, 102–103). Since there is no definitive mention of time, either in the present or the future, then one must understand "the great tribulation" to refer to all sufferings Christians face throughout the church age on account of their faithful witness (Blount, *Revelation*, 155; Kistermaker, *Revelation*, 257). The persecution they face is "a continuation of what has

Apart from worshiping God and the Lamb, along with the angels, the elders, and the four living creatures (7:11–12), these Christians are also said to "serve" (λατρεύω) in God's temple "day and night" (7:15). The verb translated "serve," λατρεύω is always used in the context of worship. The worship one engages in is not necessarily tied to a particular expression or location, but can be used of the life of the Christian in general (Rom 12:1).[281] So, also these Christians engage in worship of their God.

The basis or reason (διὰ τοῦτό) for their admittance to worship God is the substitutionary atoning death of Christ; "they have washed their robes and made them white in the blood of the Lamb" (Rev 7:14).[282] This worship is something that takes place "day and night," which is an hendiadys, meaning "endlessly" or "unceasingly" (cf. 20:10).[283] In doing so, they appear

---

already begun" (Smalley, *Revelation*, 196; so also Beale, *Revelation*, 435). Some appeal to the present tense of the participle ἐρχόμενοι ("have come") for support. Wall believes the tense indicates a looking back "over this period of history as the continual gathering together of the great multitude for the salvation of God" (*Revelation*, 120). Similarly, Charles believes the present participle should be taken as an imperfect participle, which indicates, "martyrs are *still* arriving from the scene of the great tribulation" (*Revelation*, 1.213). Although this is possible, it is perhaps more likely that one should understand the present participle as "*contemporaneous* in time to the action of the main verb" (Wallace, *Greek Grammar*, 625), the main verbs in this context [ἔπλυναν ("have washed"), ἐλεύκαναν ("made . . . white")] being in the aorist tense (Aune, *Revelation 6–16*, 473; Beale, *Revelation*, 444; Osborne, *Revelation*, 324). Although favoring this understanding, Blount does not believe the grammar is intended to indicate a "sense of time," but clearly shows the participle's "structural relationship with the main verbs" (*Revelation*, 153).

Finally, "the great tribulation" may refer to a "final affliction already occurring" (Koester, *Revelation*, 421). This view may take "the great tribulation" to be the same period of the "great wrath" depicted in Rev 12:1–17. This period began when Christ expelled Satan from heaven and will continue "until Christ returns to defeat Satan and his agents" (ibid.). Christians have the promise that they will endure suffering, but also that God will protect and keep them through such hardships until the end.

281. Hess, "λατρεύω," 3.550–551.

282. Aune, *Revelation 6–16*, 475. Beale notes that the basis of their entrance into God's presence is due to their "perseverance in Christ and resulting purity (vv. 13–14)" (*Revelation*, 439), although he seems to add the element of Christ's cross work as the reason for them praising God (ibid., 440). Similarly Osborne, *Revelation*, 326.

283. Aune, *Revelation 6–16*, 475.

to function as priest (cf. 1:5–6; 5:9–10).[284] On the other hand, those who oppose God can expect "judgment day and night (14:11; 20:11)."[285]

Near the close of Rev 7 one finds the Lamb described as the one who "will . . . shepherd" (7:17a) the "great multitude" (7:9). John has no problem envisioning a lamb that is a shepherd, any more than a lion that is a lamb. As a good shepherd, he is said to "guide them to springs of living water" (17:7b).[286]

The particular verb ποιμαίνω ("I shepherd") occurs four times in Revelation. In the other three instances (2:27; 12:5; 19:15) the shepherd is depicted as forcefully ruling over the nations.[287] However, in 7:17 ποιμαίνω clearly means to lead a flock to water, which is indicated by the context.[288]

Throughout the Hebrew Bible, God calls himself the shepherd of his people Israel (Gen 48:15; 49:24; Pss 23:1, 3; 68:7–10; 80:1; Isa 40:11; 49:10; Jer 50:19).[289] The shepherd motif was also used in the OT to articulate the responsibility of a leader to his people (2 Sam 7:7 [David]; Isa 44:28 [Cyrus]; Jer 3:15 [Israel's leaders]; Ezek 34:23–24 [Davidic Messiah]; Nah 3:18 [Assyrian leaders]; Mic 5:4 [Messiah]).[290] The writers of the NT attribute the characterization of God as a shepherd to Jesus (Matt 15:24; 25:32; Mark 14:27–28//Matt 26:31–32; Luke 19:10; Heb 13:20; 1 Pet 2:25; 5:4),[291]

---

284. Beale sees a connection between Rev 7:15 and 1:5–6; 5:9–10. All three passages describe believers as having priestly functions as a result of Christ's atoning work. This leads him to conclude that just as all Christians are made priests in 1:5–6; 5:9–10, so also are all believers envisioned in 7:15. He adds that the description of the saints in both 5:9 and 7:9 are virtually identical, which may strengthen this connection (*Revelation*, 440).

285. Koester, *Revelation*, 422.

286. Interestingly, Smalley (*Revelation*, 200) notes several images found in Rev 7:17 to reappear in 14:1–5: (1) the Lamb standing on Mt. Zion (14:1); (2) the throne is set (14:3); and (3) the faithful follow the Lamb (14:4). The picture of Mt. Zion is not especially evident.

287. Aune, *Revelation 6–16*, 477; Smalley, *Revelation*, 200; Thomas, *Revelation 1–7*, 503.

288. Koester, *Revelation*, 423; Osborne, *Revelation*, 332 n. 23. Charles believes Rev 7:17 recalls John 10:11, "I am the good shepherd" (*Revelation*, 1.217).

289. Aune, *Revelation 6–16*, 478; Charles, *Revelation*, 1.217; Koester, *Revelation*, 423; Mounce, *Revelation*, 166; Osborne, *Revelation*, 331.

290. Smalley, *Revelation*, 200.

291. Aune, *Revelation 6–16*, 477; Charles, *Revelation*, 1.217; Mounce, *Revelation*, 166; Osborne, *Revelation*, 331; Smalley, *Revelation*, 200; Thomas, *Revelation 1–7*, 502.

and the Johannine literature in particular is taken with this metaphor for Jesus (John 10:1–30; 21:15–17).[292]

Where Jesus leads his sheep, those whom God has sealed, the great multitude from every ethnic group, who have come out of the great tribulation, and whose garments are washed clean in the blood of the Lamb, is to "springs of living water." The image of living water carries further the imagery from Isa 49:10, which began in Rev 7:16.[293] Most commentators are quick to point out the unusual word order of the phrase "springs of living water" (ζωῆς πηγὰς ὑδάτων)[294] that places ζωή ("life") first for emphasis.[295] This image is shared with the Fourth Gospel (John 3:5; 4:10, 13–14; 6:35; 7:17–18, 38–39; 19:34).[296] There, as here in Rev 7:17, "living water" is linked to "eternal life," the "life of eternal fellowship with God and Christ."[297] This image is picked up later in the Apocalypse, in 21:6 and 22:1.[298] In 21:6, one hears God inviting those who are thirsty to come and receive water "from the spring of the water of life without payment." The next verse notes that the one who overcomes, one would suspect by the blood of the Lamb, "will have this heritage, and I will be his God and he will be my son" (21:7). Here the connection between the "water of life" and "eternal fellowship with God and Christ" is made explicit. Later, in Rev 22:1 one finds the source of the "water of life," that being "the throne of God and of the Lamb." It would seem, then, that 7:17, along with 21:6–7 and 22:1, states that Jesus as shepherd leads his sheep (Christians) to the source of all life,[299] God himself, to enjoy eternal fellowship with God and with himself.[300]

292. Aune, *Revelation 6–16*, 477; Mounce, *Revelation*, 166; Thomas, *Revelation 1–7*, 503. In addition to the canonical books of Scripture, Aune notes the theme of Jesus as good shepherd is also found in early Christian literature: *Barn.* 5:12; *1 Clem.* 16:1; Clement of Alexandria *Instructor* 3.101.3 (*Revelation 6–16*, 477).

293. Aune, *Revelation 6–16*, 478; Koester, *Revelation*, 423; Smalley, *Revelation*, 200.

294. Beale and McDonough note that ζωῆς can either be taken as an appositional genitive, meaning "fountains of waters which are life," or more likely as an adjectival genitive, meaning "fountains of living waters" ("Revelation," 1109).

295. Charles, *Revelation*, 1.217; Mounce, *Revelation*, 167; Osborne, *Revelation*, 332; Thomas, *Revelation 1–7*, 503.

296. Aune, *Revelation 6–16*, 478; Osborne, *Revelation*, 332.

297. Beale, *Revelation*, 442; so also Charles, *Revelation*, 1.217; Osborne, *Revelation*, 332; Smalley, *Revelation*, 201.

298. Koester, *Revelation*, 423.

299. Thomas, *Revelation 1–7*, 503.

300. Koester believes the metaphor "living water" in Revelation differs from the Gospel of John. He believes Revelation refers to a future experience, namely, the bodily

Jesus, then, is the promised Davidic shepherd, who is God himself who comes to care for his sheep and gently lead them "to springs of living water," which refers to eternal life lived in the presence of God and Christ. If he is the one leading Christians, then believers are those who follow the Lamb who is their shepherd. The theme of following is one of the chief images used in John's Gospel to depict discipleship. Even in Rev 7:17, where the verb ἀκολουθέω ("I follow") is not used, one still finds this theme on display. Christians are to be identified by the one whom they follow, the Lord Jesus Christ.[301]

Consequences of Following Jesus (Suffering)

While Rev 7:1–17 does not primarily depict a particular act of violence against the church for its faithful witness to Jesus, it does allude to suffering by way of speaking of its cessation. First, there is mention made of a "great tribulation" (7:14). As indicated previously, not all scholars are in

---

resurrection (*Revelation*, 423).

301. The timing and location of Rev 7:9–17 is a matter of debate. Some scholars believe the scene is to be taken with the image of the consummated Kingdom revealed in Rev 21:1—22:5 (Ladd, *Revelation*, 119; Osborne, *Revelation*, 326). The mention of the "temple" (7:15) and the lack of one in the New Jerusalem (21:22) create no problem. The difference "only reflects the fluidity of apocalyptic language" (Ladd, *Revelation*, 119). Beale notes the "temple" in 7:15 is not a literal "temple"; "rather, as the second part of the verse reveals, the temple now consists in the presence of the Lamb and of 'the one sitting on the throne, who tabernacles over his people' (so also 21:22)" (*Revelation*, 441). This position is based on several verbal cues found in 7:9–17 that recur in Rev 21:1—22:5 (Koester, *Revelation*, 430). In spite of these connections, some believe Rev 7:9–17 reveals "the *overall process* of those who persevere and enter into and begin to participate in the enjoyment of God's presence and eternal blessings" (Beale, *Revelation*, 443; so also Smalley, *Revelation*, 198). In other words, what is depicted is something all Christians may experience upon death, and it is something all will experience in its fullness in the consummated age. The change in verb tenses in 7:13–17 does not prove an insurmountable obstacle to this position, but actually serve to help it, since the "temporal ambiguity [is] intended to indicate an overall process" (Beale, *Revelation*, 444; so also Smalley, *Revelation*, 198. Similarly Mounce, *Revelation*, 165). Still others believe the timing and location of Rev 7:9–17 refers to the mid-point of the tribulation period (Thomas, *Revelation 1–7*, 486–487). During this period, those Christians who die of natural causes or a martyr's death go immediately to be with the Lord (Charles, *Revelation*, 1.209; Thomas, *Revelation 1–7*, 485). This view is conditioned on taking "the great tribulation" as a specific future event predicted by Daniel and Jesus. However, according to Osborne, "there is no evidence in the book that [the great tribulation] is a title for this final period" (*Revelation*, 324).

complete agreement regarding when this takes place and who undergoes it. However, all agree that θλῖψις ("tribulation") with reference to believers is used for suffering one generally endures on behalf of following Christ (1:9; 2:9, 10).[302] Here, in 7:14 those who endured "tribulation" were Christians. This is indicated by the way in which they are described: "they have washed their robes and made them white in the blood of the Lamb."

Second, 7:16 contains a list of difficult circumstances that cease to be a reality for the saints of God depicted in 7:9–17. These persons will never again experience "hunger," "thirst," nor "scorching heat." Instead, God "shelters them with his presence" (7:15).

All in all, Rev 7:15 very likely refers to God's care and protection of his people, the manner of which is described in the following verse. In 7:16 the saints are promised they will never again suffer "bodily deprivation," nor "external deprivation."[303] The certainty of this is seen in the doubling of ἔτι ("again"), which "strengthens the idea of 'never again,'"[304] but also the use of the emphatic negation subjunctive (οὐδὲ μὴ πέσῃ, "shall not strike"), which "is the strongest way to negate something in Greek."[305] These believers can be assured that they will suffer no more, because God is protecting them, as is his Son, the Lamb who will shepherd his people (7:17).[306]

It also seems that 7:16, 17b is a translation of Isa 49:10, one which is independent of the LXX.[307] The blessings initially promised to Israel are now extended to persons "from every nation, from all tribes and peoples

---

302. Osborne, *Revelation*, 324.

303. Ibid., 329, 330.

304. Ibid., 330.

305. Wallace, *Greek Grammar*, 468.

306. The use of ὅτι ("for") in Rev 7:17 appears to indicate the cause of the saints' protection and lack of suffering in 7:16. So also Osborne, *Revelation*, 331; Thomas, *Revelation 1–7*, 502.

307. Several scholars believe Rev 7:16 is a clear allusion to Isa 49:10 (Beale, *Revelation*, 441; Beasley-Murray, *Revelation*, 148–149; Keener, *Revelation*, 245; Mounce, *Revelation*, 166; Osborne, *Revelation*, 329; Thomas, *Revelation 1–7*, 501). It is also recognized as the "longest allusion to an OT passage found in Revelation" (Aune, *Revelation 6–16*, 477; so also Smalley, *Revelation*, 199).

Koester refers to it as a paraphrase of Isa 49:10 (*Revelation*, 422). Both Charles (*Revelation*, 1.216) and Smalley (*Revelation*, 199) have pointed out the differences between John's rendition of Isa 49:10 and that of the LXX. Charles goes so far as to correct the text before the reader in Rev 7:16. He does so despite a lack of manuscript evidence (*Revelation*, 1.216).

and languages" (cf. Rev 7:9).[308] The care and protection promised in 7:16 is certainly relief from physical harm and discomfort, but some scholars believe it is also a promise of "spiritual wholeness," given the way John uses the language of thirst and hunger metaphorically in the Fourth Gospel (cf. John 4:14; 6:35; 7:37).[309] If the promise is to include a spiritual element, then the blessing foretold is not so much the quenching of spiritual hunger and thirst, for Christians will continue to hunger and thirst for God in the new age, but that spiritual hunger and thirst will "always be satisfied."[310]

All of these promises testify to the fact that God's servants undergo suffering in this present age. The suffering they experience is not merely due to testifying to the gospel (see "great tribulation"), but also includes the natural impediments that all human beings experience in this fallen world. The only relief from such things is to be in the protective presence of the Lord. Osborne aptly summarizes the point of Rev 7:16, "God will deliver his followers of all the suffering they have gone through for his sake."[311]

SUMMARY

Revelation 6:1—8:5 makes several contributions to one's understanding of the theme of discipleship in the book of Revelation. In particular, Rev 7 has much to say. First, there are several ways in which Jesus' disciples are distinct from non-disciples, such as: the inclusion or exclusion of one's name in the book of life; whether or not one worships the one true God or the devil and his minions; and whose seal/mark one receives. This last distinguishing characteristic is perhaps the most well known in the Apocalypse, and comes to the fore in Rev 7. God seals his own in part, to protect them from the coming wrath, which does not preclude one from persecution; and to show who it is that belongs to him and Christ.

Second, one is reminded that Christians are servants of the living God, a theme already articulated in Rev 1. One of the ways in which believers serve God is as a kingdom of priests. Just as old covenant priests were to engage in worship before God, similarly, new covenant believers gather together to worship their God. The barrier that would otherwise

---

308. Koester, *Revelation*, 430; Thomas, *Revelation 1–7*, 501.

309. Mounce, *Revelation*, 166; so also Osborne, *Revelation*, 330; Smalley, *Revelation*, 199–200.

310. Thomas, *Revelation 1–7*, 501.

311. Osborne, *Revelation*, 331.

keep people from God's presence, their sinfulness, is washed away by the blood the Lamb (7:14). Those whom Christ has made clean may enter into God's presence and worship him.

Third, Rev 7 and verse 9 in particular indicate that Jesus' disciples are not from one particular ethnicity or background. Rather, Jesus' disciples are made up of Jewish and Gentile Christians. They include persons from every people group.

Fourth, in keeping with the imagery of following Jesus in the Gospels, Rev 7 utilizes the shepherd motif to teach that disciples of Jesus are those who follow him. They follow him because of who he is, a good shepherd who leads his sheep to "springs of living water," which serves as an image of eternal fellowship in the presence of the Father and the Son (7:17).

Finally, as has been noted earlier in the book, Jesus' disciples are not exempt from suffering. The suffering they experience may be due to persecution for faithfully following Jesus or as a result of living in a world under the curse. However, *all* saints have the promise of eternal relief from *all* suffering. It is God and his Son who are powerful to shelter their own and keep them from hunger, thirst, and the burden of the sun's scorching heat.

AN ANALYSIS OF REVELATION 8:6—11:19

As with the previous section, and for that matter, most of the depictions of God's judgment in Rev 8:6—19:5, the occasions of the theme of discipleship are not developed as they are elsewhere in Revelation. That being said, 8:6—11:19 does contribute to the theme of discipleship in Revelation. Before beginning though it may prove beneficial to give an overview of the content of 8:6—11:19, as well as a brief note about how the seals, trumpets, and bowls relate to one another.

Revelation 8:6—11:19 covers the vision of the seven trumpets (8:6—9:21; 11:15-19), as well as the second interlude in the book (10:1—11:14).[312] The trumpet plagues appear closely after the prayers of the saints (8:3-4), which may indicate they should be understood in part as God's response to their prayers for vindication (6:10-11).[313] In addition, the trumpet plagues have largely been recognized as patterned after the plagues unleashed on the Egyptians in the book of Exodus.[314] Parallels are found in the first trum-

---

312. The first interlude occurs in Rev 7:1-17.
313. Koester, *Revelation*, 436.
314. Aune goes to great lengths to show that the Exodus plague tradition in the

pet (Rev 8:7; Exod 9:22–25), the second and third trumpets (Rev 8:8–11; Exod 7:20–25), the fourth trumpet (Rev 8:12; Exod 10:21–23), and the fifth trumpet (Rev 9:1–11; Exod 10:12–15).[315] This indicates that the trumpet plagues are also God's response to sin directed toward him and his people. He will enact justice swiftly, as the rapid succession of the plagues shows.

There are basically two kinds of relationships that have been argued for with regard to the seals, trumpets, and bowls. They are parallel and simultaneous, and sequential and successive.[316] Those who interpret these events as parallel and simultaneous (sometimes referred to as recapitulation) place greater weight on the similarities found in the seals, trumpets, and bowls. While those who hold to sequential and successive generally note the differences among the three septets, and the seeming intensification of the judgments. However, most scholars hold to a mixture of the two views, with greater emphasis on recapitulation[317] or the sequential nature of the judgments.[318] The remainder of this section addresses the theme of discipleship in Rev 8:6—11:19, and specifically 11:1–13, which contains the greatest concentration of the theme of discipleship in this section.

Hebrew Bible and Judaism distilled the ten plagues of Exodus to seven (*Revelation 6–16*, 499–506).

315. Beale, *Revelation*, 465; so also Johnson, "Revelation," 672; Keener, *Revelation*, 256–258; Osborne, *Revelation*, 339. Koester believes that although the trumpets do make some allusions to the ten plagues, the greater emphasis should be placed on their parallels to Greco-Roman apocalyptic literature (*Revelation*, 445). For instance, the images of the first five trumpets reveal portent of war, a war described in Rev 9:7–19 (ibid., 452–453, 462). Koester believes the connection to Exodus is strongest in the bowl judgments (ibid., 445–446).

316. Johnson provides a concise summary of the two positions ("Revelation," 669–670).

317. Beale, *Revelation*, 121; Koester, *Revelation*, 443–445; Davis, "Seals, Trumpets, and Bowls," 149–158; Steinmann, "Tripartite Structure," 69–79.

318. Bauckham, *Climax of Prophecy*, 8–9, 15–18, 250; Thomas, *Revelation 8–22*, 525–543. Interestingly, Mounce, who holds to the telescopic theory, as does Thomas, believes "these plagues [trumpets] neither recapitulate each of the seal judgments, nor do they follow the seals in a strictly chronological sense" (*Revelation*, 176).

Distinction between Jesus' Disciples and Non-Disciples

At the sounding of the fifth trumpet[319] a "star" that had previously fallen to earth "was given the key to the shaft of the bottomless pit" (9:1).[320] This "star," which may very well have been an angel (cf. 20:1)[321] was sent from God to open the "Abyss" (NIV) where a powerful hoard of locusts went out, not to wield destruction on crops, but to harm those who "do not have the seal of God on their foreheads" (9:2–4). The implication is that those who bore God's seal on their foreheads, Christians, were protected from his wrath, which is how God's seal functions in 7:1–8. Those who lacked God's seal on their foreheads, "those who dwell on the earth" (8:13),[322] would suffer the stings of the locusts (9:5).[323]

319. The fifth trumpet appears to draw on imagery from Joel 1–2 (Beale, *Revelation*, 499; Keener, *Revelation*, 267; Koester, *Revelation*, 459–460).

320. The "bottomless pit" ("Abyss," NIV) is distinguished from Hades (the realm of the dead) and the lake of fire (the place of eternal punishment) in the book of Revelation. The abyss is "the demonic realm" (Koester, *Revelation*, 456).

321. The "star" (ἀστήρ) is thought to be either an angel of God, or Satan or a demonic being. Scholars are equally split over identification of the star. Those who view it as an angel of God include: Charles, *Revelation*, 1.238–239; Koester, *Revelation*, 456; Ladd, *Revelation*, 129; Mounce, *Revelation*, 192. Those who believe the star is Satan or a demon include: Beale, *Revelation*, 491–493; Caird, *Revelation*, 118; Johnson, "Revelation," 673.

322. The phrase "those who dwell on the earth" (τοὺς κατοικοῦντας ἐπὶ τῆς γῆς) appears to be used as a technical term in Revelation for "unbelieving idolaters" "who follow the beast . . . and both oppose and kill the saints" (Rev 3:10; 6:10; 8:13; 11:10; 12:12; 13:8, 12, 14; 14:6; 17:2, 8). God's swift judgment is about to come on them (Beale, *Revelation*, 290; Osborne, *Revelation*, 361).

323. Based on their description (Rev 9:7–11) and the place from which they originate (9:2–3), this army of locusts appears to be demonic in origin, rather than human (Aune, *Revelation 6–16*, 527; Beale, *Revelation*, 494; Johnson, "Revelation," 673–674; Koester, *Revelation*, 458). These locusts have as their "king . . . the angel of the bottomless pit. His name in Hebrew is Abaddon, and in Greek he called is Apollyon" (9:11). The king of the locusts is probably Satan or an agent of Satan. Although Satan is not called an "angel" in Revelation, he is said to wear crowns and have control over the beast from the abyss (11:7; 13:1–2; 17:8). The presence of the article (τὸν ἄγγελον, "the angel") could indicate that this particular angel is a well-known figure, Satan himself (Aune, *Revelation 6–16*, 534). Osborne believes this may be reading too much into the article (*Revelation*, 373). He argues, Satan is not called an "angel," but is the leader of fallen angels (12:7). Therefore, the one mentioned, only here in 9:11, may simply be one under Satan's sway (ibid.). Beale leaves the question unanswered, noting the "king" named "Apollyon" in 9:11 "is either the devil himself or an evil representative of the devil" (*Revelation*, 503). Mounce believes neither is correct, but instead posits, "we should probably understand the designation 'king' as no more than a detail in the larger scene of organized assault" (*Revelation*, 191).

Discipleship in the Book of Revelation

In a twist of irony, those whom the demon army torments do not "repent" of idol worship, which John calls the worship of "demons," nor do they "repent of their murders or their sorceries or their sexual immorality or their thefts" (9:20–21). The object of one's worship is used in the Apocalypse to distinguish between who is a follower of Christ (4:10; 5:14; 7:11; 11:1, 16; 13:15; 14:7; 15:4; 19:4, 10; 20:4; 22:8–9) and who is a follower of the devil (9:20; 13:4, 8, 12; 14:9, 11; 16:2; 19:20).

Another possible distinguishing characteristic of Jesus' disciples from non-disciples is the city of which they are citizens. In Rev 11 there are two cities mentioned: "the holy city" (11:2) and "the great city" (11:8). The "holy city" appears to symbolize the people of God.[324] In fact, the entire temple imagery may be used as a symbol for Christians.[325]

In the book of Revelation "the great city" is used to refer to Babylon (the city of Satan) (16:19; 17:18; 18:10, 16, 18–19, 21), Jerusalem (based on the reference to the place of Jesus' crucifixion), and even Rome (in the context of John's day). Taken together with the mention of Sodom and Egypt (11:8), Johnson believes "the great city" refers to "all places opposed to God and the witness of his servants."[326]

Revelation 9 provides three images of how one might identify a disciple of Christ from one who is not. The first, bearing God's seal, has been treated earlier. There it was seen that God's seal basically performed a threefold function, to indicate one is God's own, to preserve one's faith, and to protect one from the coming wrath. Here, though, the emphasis is squarely on being spared from God's wrath, which is in keeping with how God's seal is used in the OT (Ezek 9:4; Exod 28:36–38). Jesus' disciples can be assured that they will not face God's wrath because Christ bore it for them in their place. However, for those who fail to follow Christ, they have no protection from the judgment to come.

---

324. Beale, *Revelation*, 570–571; Bauckham, *Climax of Prophecy*, 272; Koester, *Revelation*, 486; Osborne, *Revelation*, 413.

325. Against this view of "the holy city" see Thomas, who believes "holy city" literally refers to Jerusalem (*Revelation 8–22*, 84), and Giblin, who believes the "holy city" represents the unbelieving world (*Revelation*, 439–440).

326. Johnson, "Revelation," 687; so also Keener, *Revelation*, 295; Koester, *Revelation*, 500; Osborne, *Revelation*, 426–428). Against this interpretation of "the great city" see Thomas, who believes it is also a reference to the earthly Jerusalem (*Revelation 8–22*, 94). Such an understanding appears to overlook the contrast between the two "cities," as well as the metaphorical language used throughout Rev 11:1–13.

The second image is that of idol worship, which may be the primary reason "those who dwell on the earth" are subject to the plagues. Everyone worships someone or something. In Revelation one either worships the one true God or worships the false one depicted as an unholy trinity (the beast, the false prophet, and the dragon). The false gods the people of this world follow are not able to save them and keep them secure. Just the opposite is the case. They actually encourage judgment from the one just judge, God himself. On the other hand, Jesus' disciples, who by all earthly appearances seem to be following a God who cannot save or protect them, are vindicated on the last day as God proves himself, enacting judgment on behalf of his saints. In the end, he offers the only lasting protection and safety, one that carries on into eternity.

The third image is one's citizenship. One is a citizen of either the city of God or the city of Satan. Those of the city of God acknowledge his authority, dwell in his presence, and experience his protection. Those who dwell in the city of Satan fight against God and his people, are excluded from God's presence, and will one day experience his wrath. Further, those who dwell in the city of God are characterized by living in a manner according to his word, while those of the city of Satan live after the course of this world.

Believe in Jesus

The mention of repentance has led several scholars to put forth that the purpose for God's judgment of the ungodly is to lead them to repentance (Rev 9:20), even when there is no evidence of repentance.[327] Others note the purpose is to display God's judgment and his mercy, since he does deal justly with sin, but he limits his judgment to a third (8:7–12; 9:15; 12:4) or a tenth (11:13).[328] Still others believe the purpose of God's judgments in Revelation is to harden the hearts of the wicked against God.[329] It may be that aspects of all of the above take place.

---

327. Bauckham, *Theology of Revelation*, 82, 86; Caird, *Revelation*, 124; Johnson, "Revelation," 675; Keener, *Revelation*, 272; Koester, *Revelation*, 451–452. An apparent example of repentance taking place is Rev 11:13b (Beasley-Murray, *Revelation*, 187; Caird, *Revelation*, 140; Johnson, "Revelation," 688; Koester, *Revelation*, 504, 512 Ladd, *Revelation*, 159–160). Beale does not believe 11:13b can possibly refer to the conversion of the nations, since it follows the final judgment (11:13a) when there is no more offer of salvation (*Revelation*, 607).

328. Johnson, "Revelation," 675; Keener, *Revelation*, 272.

329. Beale, *Revelation*, 472, 517.

While the individuals subject to God's wrath in Revelation do not appear to show any signs of repentance or genuine faith in Christ, it is still possible that these images were intended to elicit saving faith in the one who heard or read the content of the book. From the plagues to the offer to drink freely of the water of life at the end of the book, the reader is given a vision of two responses to Jesus, as well as two results of those responses. For those who willingly submit to Christ's rule and accept him as Savior, there is suffering in this present world, but eternal joy in the life to come. However, for those who follow after Satan and reject Christ, there is seemingly a lack of suffering, while in the age to come there is eternal torment. The disciple of Jesus witnessing these images should be led to rejoice that one day his or her suffering will come to an end, the enemies of God will be defeated, and perhaps compelled to hold out the gospel freely to others who will be subject to God's judgment.

Discipleship Language

The close of the sixth trumpet leads John to the second interlude of the book (10:1—11:14). It begins with John seeing an angel come down from heaven with a small scroll in his hand (10:1-2). The angel standing with one foot on the sea and the other on the land utters a message John is not allowed to write down (10:3-4). The angel follows this by swearing an oath, "there will be no more delay,"[330] but that in the days of the trumpet call to be sounded by the seventh angel, the mystery of God would be fulfilled, just as he announced[331] to his servants the prophets" (10:5-7).

Those to whom the mystery has been previously announced are God's "servants the prophets" (10:7). As noted earlier, the term δοῦλος ("servant," "slave") often refers to Christians in general.[332] But here, this group is given the qualifier of "prophets." Although citing different OT texts as the backdrop to 10:7, both Beale and Osborne believe this group of "prophets"

---

330. What is this "delay" that will cease? The most common understandings are: (1) the time for judgment has come (Keener, *Revelation*, 282); (2) the consummation of the age has come (Blount, *Revelation*, 195); (3) and the time of waiting for the consummation will end (Koester, *Revelation*, 480).

331. The verb translated "he announced" is εὐαγγελίζω, the term used of announcing good news. What the angel announces is the good news of God's victory over his enemies (Koester, *Revelation*, 480).

332. Aune, *Revelation 1-5*, 13; Koester, *Revelation*, 211; Osborne, *Revelation*, 54 n. 5.

includes both OT and NT prophets.³³³ Aune, on the other hand, limits the phrase to OT prophets, while Charles believes it refers to Christian prophets.³³⁴ It is at least possible that the phrase "servants the prophets" included Christians who had a prophetic role in the church.³³⁵

The designation "servants the prophets" may also help to remind Jesus' disciples that all are servants of Christ, whether pastors, teachers, or prophets. No one role is greater than any other. All are necessary for the body to function properly. All are to humbly perform their function as God has granted them the ability. The phrase may also serve to point out that Jesus' disciples have different roles and gifts, which God bestows through the Spirit at his discretion. No one role or gift is to be coveted or cherished above all others, but each one is to be used for God's glory and the good of the church.

Bear Witness to Jesus

The remainder of the analysis focuses on 11:1–13. John is instructed to "measure the temple of God and the altar and those who worship there" (11:1). He is to exclude "the court outside the temple," which is given to the nations, who will "trample on the holy city for forty-two months" (11:2). The entire imagery of the temple and holy city likely go together to represent Christians.³³⁶ The measuring of the temple functions in much the same

333. Beale cites Dan 9 as the possible background to Rev 10:7 (*Revelation*, 546), while Osborne believes 10:7 alludes to Amos 3:7 (*Revelation*, 401). The following also believe both OT and NT prophets are in view: Mounce, *Revelation*, 208; Koester, *Revelation*, 481; Roloff, *Revelation*, 125.

334. Aune, *Revelation 6–16*, 570; Charles, *Revelation*, 1.266.

335. The phrase τέσσαρες πρεσβύτεροι ("twenty-four elders) and the term ἁγίοις ("saints," "your people," NIV) occur in Rev 11:16 and 11:18 respectively.

336. Beale, *Revelation*, 570–571; Bauckham, *Climax of Prophecy*, 272; Koester, *Revelation*, 486. Ladd believes the "temple" refers to the Jewish remnant that is preserved and eventually won to Christ (*Revelation*, 150, 152–153, 159–160). Some believe the "holy city" refers to the unbelieving world (Giblin, *Revelation*, 439–440). This does not seem to fit, since the city is called "holy."

Thomas argues that the "temple" in view here is one that is literally rebuilt at the end of the age (*Revelation 8–22*, 176–177). However, there are several reasons to reject this view (Keener, *Revelation*, 287):

1. The 1,260 days (3 and one half years) is likely symbolic of the time between Christ's first and second advent (cf. Rev 12:5–6) (Keener, *Revelation*, 318–319), a period in which there was no literal temple.

2. The two witnesses addressed in this text are probably symbolic also.

way as the sealing of the saints in Rev 7. Christians are measured so that their faith is preserved; they are kept for salvation. The fact that the outer court is not measured appears to represent the persecution the church undergoes.[337] This is similar to the vision of Rev 7; those sealed have their faith preserved, but still suffer persecution from those hostile to Christ.[338] The suffering of the church is limited to "forty-two months."[339]

At that time the Lord will "grant authority to ... two witnesses" to testify for 1,260 days while wearing sackcloth (11:3). They will be given the ability to do powerful signs, and they will not be harmed until their appointed time (11:4–6). Some modern interpreters believe the "two witnesses" are in fact the literal return of Moses and Elijah,[340] while most modern

---

3. John, likely writing during a time after the destruction of the temple, probably has in mind a symbolic understanding of the temple imagery. Further, he provides no explicit details about the rebuilding of a literal temple.

4. The temple is given a symbolic meaning elsewhere in Revelation (3:12; 13:6). Johnson adds that "temple" is used figuratively elsewhere in the NT (John 2:19–21; 1 Cor 3:16; 6:19; 2 Cor 6:16; Eph 2:21) ("Revelation," 681).

5. The "holy city" is likely symbolic of the "community of those faithful to Jesus Christ" (Rev 21:2, 10; 22:19; cf. 3:12; 20:9) (Johnson, "Revelation," 683).

337. The term "nations" (ἔθνος) in the phrase "given over to the nations" (Rev 11:2) may be used as a general term for "nations" (Matt 24:9, 14; Rom 1:5; Rev 21:24, 26; 22:2), for people who are not ethnic Jews (Matt 4:15; 10:5; Luke 2:32), and even of those outside of Christ (1 Cor 5:1; 12:2; 1 Thess 4:5; 1 Pet 2:12; 3 John 7). In Revelation, though, it is often used of those opposed to God (11:18; 14:8; 19:15; 20:3). Given their action against the "holy city," it would appear this last usage is in view (Johnson, "Revelation," 682).

338. Bauckham, *Climax of Prophecy*, 272–273; Beale, *Revelation*, 557–565; Boring, *Revelation*, 143–144; Johnson, "Revelation," 681–682; Koester, *Revelation*, 485; Mounce, *Revelation*, 214–215; Osborne, *Revelation*, 411; Pattemore, *People of God*, 161.

339. The "forty-two months" (Rev 11:2) and "1,260 days" (11:3) are likely an allusion to Daniel's vision (Dan 7:25; 12:7), and may (Thomas, *Revelation 8–22*, 84–85) or may not refer to a precise length of time (three and a half years), but to what that time is characterized by, great suffering (Johnson, "Revelation," 684; Keener, *Revelation*, 292; Koester, *Revelation*, 487). Koester argues, the dynamic manner in which this time is depicted (forty-two months, 1,260 days, time, times and half a time) "work against a strict chronological interpretation" (*Revelation*, 487; so also Collins, *Cosmology and Eschatology*, 67–68).

340. Charles, *Revelation*, 1.281; Thomas, *Revelation 8–22*, 88–99. Those in favor of a symbolic view note, among other factors, the "two witnesses" are an allusions to the OT figures Joshua and Zerubbabel, who respectively bore the role of high priest and king, nomenclature similarly applied to the saints in Revelation (1:6; 5:10; 20:6) (Keener, *Revelation*, 292). This is based in part on the connection of Rev 11:4 and Zech 4:1–6, 10–14 (Johnson, "Revelation," 685). Johnson also believes there are allusions to Moses and Elijah in Rev 11:6 (ibid., 686). Thus, he accepts a symbolic understanding of the two witnesses. Koester also notes how the traits are applied equally to both witnesses, traits

interpreters believe the "two witnesses" are symbolic of "the prophetic witness of the church" or the church itself.[341] The discipleship theme of bearing witness to Jesus has already been explored in greater detail elsewhere. These two figures are a reminder to the church of the centrality of its mission to bear witness to the Lord Jesus Christ.

Consequences of Following Jesus

As a result of their testimony, the beast that "rises" from the abyss attacks, overpowers, and kills the two witnesses (11:7; cf. 6:9).[342] The abyss is the prison of demons (Luke 8:31; cf. 2 Pet 4:4; Jude 6) or the demonic realm. Revelation 11:7 contains language similar to that used in Dan 7. Both Daniel and John mention "the beast" from the abyss that overcomes God's people.[343] As described elsewhere in Revelation, there are consequences for bearing witness to Christ, namely persecution and even death (1:9; 2:9–10, 13; 6:9; 12:17; 17:6; 20:4).

---

identified specifically with Moses and Elijah. In addition, the beast's attacks are usually carried out on a larger scale (9:7, 9; 12:7; 16:14; 19:19; 20:8) and not on a limited number of individuals, in this case two. These factors lead him to conclude the two witnesses are symbolic of a much larger group (*Revelation*, 498).

341. Keener, *Revelation*, 291–292; so also Aune, *Revelation 6–16*, 603, 631; Bauckham, *Climax of Prophecy*, 166, 273–275; Beale, *Revelation*, 572–585; Beasley-Murray, *Revelation*, 183–184; Johnson, "Revelation," 685; Koester, *Revelation*, 497; Smalley, *Revelation*, 275–276. The two witnesses are also called "lampstands," which is used for the church in Rev 1:20 (Koester, *Revelation*, 497).

Additional symbolic interpretation of the "two witnesses" include:
1. The Law and the Prophets (Corsini, *Apocalypse*, 193–198).
2. Peter and Paul both executed by Nero (Randall, *Revelation*, 71).
3. Israel and the church (González and González, *Revelation*, 72).
4. Jewish and Gentile Christians (Rissi, "Kerygma," 16).
5. The end-time church (Mounce, *Revelation*, 218).

342. The term translated "rises" is the Greek present participle τὸ ἀναβαῖνον. The participle may be understood to refer to the continuous rising up of the beast throughout the history of the church's witness (Beale, *Revelation*, 588–589) or to a particular time that coincides with the final period of world history (cf. Rev 13:1; Thomas, *Revelation 8–22*, 93).

343. The use of the definite article (τὸ θηρίον, "the beast") may very well mark this as the well known beast from the abyss to recur in Rev 12, 13, and 17, that is, the antichrist (Beale, *Revelation*, 588; Osborne, *Revelation*, 424–425).

Discipleship in the Book of Revelation
Jesus as the Model for His Disciples

The two witnesses are slain, and their bodies remain on public display in the "great city ... where their Lord was crucified" (11:8).[344] The circumstances surrounding their deaths, bodily resurrection, as well as their ascension in a cloud appear to have strong parallels with the death, resurrection, and ascension of Christ. Jesus' crucifixion was a public display, so also the death of the two witnesses. Crucifixion was believed to have been degrading and shameful to the victim (cf. Mark 15:29–32; Heb 12:2).[345] In similar manner, the bodies of the two witnesses are left in the street unburied, which signifies scorn and shame.[346] Furthermore, the two witnesses are resurrected "after the three and a half days" (Rev 11:11), which may be an allusion to Jesus' own bodily resurrection that transpired "after three days" (Matt 27:63; Mark 8:31; 9:31; 10:43) or "on the third day" (Matt 16:21; 1 Cor 15:4).[347] Both Jesus and the two witnesses are taken up to heaven in a cloud (Rev 11:12; Acts 1:9–11).

The ascension of the two witnesses in a cloud (Rev 11:12) may indicate this event coincides with Jesus' second coming,[348] which would place this event after the church suffered the tribulation.[349] Although this is a possibility, Johnson and Beale favor the view that the ascension of the two witnesses does not refer to the church's meeting the Lord in the air (1 Thess 4:16–17), but to the vindication of the Lord's servants.[350] Beale bases this

---

344. Some scholars limit the "great city" (Rev 11:8) where the two witnesses suffer death to Jerusalem (Aune, *Revelation 6–16*, 618–619; Charles, *Revelation*, 1.287; Ford, *Revelation*, 180; Thomas, *Revelation 8–22*, 94). Others who argue the "great city" is figurative of those opposed to God note the "great city" is used to refer to Babylon (the city of Satan) (Rev 16:19; 17:18; 18:10, 16, 18–19, 21), Jerusalem (based on the reference to the place of Jesus' crucifixion), and even Rome (in the context of John's day). Taken together with the mention of Sodom and Egypt, Johnson believes the reference refers to "all places opposed to God and the witness of his servants" (Johnson, "Revelation," 687; so also Koester, *Revelation*, 500; Osborne, *Revelation*, 426–428). That it is also called "Sodom and Egypt" aligns it with the world opposed to God (Keener, *Revelation*, 295).

345. Koester, *Revelation*, 501.

346. Osborne, *Revelation*, 426.

347. Koester, *Revelation*, 502.

348. Johnson, "Revelation," 688.

349. Beale, *Revelation*, 598.

350. Johnson, "Revelation," 688; Beale, *Revelation*, 599; so also Koester, *Revelation*, 510–511.

on close verbal connections between Rev 4:1–2 and 11:12.[351] Osborne, on the other hand, while denying this is the final resurrection of the dead, does believe the resurrection of the two witnesses serves as a "proleptic anticipation of the 'rapture' of the church," which for him coincides with the return of Christ.[352] He notes the resurrection and ascension of the two witnesses occurs at the end of history, although the order does not exactly fit with the depiction of the final events of the age (cf. 19:1–10).[353] Regardless of the specific details, it would be difficult not to acknowledge the similarities between the two witnesses and Jesus Christ. This may serve to show how disciples of Jesus follow him not only in their manner of life and death, but also in the future bodily resurrection.

SUMMARY

Revelation 8:6—11:19 essentially reiterates discipleship themes previously articulated at greater depth elsewhere in the book. For instance, the language of God placing his seal on the foreheads of his people is picked up in 9:4 with reference to those who are not sealed. The usage of such language as "servants the prophets" (10:7; 11:18), "twenty-four elders" (11:16), and "saints" (11:18) is also repeated, as are the consequences associated with following Jesus (11:7).

However, some of these themes are articulated in new ways. The vision of the "two witnesses" and all that happens to them is depicted in terms similar to the life, death, resurrection, and ascension of Jesus (11:3–12). The mention of the death of the witnesses in "the great city . . . where the Lord was crucified" may very well be an overt attempt by the author to draw these parallels. If so, then Jesus is presented as a model for his disciples to follow in their manner of life, their suffering death, their bodily resurrection, and their future ascension to meet the Lord in the air.

Similarly, the discipleship theme of distinction between Jesus' disciples and non-disciples is not only articulated in terms previously noted like God's seal (9:4) or whom one worships (9:20–21), but also in terms of one's citizenship (11:2, 8). Christians are citizens of the "holy city," while those in opposition to God are associated with the "great city." Although this section of the Revelation may not provide the same depth with regard to the theme

351. Beale, *Revelation*, 598–600.
352. Osborne, *Revelation*, 432.
353. Ibid.

of discipleship, it nonetheless adds texture and fresh perspective to what has already been presented.

AN ANALYSIS OF REVELATION 12:1—14:20

Sometimes Rev 12:1—14:20 is viewed as the third interlude in the book of Revelation;[354] however, it is unlikely, since this section breaks with the pattern of the previous interludes, which occur between the sixth seal/trumpet and seventh seal/trumpet.[355] Revelation 12:1—14:20 occurs after the seventh trumpet and the first bowl. Revelation 12:1—14:20 is generally recognized as the center of the entire book[356] and the first major section of the second half of Revelation.[357]

It is possible to detect a seven-fold structure in this section, one that mimics the repetition of sevens found throughout the Apocalypse.[358] This possibility has led some commentators to extend the section to 15:4 based on what they believe is a seven-fold pattern identified by the occurrence of either καὶ εἶδον ("and I saw") with καὶ ἰδοὺ ("and behold") or with ὤφθη ("it appeared").[359] However, others have shown this is not necessary, since the reader was unlikely "to count unnumbered visions" and because "there are actually nine expressions for 'seeing' in this section."[360]

Regardless of whether one sees an apparent seven-fold pattern or not, the basic flow of the section may be summarized as follows. Broadly

---

354. Blount, *Revelation*, 224; Duvall, *Revelation*, 160; Ladd, *Revelation*, 166; Osborne, *Revelation*, 452; Patterson, *Revelation*, 258.

355. Boring, *Revelation*, 150. Others simply do not apply the term "interlude" to this section (Beale, *Revelation*, 621–624; Mounce, *Revelation*, 229–230).

356. Beale, *Revelation*, 621; Beasley-Murray, *Revelation*, 191; Kistermaker, *Revelation*, 351.

357. Kistermaker, *Revelation*, 351; Koester, *Revelation*, 524; Mounce, *Revelation*, 229; Smalley, *Revelation*, 310.

358. Beale, *Revelation*, 621–624; Kiddle, *Revelation*, 215; Smalley, *Revelation*, 311; Walvoord, *Revelation*, 187; Yarbro Collins, *Combat Myth*, 13–14.

359. Beale, *Revelation*, 621; Wilcock, *Revelation*, 115; Yarbro Collins, *Combat Myth*, 13–14. Beale utilizes καὶ εἶδον (Rev 13:1, 11; 14:1, 6, 14; 15:1) with καὶ ἰδοὺ (12:3) to locate the seven introductory vision formulas, while Yarbro Collins uses καὶ εἶδον (13:1, 11; 14:1, 6, 14; 15:1) with ὤφθη (12:1).

360. Koester, *Revelation*, 525; so also Bauckham, *Climax of Prophecy*, 15–18; Osborne, *Revelation*, 453. If one combines the occurrences of καὶ εἶδον, καὶ ἰδοὺ, and ὤφθη there are actually twelve expressions for seeing from Rev 12:1—15:4, and ten expressions for seeing from 12:1—14:20.

speaking, this section covers in summary fashion the birth of the Messiah through the church's involvement in end-time events. More specifically, it focuses on the false trinity (the dragon, the beast and the false prophet/second beast) that apes the one true Trinity. This group sets out to lead people astray and to war against God and his people (12:1—13:18). Those whom God has sealed persevere to the end (14:1–5), while those who are not his own are promised to drink "the wine of God's wrath, poured full strength into the cup of his anger" (14:10) unless they respond in faith to the gospel (14:6–13). Finally, this section closes with the harvest of the faithful in Christ (14:14–16) and the destruction of the wicked (14:17–20).[361]

As with previous sections there are scattered appearances of the theme of discipleship throughout 12:1—14:20. For instance, in chapters 13 and 14 one finds mention of "saints" (13:7, 10; 14:12) as a designation for the Christian. One also finds the people of God described as the symbol-laden figure of the pregnant woman who flees into the desert after giving birth (12:1-6, 13–17).[362] Mention is also made of those who "conquered" (ἐνίκησαν) over Satan "by the blood of the Lamb and by the word of their testimony" (12:11a). Earlier it was demonstrated that the νικάω word group in Revelation is almost something of a synonym for belief in Christ. So also, those who follow Christ, who even give their lives for his cause (12:11b), are overcomers, those who have declared allegiance to Christ their king. They are further identified as those who continually[363] keep God's commands (τῶν τηρούντων, "those who keep") and bear witness to Christ (ἐχόντων, "those who . . . hold to") (12:17; cf. 14:12).[364] There is also mention of wit-

---

361. See both Koester (*Revelation*, 523–525) and Osborne (*Revelation*, 452–453) for concise summaries of this section.

362. Koester provides a brief description of the four main interpretive understandings of the identity of the "woman" in Rev 12:1-6, 13-17 (*Revelation*, 542–543). These four alternatives are: (1) the historic people of God, an understanding held by numerous contemporary scholars (Beale, *Revelation*, 625–627; Mounce, *Revelation*, 231–232; Osborne, *Revelation*, 457; Smalley, *Revelation*, 315) and Koester's own position; (2) the Christian church (Roloff, *Revelation*, 145); (3) Mary, the mother of Jesus, at least as a secondary referent (Aune, *Revelation 6-16*, 712; Brown et al., *Mary*, 235–239); and (4) the Jewish community or remnant (Kiddle, *Revelation*, 219–220; Thomas, *Revelation 8-22*, 120–121).

363. Both τῶν τηρούντων ("those who keep") and ἐχόντων ("those who . . . hold to") are present tense participles, which probably "stress the ongoing perseverance of the church in obeying God and maintaining their testimony for Jesus" (Osborne, *Revelation*, 485).

364. The phrase τὴν μαρτυρίαν Ἰησοῦ may be taken as a subjective genitive, "the testimony Jesus' gave" (Mounce, *Revelation*, 242; Thomas, *Revelation 8-22*, 142), or an

ness to greater things, the greatness of the Son of Man (14:14–20),³⁶⁵ several distinctions between Jesus' disciples and non-disciples,³⁶⁶ as well as the recurring consequence for those who faithfully follow Jesus, suffering and even death (13:7, 15).

However, there is one passage in particular that has been regarded as a key text on discipleship in the book of Revelation, 14:1–5. This text has been of particular interest in two previous studies on the theme of discipleship in Revelation.³⁶⁷ This passage also contains what may be considered the most overt discipleship terminology in the entire book. The term ἀκολουθέω, a technical term for discipleship in the Gospels, occurs in its participial form in Rev 14:1–5. Therefore, this text is worthy of closer inspection to uncover what it reveals concerning being a disciple of Jesus.

---

objective genitive, "the testimony to or about Jesus" (Osborne, *Revelation*, 485; Smalley, *Revelation*, 334). It is also possible that the ambiguity of the phrase may encompass both understandings (Beale, *Revelation*, 679; Koester, *Revelation*, 554), and thus, what one has here is a plenary genitive (Wallace, *Greek Grammar*, 119–121). See also the earlier discussions on Rev 1:1–20 on this construction. The preceding phrase, τὰς ἐντολὰς τοῦ θεοῦ is in all likelihood a subjective genitive, "the commands God gives."

365. There is some debate as to whether or not the one "like a son of man" is Jesus or an angel (Rev 14:14). For those who argue the figure is an angel see: Aune, *Revelation 6–16*, 842–843; Kiddle, *Revelation*, 276–277; Morris, *Revelation* (2002), 178–179. For those who argue the figure is Christ see: Beale, *Revelation*, 771–772; Koester, *Revelation*, 623–624; Thomas, *Revelation 8–22*, 218–219.

How Jesus is presented in this section is also debated. Is he judge or redeemer? Some believe the harvest of wheat in Rev 14:14–16 is one of judgment like the cutting and trampling of the grapes (14:17–20) (Aune, *Revelation 6–16*, 842; Beale, *Revelation*, 770; Yarbro Collins, *Cosmology and Eschatology*, 192. See also Beckwith, *Apocalypse*, 662; Mounce, *Revelation*, 278; Thomas, *Revelation 8–22*, 220). However, others recognize two distinct harvests, one of the redeemed (14:14–16), and one of the wicked (14:17–20). Bauckham has offered a convincing defense of this position (*Theology of Revelation*, 94–98; see also Koester, *Revelation*, 628–629; Osborne, *Revelation*, 552; Smalley, *Revelation*, 372–373).

366. Those who bear the mark of the beast (Rev 13:17; 14:9, 11) vs. those who refuse his mark and bear God's seal (14:1). Those who worship the false trinity (13:4, 8, 12; 14:9, 11) vs. those who worship the true trinity (13:15; 14:7). Those whose names are not written in the book of life (13:8) vs. those whose names are written (this is implied).

367. Schüssler Fiorenza, "Followers of the Lamb," 144–165; Aune, "Following the Lamb," 269–284.

Come to an Understanding of Jesus' Person/and or Work

As noted earlier in this study, ἰδοὺ ("Behold!" "See!" "Listen!") is used "to highlight critical prophetic oracles."[368] Here, as earlier (1:7, 18; 3:20; 5:5), this term announces to the reader something regarding the person and work of Jesus Christ. Jesus is identified in 14:1 as "the Lamb." Of its twenty-eight occurrences in Revelation the image of an ἀρνίον ("lamb") is used mainly to represent Christ. It is found only in Johannine literature and occurs only once outside of the Apocalypse (John 21:15).[369] The Lamb standing (Rev 14:1a) recalls 5:5–6, the standing slaughtered Lamb.[370] That he is standing may also "suggest that he functions as a warrior prepared to destroy his enemies," which is revealed later in this chapter (14:14, 17–20).[371] Moreover, the Lamb of 14:1 is contrasted with the false lamb of 13:11 whose mark is needed to purchase goods (13:17). On the other hand, the true Lamb purchases for himself people from among mankind (14:4).[372] One is to give allegiance to the true Lamb and reject the false one.[373]

The Lamb is seen standing "on Mount Zion" (14:1a).[374] The mention of "Mount Zion" may very well be an allusion to Ps 2, which is one of the key

---

368. Osborne, *Revelation*, 69. Thomas adds the occurrence of καὶ ἰδοὺ in Rev 14:1 highlights "special attention to the greatness of the sight and the striking quality of the vision thus introduced" (*Revelation 8–22*, 188; see also Smalley, *Revelation*, 353).

369. Smalley, *Revelation*, 353.

370. Koester, *Revelation*, 607.

371. Aune, *Revelation 6–16*, 803; so also Osborne, *Revelation*, 525; Thomas, *Revelation 8–22*, 189. Against this understanding see Johnson, "Revelation," 720.

372. Beale, *Revelation*, 731; Johnson, "Revelation," 719; Smalley, *Revelation*, 353; see Kistemaker, *Revelation*, 400 for a detailed comparison.

373. Beale, *Revelation*, 731.

374. The occurrence of Mount Zion has led to scholarly debate regarding its location and as a result, the time and setting of Rev 14:1–5. The following locations are frequently put forward. According to Kiddle (*Revelation*, 263) and Mounce (*Revelation*, 265), heaven is believed to be the location since the sound of worship comes from heaven and is before the throne (14:2–3; 5:6–14; 7:9–17; cf. Heb 12:22–24; Gal 4:26). Another possibility is earth (Aune, *Revelation 6–16*, 803–804). Those who tend to hold to a mainly futuristic hermeneutic believe Rev 14:1–5 refers to a proleptic vision of the millennial reign (Walvoord, *Revelation*, 213–214; Thomas, *Revelation 8–22*, 189; Johnson, "Revelation," 720; Charles, *Revelation*, 2.5). Under this interpretation, Mount Zion refers to literal Jerusalem, the temple mount, Judea, or the entire land of Palestine (Thomas, *Revelation 8–22*, 191; so also Johnson, "Revelation," 719–720; Patterson, *Revelation*, 285). Still others view the text as a proleptic vision of the New Jerusalem (Beasley-Murray, *Revelation*, 222; Boring, *Revelation*, 168; Koester, *Revelation*, 616–617; Ladd, *Revelation*, 189–190). Finally, some see a blending of past, present, and future elements. According to this position the

Discipleship in the Book of Revelation

OT texts of the book (cf. Rev 2:26–27; 6:15; 11:15, 18; 12:5; 19:15) "since it depicts the triumph of the messianic king over the hostile nations."[375] What then does the identification of the Lamb with Mount Zion say about him, and how does it relate to the topic of discipleship? First, Mount Zion is identified with Jerusalem, the capital of king David where the kings of Judah reigned (2 Sam 5:6–9; Ps 2:6). In Rev 5:5–10 one finds the Lamb/Lion of the tribe of Judah. So here, in 14:1, the Lamb as king is found in his rightful place.[376] These disciples who follow the lamb wherever he goes (14:4) have pledged fealty to the one true King. Where he goes they will go, and they do because he is not only a king, but also the King of kings and Lord of lords (19:16), the absolute sovereign over all mankind. Second, Mount Zion was the center of Israelite worship, since the temple was there (Pss 9:11; 76:2; 132:13). Revelation 14:2 depicts believers worshiping the only ones worthy of worship, God and the Lamb. In addition, the offering of firstfruits (14:3–4), which was associated with the temple sacrifices, may serve only to bolster the link between Mount Zion and the temple.[377] In the book of Revelation one worships either the unholy trinity or the true Trinity. The Triune God is alone to be worshiped. He brooks no rivals. Disciples of Jesus not only pledge their lives to their King, but also worship the one true God, which in Revelation they are at times depicted doing so as priests, since they are a royal priesthood. Third, Mount Zion is referred to as a place of security and refuge (Isa 4:2–6; 24:23; 31:4; Joel 2:32; Mic 4:7). The followers of the shepherding Lamb find safety in his presence.[378] He is able to protect those entrusted to his care.

---

scene, although located on earth (Mount Zion), "anticipates a future reality" (Osborne, *Revelation*, 525; so also Beale, *Revelation*, 732; Smalley, *Revelation*, 354).

375. Bauckham, *Climax of Prophecy*, 230. Dale Brueggemann has noted the Psalms are likely a source for the book of Revelation ("Psalter in John's Apocalypse," 23). He also sees Rev 14:1 as a possible allusion to Ps 2:6 (ibid., 75).

376. Aune, *Revelation 6–16*, 803; Beale, *Revelation*, 733; Koester, *Revelation*, 616; Osborne, *Revelation*, 525.

377. Koester, *Revelation*, 616; Osborne, *Revelation*, 525.

378. Koester, *Revelation*, 616; so also Beale, *Revelation*, 732; Beasley-Murray, *Revelation*, 221; Mounce, *Revelation*, 264–265; Osborne, *Revelation*, 525; Smalley, *Revelation*, 354.

Distinction between Jesus' Disciples and Non-disciples

The Lamb has "with him 144,000" (Rev 14:1b). The 144,000 are the same group numbered in 7:4–9, "the totality of God's people throughout the ages."[379] The 144,000 are specifically distinguished from the rest of mankind, since they bear "his [the Lamb's] name and his Father's name written on their foreheads" (14:1c). Bearing the name of the Lamb and the Father is another way of referring to God's seal (7:3–8).[380] Christians bear the Father's name on their forehead (14:1c) as a sign that the Lamb has purchased them (14:4). This is the opposite of those who bear the mark of the beast on their foreheads and hands by which they are enabled to purchase goods (13:16–18).[381] The number 666 may very well represent the incompleteness of the beast and his people, as opposed to the number 144,000, which represents the completeness of the people of God.[382] These saints are sealed,

---

379. Beale, *Revelation*, 733; so also Ford, *Revelation*, 245; Johnson, "Revelation," 720; Keener, *Revelation*, 370; Mounce, *Revelation*, 265; Smalley, *Revelation*, 354. At least one ancient commentator has understood the 144,000 here as distinct from the 144,000 in Rev 7. Oecumenius believed the 144,000 in Rev 7 were Jewish believers, while the 144,000 in Rev 14 represent both Jewish and Gentile Christians (Oecumenius, *Apocalypse*, 8.7.3). Perhaps the anarthrous use of 144,000 in Rev 14 means it is to be distinguished from the articular use of the number in Rev 7? Homer Hailey notes the lack of the article before the 144,000 in Rev 14:1 should not lead one to distinguish this group from the 144,000 in Rev 7:4–9, where the article is present (*Revelation*, 302–303). Recurring images are both articular and anarthrous throughout the book (Beale, *Revelation*, 733–734; Beckwith, *Apocalypse*, 650; Smalley, *Revelation*, 354). After all, no one argues for two different "marks" (Rev 13:16–17 and 14:9).

Some commentators have argued that the 144,000 in 7:4–8 and 14:1 is a subgroup of a larger whole (Aune, *Revelation 6–16*, 804; Yarbro Collins, *Crisis and Catharsis*, 127–128; Gundry, *Tribulation*, 83; Patterson, *Revelation*, 194–199, 285; Thomas, *Revelation 8–22*, 191). Against this view and in favor of seeing both groups as one representing the entirety of the people of God see Beale, *Revelation*, 416–418.

380. Aune, *Revelation 6–16*, 804; Beale, *Revelation*, 734; Smalley, *Revelation*, 355. Aune believes the names are literally written on the disciples' foreheads and are not merely symbolic (*Revelation 6–16*, 805). However, this is not necessary since "the names and numbers in both Rev 14:1 and 13:18 are to be understood generically, and as part of John's apocalyptic imagery, rather than in any literal or primarily historical sense" (Smalley, *Revelation*, 355).

381. Beale, *Revelation*, 733–734; Koester, *Revelation*, 617; Mounce, *Revelation*, 264; Osborne, *Revelation*, 524, 525, 530; Smalley, *Revelation*, 355.

382. Beale, *Revelation*, 722. For others who understand 666 in a figurative sense see Bauckham, *Climax of Prophecy*, 398–400; Beasley-Murray, *Revelation*, 220–221; Smalley, *Revelation*, 352–353. Koester interestingly recognizes the contextual link between 666 and 144,000 in arguing for 666 being original to the text, as opposed to 616 (*Revelation*,

that is protected, from the outpouring of God's fury (14:8-11), while the rest of humanity who have the mark of the beast are the objects of God's righteous wrath (14:9-11).[383] For the disciple of Jesus Christ the picture of being sealed with God's name should offer comfort. Chiefly God's seal is a sign that the Christians are his own. They have been purchased with Christ's own blood. They no longer stand condemned and under the wrath to come. It also offers assurance, since the seal of God is not so much protection from suffering brought on by persecution or from the ill effects of living in a fallen world, but it is security of one's salvation. The Father has marked all genuine disciples as his own on the basis of his only Son bearing the marks of crucifixion.

The scene then shifts from earth to heaven, as John hears "a voice from heaven like the roar of many waters and like the sound of loud thunder" (14:2a).[384] In addition, John notes, "the voice I heard was like the sound of harpists playing their harps" (14:2b).[385] The syntactical phrasing of the

---

599), even though Koester's own view identifies 666 with Nero by way of transliterating Nero's name into Hebrew (ibid., 539-540). It may be best to view the number 666 in a figurative sense as numbers are treated similarly throughout Revelation, and due to the fact that 13:18, in which 666 occurs, contains various readings, including: 616, 646, and 656.

383. Beale, *Revelation*, 734; Thomas, *Revelation 8-22*, 192. Ownership may also be a reason for the seal (Johnson, "Revelation," 720; Osborne, *Revelation*, 525). Smalley believes the image may indicate protection (although he does not state what they are protected from) and ownership (*Revelation*, 355).

384. Aune equates the "a voice from heaven like the roar of many waters and like the sound of loud thunder" to heavenly worship and not the 144,000 on earth (*Revelation 6-16*, 806; Johnson, "Revelation," 720; Thomas, *Revelation 8-22*, 192). This may make sense since it is before God (Aune, *Revelation 6-16*, 808). Beale wonders if the mention of "heaven" may simply indicate that the new song came from God (*Revelation*, 737). In the end, he believes the 144,000 are those who learn and sing the song (*Revelation*, 737; so also Mounce, *Revelation*, 266). Smalley notes that in Rev 14:1-5 there is a blurring together of heaven and earth, so a sharp distinction between the two may not be entirely warranted (*Revelation*, 355). Smalley believes the sound, which initially comes from heaven "belongs to the angels, the whole company of the faithful in all ages, and to a redeemed creation (as in 5:13; 7:9-10)" (ibid., 355-356; so also Milligan, "Revelation," 241). Keener believes the song is sung by the 144,000 who are taken from earth to heaven (Keener, *Revelation*, 370).

385. The "harp" may anticipate the ceasing of the playing harps and singing songs in Babylon (Rev 18:22) (Koester, *Revelation*, 618).

sentence may indicate that this was one and the same sound.[386] This intense voice is identified in 14:3 as a song.[387]

Those singing sang a "new song before the throne and before the four living creatures and before the elders" (14:3a). John recounts that "no one could learn that song except the 144,000 who had been redeemed from the earth" (14:3b). There is some question regarding the meaning of the word "learn" (μαθεῖν) in this context. Does it mean to learn or to understand? Several commentators believe it best to take the infinitive μαθεῖν as "to understand" the meaning of the song.[388] Under this meaning, the reason the 144,000 can understand the song is that it "speaks of being purchased by the Lamb, which the redeemed understand because they have received the benefits of Christ's death."[389]

The 144,000 are also distinguished from those who are not disciples of Jesus by their having been "redeemed from the earth" (14:3b). While it is possible to take "earth" (γῆ) in merely a "geographical sense,"[390] it is also possible to understand "earth" as a reference to the mass of humanity out of whom the redeemed are taken. Under this understanding, Koester

---

386. Smalley takes ἡ φωνὴ as a nominative absolute, so that "the voice" ("sound," NIV) "refers to the same heavenly 'sound' which was heard at the beginning of verse 2, and further defines it" (*Revelation*, 356). Smalley's categorization of the nominative is not likely though, since the nominative absolute "*does not occur in a sentence*, but only in titles, salutations, and other introductory phrases" (Wallace, *Greek Grammar*, 50). This may be why Aune concludes ἡ φωνὴ is a pendent nominative (*Revelation 6–16*, 807). A pendent nominative "is *the logical rather than syntactical subject* at the beginning of a sentence" (Wallace, *Greek Grammar*, 51). In either case, the idea holds that "the voice" mentioned in Rev 14:2b is the same voice described in 14:2a.

387. Johnson, "Revelation," 720.

388. Aune, *Revelation 6–16*, 809; Koester, *Revelation*, 609; Smalley, *Revelation*, 357. Johnson's view seems to be in line with Aune and others when he articulates the infinitive means something like "deep listening . . . that results in learning" ("Revelation," 721). It may also be the ability to learn and sing the song (Beale, *Revelation*, 737; Mounce, *Revelation*, 266; Osborne, *Revelation*, 528).

389. Koester, *Revelation*, 609. The "new song" may be the same as the one recorded in Rev 5:9–10. Koester provides a possible verbal parallel between 5:9–10 and 14:1–5. In both texts, the Lamb is said to have purchased people (ibid., 618). The verb ἀγοράζω ("I redeem, purchase") occurs in 5:9 as an aorist active verb, in 14:3 as a perfect passive participle, and in 14:4 as an aorist passive verb. The context is also important for this position. Smalley notes that of the six occurrences of ἀγοράζω in Revelation only two references, 5:9 and 14:3–4, refer to salvation through judgment (*Revelation*, 357).

390. Aune, *Revelation 6–16*, 809–810.

reasons, "to say they are purchased from (*apō*) the earth and humankind distinguishes those who believe from those who do not (14:3-4; cf. 5:9)."[391]

Discipleship Language

In the next verse John presents three characteristics of the 144,000 (14:4). Each of these is preceded by the demonstrative plural pronoun οὗτοί ("these") and refer back to those who have been redeemed (14:3b).[392] These characteristics are treated in turn.

First, these disciples are those "who have not defiled themselves with women, for they are virgins" (14:4a). This phrase has been understood both literally[393] and figuratively.[394] If the imagery of Rev 14:4a is figurative, then it describes the church as depicted as a faithful virgin prepared to marry her betrothed.[395] These believers are depicted as those who have refused whore Babylon's advances as she peddles idolatry and godlessness, and have remained undefiled; they remain faithful to God (14:4a).[396]

---

391. Koester, *Revelation*, 609. Smalley, taking a line of reasoning similar to Koester, proposes γῆ should be translated "world," and understood in the prevailing Johannine sense of the term, meaning the world aligned against God and the things of God. Thus, he believes the phrase "who have been redeemed from the earth" refers to believers "who have been rescued by the Lamb from the world of unbelief and error, and from the tyranny of compromising behavior" (Smalley, *Revelation*, 357; so also Mounce, *Revelation*, 266).

392. Beale, *Revelation*, 737-738. Aune provides a helpful summary of the use of οὗτοί at the beginning of a sentence in Revelation, it is either used "as an interpretive explanation supplied by the author in his own person (Rev 11:4, 6, 10; 20:5, 14) or as the first word in a sentence introducing the direct discourse of a supernatural revealer (7:13, 14; 17:13, 14; 19:9; 21:5; 22:6)" (*Revelation 6-16*, 810). Here in Rev 14:4 it functions as the former.

393. Carrington, *Revelation*, 237; Draper, "Heavenly Feast," 136-137; Kiddle, *Revelation*, 267-270; Schweizer, *Lordship and Salvation*, 79; Thomas, *Revelation 8-22*, 195-197; Yarbro Collins, *Crisis and Catharsis*, 129-131.

394. Aune, *Revelation 6-16*, 848; Beale, *Revelation*, 738-741; Johnson, "Revelation," 721; Koester, *Revelation*, 618-619; Ladd, *Revelation*, 191; Mounce, *Revelation*, 267-268; Osborne, *Revelation*, 528-529; Smalley, *Revelation*, 357-358.

395. Beale, *Revelation*, 739; Koester, *Revelation*, 609, 610; Mounce, *Revelation*, 267; Schüssler Fiorenza, "Followers of the Lamb," 153; Smalley, *Revelation*, 358.

396. Beale, *Revelation*, 740; Johnson, "Revelation," 721; Koester, *Revelation*, 618; Mounce, *Revelation*, 267. Despite this conclusion, Beale believes the παρθένοι ("virgins") must be men, since it is a masculine noun (*Revelation*, 739-740). Smalley notes παρθένοι is masculine to agree with the pronoun οὗτοί ("they") and the participial phrase οἱ ἠγορασμένοι ("have been redeemed"), even though the group described as "virgins"

Second, these disciples are those who "follow the Lamb wherever he goes" (14:4b). This is conceivably the most overt discipleship language in the entire book. "Following the Lamb" indicates discipleship just as it does in the Gospels (cf. Matt 8:19).[397] The idea in Rev 14:4b is figurative and does not mean literally following Jesus around, which is a usage common in the Gospel also. The figurative use of ἀκολουθέω in the Gospels and here in Rev 14 is synonymous with being a disciple of Jesus.[398] Being Jesus' disciples includes following his way of life and teaching, as well as promoting his mission.[399] The present tense of the participle "they follow" (οἱ ἀκολουθοῦντες) may indicate continuous action.[400] Following Christ as his disciple may lead to death, but the language of following does not necessarily presuppose this meaning.[401] It entails suffering in general for one's commitment to Christ.[402]

Third, these disciples are those who "have been redeemed from mankind as firstfruits for God and the Lamb" (14:4c). The imagery here is sacrificial and invokes images of the old covenant temple with its sacrifices.[403] The terminology of "firstfruits" (ἀπαρχή) was commonly used in the LXX to refer to those who are "offered to God as a one-time contribution,"[404] and thus, someone offered to God "in the sense of being separated to him and sanctified (wholly consecrated)."[405]

The threefold description of Jesus' disciples is one of faithfulness to follow his manner of life and teaching, no matter what the cost. It also

---

are αἱ ἑκατὸν τεσσεράκοντα τέσσαρες ("the 144,000"), which is feminine. He believes the change may be "because the representatives of the twelve tribes of Israel were men" (*Revelation*, 358). Koester argues the opposite position, based on the common usage of the term παρθένος, which is used almost exclusively for a young woman or a female virgin (*Revelation*, 610).

397. Mounce, *Revelation*, 268; Schweizer, *Lordship and Discipleship*, 78.

398. Aune, "Following the Lamb," 275.

399. Mounce, *Revelation*, 268; Aune, "Following the Lamb," 275; Osborne, *Revelation*, 530.

400. Smalley, *Revelation*, 358.

401. Koester, *Revelation*, 611; Smalley, *Revelation*, 358. On the other hand, Osborne believes the phrase ὅπου ἂν ὑπάγῃ ("wherever he goes") "implies *imitatio Christi*, discipleship that involves suffering and death" (*Revelation*, 530; so also Aune, "Following the Lamb," 275–276; Aune, *Revelation 6–16*, 813–814).

402. Beale, *Revelation*, 741.

403. Bauckham, *Climax of Prophecy*, 231–232; Beale, *Revelation*, 742; Mounce, *Revelation*, 268; Osborne, *Revelation*, 530.

404. Thomas, *Revelation 8–22*, 198.

405. Johnson, "Revelation," 722.

seems as though the first two portraits (faithful virgin and following the Lamb) are grounded in the third, since God has called his own and separated them to himself to be used for his purposes. The purpose for which they have been set apart is to follow Christ faithfully. Their faithfulness to Jesus, his teaching, manner of life, and mission also serve as evidence that God has separated them for himself. These images offer assurance to any of Jesus' disciples who may struggle with the certainty of their salvation.

In addition, the imagery of Rev 14:4 is similar to what one finds in Jer 2:2–3. Both move from bridal imagery to harvest imagery.[406] Revelation 14:4 appears to use "firstfruits" in a manner similar to that found in Jer 2:2–3. While "firstfruits" in some context may refer to a select group that is part of a whole (Rom 16:5; 1 Cor 16:15), in Rev 14:4 as in Jer 2, it refers to the entire people of God.[407]

Given the allusions to Jer 2 and the common usage of the term in the LXX, it may be that these disciples are "firstfruits" in the sense of being consecrated wholly to God, which would also be in keeping with the two previous characteristics of the 144,000. All in all, the 144,000 are characterized by wholehearted fidelity to the Lamb and God, who have been redeemed, that is received salvation, from among the inhabitants of the earth.[408]

The last verse in this section, verse 5, draws together the three characterizations of the 144,000 from verse 4. Revelation 14:5 begins, "in their mouth no lie was found," which is an allusion to Isa 53:9, a text commonly identified as speaking of the messianic suffering servant. "No lie" is more than simply telling the truth, but include "faithful proclamation of God's truths as well as a refusal to surrender to Satan's deceits,"[409] which includes the worship of the beast.[410] Based on the connection to Isa 53:9 Bauckham concludes, "following the Lamb wherever he goes means imitating both his

---

406. Koester, *Revelation*, 619.

407. Beale, *Revelation*, 742–743; Kistemaker, *Revelation*, 405; Koester, *Revelation*, 619; Ladd, *Revelation*, 192; Smalley, *Revelation*, 359. Against this view of "firstfruits" see Osborne, *Revelation*, 531; Patterson, *Revelation*, 289; Yarbro Collins, *Crisis and Catharsis*, 127.

408. The imagery of "firstfruits" (Rev 14:4c) is linked to the harvest imagery with respect to salvation (14:14–16) (Koester, *Revelation*, 615). Beale highlights the salvation theme based on the use of the verb ἀγοράζω ("I redeem"), which is used elsewhere in 5:9 (its only other occurrence outside of Rev 14) "of the salvation of *all* Christians." The contexts of the verb in 5:9 and 14:3–4 are also similar (*Revelation*, 744).

409. Osborne, *Revelation*, 531; so also Smalley, *Revelation*, 360.

410. Johnson, "Revelation," 722; Thomas, *Revelation 8–22*, 198–199.

truthfulness, as the 'faithful witness'... and the sacrificial death to which this led."⁴¹¹

Finally, the disciples of the Lamb are described as "blameless" (Rev 14:5).⁴¹² The term translated "blameless," ἄμωμος (14:5) "can mean being unblemished in a physical sense and blameless in a moral sense."⁴¹³ Koester believes "both aspects are at play here."⁴¹⁴ As "firstfruits" they are blameless in the first sense, thus they may be offered in the sanctuary (Lev 21:16–24; 22:21).⁴¹⁵ As the bride, they are blameless in the second sense; they have remained pure for their husband, the Lamb.⁴¹⁶

SUMMARY

Of all the occurrences of the topic of discipleship in Rev 12:1—14:20, 14:1–5 contains a densely compacted depiction of what it means to be a disciple of Jesus Christ. Three particular themes come to the fore. First, this passage presents a vision that aids in coming to an understanding about Jesus' person and/or work. Jesus is portrayed as a "Lamb" (14:1a), which recalls earlier images of the slaughtered Lamb (5:5–6). The Lamb is one who dies a substitutionary death for the redeemed (14:4). The fact that the Lamb is standing (14:1a) may suggest that the slaughtered risen Lamb is also the divine warrior Lamb who will enact judgment on his enemies (14:14, 17–20). The Lamb is actually shown standing "on Mount Zion" (14:1a). This may very well reveal that the Lamb is the rightful heir to the Davidic throne, God to be worshiped (cf. 14:4c), and the Shepherd Lamb (cf. 7:17) who is powerful to protect and care for his sheep (14:1a).

Second, one finds in this passage several descriptions of how Jesus' disciples are distinguished from non-disciples. The "144,000" figuratively

---

411. Bauckham, *Climax of Prophecy*, 232; similarly Beale, *Revelation*, 745–746.

412. This is the sole occurrence of ἄμωμος ("blameless, without defect") in Revelation. It is used elsewhere to speak of a sacrifice without defect, the ritual purity of a priest, and one who is morally blameless (Aune, *Revelation 6–16*, 823).

413. Koester, *Revelation*, 611.

414. Koester, *Revelation*, 611–612; so also Mounce, *Revelation*, 268–269. Similarly, Aune argues that Rev 14:4a–5 form an inclusio that addresses the purity of the 144,000. Revelation 14:5 emphasizes their "moral purity," while 14:4a emphasizes their "ritual purity" (*Revelation 6–16*, 822).

415. Beale, *Revelation*, 747; Koester, *Revelation*, 612.

416. Koester, *Revelation*, 612; Osborne, *Revelation*, 531.

Discipleship in the Book of Revelation

represent "the totality of God's people throughout the ages" (14:1b).[417] They also have on their foreheads the names of the Lamb and the Father (14:1c). This is another way of referring to God's seal (7:3–8). This is different from the rest of humankind, who bear the mark of the beast (13:16–18). Like the seal in Rev 7, the names of the Lamb and the Father protect the one who bears them from the outpouring of God's wrath, while those who are marked by the beast are subject to God's judgment (14:9–11). Protection from God's wrath does not mean protection from the machinations of the false trinity (12:1—13:18). The name of the Lamb and God may also indicate believers are secured and kept from falling away. They are preserved to the end.

One also finds that only the 144,000 who have been redeemed are able to learn or understand the "new song" (14:3b). This naturally excludes those who are not part of the people of God. The reason the 144,000, and they only from among humanity, can learn or understand and sing the redemptive song (cf. 5:9–10) is that the Lamb has redeemed them "from" among those on "the earth" (14:3b).

Finally, the passage concludes with some of the most explicit discipleship language in the entire book. This language is embedded among several characteristics of "the 144,000 who had been redeemed from the earth" (14:3b). First, these disciples are those "who have not defiled themselves with women, for they are virgins" (14:4a). Disciples of Jesus Christ remain faithful to God and eschew idols. Their allegiance to God and Christ is described as the purity of a betrothed woman who eagerly anticipates and awaits her wedding day (cf. 14:5). Christians are Christ's betrothed who await the great wedding day at the consummation of the age. Second, these disciples are those who "follow the Lamb wherever he goes" (14:4b). The term ἀκολουθέω is synonymous with being a disciple of Jesus. This discipleship includes continually following Jesus' manner of life and teaching, while also promoting his mission (cf. 14:5). His way includes suffering because of his faithfulness to his own mission. So also his disciples can expect to follow him in his suffering and possibly even death. Finally, disciples are those who "have been redeemed from mankind as firstfruits for God and the Lamb" (14:4c). A disciple is one who is separated and consecrated to God. Disciples' lives are dedicated to him, to be used for his purposes.

---

417. Beale, *Revelation*, 733; so also Ford, *Revelation*, 245; Johnson, "Revelation," 720; Keener, *Revelation*, 370; Mounce, *Revelation*, 265; Smalley, *Revelation*, 354.

AN ANALYSIS OF REVELATION 15:1—16:21

Revelation 15:1—16:21 as a unit covers the seven bowl judgments. The first section of this unit is "preparatory and interpretive" of the seven plagues (15:1–8),[418] while the final section actually describes the content of each bowl and its being poured out on sinful humanity (16:1–21).[419] The first section may be divided into three parts, each of which is readily identified by Καὶ εἶδον ("And I saw"). Thus, one may separate 15:1–8 into 15:1, 15:2–4, and 15:5–8.[420] The first verse may serve as a "superscription or summary" of 15:1—16:21.[421]

Both chapters 15 and 16 have the Exodus as their background.[422] The bowl judgments that unfold in Rev 16 have several similarities to the trumpet judgments that precede them.[423] Some of these include: (1) the order of the plagues,[424] (2) their bases on the Exodus plagues, and (3) the fact that angels execute each of the septets.[425] Based on these similarities Beale argues that the trumpet and bowl judgments are "parallel literarily, the-

---

418. In support of seeing Rev 15:1-8 as a unit, the double occurrence of the aorist passive form of τελέω in 15:1 and repeated in 15:8 may form an inclusio (Aune, *Revelation 6–16*, 881; Smalley, *Revelation*, 392). Beale does not follow this division, since he takes 15:1–4 as part of the previous section (14:1—15:4). He believes 15:2–4 provides an "interlocking function" pointing back to the judgment that was announced in 14:6–13 and shown to occur in 14:14–20, but also looking forward to the bowl judgments (16:1–21), which are first introduced in 15:5–8 (*Revelation*, 784–785). Thomas notes a slightly different connection between 15:2–4 and what comes before and after it. He sees previous visions as prophetic for what takes place in 15:2–4 (= 14:1–5) and 15:1, 5; 16:1–21 (= 14:6–11, 14–20) (*Revelation 8–22*, 228).

419. Johnson, "Revelation," 728; so also Smalley, *Revelation*, 382.

420. Aune, *Revelation 6–16*, 863; Osborne, *Revelation*, 559; Smalley, *Revelation*, 382.

421. Aune, *Revelation 6–16*, 869; Beasley-Murray, *Revelation*, 233–234; Johnson, "Revelation," 728; Osborne, *Revelation*, 560; Roloff, *Revelation*, 182; Smalley, *Revelation*, 382. Thomas believes Rev 15:1 might be the summary "perhaps for the remainder of the visional portion of the book" (*Revelation 8–22*, 228).

422. The Exodus is the "strongly suggestive" background to Rev 15 (Johnson, "Revelation," 728; so also Smalley, *Revelation*, 382). The description of the seven bowls as "plagues" connects these judgments with the events of the Exodus (Osborne, *Revelation*, 561; Thomas, *Revelation 8–22*, 230). According to Bauckham, the theme of the new exodus is "one of the dominant symbolic motifs of Revelation" (*Climax of Prophecy*, 296; so also Mounce, *Revelation*, 284; Piper, "Unchanging Promises," 14–15).

423. Osborne mentions several similarities between the trumpet and bowl judgments, as well as the seal and bowl judgments (*Revelation*, 576).

424. Beale, *Revelation*, 808; so also Smalley, *Revelation*, 398.

425. Beale, *Revelation*, 809; also Beasley-Murray, *Revelation*, 238–241.

Discipleship in the Book of Revelation

matically, and temporally."[426] However, not everyone is convinced. Others acknowledge the similarities, but tend to emphasize the differences.[427]

The judgments meted out in the seven bowls have a distinct progression "from natural disasters" (bowls 1–4), "to direct judgment against the throne of the beast" (bowl 5), "to preparation for the final battle" (bowl 6), "to the beginning of the destruction of Babylon the great" (bowl 7), "which prepares for the more detailed fall of Babylon in chapters 17–18."[428] The nature of the bowls, whether to take them as literal depictions of future events or figurative of what is to come, has divided many who approach the study of Revelation.[429] It is not the purpose of this study to argue for a particular position, but to highlight and explore what the book has to contribute to the theme of discipleship.

As was the case with Rev 12:1—14:20 and earlier sections, 15:1—16:21 comprises few descriptions of the theme of discipleship. Most are covered with greater detail elsewhere in the Apocalypse. That being said, there are a few portrayals of the theme of discipleship that garner attention.[430]

Revelation 15 begins with John's witness to "another great and marvelous sign" (15:1, NIV).[431] The sign seems to be that of "seven angels with

426. Beale, *Revelation*, 809.

427. Beckwith, *Apocalypse*, 671–673, 690; Ladd, *Revelation*, 209; Thomas, *Revelation 8-22*, 247. One of the major objections to viewing the trumpets and bowls as parallel plagues is the lack of one-to-one correspondence between them. Beale recognizes that the trumpets and bowls do not have a one-to-one correspondence (*Revelation*, 810), and responds that this sort of redundancy would be odd even when the intention is to relay parallel accounts (ibid., 808). He answers the most common objections on pages 808–812.

428. Osborne, *Revelation*, 576. Thomas believes the first four judgments are characterized by personal affliction, while the final three are more global in scale (*Revelation 8-22*, 248).

429. Thomas (*Revelation 8-22*, 245–278) and Walvoord (*Revelation*, 231–242) view the events of Rev 16 as literal future events. Beale takes the content of the chapter as figurative or symbolic of present and future events (*Revelation*, 810, 812–846). Perhaps it is best or at least safest to take the position of Osborne who recognizes that one cannot state with certainty whether the plagues are intended to be literal, figurative, or some combination of the two. In any case, they are descriptions of awful events (*Revelation*, 586).

430. Although they occur in this section, the "Discipleship Language" of "saints" ("holy people," NIV) is not discussed in great detail, nor is there mention of their deaths for Christ's sake ("Consequences of Following Jesus"), since these have been treated elsewhere.

431. "Another" sign may be the third "heavenly sign, perhaps a constellation, which refers to the two previous signs or constellations referred to in Rev 12:1 and 12:3" (Aune,

seven plagues, which are the last." With this sign God will disclose his purposes for humanity.[432] The "plagues" are the bowl judgments to follow shortly (15:1, 6, 8; 16:9). They are described as "last, because with them God's wrath is complete" (15:1).[433]

Believe in Jesus

Next, John saw what looked like "a sea of glass mingled with fire—and also those who had conquered the beast and its image and the number of its name" (15:2a). The "sea of glass mingled with fire" may very well be a reference to the Red Sea crossing in the book of Exodus. This is based on the immediate context, which includes the song of Moses sung in 15:3-4, the mention of "plagues" in 15:1, which are a possible reference to the seven plagues of Exod 7-12, and the "tabernacle of testimony" in Rev 15:5, as well as later Jewish interpreters who referred to the Red Sea as a "sea of glass."[434] If the Red Sea is alluded to, then what might this mean? Since elsewhere

---

Revelation 6-16, 869; similarly Johnson, "Revelation," 728-729; Mounce, *Revelation*, 284; Smalley, *Revelation*, 382; Thomas, *Revelation 8-22*, 229). "Great and marvelous" (NIV) are only paired together in 15:1, 3 (Aune, *Revelation 6-16*, 869; Smalley, *Revelation*, 382-383; Thomas, *Revelation 8-22*, 229-230).

432. "Heavenly signs ... disclose God's purposes (Rev 12:1, 3), whereas the signs performed by the beast's agents are deceptive (13:13-14; 16:14; 19:20)" (Koester, *Revelation*, 631; similarly Mounce, *Revelation*, 284).

433. Beale takes the aorist verb ἐτελέσθη ("complete") similar to a "Hebrew prophetic perfect, [which expresses] the future, consummated occurrence of God's wrath as though it has already occurred" (*Revelation*, 788). Fanning (Fanning, *Verbal Aspect*, 269-274) and Wallace (*Greek Grammar*, 563-564) refer to this use of the aorist as *proleptic* or *futuristic*. This use of the aorist indicates the certainty with which a future event will occur (so also Thomas, *Revelation 8-22*, 231).

434. Beale, *Revelation*, 789, 791-792; Caird, *Revelation*, 197; Smalley, *Revelation*, 384; Thomas, *Revelation 8-22*, 230, 232.

Osborne believes the "sea of glass mingled with fire" points back to Rev 4:6 and the "sea of glass" before the throne of God (Osborne, *Revelation*, 561; so also Giblin, "From and before the Throne," 510-511; Thomas, *Revelation 8-22*, 232). The "sea of glass" alludes to the waters in Gen 1:7; the bronze sea in the temple (1 Kgs 7:23-26); and the "vault, sparkling like crystal, and awesome" above the four living creatures (Osborne, *Revelation*, 561-562; see also Smalley, *Revelation*, 384 who notes this as a possibility, but in the end goes with the Exodus motif based on the multiple allusions to the Exodus event in Rev 15-16). The inclusion of "fire" points to God's judgment, which is yet to come (20:11-15). Osborne finds the view that this phrase is an allusion to the Red Sea to be "too allegorical" (*Revelation*, 562).

the "sea" "connotes cosmic evil,"[435] and "fire" divine judgment,[436] it may be that Rev 15:2 reveals that the divine Lamb has executed judgment over the beast that came out of the sea (13:1–10). Only because of his victory are those who follow him also able to overcome the beast, its image, and its number (15:2).[437]

Those "who had conquered [τοὺς νικῶντας] the beast and its image and the number of its name"[438] are revealed "standing beside" the glassy sea.[439] As noted earlier in this chapter νικάω ("I overcome, am victorious") may include salvific undertones. Those who place faith in Christ and remain faithful to him are those who are declared victorious in the letters to the seven churches (2:7, 11, 17, 26–28; 3:5, 12, 21). The promises attached to those who overcome "relate to participation in the kingdom of God, as described in the closing vision of Revelation."[440] If Rev 15–16 points to events

---

435. Beale, *Revelation*, 789; so also Smalley, *Revelation*, 384.

436. The term πῦρ ("fire") in almost every case (except Rev 13:13) refers to God's judgment (Beale, *Revelation*, 789; Bauckham, *Climax of Prophecy*, 296; Osborne, *Revelation*, 562; Smalley, *Revelation*, 384; Thomas, *Revelation 8–22*, 232). Koester believes it is possible for "fire" to refer to God's judgment, as well as "the trials that test faith (Rev 3:18; 1 Pet 4:12)" (*Revelation*, 631).

437. Beale, *Revelation*, 790; Smalley, *Revelation*, 384.

438. Koester believes the preposition ἐκ "could imply that they separate themselves from or are saved from the beast, though it may simply be a way of saying they triumph over the beast (12:11)" (*Revelation*, 631). Both Beale (*Revelation*, 790) and Smalley (*Revelation*, 385) believe the phrase refers to the saints being victorious because they have separated themselves from the deceptions of the beast (similarly Thomas, *Revelation 8–22*, 233). Aune believes the phrase is a possible *Latinism*, a word or phrase translated from a Latin source, and thus, would be translated "victorious over the beast" (Aune, "Latinism in Revelation 15:2," 691–692).

439. Those who are victorious either stand "on" (NASB) or "beside" (NIV, ESV) the glassy sea. Both are possible translations of ἵστημι and ἐπί with the accusative case. Although Rev 10:5, 8 include ἵστημι and ἐπί with the genitive case, this may be a closer parallel, since an angel is seen standing "on the sea." The composition of the sea may also point in the direction of standing "on the sea," rather than "beside" it (Beale, *Revelation*, 791; Johnson, "Revelation," 729; Mounce, *Revelation*, 286; Smalley, *Revelation*, 385; Thomas, *Revelation 8–22*, 234). Wallace in his discussion on prepositions does not include the gloss "beside" or "at" in the case of ἐπί with the accusative case (Wallace, *Greek Grammar*, 376). Bauckham wonders if the ambiguity is intended. The victors stand on the sea of glass, since this is the floor of heaven (*Climax of Prophecy*, 296; so also Aune, *Revelation 6–16*, 872; Osborne, *Revelation*, 562 n. 6). There may also be an allusion to the Red Sea crossing, which describes the Israelites walking between the walls of water, and thus, beside the water, rather than on it (Bauckham, *Climax of Prophecy*, 296–297). Koester believes "beside" fits the allusions to the Red Sea crossing (*Revelation*, 632).

440. Beasley-Murray, *Revelation*, 78. Mounce notes several rewards promised to

that take place at the end of the age, then it may be possible to view the description of those "who had conquered" as a window into these promises that are bound up with God's coming and consummated kingdom. At the very least, one may identify these overcomers experiencing their heavenly reward.[441]

This depiction of the overcomers would be a welcome sight to any and all of Jesus' disciples living in this fallen world. Not only are they the target of abuse, both verbal and physical, from the unbelieving world around them, but they also deal with the same effects of the fall that all persons must suffer, whether sickness or the loss of loved ones. But disciples of Jesus of all people have reason to remain faithful to Christ, and one of them is mentioned in 15:2. They are given a vision of victory over the beast and its image and its number. Although they may suffer loss in this life, they may know that in the end they win. They are victorious because Jesus has already decisively won the victory through the cross.

Distinction between Jesus' Disciples and Non-Disciples

The victorious are also engaged in playing "harps" and singing "the song of God's servant Moses and of the Lamb" (15:2b–3a, NIV).[442] The "harps of God" (κιθάρας τοῦ θεοῦ) can be taken as an objective or subjective genitive. If objective, then the harps are those played for God as an act of worship. If subjective, then the harps are those God gives to those who are victori-

---

those who are victorious over the beast and its image and its number (*Revelation*, 285).

441. Beale believes the location of the scene presented in Rev 15:2ff is heaven (*Revelation*, 791; so also Aune, *Revelation 6–16*, 863; Smalley, *Revelation*, 382). Beale also believes the idea of the resurrection is included based on 15:2-4 being linked to other depictions of the resurrection (4:6; 5:5–9) (*Revelation*, 791; so also Osborne, *Revelation*, 562 n. 6). Beale also notes how some Jewish writers interpreted the Red Sea event to imply "the resurrection of the Israelite singers to sing once again in the new age" (*Revelation*, 792; so also Johnson, "Revelation," 730 n. 3).

442. The fact that this group is holding "harps" seems to link them to the 144,000 in Rev 14:1–5, where harps are also found. All of the people of God are in view (Beale, *Revelation*, 791; Johnson, "Revelation," 729; Osborne, *Revelation*, 563 n. 7; Smalley, *Revelation*, 384–385). Walvoord believes those holding harps in 15:2 are a remnant of those the beast martyred in 13:1–10, many of whom are Israelites (*Revelation*, 227), while Charles identifies them as literal martyrs (*Revelation*, 2.32–33; so also Bauckham, *Climax of Prophecy*, 296). Thomas identifies them as those the beast killed during the great tribulation (13:7) (*Revelation 8–22*, 233). Koester notes the group includes martyrs and all who have been faithful (*Revelation*, 634).

ous. Osborne believes it is possible to understand the phrase as a genitive of source (similar to subjective genitive) or a possessive genitive, meaning they are God's harps. In light of the song that is sung (15:3b-4), he prefers objective genitive.[443] If this is correct, then what 15:3-4 describes is Christians, those who are disciples of Jesus Christ, engaged in worship of the one true God. This is the opposite of what is found in 16:2. There those who stand condemned and poised to receive God's wrath are identified as those "who bore the mark of the beast and *worshiped* its image" (emphasis added). One group worships the one true God, while the other worships a false god; both receive their just rewards.

The song the saints sing is called the song of Moses and the Lamb.[444] This song is a hymn of praise[445] drawn together from several OT allusions[446] and directed primarily to the Lamb, for his marvelous deeds of redeeming his people, and of his greatness and worthiness to receive worship from all

---

443. Osborne, *Revelation*, 563; so also Beale, *Revelation*, 791. There are similarities between the subjective genitive, genitive of source, and possessive genitive. When all three are possibilities, then the subjective genitive "should be given priority" (Wallace, *Greek Grammar*, 109).

444. Thomas believes there are two songs: the song of Moses, which is not quoted, and the song of the Lamb, which is recorded in Rev 15:3-4 (*Revelation 8-22*, 235). Koester states that most scholars believe the songs are one (*Revelation*, 632).

445. Leonard Thompson identifies Rev 15:3-4 as one of only two passages in Revelation that "are explicitly identified as hymns." The other is Rev 5:9-10 ("Hymns," 459). Johnson, likewise, identifies 15:3-4 as "liturgy ... no doubt from the early Christian church" ("Revelation," 730; so also Mounce, *Revelation*, 286; Smalley, *Revelation*, 382).

446. The song in Rev 15:3-4 possesses traits similar to the song of Moses in Exod 15:1-18 (redemption) and Deut 32 (judgment) (Beale, *Revelation*, 792-793; Beasley-Murray, *Revelation*, 235; Koester, *Revelation*, 634). Ford believes the closest parallels are to Deut 32 (*Revelation*, 257). On the other hand, Bauckham emphasizes the allusions to the Red Sea, and thus concludes that Exod 15 is the primary background (*Climax of Prophecy*, 297, 306; so also Mounce, *Revelation*, 285; Smalley, *Revelation*, 382, 386; Thomas, *Revelation 8-22*, 235). Mounce notes that nearly 80 percent of the song includes an allusion to some OT text (*Revelation*, 286; see also Aune, *Revelation 6-16*, 874; Beale, *Revelation*, 794; Johnson, "Revelation," 729; Koester, *Revelation*, 634; Smalley, *Revelation*, 386). Schüssler Fiorenza believes John sampled the language and themes of the OT, but did not intend for his words to be connected to any particular set of texts (*Revelation*, 135). Bauckham notes this view fails to consider fully "the remarkable wealth of meaning John has packed into his dense text" (*Climax of Prophecy*, 298).

peoples.[447] Some will fear and worship him gladly, while others will do so unwillingly.[448]

The remainder of Rev 15 describes the seven angels whom God commissions to pour out the bowls of his wrath on the ungodly (15:5–8).[449] What follows is the enactment of God's justice against sinful humanity (16:1–21).

Consequences of Following Jesus

Revelation 16:5–7 includes a rather abrupt deviation from the revealing of the seven bowl judgments. Some believe this passage contains an example of a "judgment doxology," which is "a brief hymnic passage that provides general or specific justification for the judgment of God."[450] Whether or

---

447. The καὶ ("and") in the phrase "Moses and of the Lamb" (NIV) is an epexegetical καὶ (Beale, *Revelation*, 792; Koester, *Revelation*, 632; Osborne, *Revelation*, 564; Smalley, *Revelation*, 385–386). Also, the genitive phrase καὶ τὴν ᾠδὴν τοῦ ἀρνίου ("and the song of the Lamb," NASB) is likely an objective genitive, meaning the song about the Lamb or the song for the Lamb (Aune, *Revelation 6–16*, 873; Osborne, *Revelation*, 564; Smalley, *Revelation*, 386). Beale believes if one must choose, it may be a subjective genitive, since the preceding parallel genitive phrase ("the song of God's servant Moses," NIV) is likely subjective, meaning the song Moses sang (*Revelation*, 793; so also Thomas, *Revelation 8–22*, 236). In the end though, he would rather leave the phrase ambiguous, as do most English translations (Beale, *Revelation*, 793).

If the song is mainly about the Lamb, then it is likely to focus on the Lamb's sacrifice for the redemption of the nations (Osborne, *Revelation*, 564). According to Mounce, the song "celebrates [God's] righteous and redemptive activity beginning with Moses and culminating with the Lamb" (*Revelation*, 285).

448. Revelation 15:4c [the third ὅτι (*hoti*) clause of 15:4] possibly provides the ground or basis for fearing and worshiping the Lord (Beale, *Revelation*, 798; Osborne, *Revelation*, 568). Thomas sees this ὅτι clause as the reason "all nations will come and worship" God (*Revelation 8–22*, 238–239). God's "righteous acts" include both redemption and judgment (Beale, *Revelation*, 798–799). Bauckham notes that both redemption and judgment are clearly displayed in Exod 15, while in Rev 15 judgment is noticeably articulated, while redemption is "presupposed" (*Climax of Prophecy*, 301; so also Thomas, *Revelation 8–22*, 239). Osborne believes the emphasis should be on God's redemptive "righteous acts," and thus takes the phrase as mostly positive (*Revelation*, 568; so also Aune, *Revelation 6–16*, 876; Charles, *Revelation*, 2.36; Smalley, *Revelation*, 389). Ford believes the emphasis is on God's judgment (*Revelation*, 257). Beale believes both believers and unbelievers will fear the Lord and worship him. Some will do so willingly (Christians), while others will do so forcibly (cf. Phil 2:9–11) (*Revelation*, 799).

449. Beale, *Revelation*, 802. Aune sees their commissioning taking place in 15:7 (*Revelation 6–16*, 879).

450. Aune, *Revelation 6–16*, 885; so also Smalley, *Revelation*, 402; Yarbro Collins,

not this is an example of a judgment doxology, the passage does reveal something of who God is and the basis for his judgment against those who follow the beast. The angel declares God is righteous (δίκαιος) and holy (ὅσιος) in his judgments (16:5a). The basis or ground (ὅτι, "for," "because") for this declaration of God's attributes is the fact that he has "judged these things" (NASB) (ταῦτα ἔκρινας).[451] "These things" (NASB) God judges are at least the murder of God's people (16:6a), but may include all sins mentioned in the book.[452] The identification of God as "who is and who was" (16:5b) indicates he is sovereign over all human history.[453]

God is also holy and just because he has dealt with those who have "shed the blood of saints and prophets" (16:6a).[454] As with the first bowl, the punishment of those who killed God's "saints" and "prophets" fits the crime (*lex talionis*).[455] They spilled blood, so God has "given them blood to drink" just as "they deserve" (16:6b).[456] Several NT texts indicate that the murder of God's prophets is reason for divine judgment on the perpetrators (Matt 23:31, 37; Acts 7:52; Rom 11:3; 1 Thess 2:15; Heb 11:35–37).[457] Revelation 16:6 may indicate that God has finally answered the prayers of the saints who cried out from under the altar in 6:9–11.[458] They desired God

---

"Apocalypticism," 367–381. A "judgment doxology" contains three parts: (1) confession of sin, (2) an affirmation of God's righteousness, and (3) the justice of his punishment. The difficulty with this designation is that there is no one biblical text that includes every element, Rev 16:5–6 included (Osborne, *Revelation*, 581).

451. Aune, *Revelation 6–16*, 856; Osborne, *Revelation*, 582 n. 7; Thomas, *Revelation 8–22*, 253.

452. Osborne, *Revelation*, 583. Thomas excluded earlier judgments (*Revelation 8–22*, 253). Smalley maintains that the ὅτι clause is not causal, but rather should be understood as a verbal clause, so that "these things" (NASB) points to the previous bowl judgments (Rev 16:2–4) or perhaps all seven (*Revelation*, 403).

453. Beale, *Revelation*, 818; Smalley, *Revelation*, 402.

454. The second ὅτι clause further elucidates the ground for the declaration of God's righteous and holy character (Beale, *Revelation*, 818; Osborne, *Revelation*, 583; Thomas, *Revelation 8–22*, 253).

455. Aune, *Revelation 6–16*, 887; Thomas, *Revelation 8–22*, 254.

456. Charles takes αὐτοῖς ("they") in the phrase αἷμα αὐτοῖς as reciprocal "one another's blood" (*Revelation*, 2.120). This appears to be an unparalleled use of the pronoun αὐτός. If the author wanted to indicate a reciprocal relationship he could have used ἀλλήλων ("one another"). He sees this verse as descriptive of fighting that takes place between Rome and her allies. They will do each other in. That is their judgment (ibid., 2.123).

457. Osborne, *Revelation*, 583; Smalley, *Revelation*, 404.

458. Here in Rev 16:6a one group, not two is probably in view. Those who have been

to vindicate their deaths at the hands of wicked people.[459] Revelation 16:6 serves to remind the reader of the potential threat all of Jesus' disciples may have to endure. Jesus promised no less to his disciples. If people persecuted him, they could also expect to be persecuted (John 16:20).

Twice during the course of the bowl judgments the ungodly are said to have refused to repent (Rev 16:9, 11). One of the questions that come to the surface when reviewing the response of the wicked to God's judgment is whether or not they could have actually repented of their ways. The question is not an easy one to answer, as are many of the questions that arise from the study of the Apocalypse. Yarbo Collins thinks the refusal to repent in 16:9, 11 "seems to be almost predetermined from the point of view of the author of Revelation" (cf. 22:10–11). Therefore, "the time for repentance is already past" at the time of the seal, trumpet, and bowl judgments.[460] She sees this throughout Revelation, with the exclusion of 11:13, which she believes is the repentance and conversion of some of the Jewish people.[461] Thomas seems to agree, since he sees those who are afflicted with these plagues as "a hopeless case."[462] Osborne disagrees, noting the phrase "give him glory" "signifies conversion," which means the ungodly pictured in Rev 16 are presented with the opportunity to repent and be

---

killed are the people of God, who include among their number some who exercise prophetic gifts (Mounce, *Revelation*, 295; Osborne, *Revelation*, 584; Smalley, *Revelation*, 403 Thomas, *Revelation 8–22*, 253).

459. The "altar" mentioned in Rev 16:7 may be a reference to the altar under which the souls of the martyrs cried out to God for justice (6:9–10). Beale basis this position on verbal links between 16:5 and 6:10, as well as the occurrences of "altar" elsewhere in Revelation, which are "a development of the reference to the 'altar' in 6:9 and refers to the judgment petitioned for by those under the altar (8:3–5; 9:13; 14:18)" (*Revelation*, 820; so also Aune, *Revelation 6–16*, 820; Charles, *Revelation*, 124; Ladd, *Revelation*, 211; Mounce, *Revelation*, 295). Osborne believes the voice from the altar is an angel (λέγοντος is a present singular participle) who presented the prayers of the saints to God in 8:3–5 (*Revelation*, 585). Beale states that even though the participle "saying" (λέγοντος) is singular, it is possible that "the voice represents the corporate declaration" of the souls (plural) from under the altar (*Revelation*, 820; so also Koester, *Revelation*, 648; Smalley, *Revelation*, 404). Aune suggests the voice is of one of the saints under the altar (*Revelation 6–16*, 888). Others believe the altar is personified, so that it actually speaks (Charles, *Revelation*, 2.124; Ladd, *Revelation*, 211; Mounce, *Revelation*, 295; Roloff, *Revelation*, 189; Thomas, *Revelation 8–22*, 254).

460. Yarbro Collins, "Apocalypticism," 371.

461. Ibid., 371–372.

462. Thomas, *Revelation 8–22*, 258.

saved.⁴⁶³ Koester sees even this judgment as a picture of God's mercy, since those who are burned with fire are not killed, but able to respond to God's judgment (16:8–9). He concludes, their failure to repent does not mean they lack the opportunity.⁴⁶⁴

Their failure to repent may point to an additional distinction between Christ's disciples and non-disciples found in Rev 16. Earlier, in several of the letters to the seven churches of Asia Minor, Jesus extends the opportunity for the church to repent of its ways and return to rightly following him (2:5 [2x], 16, 22; 3:3, 19). For instance, to the church at Laodicea Jesus' offer of repentance is couched as an example of his loving discipline for his disciples (3:3). Elsewhere, Jesus' words are coupled with a warning of judgment. To the church in Ephesus he calls for repentance and promises that if they do not repent, he will come and take away their lampstand (2:5). Now, the text does not say whether or not these churches repented of their ways, but it is highly likely that some in the church, having heard the letter read, did repent. However, this is not the case for those who have been presented with awful displays of God's justice (16:9, 11, 21). Like Pharaoh and the Egyptians before them, God's judgment on their sinfulness serves only to harden them against him and his ways.⁴⁶⁵ This may reveal that those who are truly Christ's disciples respond positively to warnings and discipline, while the unbelieving world spirals further down into its own sinfulness and away from following Jesus.

---

463. Osborne, *Revelation*, 587.

464. Koester, *Revelation*, 655.

465. There is a continual hardening of their heart against God, which is similar to the reaction of Pharaoh to the ten plagues of Exodus (Beale, *Revelation*, 825; Osborne, *Revelation*, 588; Smalley, *Revelation*, 407). This leads Beale to conclude, "contrary to the assessment of some, the lack of repentance here and throughout chapter 16 (vv. 9, 11, 21) is not penultimate or reversible but irremediable according to the theological pattern of the hardening of Pharaoh and the Egyptians" (*Revelation*, 825). If Beale's reasoning is correct, then perhaps the aorist verb μετενόησαν should be taken as a *consummative aorist*, which reflects the final or completed result of an action (Wallace, *Greek Grammar*, 559). Robertson (*Grammar*, 834) notes that some grammarians refer to the consummative aorist as "resultant aorist". Osborne seems to argue the opposite based on the occurrence of μετανοέω ("I repent, change my mind"). He views repentance as a major purpose of the three judgment septets (*Revelation*, 589). The fact that they failed to repent shows there was a possibility that they could repent.

Come to an Understanding of Jesus' Person and/or Work

The bowls continue to progress rapidly until the sixth is poured out (16:12). In the midst of armies preparing for battle (16:14), Jesus speaks to his own, offering encouragement for them to endure during these final days, "Behold [Ἰδοὺ], I am coming like a thief!" (Rev 16:15a) It has been shown that ἰδοὺ is used to relate something about the person and work of Jesus Christ, and such is the case here. Osborne takes the present tense verb ἔρχομαι ("I come") as a *futuristic present*, a usage of the present tense to describe the certainty of a future action or event.[466] Jesus spoke similarly of his second coming in the Gospels.[467] Aune believes 16:15 is an interpolation of 3:3, which also speaks of Jesus coming like a thief. His view is based on what he thinks is a disruption of the content of 16:14 to 16:16.[468] However, the place of 16:15 functions in a fashion similar to earlier exhortations in 13:9 and 14:12, which call on believers to remain faithful.[469] Jesus' coming will be sudden and unexpected, particularly for those who are not his own, those who do not expect him to return. It is also possible that his words are directed toward his disciples, as he desires to wake up his church, for them to make themselves ready for his sure return, which fits with the reason Jesus uses the same image in 3:3.[470]

Discipleship Language

Jesus continues his words of encouragement for his disciples to remain steadfast: "Blessed is the one who stays awake, keeping [τηρῶν] his garments on, that he may not go about [περιπατῇ] naked and be seen exposed!" (16:15b) This is the third of seven beatitudes in the book (1:3; 14:13; 16:15; 19:9; 20:6; 22:7, 14).[471] For Jewish persons to be naked was shameful (Gen

---

466. Osborne, *Revelation*, 593; for more on the futuristic present see Fanning, *Verbal Aspects*, 221–226; Wallace, *Greek Grammar*, 535–537.

467. For a thorough look at this see Bauckham, *Climax of Prophecy*, 104–109.

468. Aune, *Revelation 6–16*, 896.

469. Beale, *Revelation*, 836; Koester, *Revelation*, 659; Smalley, *Revelation*, 411.

470. Koester, *Revelation*, 667. Thomas believes Christ's words are not for the church or any group of Christians, since the church would already be safe (Rev 12:13–17) and those who experienced martyrdom (13:15; 14:1–5, 13; 15:2) would have already come and passed. These words should be seen as an invitation to repent and truly believe in Christ (*Revelation 8–22*, 267).

471. Aune, *Revelation 6–16*, 896; Koester, *Revelation*, 659; Osborne, *Revelation*, 593;

2:25; 3:3; 9:20–25). Here in Rev 16:15b, though, it is connected to being prepared for Christ's return. The kind of preparation envisioned likely has to do with remaining faithful to Christ.[472] Smalley sees the verb τηρέω ("I keep") used metaphorically with the noun ἱμάτια ("garments") only here in Revelation.[473] To remain clothed is a metaphor for remaining steadfast in one's worship of God in the face of the idolatrous seductions of the beast.[474] Likewise, nakedness is used of idolatry in the OT (cf. Isa 20:1–6; Ezek 16:36; 23:29; Nah 3:4–5).[475] The call Jesus issues is for them to "not walk [περιπατῇ] about naked" (NASB). The verb περιπατέω ("I walk") may be used for actual walking or figuratively for one's manner of living. Earlier with regard to the use of the verb in Rev 3:4, both Aune and Smalley indicated that in the NT "walking" is often synonymous with discipleship.[476] In this case, Jesus challenges his church not to walk in a manner that will leave them "naked" and "exposed," which in this context appears to be succumbing to idolatry.[477] Instead, they are to be clothed with good works, those deeds that show evidence of their commitment to follow after Christ (3:4–5, 18; 19:8–9).[478]

The remainder of Rev 16 depicts the gathering for the great battle between Satan's forces, represented by the "kings of the whole world," and the

---

Smalley, *Revelation*, 411; Thomas, *Revelation 8–22*, 267.

472. Beale, *Revelation*, 837; Koester, *Revelation*, 660; Osborne, *Revelation*, 593.

473. Smalley, *Revelation*, 411.

474. Beale, *Revelation*, 837; Smalley, *Revelation*, 411.

475. Smalley, *Revelation*, 411.

476. Aune, *Revelation 1–5*, 222; Smalley, *Revelation*, 84.

477. The verb περιπατῇ is in the present tense and should probably be taken as a *gnomic present*, which indicates the statement is "general, timeless fact" that should occur at "*all* times" (Wallace, *Greek Grammar*, 523).

478. Ibid., 412. This may also indicate the discipleship category, "Marks of Discipleship," of which bearing much fruit is a characteristic.

Lord God at Armageddon.⁴⁷⁹ It is at Armageddon that the Lord will fight and defeat the forces of evil once and for all.⁴⁸⁰

The seventh and final bowl is poured out "into the air" (16:17a) and is accompanied by several phenomena: a voice from the temple declaring, "It is done," a great storm, an earthquake, and gigantic hailstones (16:17b–21a),⁴⁸¹ at which people do not repent or cry out for mercy, but who defiantly curse (ἐβλασφήμησαν, "they blasphemed," NASB) God (16:21b). This verse shows that sinful humanity has aligned itself with the false christ (the first beast), who also blasphemed God (13:5–6).⁴⁸² They have become like the one they worship (13:12).

SUMMARY

The few instances of the theme of discipleship in 15:1—16:21 display some of the same themes that occurred earlier in the book. For instance, the discipleship language of "saints" (16:6) and the distinguishing features of Jesus' disciples from non-disciples include the "mark of the beast" (16:2). However, that does not mean there is not something to be gained from analyzing 15:1—16:21 for discipleship motifs. The discipleship language of being victorious is fleshed out even more. Those who are victorious are so over "the beast and its image and the number of its name" (15:2). They have not succumbed to the ploys of the enemy to follow after him, but have remained faithful to God. For their faithfulness in overcoming they will enjoy eating from the tree of life (2:7), protection from the second death (2:11), receive the hidden manna (2:17), they will rule over the nations (2:26), be clothed in righteousness (3:5), become pillars in God's temple (3:12), and reign with Christ (3:21). This leads Mounce to exclaim, "little wonder that

---

479. The name "Armageddon" appears to be the combination of two Hebrew words, "*har*, meaning hill or mountain, with the name Megiddo, a city in northern Israel" (Koester, *Revelation*, 660). The exact location and meaning of Armageddon is hotly debated. For a list of possible geographical and etymological interpretations see: Jauhiainen, "Armageddon," 381–393; Osborne, *Revelation*, 594–595. Rather than attempt to identify a particular geographical location, it may be best to go with Koester's straightforward conclusion: Armageddon refers to the "mountain of Megiddo" (*Revelation*, 661; so also Beale, *Revelation*, 840).

480. Beale, *Revelation*, 841; Koester, *Revelation*, 660; Osborne, *Revelation*, 595–596.

481. Thomas does not view this as the end of the seventh bowl, which he believes is resumed in Rev 19:11 (*Revelation 8–22*, 277).

482. Koester, *Revelation*, 669.

they break out in song!"[483] God will reward those who remain faithful to him.

Discipleship language also occurs near the end of the section in 16:15b where Christ encourages his disciples not to walk according to the pattern of this world, but instead to set out to follow Christ. The disciple's manner of life is to depict a resolute acceptance of Jesus' lordship and an equally steadfast rejection of the enemy's pull and sway over one's life.

In addition, 15:3–4 and 16:2 bring to light a contrast between those who are followers of Jesus and those who do not follow after him. In 15:3–4 one finds the saints of God praising and worshiping the one true God for his great acts that reveal his just and holy nature. These disciples willingly give themselves in worship of God. On the other hand, 16:2 mentions those who "bore the mark of the beast and worshiped its image." One is going to worship someone or something. And in the case of those described in 16:2, they worship a false god, one who they hoped would provide stability and sustain them, but in the end is found wanting. The beast is unable to stop the torrent of judgment God pours out on them. Rather than repent and turn to God, these same people curse him for the punishments that afflict them (16:9, 11, 21). On the other hand, when the Lord Jesus extended forgiveness to several of the churches of Asia Minor (2:5 [2x], 16, 22; 3:3, 19), more than likely several of them repented. Joyful, heartfelt worship and humble repentance is to be characteristic of all of Jesus' disciples.

Finally, Rev 16:15a provides another glimpse of who Christ is in his person and work. In this passage Jesus declares that he is coming as a thief (cf. 3:3). This reveals that he is coming again. He promised to return for his church, to judge the living and the dead, and he will keep his word. But he is also coming suddenly and unexpectedly for those who are not his own. Those who follow him are to be prepared for his coming, being found honoring his name in all they say and do.

AN ANALYSIS OF REVELATION 17:1—19:5

This section of Revelation covers the final defeat of Babylon and the beast (17:1–18), a series of laments and warnings regarding Babylon's fall (18:1–24), and the praise of the saints over her demise (19:1–5). The allusions to the theme of discipleship occur sporadically throughout this section. Most of these instances have been treated earlier with greater detail, and others

---

483. Mounce, *Revelation*, 285.

have become commonplace and thus do not need to be discussed further.[484] Therefore, the analysis of this section highlights two particular aspects of the theme of discipleship.

The angel begins by introducing the main characters of the vision, namely, the prostitute, the kings of the earth, and the beast (17:1–3). Next, the angel further describes the great prostitute, "Babylon the great" in all of her "opulence"[485] and bloodthirstiness,[486] for the death of God's people (17:4–6).[487] The angel finally sets out to interpret the vision for John, which includes the beast who is the antitype of God, the "seven heads are seven mountains on which the woman sits,"[488] and the "ten kings" who had not yet "received royal power" (17:7–14).

Discipleship Language

John also witnesses "ten kings" that join together in an unholy coalition to "make war on the Lamb" (17:12–14).[489] It is God, not the beast, who ulti-

---

484. For instance, discipleship language such as "saints" (Rev 17:6; 18:20, 24) and "servants" (19:2, 5) can be found, the theme of bearing witness to Jesus (17:6), as well as consequences of following Jesus (17:6; 18:24). Some instances of the theme of discipleship are treated at greater length in subsequent sections [i.e., "Membership and Election of the People of God," specifically the language "my people" (18:4; cf. 21:3)].

485. Koester, *Revelation*, 673. Beale believes the fact that both the beast and the prostitute are clothed with red may suggest they are to be identified with the red dragon (Rev 12:3), the devil himself. Satan is the one undergirding their power (*Revelation*, 853). So also Mounce, *Revelation*, 310.

486. Aune, *Revelation 17–22*, 937; Koester, *Revelation*, 675; Thomas, *Revelation 8–22*, 290–291.

487. For a brief overview of Babylon in the history of interpretation see Koester, *Revelation*, 637–641.

488. The "seven heads" are typically identified as kings or national leaders (Rev 17:10), whether of Rome or other nations (Beckwith, *Apocalypse*, 707–708; Boring, *Revelation*, 183–184; Caird, *Revelation*, 216–219; Kiddle, *Revelation*, 349–351). The "seven mountains" have been interpreted as Rome, any political kingdom in opposition to Christianity (Mounce, *Revelation*, 315; Wall, *Revelation*, 207), seven successive kingdoms (Ladd, *Revelation*, 227–228; Seiss, *Apocalypse*, 392; Thomas, *Revelation 8–22*, 296), figuratively of the completeness of the world's kingdoms (Aune, *Revelation 17–22*, 948; Beale, *Revelation*, 868–869; Beasley-Murray, *Revelation*, 256–257), or some combination of these views (Bauckham, *Climax of Prophecy*, 406–407; Osborne, *Revelation*, 620; Smalley, *Revelation*, 437).

489. Aune, *Revelation 17–22*, 950; Koester, *Revelation*, 679; Thomas, *Revelation 8–22*, 300.

mately grants these kings brief authority in order to destroy the prostitute (17:16).⁴⁹⁰ The coalition submits to the beast and gives it "their power and authority" (17:13). The singular purpose of the kings and the beast is to defeat the Lamb and his forces, but they will lose, because (ὅτι) the Lamb "is Lord of lords and King of kings," meaning he and he alone is sovereign over all (17:14).⁴⁹¹

Those who follow the Lamb into battle to engage the enemy are "with him" (17:14). This language may indicate discipleship. It is similar to the image of following or walking with Jesus used elsewhere (3:4; 7:17; 14:4; 16:15). The connection to the 144,000 of Rev 7 and 14 with these who are "with him" may strengthen the assertion that this is indicative of discipleship language in Revelation.⁴⁹² Those who are "with him" may take up the fight against the enemy of the Lord.⁴⁹³

Membership and Election of the People of God

Perhaps no verse in Revelation more clearly points to the theme of election of the people of God than 17:14. Christians are described in 17:14 as "called" (cf. Rom 1:6; 1 Cor 1:24), "chosen" (cf. 1 Pet 2:9), and "faithful" (cf. Rev 1:5; 2:10, 13).⁴⁹⁴ This is the only occurrence of κλητός ("called") and

---

490. Aune, *Revelation 17–22*, 952; Beale, *Revelation*, 879; Osborne, *Revelation*, 622. Smalley acknowledges that God is the ultimate source of the kings' authority according to Rev 17:16, but still believes in 17:12 their authority is derived from the devil (cf. 13:2) (*Revelation*, 437–438). So also Thomas, *Revelation*, 301.

491. Koester, *Revelation*, 692; Smalley, *Revelation*, 438. Koester believes this passage "anticipates the battle of Rev 19:11–21" (Koester, *Revelation*, 679; so also Osborne, *Revelation*, 623; Thomas, *Revelation 8–22*, 302).

492. Aune, *Revelation 17–22*, 952; Koester, *Revelation*, 679; Schüssler Fiorenza, "Followers of the Lamb," 151–152; Smalley, *Revelation*, 438. Kistermaker refers to this group as the "Lord's followers" (*Revelation*, 476).

493. Several scholars believe the Lamb's followers fight with him in battle (Aune, *Revelation 17–22*, 956; Ladd, *Revelation*, 232; Mounce, *Revelation*, 319; Osborne, *Revelation*, 624). Aune takes "with him" as evidence of this. This is based on the idea of two types of apocalyptic holy war texts: one in which God wins the victory alone and his people are passive (Exod 14:13–14; 2 Kgs 19:32–35; Isa 37:33–36; 2 Chr 20), and another in which his people join the fight and participate in the victory (Joel 3:11b; Zech 14:5b). For more on apocalyptic holy war texts see Bauckham, *Climax of Prophecy*, 210–213. Against this view see Koester, *Revelation*, 680.

494. Koester, *Revelation*, 679.

ἐκλεκτός ("chosen") in Revelation.[495] Those who are "with" the Lamb belong to him and to God because he has graciously called and chosen them.[496]

Finally, the angel describes to John the destruction of the prostitute at the very hands of those who submitted to her authority (17:15–18). This is followed by an angelic[497] announcement of Babylon's demise (18:1–3) and a call for God's people to remain faithful lest they too fall as Babylon did (18:4–8). The angel's message is followed by a threefold woe over Babylon's demise (18:9–19). Those who profited most from Babylon's sins each take up singing one of the dirges.[498] The first to sing are "the kings of the earth" (18:9–10), followed by "the merchants of the earth" (18:11–17a), and finally those who made their living from the sea (18:17b–19).[499]

The final destruction of Babylon depicted in 18:21–24 is interrupted by a voice calling on all of God's people to rejoice over Babylon's destruction (18:20). Those who are encouraged to rejoice may be either in heaven or on earth, or perhaps both.[500] Typically the basis or ground for their rejoicing is narrowed[501] to either God's judgment of Babylon, based on the accusations she laid against God's people,[502] or his pronouncement of judgment against Babylon on behalf of the saints.[503] The former fits with the principle of retribution found throughout Rev 16–17 and 18:6, and so may be intended here, although one cannot be certain. In either case, God has judged Babylon; only the execution of her sentence awaits.

---

495. Aune, *Revelation 17–22*, 955; Smalley, *Revelation*, 439.

496. Osborne, *Revelation*, 624; Smalley, *Revelation*, 439.

497. Beale notes the voice may be that of God, Christ, or an angel representing God (*Revelation*, 898). Smalley does not believe "God" is likely since it would have him speaking of himself in the "third person" (*Revelation*, 446). For the same reason Mounce believes an angel is the voice (*Revelation*, 327). Aune (*Revelation 17–22*, 990) and Charles (*Revelation*, 2.97) identify the voice as that of Jesus.

498. Mounce, *Revelation*, 331; Osborne, *Revelation*, 644.

499. Ezekiel 26–27, the fall of Tyre, may be the backdrop to Rev 18:9–19 based on several similarities, including those who express lament (Beale, *Revelation*, 905; Mounce, *Revelation*, 331).

500. Mounce (*Revelation*, 336) and Thomas (*Revelation 8–22*, 341–342) believe the location is heaven, while Beale (*Revelation*, 916) and Osborne (*Revelation*, 653–654) believe both heaven and earth are in view.

501. Beale provides several more possibilities (*Revelation*, 917).

502. Aune, *Revelation 17–22*, 1008; Caird, *Revelation*, 228–230; Smalley, *Revelation*, 461.

503. Thomas, *Revelation 8–22*, 342–343.

This section closes with a heavenly scene of rejoicing over Babylon's end (19:1–5). Those pictured praising God are a "great multitude in heaven"[504] (19:1–3), and the "twenty-four elders and four living creatures" (19:4). Earlier the "twenty-four elders and four living creatures" were shown together worshiping the Lamb for his worthiness to loose the scrolls (5:6–10). In 19:4 they again prostrate themselves, this time before the throne of God, and affirm the earlier praise of the multitude (19:1–3).

Finally, a "voice" coming "from the throne" exhorts all God's "servants" to praise God (19:5).[505] Elsewhere in the book, the term "servant" is used of disciples of Christ in general and should be understood the same here. God's servants, Jesus followers, are made up of people from various social class distinctions, both "small and great." The reason they are entreated to praise God may be for the very the same reasons indicated in 19:2.[506] Most identify the location of this body of believers as earth,[507] while some believe they are in heaven.[508] Regardless of the precise location, the text teaches that all of God's people, all those who follow after the Lord Jesus Christ, are continually to join in praise of him.[509]

---

504. The "great multitude" may consist of angels (Aune, *Revelation 17–22*, 1024. Ladd, *Revelation*, 244; Thomas, *Revelation 8–22*, 355; Wall, *Revelation*, 220) and the entire people of God that includes the saints, apostles, and prophets (cf. Rev 18:20) (Beale, *Revelation*, 926). The entirety of the people of God may be more likely, given the context. In 18:20 the angel enjoins the people of God to rejoice and praise God for his judgment of Babylon, and in 19:2 the song of the "great multitude" is taken up with this theme. Further, the declaration of God's salvation (19:1) would be fitting of those he has redeemed, rather than angels (Koester, *Revelation*, 726; Mounce, *Revelation*, 341).

505. Some have understood the voice to be that of God or Christ (Beale, *Revelation*, 930), one of the twenty-four elders or the four living creatures beside the throne (Beckwith, *Apocalypse*, 721; Charles, *Revelation*, 2.124; Kiddle, *Revelation*, 378), or even an angel [Smalley notes this as a possibility (*Revelation*, 480)]. Most likely the voice is not that of God, since he would be speaking of himself in the third-person (Aune, *Revelation 17–22*, 1027; Osborne, *Revelation*, 666). Although one of the twenty-four elders or four living creatures are possible sources, perhaps it is best to come down with Aune who concludes, "the phrase 'from the throne' at the very least indicates the divine authorization of the speaker" whoever it may be (Aune, *Revelation 17–22*, 1027; so also Osborne, *Revelation*, 666; Smalley, *Revelation*, 480).

506. Beale, *Revelation*, 930.

507. Aune, *Revelation 17–22*, 1027; Kistemaker, *Revelation*, 511; Mounce, *Revelation*, 343; Osborne, *Revelation*, 666; Smalley, *Revelation*, 480.

508. Thomas, *Revelation 8–22*, 362.

509. The present tense of the imperative αἰνεῖτε ("praise") may indicate this (Wallace, *Greek Grammar*, 485).

SUMMARY

While only a couple of aspects of the theme of discipleship in this section were highlighted, several recurred; chief among them was discipleship language like "saints" (17:6; 18:20, 24) and "servants" (19:2, 5). On two occasions the description "saints" and on another occasion the term "servants" were coupled with mention of the suffering God's people endured for their commitment to follow Jesus (17:6; 18:24; 19:2). This reminds God's people that a servant is not greater than his master (John 15:20; cf. 13:16).

In addition, the term "servants" was found in the context of worship, in particular, an exhortation for all of God's people, from the greatest to the least, to worship God for his righteous judgment of Babylon (Rev 19:5). This is not the first time one of the themes of discipleship outlined in this study has been linked to worship, nor is it likely that it will be the last.

The two particular features of the discipleship motif in Revelation addressed in this section included the discipleship language "with him" (17:14), and membership and election of the people of God (17:14). The prepositional phrase "with him" appears to be used in the same vein as what is recognized as traditional discipleship language, like "following." With regard to membership and election of the people of God, the terminology of 17:14 could not be clearer. Those who are with Jesus are "called and chosen and faithful." Those who are with Jesus, who follow him as his disciples, do not do so according to their own efforts. Jesus, contrary to the majority of rabbis, called his own disciples. He chose them to enter into his discipleship. And so is the case with all who are with Jesus, all who have been invited to pattern their lives after his, and to fight the good fight under his Lordship (17:14).

AN ANALYSIS OF REVELATION 19:6—20:15

Revelation 19:6—20:15 takes the reader to the precipice of the last days. It begins with the bride preparing herself for the day of her wedding (19:6-8) and invitations sent out for guest to join the wedding feast (19:9-10).[510]

---

510. Revelation 19 on several occasions refers the wedding of the Lamb and his bride. The bridal imagery is especially thick in 19:6-9, but may also occur in 19:17. Similar imagery is repeated in 21:2, 9; 22:17. The imagery of Israel as God's bride occurs primarily in the OT prophetic literature (Isa 49:18; 54:5, 11–12; 61:10; 62:5; Jer 31:32). Fekkes believes the likely OT background to the bridal imagery in Rev 19:7-9; 21:2, 9, 18–21 is Isa 61:10 and 54:11–12 (Fekkes, "Isaian Nuptial Imagery," 269). Fekkes notes several

Before the wedding or feast may take place, though, the groom, the Lord Jesus Christ must come to vanquish his enemies, the beast and the false prophet and their allies in battle (19:11–21).[511] This vision is followed by one of Satan, the third member of the unholy trinity, being bound and later consigned to the lake of fire like all who rebel against God (20:1–10). The section concludes with a revelation of the judgment of the dead (20:11–15). Since it is not the purpose of this study to argue for a particular millennial position, the focus of this section is relegated to those passages that relate to the theme of discipleship in Revelation.[512]

Discipleship Language

This section begins with John hearing a sound like a "great multitude, like the roar of many waters and like the sound of mighty peals of thunder" praising God (19:6). This group is likely believers, based on the most recent description of a "great multitude" in 19:1 and verbal parallels found in 14:2–3.[513] The reason they praise God is "for [ὅτι] the marriage of the Lamb has come, and his Bride has made herself ready" (19:7b).[514]

---

aspect of the bridal imagery of Rev 19:7–9 that are found in antecedent Scripture, and particularly in Isa 61:10 and 54:11–12 (ibid., 270, 273, 275–282).

511. Some question whether those killed are limited to the army of the beast or if all earth dwellers are destroyed. Osborne believes the army is destroyed, leaving others alive to follow the dragon (Rev 20:7) during the millennium (20:1–10) (*Revelation*, 688). However, Koester (*Revelation*, 768), Boring (*Revelation*, 200), and Bauckham (*Theology of Revelation*, 102–103) believe the scenes of redemption and judgment are best understood rhetorically. The scenes of judgment and destruction serve to warn people of the sure end of all who oppose God, while the scenes of salvation urge people to continually follow Christ.

512. For a brief description of the various millennial perspectives one may wish to consult chapter 1 of this study or the brief overview provided in Osborne, *Revelation*, 696–697. For a helpful overview of the history of interpretation concerning Rev 20 see Koester, *Revelation*, 741–750.

513. In Rev 14:2–3 one finds a sound from heaven also likened to "the roar of many waters and like the sound of mighty peals of thunder." In 14:1–5 only the 144,000, that is, the entirety of the people of God, were able to sing the "new song" (14:3). This may indicate that the "great multitude" in 19:6 are also believers (Osborne, *Revelation*, 671–672).

514. Koester notes the different kind of imagery associated with Rev 19:7. There is the wedding imagery of first century Judaism with its yearlong betrothal period when the man made preparations for their new life together, and the woman pledged to remain faithful. Only after this period of time would the two celebrate their union with wedding guests. Second, there is the imagery of God as a husband, which is found in both the OT

Osborn takes the verb ἦλθεν ("has come") as a consummative aorist, which "emphasizes the arrival of the great event."⁵¹⁵ Thomas, on the other hand, takes ἦλθεν and ἡτοίμασεν ("has made ready") as proleptic or futuristic aorist. He views this as a latter event, since it does not fully come until the "consummation of the thousand years (20:3)," although he acknowledges that from "the perspective of the culmination of the seventh-bowl events [which he takes as 19:21], the marriage has come at last."⁵¹⁶

Christ coming refers to his *parousia*, when he will join with his bride, the church, and will inaugurate the great marriage supper of the Lamb.⁵¹⁷ Not much should be made of the term often translated "bride," γυνὴ, which is usually rendered "wife." This does not mean the bride and groom are already married, since it is possible to use γυνὴ for someone's wife even during the betrothal period (Matt 1:20).⁵¹⁸

That the "Bride has made herself ready" (Rev 19:7b) refers to her faithfulness and perseverance during the betrothal period. This is the only place the church is said to have prepared itself. Although precisely how she is to prepare herself is not mentioned, it may be that she has prepared herself by remaining "faithful" (2:10, 13; 13:10; 14:12; 17:14), consistently bearing witness to Jesus and keeping the teaching of Jesus (1:9; 6:9; 12:11, 17; 20:4), persevering through suffering (1:9; 2:2–3, 19; 3:10; 13:10; 14:12), and obeying God's commands (12:17; 14:12).⁵¹⁹

The wedding imagery continues with the bride being "given" (NIV) "fine linen, bright and pure" "to clothe herself" (19:8a). The verb ἐδόθη ("was given," NIV) is passive tense and likely points to God as the unnamed subject. He as sovereign initiates the marriage of the church to the Lamb.⁵²⁰

---

and NT (Ezek 16:8; cf. Jer 31:32; Isa 54:5; Hos 2; Eph 5:22–33). Third, Jesus is likened to the bridegroom (Matt 19:15; Mark 2:19–20; Luke 5:34–35; John 3:39; 2 Cor 11:2). Finally, the wedding imagery may be used with reference to eschatological salvation and the consummation of the Kingdom (Isa 25:6; 61:10; Matt 8:11–12; Luke 13:28–29; cf. Mark 14:25; Matt 26:29; Luke 22:18; 2 Cor 11:2) (Koester, *Revelation*, 728–729. See also Beasley-Murray, *Revelation*, 273–274). The last two feature prominently in Revelation.

515. Osborne, *Revelation*, 672. For more on the consummative aorist see Wallace, *Greek Grammar*, 559–561. According to Wallace's discussion of the consummative aorist, it is not clear whether or not the two aorists in Rev 19:7b (ἦλθεν and ἡτοίμασεν) should be understood in this manner.

516. Thomas, *Revelation 8–22*, 365; so also Mounce, *Revelation*, 347.

517. Mounce, *Revelation*, 347.

518. Ladd, *Revelation*, 247; Mounce, *Revelation*, 347.

519. Osborne, *Revelation*, 674.

520. Beale states that on several occasions (Rev 6:2, 4, 8, 11; 7:2; 8:2, 3; 9:1, 3, 5; 11:1,

The remainder of the verse explains what the image of the "fine linen" (βύσσινον) represents: "the righteous deeds of the saints" (τὰ δικαιώματα τῶν ἁγίων) (19:8b). If the fine linen represents "the righteous deeds of the saints" that she has done to make herself ready, then how can they also be something God has given? This apparent contradiction is normally handled in one of two ways.[521] First, it is possible to view the "righteous deeds" as evidence of one's salvation.[522] The garments the bride wears have already been cleansed in the blood of the Lamb (7:14; 22:14). Therefore, there is no works righteousness here, but simply fruit that is consistent with one's faith in Christ. A similar idea is found in Paul: one is saved by God's grace for good works, which God has prepared for his people to do (Eph 2:8–10). Second, some have taken the "righteous deeds" as God's just deeds on the believer's behalf. These are God's just and saving actions on behalf of his people.[523] Some take the ambiguous nature of the phrase as a possibility that both ideas are in view.[524] The syntax of the sentence allows for either. Those who support the first view take the genitive phrase τὰ δικαιώματα τῶν ἁγίων as a subjective genitive, meaning the righteous deeds the saints perform. If one is inclined to affirm the second position, then the genitive phrase is understood as an objective genitive, meaning the righteous deeds done for the saints.

The wedding imagery of Rev 19:7–9 concludes with mention of the invitation of the wedding guests (19:9). The angel instructs John to write: "Blessed are those who are invited to the marriage supper of the Lamb" (19:9a). While 19:7–8 portrays Jesus' disciples as his betrothed, here they are identified as wedding guests. Such mixing of metaphors is common in apocalyptic literature. If John is indeed mixing his metaphors, then God's relationship with the church is presented in two complementary ways. The church is presented as the people of God, both corporately and individually.[525] Just as God gave the garment to his bride, so also he is described here as

---

2; 12:14; 13:5, 7, 14, 15; 16:8; 20:4) in Revelation ἐδόθη with the dative indicates "sovereign provision" (*Revelation*, 943). So also Osborne, *Revelation*, 674.

521. Charles's way of dealing with the difficulty of the text is to identify it as a later gloss (*Revelation*, 2.127–128). So also Aune, *Revelation 17–22*, 1030.

522. Beasley-Murray, *Revelation*, 274; Koester, *Revelation*, 730–731; Mounce, *Revelation*, 347–348; Osborne, *Revelation*, 684; Roloff, *Revelation*, 212–213; Thomas, *Revelation 8–22*, 370–371.

523. Beale, *Revelation*, 935–938; Ford, *Revelation*, 311.

524. Beale, *Revelation*, 936, 941–942; Smalley, *Revelation*, 484.

525. Beale, *Revelation*, 945; Caird, *Revelation*, 234; Smalley, *Revelation*, 485. However,

inviting (κεκλημένοι, "who are invited") the guest to the wedding banquet.[526] This is similar to how those who were with Christ were described in 17:14 as his "called and chosen and faithful." It appears that election may be in mind here in 19:9a as it was in 17:14. The root of the participle "invited" is καλέω, which is used in the NT as a call to salvation (Matt 9:13; Rom 8:30; 9:24; 1 Cor 1:9; 2 Thess 2:14).[527]

The angel concludes, "these are the true words of God" (Rev 19:9b). This expression is similar to what one finds in the Pastorals: "the saying is trustworthy and deserving of full acceptance" (1 Tim 1:15; 3:1; 4:9; 2 Tim 2:11; Titus 3:8). Some take this statement to refer to the content of the entire book,[528] the book from chapter twelve to the end,[529] while others to a section of Revelation (17:1—19:8),[530] the wedding imagery (19:7–9),[531] and still others to the beatitude (19:9).[532]

In response to the angel's message John falls down to worship him (19:10a). However, the angel will have none of it, since he is a fellow servant with John and all Christians "who hold to the testimony of Jesus" (19:10b). Rather, John should "worship God." John is not to worship others who are also tasked with bearing witness to Jesus.

Wedding imagery also occurs in 19:17-18, where an angel invites birds to "gather for the great supper of God, to eat the flesh of kings, the flesh of captains, the flesh of mighty men, the flesh of horses and their riders, and the flesh of all men, both free and slave, both small and great." The text appears to be an allusion to Ezek 39:17–20. Some equate this meal

---

not everyone takes this view. Both Thomas (*Revelation 8-22*, 371–373) and Walvoord (*Revelation*, 270–273) see two groups. The bride is identifies as the church, while the invited guests, at least in the case of Walvoord, refer to old covenant saints (*Revelation*, 270–273).

526. Several commentators take κεκλημένοι as a divine passive: Ladd, *Revelation*, 250; Osborne, *Revelation*, 675; Thomas, *Revelation 8-22*, 371.

527. Beale, *Revelation*, 945; Ladd, *Revelation*, 250. Against see Johnson, "Revelation," 756.

528. Smalley, *Revelation*, 485–486.

529. Kiddle, *Revelation*, 381; Roloff, *Revelation*, 213.

530. Beasley-Murray, *Revelation*, 275; Mounce, *Revelation*, 349; Thomas, *Revelation 8-22*, 374.

531. Beale, *Revelation*, 945; Ladd, *Revelation*, 250; Johnson, "Revelation," 756; Osborne, *Revelation*, 676.

532. Wall, *Revelation*, 223.

with the wedding banquet to which others are invited in Rev 19:9,[533] while others believe the "great supper of God" means the supper is God's in the sense that he is the one who provides it, and not the same meal.[534] Others believe there is an intentional contrast between the two meals and therefore take the banquets as two distinct meals.[535] If 19:17 is a reference to the same meal, then it is possible that this eschatological meal expresses two realities. For those who are followers of Christ (the bride), the meal is a joyful celebration of the consummated Kingdom, and perhaps of the just judgment against God's enemies. For those who have fought against Christ and his people, the meal is the announcement of their demise and just end.[536]

Although it goes beyond the limits of Rev 19–20, similar bridal imagery appears in 21:2, 9. Therefore, it is addressed at this time. The term for "bride" (νύμφη) occurs in 21:2, 9. Most see this imagery as a continuation of the wedding imagery of 19:7–9. But how do the two passages complement one another? Is the New Jerusalem the home of the saints, or is it the saints themselves?

Gundry argues the New Jerusalem is the saints and not a place in which the saints dwell. His most noteworthy evidence includes the identification of those who overcome in 3:12 as "a pillar in the temple of my God." Christians are identified with a particular structure, the temple of God, his dwelling place with humanity.[537] A similar image of God dwelling with his people is taken up in 21:3, which is the immediate context of the bridal imagery of 21:2.[538] He also seems to understand 21:22 as reminiscent of language Jesus uses in his high priestly prayer of his disciples' union with him and the Father (John 17:21–23), which furthers the idea of Rev 21:2–3.[539] In addition, he notes that the language of 21:2, 9 has close parallels to 19:7–9.[540]

---

533. Beale, *Revelation*, 965; Koester, *Revelation*, 759; Roloff, *Revelation*, 220. Both Beale (*Revelation*, 965) and Smalley (*Revelation*, 497) note the two texts are linguistically linked by the phrase εἰς τὸ δεῖπνον ("to the marriage supper").

534. Mounce, *Revelation*, 357–358.

535. Aune, *Revelation 17–22*, 1063; Ladd, *Revelation*, 257; Osborne, *Revelation*, 687; Thomas, *Revelation 8–22*, 393–394.

536. Beasley-Murray, *Revelation*, 282.

537. Gundry, "New Jerusalem," 256.

538. Ibid., 257.

539. Ibid., 262.

540. Ibid., 257. See also Kevin E. Miller who takes all of Rev 19–22 as a depiction of the church as the bride of Christ ("Nuptial Eschatology," 301–318).

Mounce along similar lines connects this building imagery with the depiction of the saints as the temple of God in 1 Cor 3:16–17.[541]

Both Beale and Smalley separate the bridal imagery from the mention of the New Jerusalem. For them, the New Jerusalem is identified with God's "covenant fellowship, which God shares with his people in the new creations."[542] Aune likewise does not identify the New Jerusalem as God's people since: (1) the city is compared to a bride (Rev 21:2) and is not the bride itself, (2) the saints are to inherit the city (21:7), and (3) "the city is described as a place the saints dwell (21:24–26)."[543]

Osborne, on the other hand, argues the imagery of the city is intended to provide a contrast with Babylon, which is depicted as both a people and a place. So also, the New Jerusalem is a city in which God's people will dwell with him, as is evidenced in 21:2–3. It is also a place the saints will inherit (21:7–8), and the glory of the nations will be brought into it (21:24, 26). The New Jerusalem is also identified with the people of God themselves in 21:9–14, since there it is called "the Bride, the wife of the Lamb" (21:9), and its construction consists of the entirety of the people of God, where the

---

541. Mounce, *Revelation*, 382. Jan Fekkes III also argues for the bridal imagery as applied to the church extending from Rev 19–21, but along slightly different lines. Following a discussion of the specific bridal imagery from Rev 19–21, primarily as it relates to Isa 61:10 and 54:11–12, Fekkes concludes that there are three bridal units in Revelation: 19:7–9; 21:2; and 21:18–21, which are linked with one another by "connecting words: ἑτοιμάζω ('I make ready') (19:7) → ἑτοιμάζω – κοσμέω ('I adorn') (21:2) → κοσμέω (21:19)" ("Isaian Nuptial Imagery," 283). This move leads him to attribute the picture of the New Jerusalem in 21:18–21 as figurative, not necessarily of a city, but of a woman referred to as a city, which in this case is the bride of Christ, the people of God (ibid., 284–286). Furthermore, Fekkes sees the nuptial imagery of Rev 19–21 consistent with the betrothal and wedding period of the first century Jewish context. First is "the planning and final preparations stage: a formal wedding announcement is given; the marriage supper is arranged; and the guest list is finalized" (19:7–9). Second is the marriage ceremony itself (21:2). Finally is the descriptions of the bride's dress, her adornment, which is "anticipated in 21:2, 9" (21:18–21) (ibid., 283). First, he bases this on the depiction of the "great prostitute" (17:4; 18:16), which he believes is to be contrasted with the bride of Christ (21:18–21). Second, he sides with interpreters of Isa 54:11–12 who believe the imagery may have been used to suggest that Zion is an adorned woman. Finally, he looks to extrabiblical literature (*Jos. Asen.*) where a woman, who is previously described as a city, is later pictured as a beautifully adorned bride, similar to the imagery of Rev 21:18–21 (ibid., 283–285).

542. Smalley, *Revelation*, 536; so also Beale, *Revelation*, 1045.

543. Aune, *Revelation 17–22*, 1122.

Discipleship in the Book of Revelation

twelve tribes and twelve apostles are the gates and foundations of the city (21:12–14).[544]

What, then, might all of this wedding and bridal imagery contribute to one's understanding of discipleship? First, the image of the "bride" is clearly used to depict the people of God. It is unlike other discipleship language used earlier in the book (saints, servants, follow, etc.). This imagery superintends the remaining observations, which is why it falls under the heading of "discipleship language." Second, the way the bride is portrayed says something about how disciples of Jesus Christ are to look and respond to him. The bride is revealed as a faithful woman, who keeps her vow to her betrothed (19:7b). So also the church, individually and corporately, is to remain pure and undefiled. It is not to go after other gods, but to remain faithful to its husband and Lord, Jesus Christ. Third, the church shows evidence of its faithfulness to its Savior through "the righteous deeds" it does (19:8). These good deeds do not save, but rather show evidence of the salvation God has won for his people through his Son. Fourth, as invited guests to the wedding supper of the Lamb, the body of Christ are the elect of God (19:9a). He has graciously chosen them for himself (cf. 17:14). Therefore, the proper response is always worship for what God alone has accomplished (19:10a). Finally, disciples of Jesus Christ are to bear witness to him, motivated by the Spirit (19:10c).

Witness to "Greater Things"

Revelation 19:11–16 provides a picture of the risen Christ, glimpses of which have occurred elsewhere (1:16; 2:15–16, 18; 5:5; 14:1, 14, 17–20; 17:14). The scene shifts abruptly from the wedding supper to the image of a rider atop a white horse poised for battle (19:11). The imagery is thoroughly Jewish and reflects their "tradition of a warrior Messiah."[545] And yet, the idea of Christ coming again to punish his enemies is not out of step with the NT (Matt 25:41; 2 Thess 1:7–8). The truth is that Jesus is revealed

---

544. Osborne, *Revelation*, 733; so also Thomas, *Revelation 8–22*, 442.

545. Mounce, *Revelation*, 351. Both Beale and Mounce believe Jewish apocryphal literature stands behind the image of Christ as warrior Messiah. Beale (*Revelation*, 950) believes 3 Macc 2 serves as the likely background, while Mounce (*Revelation*, 351) thinks 2 Bar 72 and *Pss. Sol.* 17:23–27 stand behind Rev 19:11–16. Aune (*Revelation 17–22*, 1048–1050) notes several possible extrabiblical allusions including Wis 18:15 and *T. Mos.* 10:3–7. He also includes Isa 63:1–3, where God is described as "a blood stained divine warrior" (ibid., 1048).

as both conquering warrior and the joyous hope of the saints with reference to his second coming (2 Thess 1:9–10).⁵⁴⁶ Christ is coming again both to judge the wicked and deliver his own.⁵⁴⁷

The "white horse" likely symbolizes purity and holiness, as well as a victorious conqueror.⁵⁴⁸ The name of the rider is "Faithful and True" (Rev 19:11b).⁵⁴⁹ If this is a title, it is the first of four in 19:11–16. Jesus is called the "faithful and true" witness in 3:14. There, as here, it occurs in the context of judgment. Jesus is shown to be "faithful to his promises [to judge and deliver] and will in due time vindicate the faith of all who place their confidence in him."⁵⁵⁰

Next, John describes Jesus' eyes and head: "his eyes are like a flame of fire, and on his head are many diadems" (19:12a). Jesus' eyes depicted as "a flame of fire" has occurred earlier in the book (1:14; 2:18). There, as here, the image points to his ability to penetrate the hearts of people, knowing their thoughts, but also suggest the ability to destroy with his gaze.⁵⁵¹ That he has "many diadems" ("many crowns," NIV) indicates his absolute sovereignty over all created things.⁵⁵² Some see a contrast between the description of the dragon (12:3) and the beast (13:1) who also wore crowns. While Christ's many crowns indicate his total sovereignty, the crowns of the dragon and the beast were limited, as was their authority.⁵⁵³

Christ also has a "name written on him that no one knows but he himself" (19:12b, NIV).⁵⁵⁴ What is this name? Is it the name "the Word of God"

---

546. Mounce, *Revelation*, 351.

547. Koester, *Revelation*, 754.

548. Koester, *Revelation*, 753; Mounce, *Revelation*, 352. Beale believes "white" may also convey the idea of "juridical vindication of truth through judgment," in keeping with Rev 14:14 and 20:11 (*Revelation*, 950).

549. Scholars are divided on whether or not καλούμενος πιστὸς καὶ ἀληθινός ("called Faithful and True") are original to the text. Aune (*Revelation 17–22*, 1042) and Smalley (*Revelation*, 471–471) believe the participle καλούμενος is not original, while Koester (*Revelation*, 753) believes its omission in some manuscripts was accidental, and therefore, it should be included. Metzger notes the committee included the reading καλούμενος πιστὸς καὶ ἀληθινός because it is thought to have been either accidentally or purposefully omitted (*Textual Commentary*, 685–686).

550. Mounce, *Revelation*, 352.

551. Beale, *Revelation*, 951–952; Koester, *Revelation*, 754; Mounce, *Revelation*, 353.

552. Koester, *Revelation*, 754.

553. Beale, *Revelation*, 952; Caird, *Revelation*, 241; Mounce, *Revelation*, 353.

554. Some scholars conjecture as to where the name is found. Some believe it is engraved on his crown (Beale, *Revelation*, 955; Smalley, *Revelation*, 489), while others

or "King of kings and Lord of lords?" Koester provides three of the most common answers. First, the name is that which appears on his robe, "King of kings and Lord of lords" (19:16b). The idea is that the passage moves from secrecy to disclosure in the same context. In 17:5 the name of the great prostitute is called a mystery, but a mystery that is shortly revealed; her name is Babylon the Great.[555] Second, it may be a name that will remain unknown until the end of the age.[556] Finally, some take this secret name to be the divine name of God, the *tetragrammaton*.[557] Beale also wonders if the secret is not so much the name itself, but the meaning of the name. He believes the "name" (singular) should be understood figuratively, so that the significance of the "name" is relative to the experience of the individual, whether he be one of the redeemed or one of the reprobate.[558] The secrecy of his name may also indicate the inability of finite human minds to fully comprehend who Jesus truly is.[559] While one cannot be certain, perhaps it is best to side with one of the figurative meanings, either that of Beale or Beasley-Murray, as they seem to be have fewer difficulties.

The image of Christ moves from his head to his clothing, which is a "robe dipped in blood" (19:13a). Isaiah 63:1–3 is the possible background to this image. The Isaiah passage focuses on God's judgment of Edom, whom God tramples as grapes in a wine press, which results in their blood splattering on his garments. The image is of the wicked thrown into the winepress of God's judgment (Rev 14:17–20). The one obstacle this view must overcome is that the time of judgment envisioned in Rev 19 has yet to take place (19:17–21), although Christ's robe is already stained with blood. Some work around this problem by noting the blood on Jesus' garments anticipates the judgment of sinners in 19:17–21.[560] Beale points to the "nature of the prophetic genre, which describes future events as past or present in

---

believe it is written on his head (Alford, *Greek Testament*, 4.727), and still others believe it is on his robe (Koester, *Revelation*, 755).

555. Koester, *Revelation*, 755.

556. Aune, *Revelation 17–22*, 1056; Osborne, *Revelation*, 682; Thomas, *Revelation 8–22*, 385.

557. Beale, *Revelation*, 954; Smalley, *Revelation*, 490–491.

558. Beale, *Revelation*, 956; so also Smalley, *Revelation*, 491. Similarly Johnson, "Revelation," 758.

559. Beasley-Murray, *Revelation*, 279–280; Mounce, *Revelation*, 353.

560. Aune, *Revelation 17–22*, 1057; Mounce, *Revelation*, 354; Roloff, *Revelation*, 218; Thomas, *Revelation 8–22*, 386.

order to stress the certainty of their occurrence."[561] However, some are still convinced that the blood on Jesus' robe is either that of the saints[562] or his own blood of redemption.[563] The most likely alternative is to understand the blood as Jesus' own. Those arguing for this position note that his blood brings "victory over evil (12:11)."[564] They also stress the battle has yet to take place, so that the blood of Jesus' enemies is not in view. The greatest difficulty with this position is the strong allusion to Isa 63:1–3, which speaks clearly about judgment of God's enemy. Although both Boxall and Koester recognize Rev 19:13 alludes to Isa 63:1–3, they believe it is recast for John's own distinct purposes.[565] In the end, it seems more plausible that the blood is of Jesus' enemies, given the allusion to Isa 63 and the previous image of judgment depicted as a wine press in Rev 14.[566]

John also mentions that the warrior's name is "the Word of God" (19:13b). This is the only occurrence in Revelation where "Word" functions as a title for Christ, similar to what one finds in John 1:1, 14.[567] While in John the "Word" refers to Jesus' self-disclosure to humanity, here in Rev 19:16b it indicates the manner in which he executes judgment, by his word (cf. 19:15a).[568]

John also sees "the armies of heaven, arrayed in fine linen, white and pure" following Jesus. They too are riding "white horses" (19:14). The heavenly army is composed of either angels[569] or God's people,[570] or perhaps both.[571] It is likely that the best alternative is the last one since Scripture indicates that angels accompany Christ at his second coming (Matt 13:41; 16:27; 25:31; 1 Thess 3:13; 2 Thess 1:7; Jude 14), as do his elect (Rev 17:14).

---

561. Beale, *Revelation*, 959.

562. Caird, *Revelation*, 243–244. Caird bases this on the unconvincing interpretation that Rev 14:17–20 refers to the blood of the martyrs (ibid., 192–195).

563. Boxall, *Revelation*, 274; Koester, *Revelation*, 755–756.

564. Koester, *Revelation*, 756.

565. Boxall, *Revelation*, 274; Koester, *Revelation*, 756.

566. Osborne's provides a brief and helpful defense of this view (*Revelation*, 682–683).

567. Aune, *Revelation 17–22*, 1058; Koester, *Revelation*, 756.

568. Aune, *Revelation 17–22*, 1058; Beale, *Revelation*, 958; Koester, *Revelation*, 757; Mounce, *Revelation*, 354.

569. Beasley-Murray, *Revelation*, 281; Ladd, *Revelation*, 255; Roloff, *Revelation*, 219.

570. Beale, *Revelation*, 960; Charles, *Revelation*, 2.135–136; Smalley, *Revelation*, 493; Wall, *Revelation*, 231–232.

571. Mounce, *Revelation*, 354; Osborne, *Revelation*, 684.

Discipleship in the Book of Revelation

In addition, Revelation depicts both angels (4:4; 15:6) and God's people (3:4-5; 6:11; 7:9, 13-14; 19:8) wearing white garments.[572]

Revelation 19:14 may include discipleship language, namely, ἠκολούθει ("were following"). This is only one of two instances in Revelation where ἀκολουθέω ("I follow") is applied to believers following Jesus (cf. 14:4). As in 14:4, it may indicate discipleship. In 14:4 Jesus' disciples were said to follow him wherever he goes. In 19:14 where he goes is into battle.[573]

Revelation 19:15 includes three activities of Jesus taken from the OT. The three images taken together portray "the total conquest and destruction the returning Christ will achieve over the nations."[574] First, he is said to "strike down the nations" with a "sharp sword" that comes "from his mouth" (19:15a). Second, Jesus is said to "rule them with a rod of iron" (19:15b). Third, the final activity is treading the "winepress of the fury of the wrath of God the Almighty" (19:15c; cf. 14:17-20).[575]

This scene comes to a close mentioning the name written on Jesus' "robe,"[576] "King of kings and Lord of lords" (19:16). That Jesus is "King of kings and Lord of lords" indicates that he is sovereign over all (cf. 17:14).[577] Both in the OT (Deut 10:17; Ps 136:2-3; Dan 2:37, 47; 8:25; 11:36) and NT (1 Tim 6:15) similar titles are always used of God.[578]

What might this vision of Christ contribute to the theme of discipleship in Revelation? As noted earlier in this chapter, Jesus promised his

---

572. Osborne, *Revelation*, 684.

573. Osborne questions whether or not the heavenly army fights with Christ or if Christ singlehandedly wins the battle (*Revelation*, 684). Thomas seems to indicate that Christ alone fights (*Revelation 8-22*, 389), while Miller maintains, "armies ... fight along with their leader," and argues accordingly ("Nuptial Eschatology," 315-316).

574. Osborne, *Revelation*, 684.

575. Osborne takes the phrase τοῦ θυμοῦ as an epexegetical genitive and τῆς ὀργῆς as an adjectival genitive, leading to the translation of Rev 19:5c, "He treads the winepress, namely, the furious wrath of God almighty" (*Revelation*, 685). Wallace seems to categorizes each accordingly: τοῦ θυμοῦ as a genitive of apposition (*Greek Grammar*, 95) and τῆς ὀργῆς as attributive genitive (ibid., 86-87). So also Aune, *Revelation 17-22*, 1044; Beale, *Revelation*, 963. Aune notes that this is the longest string of genitives in the book (ibid., 1062).

576. Aune takes the καὶ as epexegetical or ascensive, so that "on his thigh" explains "on his robe," meaning the name was written underneath his robe where the robe covers his thigh, as when riding a horse (*Revelation 17-22*, 1044; so also Koester, *Revelation*, 759; Osborne, *Revelation*, 686; Thomas, *Revelation 8-22*, 390).

577. Johnson, "Revelation," 760.

578. Osborne, *Revelation*, 686; Thomas, *Revelation 8-22*, 391.

disciples that they would be witnesses to "greater things," namely, "revelations of God's glory in Christ."[579] Even as Rev 1:12–16 and Jesus' identification to the seven churches of Asia Minor (2:1, 8, 12, 18; 3:1, 7, 14) may have provided a picture of such revelations for John, so also this image of Jesus in 19:1–6 may be included among the "greater things" his disciples would see. The connection between the two earlier visions and the vision of Jesus in Rev 19 are the robe he wore (1:13; 19:16), his eyes that blazed like fire (1:14; 19:12; 2:18), the sword coming out of his mouth (1:16; 19:15; cf. 2:13), and his identification of himself as "holy and true" (3:7) and the "faithful and true witness" (3:14), which are encompassed in the title "Faithful and True" (19:11). These bookends of images remind not only John's audience, but also all disciples of Jesus Christ of his authority over all things and all peoples. To those Christians who may be suffering because of their identification with Christ, the image of Jesus in 19:1–6 should be of great comfort. Their suffering is not in vain. Those who seem to be escaping punishment for their crimes will one day have to answer to the Lord himself, who will judge and destroy those who have rebelled against him and persecuted his church. Moreover, the image of the warrior Messiah should encourage the persecuted church to continue to follow after Christ, for in the end he will be seen by all to be the King of kings and Lord of lords. Who they follow is absolutely worth following. They may also be encouraged that he has heard their prayers, as he has the prayers of the saints under the altar (6:10–11), and will one day avenge his holy people. Since he is the one to avenge his people, there is no room for revenge. Vengeance is the Lord's, and he will repay it accordingly (Deut 32:35; Rom 12:19).

Distinction between Jesus' Disciples and Non-Disciples

The next text related to the theme of discipleship occurs in Rev 20:12–13 in the context of the "great white throne" judgment (20:11). God is the one who sits in judgment,[580] or possibly the Father and the Son are both engaged in judgment.[581] John not only sees one sitting on a "great white throne," but also the "dead, great and small, standing before the throne" (20:12a). The people standing before the throne are either all of humanity,[582]

---

579. Köstenberger, *John*, 87.
580. Koester, *Revelation*, 779.
581. Beale, *Revelation*, 1031; Osborne, *Revelation*, 720; Thomas, *Revelation 8–22*, 429.
582. Mounce, *Revelation*, 376; Koester, *Revelation*, 779.

possibly the saints of God with the unbelievers mentioned in 20:13–14,[583] or only the reprobate.[584]

The "books were opened" and "another book was opened, which is the book of life" (20:12b). The first group of books is often taken to contain the deeds of unbelievers[585] and possibly believers as well (cf. Isa 65:6; Dan 7:10; Mal 3:16), since elsewhere believers are also identified as "great and small" (Rev 19:18).[586] If it includes the works of believers, then these provide the basis for which they will be rewarded.[587] The second book, "the book of life," was also opened (cf. Dan 12:1–2). In Revelation, "the book of life" is often found in contexts that speak of those whose names are not included in it (Rev 3:5; 13:8; 17:8; 20:15), but it may have positive associations (21:27). The names in the book of life are those who have received "the gift of life with God."[588] Mounce remarks on the difficulty associated with determining the relationship between the two books.[589] One way to clear it up is to understand the phrase "the dead were judged by what was written in the books, according to what they had done" (20:12c) as a reference to the first set of "books" that were opened, the books of deeds.[590] Even if the books and the book of life are those that were opened up, it does not mean that the fitness of one's entrance into the New Jerusalem is based on one's good works. In fact, no one's works are sufficient to enter the kingdom of God.[591] The works one does serve as evidence of where one's allegiance is. If one's name is recorded in the book of life, then one will have corresponding good works to show evidence of it in the books of deeds. The two go hand in hand (cf. 19:8).[592]

Next, John sees the "sea" give up its dead, and "Death and Hades" give up the dead that were in them, and "they were judged, each one of them, according to what they had done" (20:13). Some take this as the judgment

---

583. Both Beale (*Revelation*, 1034) and Osborne (*Revelation*, 721) mention this as a possibility.

584. Thomas, *Revelation 8–22*, 430–431.

585. Koester, *Revelation*, 780; Thomas, *Revelation 8–22*, 431.

586. Beale, *Revelation*, 1033.

587. Osborne, *Revelation*, 722.

588. Koester, *Revelation*, 780.

589. Mounce, *Revelation*, 376–377.

590. Aune, *Revelation 17–22*, 1102.

591. Ladd, *Revelation*, 274.

592. Smalley, *Revelation*, 517; Wall, *Revelation*, 241.

of the unrighteous,⁵⁹³ while others wish to include all of humanity.⁵⁹⁴ Although the judgment of people occurs in 20:12, this does not mean that 20:13 is out of order as Charles maintains.⁵⁹⁵ Aune understands 20:12–13 as an instance of "*hysteron-proteron*, i.e., the arrangement of events in the reverse of their logical order."⁵⁹⁶ He finds occurrences of this in 3:3, 17; 5:5; 6:4; 10:4, 9; 22:14.⁵⁹⁷ After giving up their dead, both "Death and Hades were thrown into the lake of fire" (20:14). The "lake of fire" is the final punishment of the wicked after their resurrection at the close of the age (2:11; 20:6, 14; 21:8).⁵⁹⁸ It is "eternal and final" death (20:10; cf. Matt 3:12; Mark 9:43; Luke 3:17; Rev 14:10–11),⁵⁹⁹ complete separation from the joy of God's presence.⁶⁰⁰

This section comes to a close with a warning to those whose names are not found written in the book of life. They will follow death and Hades into the lake of fire (Rev 20:15). It is also possible, and perhaps more likely, that 20:15 should be understood as an appeal on the part of John to encourage his audience, the church, to heed what he says, for in doing so one may receive eternal life.⁶⁰¹ The appeal is geared toward perseverance of the saints in their walk with Christ.

Beale asks the question, "What is it about the 'book of life' that spares them?"⁶⁰² He finds his answer in 21:27 (cf. 13:8); the book of life is "the Lamb's book of life." There are two genitive phrases contained in the prepositional phase ἐν τῷ βιβλίῳ τῆς ζωῆς τοῦ ἀρνίου ("in the Lamb's book of life"). The first τῆς ζωῆς ("of life") may be a genitive of apposition, meaning

---

593. Osborne, *Revelation*, 723; Thomas, *Revelation 8–22*, 432–433.

594. Aune, *Revelation 17–22*, 1103; Beale, *Revelation*, 1034; Smalley, *Revelation*, 518.

595. Charles, *Revelation*, 2.194–198.

596. Aune, *Revelation 17–22*, 1102.

597. Smalley argues along different lines that it is not necessary to believe Rev 20:13 originally occurred before 20:12 (*Revelation*, 518).

598. Koester, *Revelation*, 781.

599. Keener, *Revelation*, 470; Roloff, *Revelation*, 232. Against eternal punishment see Harrington, *Revelation*, 206.

600. Beale, *Revelation*, 1036.

601. Revelation 20:15 is a first class conditional sentence "in which the author attempts to get his audience to come to the conclusion of the apodosis (since they already agree with him on the protasis). It thus functions as a tool of persuasion" (Wallace, *Greek Grammar*, 692).

602. Ibid., 1037.

this is the book that is life.[603] The second genitive phrase τοῦ ἀρνίου ("of the Lamb") is either a possessive genitive or a genitive of source, either of which has the idea that life is found in the Lamb.[604] It is important for one's name to be in the book precisely because of whose book it is and what he has done for those whose names are in it. Beale draws this connection together noting, "the 'life' granted the saints in association with the book comes from their identification with the Lamb's righteous deeds, and especially his death, which means likewise that they are identified with his resurrection life (cf. 5:5–13). They do not suffer judgment for their evil deeds because he has already suffered it for them: he was slain on their behalf."[605] However, for those whose names are not in the "book of life" their only ground for God accepting them is their own deeds, which in the end cannot save them from destruction.

SUMMARY

Revelation 19:6—20:15 contains several references to the theme of discipleship as articulated in chapter three. This section included an analysis of discipleship language, in particular the imagery of the "bride" of Christ (19:6–9, 17; 21:2, 9; 22:17). Additional aspects of discipleship language that were not specifically addressed in this section include "servant" (19:10) and "saints" (19:8; 20:9). The depiction of the church, both corporate and individual, as the bride of Christ has a rich history in the NT. However, the use of such language in Revelation is essentially limited to the closing chapters of the book. Two reasons for this are the presentation of Jesus as the bridegroom and the use of wedding imagery with reference to eschatological salvation and the consummation of God's kingdom. With Rev 19 the picture of Christ's second coming comes more into focus. Since this is the case, it makes sense that wedding imagery would be utilized at this place in Revelation. What one may learn from the identification of "bride" with Jesus' disciples relates to how they respond to him (they are to faithfully follow him), how they live their lives (they produce good works, which evidence their faith in Christ and bear witness to him by the power of the Spirit), and the relationship they have with him (he has graciously chosen them).

---

603. Smalley seems to understand it this way (*Revelation*, 517).
604. Beale, *Revelation*, 1037.
605. Ibid.

The discipleship motif of witness to "greater things" was also discussed in this section. It is interesting to see how this vision of Christ in 19:11–16 repeats much of the same imagery introduced in the first three chapters of the Apocalypse. The "greater things" to which John bore witness were a vision of the Lord Jesus Christ, not as a slain Lamb, but as the Messianic divine warrior come to fight his enemies and win. For the disciple of Jesus this picture should elicit hope, rather than lead one to recoil at the bloody spectacle, for those who suffer in this world do not suffer in vain. Their Lord will return to exact justice for their suffering at the hands of wicked people. Not only will they escape his wrath, but they will also be victorious with him. They are also reminded of his faithfulness to his promises to his people. He will set all wrongs to rights, but not yet. This will come in its fullness at his second coming.

The "book of life" (20:12, 15) or "Lamb's book of life" (21:27; cf. 13:8) provides evidence of the discipleship theme of distinction between Jesus' disciples and non-disciples. Several other images occur in this section that fall under this category, including: the mark of the beast versus those who bear God's seal (19:8; 20:4), worship of the beast versus those who worship God alone (19:4, 10, 20; 20:4), and being made holy by Christ's own blood (7:14; 22:14) versus those who remain stained by sin, which the imagery of clean garments versus spoiled garments appears to suggest (19:8; cf. 3:4; 18:2). In particular, the imagery of having one's name included or excluded from the book of life was discussed (20:12, 15). Having one's name in the Lamb's book of life results in eternal life and entrance into the New Jerusalem, while those whose names are not found therein are cast into the lake of fire, forever excluded from the joyous presence of God. John attempts to persuade his audience, which includes all true disciples of Jesus, to persevere in their faith, for in doing so they show evidence of their salvation and can be assured that their names are recorded in the book of life.

Two additional aspects of discipleship in Revelation that occur in this section, but were not discussed because they have been treated elsewhere, are bearing witness to Christ (20:4) and consequences of following Jesus, which in the case of 20:4 is to suffer death. Those who died in this manner were raised to resurrection life and reign with Christ (20:4, 6), and function as "priests of God" (20:6). To disciples facing death for bearing witness to Christ this would be of great comfort. They would be reminded that this world is not the end, and that they may anticipate rewards, which include a resurrected body and being in Christ's presence.

Discipleship in the Book of Revelation

AN ANALYSIS OF REVELATION 21:1—22:5

The next to last section of the book of Revelation includes a description of a new heaven and a new earth (Rev 21:1),[606] the inauguration of the New Jerusalem (21:2), God's declaration to his people of his immediate and permanent presence with them (21:3–8), a symbol-laden description of the New Jerusalem as the Holy of holies (21:9–27), and the new order as a restored Garden of Eden (22:1–5). The following analysis is essentially focused on 21:3–8, since several discipleship themes are tightly compacted into this small number of verses, and additional themes have been treated earlier in this study.[607]

Revelation 21:3–8 provides a summary of the entire book.[608] This passage contains several allusions to antecedent Scripture, including several OT texts, most of which are drawn from Isa 60 and 65, Ezek 40–48, and Gen 1–3,[609] and even references to earlier passages from Revelation. With regards to the associations of Rev 21:3–8 with earlier passages in the book, this text seems to be a reiteration and expansion of what is promised in 7:15–17. In addition, there are several links to the seven churches of Asia Minor. In Rev 21 one finds the fulfillment of Jesus' promises to those

---

606. There is some disagreement concerning whether or not the earth in the age to come is completely new or a renewed earth. Several commentators opt for "new" meaning a completely new order of things, so much so that the previous earth is burned up and completely done away with (Beasley-Murray, *Revelation*, 307; Roloff, *Revelation*, 235; Mounce, *Revelation*, 375; Thomas, *Revelation 8-22*, 439). Others believe the "new" earth is simply a renovation of the old order. The earth is renewed or reborn (Bauckham, *Theology of Revelation*, 49–50; Caird, *Revelation* 265-266; Ford, *Revelation*, 364-365; Wall, *Revelation*, 247; Aune, *Revelation 17-22*, 1116–1120). Others attempt to show that although the earth is "new," it does not lack continuity with the old earth, much like the glorified bodies of the saints are new but seem to have continuity with the old body, at least by way of their appearance (both are physical bodies and are recognizable, as in the case of Jesus' resurrected body). Osborne is an example of someone who views continuity, but still believes the earth is totally new (*Revelation*, 730). On the other hand, Beale (*Revelation*, 1040) and Koester (*Revelation*, 795, 803) are examples of those who recognize continuity and understand the new earth as one being renewed.

607. An additional reason for focusing on Rev 21:3–8 is that this section serves "simultaneously as an introduction to and an exposition of the following visionary section depicting the New Jerusalem (21:1 is taken up in 22:1–5; 21:2 in 21:9–11; 21:3 in 21:22f and 22:3; 21:4 in 22:2; 21:6 in 22:1; 21:7 in 22:4; 21:8 in 21:26f and 22:3)" (Schüssler Fiorenza, *Revelation*, 109).

608. Michaels, *Revelation*, 235.

609. Johnson, "Revelation," 776; Osborne, *Revelation*, 727. Mounce emphasizes the allusions to Gen 1–3 (*Revelation*, 379).

churches. For instance, those who overcome receive the tree of life (2:7; cf. 22:2); the saints get the right to rule the nations (2:26; cf. 22:5), and are united with God in the New Jerusalem (3:12; cf. 21:2, 9–27).[610]

Revelation 21:3–8 begins with John hearing an unnamed voice call out from the throne (21:3). This is not the first unnamed voice John has heard. This one is loud (cf. 11:12; 12:10; 16:1, 17) and stands alone. Although it is possible for the unidentified voice to be God's, since God is the one who sits on his throne (21:5),[611] this is unlikely since he is referred to in the third person (21:3; cf. 19:5).[612] In addition, the voice in 21:5 comes from one "seated on the throne," which provides juxtaposition with the voice of 21:3 that calls out "from the throne." In 21:5 the voice is most likely God's. In 21:3 Jesus or an angel is also a possibility,[613] but it may be best to conclude whoever the speaker is, he speaks as one authorized to speak on God's behalf as in 19:5.[614]

Union with Christ

The voice announces, "the dwelling place of God is with man" (21:3a). The noun σκηνὴ ("dwelling place")[615] is used in the LXX for the tent (Exod 33:7–11) or tabernacle (25:9) in the wilderness, where God dwelt in the midst of Israel.[616] The verb from the same root σκηνόω ("I dwell") also occurs in Rev 21:3 and may refer to "God's covenant" with his people.[617] The passage seems to be an allusion to either Lev 26:11–12 or Ezek 37:27.[618]

---

610. Johnson, "Revelation," 776; Smalley, *Revelation*, 541–542; Osborne, *Revelation*, 736.

611. Beale, *Revelation*, 1046.

612. Aune, *Revelation 17–22*, 1122; Thomas, *Revelation 8–22*, 443.

613. Smalley believes it is the voice of an angel (*Revelation*, 537). So also Osborne, *Revelation*, 733.

614. Koester, *Revelation*, 797.

615. Some scholars believe the term σκηνὴ alludes to the Hebrew term *shekinah*, used for God's presence (Mounce, *Revelation*, 383; Osborne, *Revelation*, 734; Smalley, *Revelation*, 538; Thomas, Revelation 8–22, 444). Koester disagrees "since the term *shekinah* was not commonly used before the second century (Koester, *Revelation*, 797; see also Mounce, *Revelation*, 383).

616. Koester, *Revelation*, 797; Mounce, *Revelation*, 383; Thomas, *Revelation 8–22*, 443.

617. Koester, *Revelation*, 797.

618. Beale, *Revelation*, 1046; Smalley includes several other OT allusions (Exod 29:45;

The voice continues, God "will dwell with them, and they will be his people, and God himself will be with them as their God" (Rev 21:3b).[619] This language recalls God's covenant with Israel (Jer 7:23; 30:22; 31:1, 33; 32:38; Ezek 11:20; 36:28; 37:23) and his promise to dwell with the church (2 Cor 6:16). Revelation 21:3b is a fulfillment of that promise.[620] While the ESV translates the plural λαοί "people," which is perfectly acceptable, perhaps it should be translated as a plural noun ("peoples") in order to make the connection to the "persons from every tribe and language and people and nation" (NIV, cf. 5:9; 7:9; 14:6) who will inhabit the New Jerusalem.[621]

The union of God with his people is emphasized all the more by the repetition of God being "with" or "among" (μετά) his people.[622] This underscores the fact that in the new age God is present with his people. The fellowship the Triune God experiences with his people will be unbroken, unhindered, and eternal.[623]

One of the discipleship themes that make up the coding frame is union with Christ. Up until this point, Revelation has not included a clear reference to this theme, although perhaps it has been assumed throughout the book. But here, in 21:3 the language used is a clear depiction of the discipleship theme of union with Christ. In the Pauline epistles union with Christ includes a "whole host of experiences" the believer shares "with Christ," including: "suffering (Rom 8:17); crucifixion (Gal 2:20); death (Col 2:20); burial (Rom 6:4); quickening (Eph 2:5); resurrection (Col 3:1); glorification and inheritance (Rom 8:17)."[624] In Rev 21:6 the emphasis is on God being present with his people and they with him. The idea of abiding with Christ that is so prominent in John's Gospel, of personally communing with Jesus, is heightened in this text. The kind of union with Christ envisioned here is not only of the fellowship one experiences with him through the internal presence of the Holy Spirit, but is perhaps more akin to what Jesus' earthly

---

Ps 46:4; Jer 31:33; Zech 2:10–11; 8:8) (*Revelation*, 537). So also Osborne, *Revelation*, 734.

619. The phrase "as their God" (αὐτῶν θεός) is a textual variant. The ESV and NIV include this reading, while the NASB goes with a different reading. The ESV and NASB include footnotes recognizing additional readings.

620. Koester, *Revelation*, 797–798.

621. Beale, *Revelation*, 1047; Koester, Revelation, 798; Smalley, *Revelation*, 538; Osborne, *Revelation*, 734; Thomas, *Revelation 8–22*, 444.

622. Thomas believes Rev 21:3 echoes 7:15, but μετά replaces ἐπί in 21:3. For Thomas, the change to μετά "suggests an even closer bond of fellowship" (*Revelation 8–22*, 433).

623. Burke, *Message of Sonship*, 230.

624. Erickson, *Christian Theology*, 962.

disciples experienced in Christ's first advent. They were daily present with him in the flesh. It appears that 21:6 leaves room for Jesus' disciples to once again, one day experience this sort of relationship with him, one in which he dwells in their midst physically and they with him. For Jesus' disciples this experience of unfettered access to him should cause great joy and hope. The present joy his disciples experience in their current state of being in his presence through the Spirit is but a foretaste of the full-blown reality that awaits them in the *eschaton*. The effects of sin on Jesus' disciples and this broken world keep Jesus from fully uniting with his bride, the church. However, his disciples have hope as they eagerly await the consummation of his Kingdom, including the reality of dwelling unhindered in the presence of God forever.

The suffering associated with this world will come to an end, never to affect the people who dwell in God's presence (21:4a). God is personally depicted as wiping away the tears of his beloved children.[625] The "former things" (21:4b) refers either to the previous line of thought: death, mourning, crying, and pain (21:4a),[626] or to "the disappearance of the first heaven, the first earth, and the sea" (21:1).[627] The description of the *new* order of things is couched in terms of "what it replaces [rather] than by an attempt to describe what is largely inconceivable in our present state."[628] These things will cease in the new age.

For what is possibly only the second time in the book, God speaks (21:5; cf. 1:8).[629] God announces he is making[630] "all things new," and com-

---

625. Johnson calls this a "touching metaphor of motherly love" ("Revelation," 780). Thomas highlights the fact that the phrase "every tear" (πᾶν δάκρυον) is singular, which "focuses on God's great compassion for the individual even to the point of noticing infinitely small minutia" (*Revelation 8–22*, 445).

626. Koester, *Revelation*, 798; Mounce, *Revelation*, 383.

627. Aune, *Revelation 17–22*, 1125; Roloff, *Revelation*, 236; Smalley, *Revelation*, 539.

628. Mounce, *Revelation*, 383–384; so also Smalley, *Revelation*, 539; Thomas, *Revelation 8–22*, 445.

629. Johnson, "Revelation," 780; Mounce, *Revelation*, 384; Smalley, *Revelation*, 539; Osborne, *Revelation*, 736. Against see Beasley-Murray who believes God is still relaying his message through an intermediary (*Revelation*, 312). Thomas believes there are two persons who speak to John in Rev 21:5–8. The first voice is God who declares, "I am making all things new." The second voice is an angel who instructs John to "write this down." Finally, God resumes as the speaker in Rev 21:6 (*Revelation 8–22*, 447).

630. The verb ποιῶ is present tense and should be taken as a futuristic (prophetic) present, thus guaranteeing that it will come to pass (Wallace, *Greek Grammar*, 535). Both Beale (*Revelation*, 1053) and Osborne (*Revelation*, 736) understand the present this way.

mands John to record these things because they are "trustworthy and true" (21:5). Even as God is trustworthy and true (6:10; 15:3), so also are his words (21:5b; 22:6).[631]

God declares, "They have come to be" (γέγοναν)[632] (author's translation) (21:6a). The announcement likely refers to "the eschatological events that are part of the eternal plan of God,"[633] which include both judgment and salvation.[634] Thomas specifically believes the perfect tense verb refers to everything God is making new in 21:1–5, and in particular, 21:5a.[635] God draws attention to his role as absolute sovereign and Creator of everything with the titles, "the Alpha and the Omega, the beginning and the end" (21:6b).[636]

Believe in Jesus

God is the source of all life, and as such he is able to give water "from the spring of the water of life" (21:6c). This is possibly an allusion to Isa 55:1. Living water is flowing water that one might find in a spring, as opposed to still water that may be found in a cistern (Gen 26:19; Lev 14:6). But that is not exactly what the text describes. It refers to "the spring of the water of life." The source of the spring is the throne of God (Rev 22:1), and the water of life flows through the New Jerusalem (22:2). Koester finds a distinction between the "living water" featured prominently in John's Gospel as a metaphor for eternal life mediated by the Spirit, and drinking from "the water of life" in Revelation, which he takes to mean "resurrection to endless life in God's presence."[637] Smalley appears to take the two ideas as synonymous, both referring to spiritual life or eternal life in the presence of God and Christ, received by faith in Jesus.[638] In the end, both Koester and

---

631. Aune believes the phrase πιστοὶ καὶ ἀληθινοί ("trustworthy and true") is an *hendiadys*, that is, two words used to form one idea (*Revelation 17-22*, 1126). So also Smalley, *Revelation*, 540.

632. The verb γέγοναν is perfect plural, which the ASV attempts to convey, "they are come to pass." So also Beale, *Revelation*, 1054; Thomas, *Revelation 8-22*, 448.

633. Aune, *Revelation 17-22*, 1126; so also Johnson, "Revelation," 780; Mounce, *Revelation*, 385; Osborne, *Revelation*, 738.

634. Beale, *Revelation*, 1054–1055; Smalley, *Revelation*, 540.

635. Thomas, *Revelation 8-22*, 448; so also Beale, *Revelation*, 1054.

636. Bauckham, *Theology of Revelation*, 26; Beale, *Revelation*, 1055.

637. Koester, *Revelation*, 800.

638. Smalley, *Revelation*, 541; so also Beale, *Revelation*, 1056; Osborne, *Revelation*,

Smalley seem to be in general agreement as to the meaning of "the water of life" in 21:6c. While Smalley hints at the idea of faith in Jesus to receive "the water of life," Osborne overtly views God's offer of "water" as "an invitation to the unsaved."[639] The genitive phrase τοῦ ὕδατος τῆς ζωῆς ("the water of life") may be a genitive of apposition, meaning the water that is life.[640] Aune notes several verbal parallels between 21:6c and John 4:4–16.[641] Despite these similarities, he believes this does not show dependence, but instead a common background.[642]

The discipleship theme of believing in Jesus has been rare in Revelation. And while Rev 21:6c does not depict someone coming to faith in Christ for salvation, the idea may still be present, particularly if Osborne is correct that the "water of life" God offers is an "invitation to the unsaved."[643] In this sense, it appears at least possible that what God offers is to experience eternal life, through belief in his Son, which is similar to Jesus' offer to the woman at the well in John 4. For that matter, one may include the numerous distinctions between Jesus' disciples and non-disciples scattered throughout Revelation. In each instance they provide a choice to the reader, to either follow Christ or follow the course of this world. In this way Revelation is an evangelistic book, calling on its readers to come to Christ and follow him, and for those who are already his disciples, to remain resolute in their commitment to Jesus' discipleship.

Membership and Election of the People of God

The language of sonship that God directs to the redeemed indicates "the affection with which he cherishes us as his children."[644] Amidst the symbolic language associated with the descriptions of a new heaven and a new earth, there is the concrete language of family. Osborne takes 21:7b as a summary of the Abrahamic covenant (Gen 17:7) and the Davidic covenant (2 Sam 7:14).[645] Thus, the language God uses is covenantal in nature and consistent

---

738–739.

639. Osborne, *Revelation*, 738.
640. See Smalley, *Revelation*, 541.
641. Aune, *Revelation 17–22*, 1128–1129.
642. Aune, *Revelation 17–22*, 1129; so also Koester, *Revelation*, 800.
643. Osborne, *Revelation*, 738.
644. Burke, *Message of Sonship*, 226.
645. Osborne, *Revelation*, 740.

with the idea of election of his people. The difficulties of this life, no less than suffering persecution for the name of Christ, will cease to be a reality for Jesus' disciples in the age to come (Rev 21:4). However, those hearing or reading the Apocalypse still live in the midst of a fallen and broken world, thus the motivation to persevere through suffering and to be victorious, since it is the "victorious[646] [that] will inherit all this," the "all this" referring to 21:1–6 (21:7a, NIV).[647] The one who is victorious is so because the Son was victorious. It is being in relationship with him that results in his disciples, God's children,[648] receiving the inheritance and experiencing the joys associated with a new heaven and a new earth.[649]

Distinction between Jesus' Disciples and Non-Disciples

Although the redeemed are God's adopted sons and daughters, there are those who stand outside of this relationship (21:8).[650] The vice list in 21:8 may be compared to the "positive quality possessed by members of the new Jerusalem, and acknowledged already among the churches addressed in the seven oracles of Rev 2–3."[651] God's children experience the benefits of dwelling in his presence, the cessation of sorrow and mourning and death (21:4). However, for everyone else, misery and sorrow and pain will not

---

646. The NIV translates the singular present participle ὁ νικῶν as a plural, "those who are victorious," which is perfectly acceptable.

647. Burke, *Message of Sonship*, 229; Johnson, "Revelation," 780; Koester, *Revelation*, 800; Smalley, *Revelation*, 542. Aune restricts "all this" (ταῦτα) to the benefits of Rev 21:4 (*Revelation 17–22*, 1129). Mounce believes "all this" refers to the promises of Rev 2–3 (*Revelation*, 385–386; so also Beale, *Revelation*, 1057–1058). Osborne takes a much broader referent of "all this" to refer to all of God's promises, "since this [Rev 21:3–8] is in effect a summary of the book" (*Revelation*, 739).

648. The term the NIV translates "children" (υἱός) is actually singular, rather than plural. Smalley believes it is acceptable for a singular to include a corporate dimension, particularly in light of a possible allusion to 2 Sam 7:14, where the singular "son" also includes a corporate dimension (*Revelation*, 542).

649. Beale, *Revelation*, 1057–1058; Smalley, *Revelation*, 542.

650. Smalley believes Rev 21:8 could be "an interpolated comment" of John, rather than the voice of God (*Revelation*, 542).

651. Smalley, *Revelation*, 544; so also Beale, *Revelation*, 1059. Smalley notes the following comparisons: cowardly vs. fearless (Rev 2:10) and conquerors (3:21); faithless vs. faithful (2:19); the vile, murderers, sexually immoral, sorcerers vs. unsoiled (3:4), persevering (3:8); idolaters vs. those who have not denied Christ's name (3:8); and liars vs. those who keep Jesus' word (3:10) (*Revelation*, 544).

cease, but will continue for eternity (21:8; cf. 14:10–11; 20:10).[652] This is their inheritance (τὸ μέρος αὐτῶν).[653]

SUMMARY

Revelation 21:1—22:5 includes several references to the theme of discipleship, the greatest concentration of which occurs in 21:3–8. Apart from those discipleship themes addressed in the previous analysis, the following also occurred: the marks of discipleship, specifically obeying God's word (21:5), believing in Jesus, which may be evidenced through the language of overcoming (21:7), the discipleship language of "servants" who "serve" (22:3), and the distinguishing of Jesus' disciples from non-disciples through imagery of the book of life (21:27) and the Lamb's name being on his disciples' foreheads (22:4). But what of the rest included in the former analysis? What do they contribute to the idea of discipleship in Revelation?

First, the imagery of union with Christ, in Rev 21:3 indicates the close relationship between the Lord and his followers. The imagery revealed in this verse is of God being with his people, similar to his being present with his old covenant people through the tabernacle in the wilderness, and perhaps closer to what John describes in the first chapter to his Gospel, of the Word coming to dwell among people (John 1:14). In his earthly ministry, Jesus was daily with his disciples and they with him. The imagery of Rev 21:3 of constantly being in God's presence is similar to the relationship Jesus experienced with his first disciples. However, while Jesus left his disciples to return to the Father, and along with the Father sent the Holy Spirit to abide in his disciples, the picture in Revelation is of unending close personal fellowship with the Father and the Son (cf. 21:22). As noted in the analysis of this section, for the disciple of Jesus Christ this future reality may be a source of hope, as his disciples eagerly anticipate the experience of full joy in his presence forever.

Second, God's offer of "the water of life" is one he extends to two groups: those who have yet to drink from its fountain, and those who are his own, whose thirst for God is satisfied by him. To the one who is not a

---

652. Beale argues that the antithesis between "first" and "second," and "old" and "new" suggests a contrast between the time of incompletion (this present age) and the consummated age to come. In the case of Rev 21:8, the "second death" is final and fixed, and thus, eternal (*Revelation*, 1060–1061).

653. Thomas, *Revelation 8–22*, 452.

disciple of Jesus, this offer to drink of the water of life is an offer to believe in Jesus alone for one's salvation. To his disciples who currently freely drink from the free gift of God, the offer to partake of this water is to spur one to remain faithful to Christ and to remind one that true life is found only in Jesus. As such, one is to daily seek to drink from him, to find one's spiritual nourishment from him, to continually feast on his presence.

Third, the language of sonship found throughout Scripture and here in 21:7 points to God's election of the disciple. If one is a disciple of Jesus Christ, then one is God's child. To his children he promises that one day they will experience the cessation of all suffering and the unending presence of God (21:1–6). And this is something they may be assured of even now, since the word of the one who declares this is "trustworthy and true" (21:5). Although one may experience hardships in this life, there is coming a day when sorrow will give way to unadulterated joy.

Finally, once again Revelation presents a vision of how Jesus' disciples are distinguished from non-disciples. Earlier in the book the differences were largely situated around the character of the individual. One is faithful, while the other is faithless. Something like that is described in 21:7–8 as well. Jesus' disciples are called "conquerors," while those who are not his disciples are described as "the cowardly, the unbelieving, the vile, the murders, the sexually immoral, those who practice magical arts, the idolaters and liars" (21:8, NIV). But more than that is at stake here. For those who are victorious pain ends and they dwell with God in the New Jerusalem forever (21:1–4). However, for those who are not Jesus' disciples, they will continue to experience unending suffering in the lake of fire (21:8) as they find themselves outside of the city of God (21:27). The reward and realization of one's present life, either as a follower of Christ or as a follower of the prince of the power of the air, is a distinction that will echo through the corridors of eternity.

AN ANALYSIS OF REVELATION 22:6–21

The revelation to John draws to a close by noting the trustworthiness of the book's contents (Rev 22:6–7), followed by commands from an angel (22:8–11), the final sayings of Christ (22:12–20), and a benediction (22:21). There are numerous parallels between the epilogue (22:6–21) and prologue

(1:1–20).[654] In a way the epilogue and the prologue form an inclusio of the entire book.[655]

Revelation 22:6–21 begins with an unnamed voice speaking to John. Some have identified this voice as none other than Christ;[656] others believe it is that of an angel (NIV, ESV), perhaps the interpreting angel for the entire book,[657] or the angel who showed John the New Jerusalem in 21:9, 15 and 22:1.[658] The angel that recently appeared in Rev 21 is probably in view. The angel declares the trustworthiness of the revelation John received and the purpose for which it was sent, "to show [δεῖξαι] his servants what must soon take place" (22:6). The "servants" are all Christians, in keeping with how δοῦλος is used throughout the book (1:1; 2:20; 7:3; 19:2, 5, 10; 22:3, 9).[659]

Come to an Understanding of Jesus' Person and/or Work

Christ and his words to the church feature prominently in the epilogue (22:7, 12–19). In both 22:7 and 12 Jesus' words are introduced with the particle ἰδού ("See!" "Behold!"), which is used "to highlight critical prophetic oracles,"[660] and is often used to relate something to the reader about Jesus' person and work (1:7, 18; 3:20; 5:5; 14:1, 14; 16:15; 19:11; 21:3, 5; 22:7, 12).

The phrase "Behold, I am coming soon" (ἰδοὺ ἔρχομαι ταχύ) is repeated in this section (22:12, 20), and occurs earlier in 2:16 and 3:11.[661] Similar terminology occurs in 22:6, 10, and 17.[662] A blessing accompanies Jesus'

---

654. Some include: "show his servants" (Rev 1:1; 22:6), authenticating the books from God (1:1; 22:6), "what must soon take place" (1:1; 22:6), beatitude (1:3; 22:7), "words of the prophecy" (1:3; 22:7, 10), keeping the words of the book (1:3; 22:7), "I am coming soon" (1:3, 7; 22:7, 12, 20), the challenge to be faithful (1:3, 6; 22:7, 9, 11, 14, 17), and "the Alpha and the Omega" (1:8; 22:13) (Osborne, *Revelation*, 777–778. See also Thomas, *Revelation 8–22*, 494).

655. Aune takes the similarities between 1:1–3 and 22:6–7 as evidence of an inclusio of the entire book (*Revelation 17–22*, 1188).

656. Charles, *Revelation*, 2.217.

657. Aune, *Revelation 17–22*, 1182; Smalley, *Revelation*, 567.

658. Beale, *Revelation*, 1123; Beasley-Murray, *Revelation*, 334; Koester, *Revelation*, 837; Mounce, *Revelation*, 403; Osborne, *Revelation*, 780; Thomas, *Revelation 8–22*, 495.

659. Bauckham, *Climax of Prophecy*, 85–86.

660. Osborne, *Revelation*, 69.

661. In Rev 2:16; 3:11; and 22:20 the phrase lacks ἰδού.

662. There is some question as to what it means that Jesus is coming soon. Several commentators believe it refers to Jesus' immanent return (Aune, *Revelation 17–22*, 1184; Blount, *Revelation*, 402; Mounce, *Revelation*, 404; Osborne, *Revelation*, 781–782;

announcement of his second coming (22:7), as well as an encouragement or warning (22:12), depending on the relationship of the individual to Christ (22:7, 12). In the first instance, Jesus' blessing is directed to the one who obeys his teaching. In the second instance, Jesus promises rewards for each person according to the works they have done in this life. A "reward" (NIV) (μισθός) can refer to something either positive or negative.[663] In both the OT and NT, God is the one who judges people to repay them for their works (Pss 28:4; 62:12; Prov 24:12; Jer 17:10; Rom 2:6; 2 Tim 4:14; Rev 20:11–14), but here it is ascribed to Christ (Rev 22:12).[664] Elsewhere, Jesus is portrayed as an eschatological judge (Matt 16:27; John 5:22; Acts 10:42; Rom 2:16; 2 Thess 1:7–11), and Rev 22:12 (cf. 2:23) falls in line with that tradition.[665] For Christians their reward is the fullness of their salvation, and for the unrighteous there is only judgment.[666] His coming soon acts as the basis for "ethical commitment" (22:10–12; cf. 2 Pet 3:11–14).[667] For disciples of Jesus Christ the promise of rewards and the threat of judgment may serve to motivate them to continue to follow faithfully after him.

This section also includes several titles the Lord attributes to himself. As in Rev 21:6b, the compound title, "the Alpha and the Omega, the first and the last, the beginning and the end" should probably be taken together as one title. It is significant that God also declares himself to be "the Alpha and the Omega" (1:8), "the beginning and the end" (21:6), and the "first and the last" (Isa 44:6; cf. 41:4; 48:12). Since Jesus too claims this for himself, it clearly identifies him with the one true God. Even as God is absolutely sovereign and the creator of everything, so also is Jesus. Even as God is eternal, so also is the Son. Even as the Father is the "origin and goal of all history," so is Christ.[668] This picture of Jesus would be of encouragement to the disciples of Jesus Christ, since the one they follow is in control of all

---

Thomas, *Revelation 8–22*, 497), while Beale seems to hold that it refers to Jesus' coming to the church in "blessing and judgment" throughout the present age that will be consummated at his second coming (Beale, *Revelation*, 1127; so also Koester, *Revelation*, 851). Beale also notes that Jesus' second coming is soon in the context of salvation history. The next event after Pentecost is his second coming (*Revelation*, 1135).

663. Koester, *Revelation*, 841; Osborne, *Revelation*, 788; Thomas, *Revelation 8–22*, 504–505.

664. Koester, *Revelation*, 841.

665. Aune, *Revelation 17–22*, 1218–1219; Ladd, *Revelation*, 292.

666. Mounce, *Revelation*, 407; Smalley, *Revelation*, 572.

667. Osborne, *Revelation*, 787; so also Beale, *Revelation*, 1138.

668. Bauckham, *Theology of Revelation*, 27, 55.

things, including human history, which is moving to a glorious end for all who submit to and serve Christ.

In Rev 22:16b Jesus calls himself the "root" of David, a messianic title found in Isa 11:1-5 and one that occurred earlier in Rev 5:5. In Isa 11 the root of David is a militaristic leader (11:4). This understanding would be compatible with the immediate context of Rev 22:16b, which describes the judgment of the wicked (22:14). The "descendant of David" may be an allusion to 2 Sam 7:12, in which God promised David that one of his descendants would reign on his throne forever. Jesus fulfills this promise as the forever Davidic king whose rule will see no end. The final title "bright morning star" is an allusion to Balaam's oracle that stated a ruler would come from the line of Jacob to rule the nations (Num 24:17). Jesus is the one who not only rules over the nations, but swiftly defeats them.[669] This vision of Christ affirms that he is the Messiah King he said he was during his first advent. As such, his disciples can be assured of his judgment of the wicked, many of whom set their hearts to rebellion against God and the persecution of his church.

Marks of Discipleship (Keep Jesus' Teaching)

Revelation 22:7b contains the sixth of seven beatitudes in the book (1:3; 14:13; 16:15; 19:9; 20:6; 22:7, 14). Here and in 1:3 the blessing is not defined, although some general understanding of one's well-being is probably in mind,[670] or perhaps the consummation of salvation as evidenced from "blessed" in 14:13; 16:15; 19:9; 20:6 and 22:14.[671] Like 1:3 and 16:15 the blessing is for the one who "keeps the words of the prophecy of this book" (22:7b; cf. 22:9, 18–19).[672] The verb τηρέω ("I keep") refers to being obedient to do something, which in this case is keeping "the words of the prophecy of this book."[673] Since this revelation has come from Jesus, then the book refers to everything John recorded, all that Jesus disclosed to him in the book of Revelation (cf. 1:1–2).

---

669. Osborne, *Revelation*, 793.
670. Koester, *Revelation*, 130.
671. Beale, *Revelation*, 1127.
672. Osborne, *Revelation*, 782.
673. Osborne believes the genitive phrase οὓς λόγους τῆς προφητείας τοῦ βιβλίου τούτου ("the words of the prophecy of this book") is an epexegetical genitive [genitive of apposition], which further defines the kind of "words" that are to be kept (ibid.).

Discipleship in the Book of Revelation

Because these words are from Jesus, this may be an instance of one of the marks of discipleship, namely, keeping Jesus' words. By keeping Jesus' words his disciples show their undying faithfulness to him.[674] Jesus' disciples are promised a blessing if they obey his words. The time of this blessing is not defined, so that it may be something Jesus' disciples experience in the present, as well as at his second coming. For those who would have endured hardship and perhaps witnessed the relatively comfortable lives of the ungodly, the beatitude would remind them that obeying Christ's words and remaining in right fellowship with him is of greater value than any momentary creature comforts or even the absence of suffering. But the blessing is likely for the future as well and may have related to the persecution and injustice Jesus' disciples faced in this present world. One day such suffering would come to an end; Jesus' faithful servants would be vindicated, and could expect the blessing of fellowship with him in the New Jerusalem. Whether one were to emphasize present or future blessings, the intent appears to be that disciples of Jesus are to encourage one another, based on Jesus' promised blessing, to persevere to the end "knowing that God views such people favorably and will bring them to a better future."[675]

John indicates that he is the one who "heard and saw" the prophecy he wrote down (22:8a). Just as he did in 19:10, John falls before the angel to worship him, but is quickly reprimanded for doing so and commanded to "Worship God" (22:8b–9).[676]

The angel follows up this command with a prohibition: "do not seal [μὴ σφραγίσῃς] up the words of the prophecy of this book, for the time is near" (22:10). The angel follows this with some of the most difficult words in the book (22:11). For some scholars the language speaks to the certainty of what will take place,[677] while others attempt to soften the angel's words.[678]

---

674. Koester, *Revelation*, 839; Osborne, *Revelation*, 782.

675. Koester, *Revelation*, 132; so also Boring, *Revelation*, 67.

676. "God" (τῷ θεῷ) is fronted for emphasis. The article with God may express that this God is unique as compared to other gods (monadic use of the article). Often the verb προσκυνέω ("I worship") occurs with the dative case "when true deity is the object of worship," as is the case in Rev 22:9, τῷ θεῷ προσκύνησον (Wallace, *Greek Grammar*, 172).

677. Beale, *Revelation*, 1132.

678. This is done in various ways. For instance, Koester emphasizes the rhetorical function of this verse, which was intended to lead the ungodly to cease in their ways and to follow after Christ, and for the righteous to remain faithful. It is an appeal, rather than a statement of one's fixed position (*Revelation*, 853; so also Beasley-Murray, *Revelation*, 338; Smalley, *Revelation*, 571–572). Hendricksen essentially views the imperatives as permissive imperatives (*More Than Conquerors*, 208. For more on permissive

It is interesting that those who represent both positions believe the language used in Rev 22:11 has a rhetorical function. The question of intent remains. While one cannot be certain, it is at least possible that this verse is intended to awaken the elect remnant, who are unbelievers prior to coming to faith in Christ, to saving faith, and to encourage those who follow Christ to remain steadfast in their commitment to him.

Distinction between Jesus' Disciples and Non-Disciples

Revelation 22:14a is the seventh and final beatitude in the book.[679] Here the implied unclean persons are distinguished from "those who wash their robes." Under the old covenant physical uncleanness required washing to purify oneself or one's clothes (Lev 11:25; 13:6; 14:8; Num 31:24). Uncleanness could also be the result of sin and so not only required ritual washing, but also the appropriate sacrifice to atone for one's sin (Num 8:21). Here in Rev 22:14, "washing is a metaphor for the removal of sin that occurs through repentance and faith in the redemptive action of Christ."[680] As such, it refers to all Christians,[681] and not only Christian martyrs as some contend.[682] This verse almost certainly does not refer to water baptism, since the participle οἱ πλύνοντες ("those who wash") is in the present tense, which may indicate consistent "repentance and faith rather than the single washing of baptism, which was done to a person by someone else."[683] Given this

---

imperatives see Boyer, "Classification of Imperatives," 37; so also Thomas, *Revelation 8–22*, 502–503). Mounce (*Revelation*, 406) and Ladd (*Revelation*, 292) believe the end is so near that the opportunity to change one's ways will not exist. Ramsey Michaels believe the passage speaks to the reality of good and evil until the second coming of Christ and does not pertain to individual persons, per se (*Revelation*, 252–253).

679. Smalley believes in Rev 22:14–15 that John is the speaker, not Christ (*Revelation*, 573). John also gives a beatitude at 1:3 and 20:6.

680. Koester, *Revelation*, 842; so also Aune, *Revelation 17–22*, 1219; Osborne, *Revelation*, 789; Thomas, *Revelation 8–22*, 506. Similarly Smalley, who believes the metaphor refers to ongoing moral and spiritual renewal (*Revelation*, 573). Johnson believes this image symbolizes "salvation that involves obedience and discipleship" ("Revelation," 788). Similarly, Mounce attributes the image of washing one's robes to faithfulness to Jesus and a refusal to submit to the beast (*Revelation*, 407). It would appear that he has Rev 3:4 in mind. Beale seems to follow Mounce (*Revelation*, 1139).

681. Beale, *Revelation*, 1140; Beasley-Murray, *Revelation*, 340; Thomas, *Revelation 8–22*, 506.

682. Caird, *Revelation*, 285.

683. Koester, *Revelation*, 842; so also Aune, *Revelation 17–22*, 1220.

is the case, it is unlikely that it refers to them having washed their robes in the blood of the Lamb (7:14), although it is certainly the basis for them continuing to wash their own garments.[684]

Those who live a life of repentance and faith can expect to be rewarded with access "to the tree of life" and may enter "the city" (22:14b).[685] The ground for access "to the tree of life" and the ability to enter "the city" is the atoning blood of Christ and not one's works.[686] The works serve to indicate who is worthy to enter, but are not the basis of one's worthiness.[687] The tree of life points back to Gen 1–3, where eating of its fruit was associated with eternal life in the presence of God (cf. 3:22–24). This is likely the meaning here.[688] The city in which they may enter is the city of God, the New Jerusalem (Rev 22:3, 11).[689] It is also possible to understand entering into the city as another way of referring to the imagery of access to the tree of life.[690] If this is the case, then both refer to experiencing full salvation, which includes dwelling in the presence of God forever.

Revelation 22:15 offers a comparison to those described in 22:14 and provides an example of negative rewards (cf. 22:12). While those who continue to live lives characterized by repentance and faith in Christ experience eternal fellowship with God, those who are "the dogs and sorcerers and the sexually immoral and murderers and idolaters, and everyone who loves and practices falsehood" are not granted access to fellowship with God (22:15), since they are consigned to the lake of fire (20:15; 21:8).[691] The comparison between those in 22:14 and those in 22:15 begins with identifying who is clean and unclean. In 22:14 there are those who wash their robes, while in 22:15 there are those who are identified as dogs, who

---

684. Ladd, *Revelation*, 293; Osborne, *Revelation*, 790.

685. The ἵνα clause may be purpose or result, although result seems to be more likely since it is connected to one's reward. Osborne thinks it indicates result (*Revelation*, 790 n. 10).

686. Smalley, *Revelation*, 574.

687. Beale, *Revelation*, 1139.

688. Aune, *Revelation 17–22*, 1222; Koester, *Revelation*, 842; Ladd, *Revelation*, 293; Osborne, *Revelation*, 790; Smalley, *Revelation*, 574.

689. Aune believes the language of entering into the city is metaphorical of entering into the kingdom of God, and therefore, refers to salvation (*Revelation 17–22*, 1222). So also Beale, *Revelation*, 1140; Mounce, *Revelation*, 407.

690. Mounce, *Revelation*, 407.

691. Beale, *Revelation*, 1142; Beasley-Murray, *Revelation*, 341–342; Thomas, *Revelation 8–22*, 507.

ate unclean things (Exod 22:15).[692] The designation "dog" is often used of wicked persons and those who practice unrighteousness (Ps 22:16, 20; Phil 3:2).[693] It is possible that it refers specifically to those who engage in cult prostitution (Deut 23:17–18) and would therefore parallel "the sexually immoral" in Rev 21:8.[694] To call someone a dog is to associate him with all things that make one unclean (cf. 21:8, 27) and therefore an unbeliever. The remainder of the list picks up on items mentioned earlier in 21:8. As was the case in 22:14, the participles in 22:15 (φιλῶν, ποιῶν) are in the present tense and imply repeated or habitual behavior. This is not the description of someone struggling to overcome besetting sin, but someone who willfully followed the course of this world, rather than the way of God, which may be applied to those inside (false Christians) and those outside of the church.[695]

As noted earlier, one of the things that distinguish Jesus' disciples from non-disciples is their action in response to him, as well as the future they can expect to inherit. Here, Jesus' disciples are characterized by lives of repentance and faith in Christ, and their reward is dwelling joyfully in the presence of God forever. This does not mean that Jesus' disciples do not succumb to temptation and sin, since they recognize their need to be washed; they repent of their sins. In doing so, Christians recognize they are weak and dependent on God. They cannot faithfully follow Christ of their own initiative, but need his continued help through the indwelling Holy Spirit, and the ordinary means of grace like prayer, Scripture reading, and regular fellowship with the saints.

Believe in Jesus

In Rev 22:17 the "Spirit and the Bride"[696] extend an offer to come and experience "the free gift of the water of life" (NIV). The relationship between

---

692. Koester, *Revelation*, 842; Smalley, *Revelation*, 574.

693. Johnson, "Revelation," 788; Ladd, *Revelation*, 294; Mounce, *Revelation*, 408.

694. Aune, *Revelation 17–22*, 1222–1223; Charles, *Revelation*, 2.178; Ford, *Revelation*, 345, 347.

695. Beale, *Revelation*, 1141.

696. The identity of "the Spirit and the Bride" is variously interpreted. Some believe it refers to Christ (Osborne, *Revelation*, 787), the Holy Spirit and Christ (Beasley-Murray, *Revelation*, 335), the Spirit and the church (Beale, *Revelation*, 1148; Harrington, *Revelation*, 91, 225–226), the prophetic spirit of the church and the church (Bauckham, *Theology of Revelation*, 117–118; Kiddle, *Revelation*, 456; Roloff, *Revelation*, 252; Smalley, *Revelation*, 578), the Spirit through John and the church (Aune, *Revelation 17–22*, 1228;

the call to "come" in 22:17a and to drink of the water of life in 22:17b has been variously interpreted.[697] The position that finds the greatest support is the one that takes the first two imperatives as directed to Christ to come, while the last two are directed to unbelievers.[698] Thus, the passage includes a request from believers for Jesus to come and an appeal to unbelievers to accept God's free gift of salvation while there is still time.

This final appeal is in line with the heart of God that takes no pleasure in the death of the wicked, but would rather see his image bearers live (Ezek 18:23, 32; 33:11; cf. 2 Pet 3:9). It is also in keeping with Jesus' heartbrokenness over the lostness of the inhabitants of Jerusalem expressed in the Gospels: "O Jerusalem, Jerusalem, the city that kills the prophets and stones those who are sent to it! How often would I have gathered your children together as a hen gathers her brood under her wings, and you were not willing!" (Matt 23:37; cf. Luke 13:34) Jesus' desire should be the longing of his disciples as well. The lostness of humanity and the sureness of the final judgment should compel Jesus' disciples to offer the gospel freely as Jesus offers it freely to those who stand in opposition to him.

Jesus continues by offering a warning to anyone who might add to or take away from the content of the book (Rev 22:18–19).[699] This may refer to either tampering with the text itself, or more likely a warning against falsifying "the scroll's message by one's teaching or manner of life," so as to lead others into idolatry.[700] The consequences for doing so are dire. Those who add to the scroll can be assured of experiencing the "plagues described

---

Koester, *Revelation*, 856), and the Spirit of Christ and the church (Charles, *Revelation*, 2.179).

697. The following is a sampling of the most often cited interpretations: a call to repent and to come to faith in Christ (Ladd, *Revelation*, 294–295; Mounce, *Revelation*, 409), a response to Jesus announcing his coming and participation in the Eucharist (Aune, *Revelation 17–22*, 1228–1229, 1237; Roloff, *Revelation*, 252–253), a command to the people of God to persevere to receive one's reward (Beale, *Revelation*, 1149–1150), and a call to repentance and for Christians to commit to persevere (Osborne, *Revelation*, 794).

698. Beasley-Murray, *Revelation*, 343–345; Smalley, *Revelation*, 577; Thomas, *Revelation 8–22*, 511–513.

699. Some take the speaker as John (Roloff, *Revelation*, 253; Smalley, *Revelation*, 583; Wall, *Revelation*, 268), however, the speaker is probably still Christ since he is the speaker of Rev 22:16 and the witness in 22:20 (Koester, *Revelation*, 844; Mounce, *Revelation*, 410; Osborne, *Revelation*, 794).

700. Koester, *Revelation*, 844; so also Beale, *Revelation*, 1151; Smalley, *Revelation*, 584; Thomas, *Revelation 8–22*, 515–516.

in this book" (22:18). As for those who take away from its content "God will take away his share in the tree of life and in the holy city" (22:19).[701] In both instances, the consequences are those that await all unbelievers.

Perhaps in response to the appeal of his disciples in 22:17a, Jesus promises that he is "coming soon" (22:20a; cf. 22:7, 12). While the revelation was delivered through an angel to John and then to the churches, this does not discount that the ultimate source of the revelation is Jesus, "who testifies to these things" (22:20a). John responds with "Amen. Come, Lord Jesus!" (22:20b) His hopeful expectation is for the second coming of Christ. The book closes with a standard benediction, "the grace of the Lord Jesus be with all. Amen" (22:21).

SUMMARY

As was the case in previous sections of the book, this analysis was limited in its scope, and therefore did not consider some of the discipleship themes that were addressed earlier. However, those that were addressed serve to expand on themes discussed previously.

First, with reference to coming to an understanding of Jesus' person and/or work Rev 22:7, 12 in particular emphasized the certainty of Jesus' *parousia*. Not only is this truth affirmed, but it also describes what he brings with him, rewards. These rewards are based on one's actions during this life. For the disciple of Jesus Christ the prospect of rewards may serve to motivate one to love and good deeds. It may also serve as a reminder that one's actions in this life carry with them inescapable consequences. Those who live after the course of this present world, can expect an entirely different kind of reward. This too may stimulate the disciple to make every effort to put sin to death in one's own life.

Second, the additional disclosure of Jesus' claim as the Davidic Messiah affirms the picture one finds in the Gospels. The particular picture of the Messiah in 22:16b is of a coming judge who will surely deal swiftly with the wicked of this world. Jesus' disciples can rest assured that evil will not continue to operate seemingly unabated, but will come to an abrupt end when their Savior returns.

---

701. Osborne believes this is something that could potentially happen to anyone in the church, both regenerate and unregenerate persons (*Revelation*, 796–797), while Beale believes it is only possible for those who claim to be Christians but in reality are not (*Revelation*, 1153).

Discipleship in the Book of Revelation

Third, Jesus' disciples are those who keep his teaching. This theme was discussed earlier in this study, but it seemed fitting to discuss it once again, since it is repeated in 22:7, 9. In the case of 22:7, keeping Jesus' teaching results in a blessing. This blessing may be something experienced prior to his second coming and when he returns. Keeping Jesus' teaching in this fallen world usually means being out of step with the world. This can cause difficulty and strife for the disciple who follows Christ's word. And while this result is stressed elsewhere in Scripture (cf. John 15:18–25), the emphasis here is on the blessing one receives. The momentary difficulties one experiences for living in accordance with Jesus' teaching cannot compare to the blessing that he will grant to those who faithfully follow his word.

Fourth, one of the discipleship themes that has been a constant throughout the Apocalypse is distinctions between Jesus' disciples and non-disciples. The comparisons include not only the actions indicative of one who follows after Jesus and one who follows after the enemy, but it also includes what can be expected of living in a certain manner. Here in Rev 22:14–15 the distinctions between the eternity of Jesus' disciples and his non-disciples could not be any more clear. With these ends in view, Jesus' disciples are encouraged to continue to follow hard after him, knowing full well that they will experience an eternity with the one true God.

Finally, the discipleship theme of believing in Jesus occurs once again. It is quite fitting that the conclusion of the book of Revelation includes an appeal to all who are thirsty to find their thirst quenched by the satisfying water of life. This appeal is in line with Jesus' parting words to his disciples in Matt 28:19–20. They are to go and make more disciples of Jesus, and the message they herald is the free offer of the gospel, which is figuratively alluded to in Rev 22:17b. And just as Jesus' first disciples were commanded to go and proclaim the good news in light of the authority Jesus received from his Father (Matt 28:18), so also are his disciples to carry the gospel message with them, knowing that Jesus is absolutely sovereign over all (Rev 22:13). They are to trust the results of gospel proclamation to him and to go under his authority as his emissaries, authorized with his message.

5

Conclusion

INTRODUCTION

This chapter provides an overall survey of the research, as well as a synthesis of the exegetical conclusions on the theme of discipleship in the Apocalypse. This synthesis includes how the theme of discipleship as it is revealed in Revelation might be applied to the disciple of Jesus Christ. This chapter concludes with some recommendations for future research.

SUMMARY OF RESEARCH

Chapter 1 identified the need for an analysis of the theme of discipleship in Revelation. The method for this analysis is a content analysis of the book of Revelation. It also proposed and concluded that discipleship, although not exactly synonymous with either Christian education or Christian spiritual formation, does share a striking affinity with both disciplines' emphasis on the need for a holistic educative process for Christian growth and maturity into the image of Christ. The study consists of three areas of investigation: (1) an overview of the forms of discipleship in the ancient world, including the NT, (2) current research on the theme of discipleship in the Gospel of John, and (3) investigation of the theme of discipleship in the book of Revelation. The research questions are as follows:

Conclusion

1. What forms of discipleship existed in the ancient world?
2. How is the theme of discipleship developed in the Gospel of John according to current research?
3. How is the theme of discipleship developed in the book of Revelation?

Chapter 2 contained an overview of the forms of discipleship in the ancient world, including the NT. It explored the historical background to NT discipleship through a summary of the forms of discipleship in the ancient Greco-Roman world largely through the use of its terminology, and in Judaism through its terminology, as well as through certain relationships in the world of Judaism. Next, it provided an overview of the characteristics of NT discipleship, beginning with relevant terminology used in the Synoptic Gospels and the NT Epistles, followed by a look at Jesus' distinct form of discipleship, and concluded with discipleship as articulated in the Epistles.

Chapter 3 consisted of a review of the recent scholarly literature on discipleship in the Gospel of John and the development of a coding frame to be used for analysis of Revelation. The coding frame utilized to explore the theme of discipleship in Revelation was developed from the literature on discipleship in John. Although the methods utilized to study the concept of discipleship in the Fourth Gospel vary, these works have focused on many of the same pericopae and have arrived at similar conclusions regarding discipleship in John's Gospel. The themes most often represented were utilized in the construction of the coding frame.

Chapter 4 is an application of the coding frame developed in chapter three. This chapter was divided into twelve sections, corresponding to an outline of the book of Revelation. The exegetical analysis of several of the selected pertinent texts related to the theme of discipleship are accompanied by brief vignettes of what Revelation may contribute to Jesus' disciples' walk with him today.

SYNTHESIS

In this section each of the discipleship themes articulated in Revelation is handled in turn to provide a picture of how the theme of discipleship is developed in the book. But first, it may prove helpful to provide a brief analysis of the frequency of particular themes, as well as where they occur in Revelation. Some preliminary reasons are provided for these results.

With regard to the occurrences of the theme of discipleship in Revelation, certain sections of the book are better represented than others. The greatest concentration of the theme of discipleship happens to be in the first three chapters of Revelation, in particular Rev 2–3. The reason for this is almost certainly due to the fact that in these chapters the seven churches of Asia Minor are addressed. The second highly concentrated area of the book is the final two chapters of Revelation. This is probably because Rev 21–22 has several parallels with the letters to the seven churches, which frequently touch on discipleship. The fewest occurrences of the theme of discipleship take place in Rev 4–5, 8–10, 12, and 15–16. This is not to say that these chapters are devoid of the topic, but they simply happen to have the fewest occurrences. This may be due to the content of these chapters, most of which cover the seal, trumpet, and bowl judgments, which place a greater emphasis on God's wrath poured out on unbelievers.

There are also greater occurrences of some aspects of the coding frame as compared to others. For instance, discipleship language frequently occurs in the book, while union with Christ is basically relegated to one place in particular (21:3). Of the discipleship language found in the book, disciples of Jesus are most often referred to as "servants" or those who are "serving" him. A second group of themes that occur often but with slightly less frequency than discipleship language include: distinction between Jesus' disciples and non-disciples, consequences of following Jesus, and coming to an understanding of Jesus' person and/or work. The comparisons between Jesus' disciples and non-disciples may have been due to the rhetorical function of the book, as motivation to encourage Christians to remain faithful to Christ, and for unbelievers to wake up from their state of lostness, so that they may repent and believe the gospel. The theme of consequences of following Christ, namely suffering, is a constant in the NT, and so it should be no surprise to find it here in the final book of the canon. Finally, the theme of coming to an understanding of Jesus' person and/or work is concentrated in the visions of the exalted Christ that are scattered throughout the book.

Discipleship Language

The language used with reference to Jesus' disciples in the Apocalypse is quite diverse. Prominent among the language that occurs is δοῦλος ("servant"), σύνδουλός ("fellow servant") and λατρεύω ("I serve"). In Revelation,

Conclusion

servants include Moses (15:3), John (1:1), prophets (10:7; 11:18), an angel (19:10; 22:9), and most frequently Christians (1:1; 2:20; 7:3; 19:2, 5; 22:3, 6). Those who serve are first and foremost servants of God and Christ. The servants also exhibit humility. Whether one is the great prophet and leader Moses, or the apostle John, or someone exhibiting prophetic gifts, or even a spectacular angelic being, at the most basic level, all are servants. These servants also serve other Christians. This may be alluded to through the phrase "his/your servants the prophets" (10:7; 11:18). First, they are identified as servants of God and Christ ("his/your"). But they also may serve others. In the NT the gift of prophecy is to be exercised for the edification of the body of Christ (1 Cor 12:7; 14:3, 31). So Christ's disciples are to serve him, but also to serve him by serving other brothers and sisters in Christ.

The Revelation also identifies disciples as ἅγιοι ("saints" or "God's people," NIV). This and the imagery of disciples as "virgins" (Rev 14:4) and Christ's betrothed "bride" who has prepared herself for her wedding (19:7) highlight the faithfulness and holiness of God's people. Believers are set apart and made holy on account of what God has done in Christ. This idea is expressed in the imagery of their being "firstfruits" offered to God (14:4). This is sometimes referred to as positional sanctification. But disciples of Jesus are also called to be holy, to live a life of holiness. They are to live in accordance with their new position in Christ as holy to the Lord.[1] This idea is also picked up in the imagery of not walking about naked (16:15). Disciples are to live in line with the ethical demands of Christ. In the context of 16:15, this means not succumbing to idolatry and remaining clothed with good works, those deeds that show evidence of one's commitment to follow after Christ (3:4–5, 18; 19:8–9).[2]

Perhaps the most overt discipleship terminology in the entire book, or at least that which is more closely associated with the language of the Gospels, is that of following Christ. This language is utilized sparingly in Revelation (7:17; 14:4; 17:14). Jesus' disciples follow their good shepherd because he leads them to drink "living water" (7:17), which, when taken along with 21:6–7; 22:1, means that Jesus leads all Christians to the source of all life, God himself, to enjoy eternal fellowship with God and Christ.[3] His disciples also follow him because he promises protection and the cessation of all suffering (7:15–17). What they follow is Jesus' manner of life and

---

1. For more on this aspect of sanctification see Peterson, *Possessed by God*.
2. Smalley, *Revelation*, 412.
3. Thomas, *Revelation 1–7*, 503.

his teaching, as well as promoting his mission (14:4–5).[4] Following Jesus does not mean an easy existence in this present life, for following Jesus' way of life may include following him in his manner of death.

Union with Christ

This is the least overt discipleship theme in the entire book. The clearest example occurs in Rev 21:3, where a voice announces, "the dwelling place of God is with man. He will dwell with them, and they will be his people, and God himself will be with them as their God." The term σκηνή ("dwelling place") is used in the LXX for the tent (Exod 33:7–11) or tabernacle (25:9) in the wilderness, where God dwelt in the midst of Israel.[5] The verb from the same root σκηνόω ("I dwell") occurs in John 1:14, with reference to the incarnation. The verb also occurs in Rev 21:3 and may refer to "God's covenant" with his people.[6] The union of God with his people is emphasized all the more by the repetition of God being "with" or "among" (μετά) his people.[7] This underscores the fact that in the new age God is present with his people. The fellowship the Triune God experiences with his people will be unbroken, unhindered, and eternal.[8]

Although the vision is of future dwelling with God and Christ in the new heaven and new earth, Jesus' disciples dwell with him now through the internal presence of the Holy Spirit. And although this is true of all of his disciples, this does not mean that this reality is always fully realized. In this present world sin and the effects of sin on this world hinder one's ability to fully recognize Christ dwelling within his people. Often the cares of this world are more readily experienced than the closeness of Jesus with his disciples. These things seem to occupy one's attention and make it difficult to abide with Christ. However, a day is coming in which Jesus' dwelling with his disciples will be unhindered by the damaging effects of sin, for God will cause all such effects to cease in the age to come (21:4–5). Then

---

4. Aune, "Following the Lamb," 275; Mounce, *Revelation*, 268; Osborne, *Revelation*, 530.

5. Koester, *Revelation*, 797; Mounce, *Revelation*, 383; Thomas, *Revelation 8–22*, 443.

6. Koester, *Revelation*, 797.

7. Thomas believes Rev 21:3 echoes 7:15, but μετά replaces ἐπί in 21:3. For Thomas, the change to μετά "suggests an even closer bond of fellowship" (*Revelation 8–22*, 433).

8. Burke, *The Message of Sonship*, 230.

Jesus' disciples will be able to experience unfettered access to the Lord of life and truly and fully dwell with him forever.

Come to an Understanding of Jesus' Person and/or Work

The book of Revelation contains several visions of the exalted Christ. Several of these are identified with ἰδού ("Behold!" See!" "Listen!") (1:7, 18; 3:20; 5:5; 14:1, 14; 16:15; 19:11; 21:3, 5; 22:7, 12), although not all of them are (2:7, 11, 17, 29; 3:6, 13, 22). Jesus is revealed to be coming soon, both in blessing and judgment (1:7; 22:7, 16), the eternal sovereign Lord over all (22:12), including death and Hades (1:18), and the triumphant crucified living Lord (5:5, 6, 9, 12) who is absolutely worthy to receive worship (5:8–14).

Two particular aspects of this discipleship theme relate to following Jesus today. First, in each of the letters to the seven churches of Asia Minor, Jesus announces a promise to the one who overcomes (2:7, 11, 17, 29; 3:6, 13, 22). These promises are one of the ways in which the Lord motivates his disciples to continue in his discipleship. The problems each of the churches faces are momentary struggles; however, the promises are eternal in nature. For any of Christ's disciples facing suffering or difficulties in this world, Jesus would call on them not to ignore their present circumstances, but to view them in light of eternity. He calls his own to take the long view.[9] Second, Jesus speaks to each church through the Holy Spirit by means of a prophet, in the case of the seven churches of Rev 2–3 the apostle John. Jesus continues to speak to his disciples through the Holy Spirit, not necessarily through prophetic gifts (although he may), but he speaks authoritatively through his Spirit-inspired word, the Bible. The ability to hear, that is, listen to the teaching of Scripture and obey it, is something that distinguishes Jesus' disciples from non-disciples. Only those who are in a discipling relationship with him hear his voice and follow him (cf. John 10:4–5).

Believe in Jesus

It was mentioned earlier that the book of Revelation does not include a single occurrence of the verb πιστεύω ("I believe"). Nor are there any instances of people experiencing initial salvation, transforming from unbelievers

---

9. Carson, *How Long, O Lord?*, 238–246.

to believers. Some scholars even deny the concept of saving faith in Revelation.[10] However, that that does not mean the idea of belief in Jesus for salvation is not present. For instance, the verb νικάω ("I overcome, am victorious") may include salvific undertones (Rev 2:7, 11, 17, 26–28; 3:5, 12, 21; 15:2). Those who remain faithful to Christ are promised to experience blessings that are associated with the end of the age.

It is also possible to take the term πίστις ("faith") in 2:13, 19 as a reference to the salvation of the saints in Pergamum and Thyatira. In the case of the disciples in Pergamum and Thyatira, their faith in Christ was expressed by continuing to be faithful to him in the midst of conflict. Although they are not shown coming to faith, their lives show evidence of their having repented of sin and believing the gospel.

Perhaps the clearest depiction of this discipleship theme is the free offer to drink from the water of life in 21:6 and 22:17. To drink from the water of life is to receive the eternal life Jesus offers, which is received by faith.[11] In each instance, an appeal is made to unbelievers.[12] So while these verses do not picture an individual or group receiving initial salvation, they do describe an appeal from God himself (21:6) and from his people (22:17) for others who are outside of Christ to come to him in faith. This appeal is in line with Jesus' parting words to his disciples in Matt 28:19–20. They are to go and make more disciples of Jesus, and the message they herald is the free offer of the gospel, which is figuratively alluded to in Rev 22:17. And just as Jesus' first disciples were commanded to go and proclaim the good news in light of the authority Jesus received from his Father (Matt 28:18), so also are his disciples to carry the gospel message with them, knowing that Jesus is absolutely sovereign over all (Rev 22:13). They are to trust the results of gospel proclamation to him and to go under his authority as his emissaries, authorized with his message.

Membership and Election of the People of God

There are relatively few instances of this discipleship theme in Revelation; however, several of them occur in Rev 2–3. In both 2:17 and 3:12 the

---

10. Boring, *Revelation*, 95. Boring states, "the whole word-group for faith and believing . . . never has the Pauline meaning of 'obedience in personal trust that mediates our relationship to God.'"

11. Beale, *Revelation*, 1056; Osborne, *Revelation*, 738–739; Smalley, *Revelation*, 541.

12. Osborne, *Revelation*, 738.

Conclusion

disciple of Christ is promised a "new name." The background for Christ giving a "new name" to the believer is rooted in the OT (cf. Gen 32:28; Isa 62:2; 65:15). What is promised in Rev 2:17 and 3:12 may be similar to what occurred in the OT as God at times gave a new name to those with whom he had entered into a covenant relationship (e.g., Abraham and Israel).[13] Revelation 2:17 and 3:17 is a promise to Christians in general, for the one who perseveres to the end will receive a new name. The fact that this name is given at the consummation does not mean one is not currently a disciple of Jesus. The new covenant relationship is experienced now, but will be more fully realized in the *eschaton*.[14]

Jesus also promises to those believers who persevere at Sardis to have their names kept in or not removed from the book of life (3:5; cf. 13:8; 17:8; 20:12, 15; 21:27). The names of those included in the book are in covenant relationship with God through Christ, "who was slain from the creation of the world" (13:8, NIV). The names of those in the book of life are "believers whose salvific destiny has been determined because their names have already been written in the book before the foundation of the world."[15] They are the elect people of God.

Jesus' promises are granted to those who are victorious (21:7). Their ability to be victorious may be grounded in the assurance of their salvation. The disciples who have accepted the reality that they are God's elect have the assurance that he will grant them the strength to follow Christ faithfully, even while suffering for him. God's election does not give one a reason to be idle, but it energizes the disciple to live for Christ, confident that what he has begun he will also bring to completion. The emphasis is not on what the disciples can do in their own power, but ultimately on what God has done. It is Christ who has called and chosen his disciples from out of the world (17:14). Their faithfulness is grounded in the certainty of his calling, in his making them his beloved children (21:7).

---

13. Beasley-Murray, *Revelation*, 88; Hemer, *Seven Churches of Asia*, 102–103; Thomas, *Revelation 1-7*, 202. Beale does not reject this aspect of the giving of a "new name," although he still believes the name given is that of God/Christ (*Revelation*, 255). Others who believe the name is a personal "new name" given to the Christian differ in their meaning. Mounce believes the name is new in quality and "appropriate to the New Age" (*Revelation*, 83). Smalley hints at the covenantal aspect, but comes short of clearly speaking in favor of it. He believes the giving of a "new name" symbolizes "entrance into new life and status" (*Revelation*, 71).

14. Hemer, *Seven Churches of Asia*, 103; Smalley, *Revelation*, 71.

15. Beale, *Revelation*, 279. Against see Osborne, *Revelation*, 183 n. 3:5.

Bear Witness to Jesus

In the book of Revelation there are several individuals who testify, apart from John in 1:2, 9. Jesus is one who testifies (1:5; 3:14; 22:20), as does Antipas (2:13), the "two witnesses" (11:3), those who suffered and died because of their testimony about Jesus (1:9; 6:9; 11:7; 12:17; 17:6; 20:4), and Christians in general (12:11, 17; 19:10). What John specifically testifies to is "the word of God and the testimony of Jesus Christ" (1:2, 9). As noted earlier, this phrase indicates that what John bore witness to was the word *about* God that was also *from* God and the testimony *about* Jesus that was also *from* Jesus.[16] This is in keeping with the Great Commission (Matt 28:19-20). Since the Great Commission is intended for all disciples of Jesus, and Revelation indicates that Christians in general engaged in the testimony about Jesus, it appears that bearing witness to Jesus' life and teaching and the salvific significance of it is the ministry of all Christians. As is often the case in Revelation, those who bear witness to Jesus are persecuted for doing so (Rev 6:9; 11:2, 7; 12:17; 20:4). So Jesus' disciples are engaged as witnesses to the truth of the gospel knowing full well that they may suffer at the hands of those who are opposed to their message.

Some of the discipleship themes relate to one another. For instance, bearing witness to Christ relates to consequences of following Jesus, because so often those who bear witness are persecuted. Similarly, the theme of belief in Jesus also relates to bearing witness to Jesus. One of the interesting ways this works out is through those passages that note the failure of people to repent when they experience God's wrath (9:20-21; 16:9, 11; cf. 16:21). Many of the plagues that befell the ungodly were natural disasters, and yet those who suffered them somehow recognized the hand of God in sending them. How did they know this? Perhaps the church engaged in witnessing to the surrounding culture, making them aware that the plagues were God's judgment against sin, and therefore, they called the inhabitants of the earth to repent. The church may have been following Christ's example in Luke 13:1-5, when he noted that any disaster was a wake up call to repent. It is also possible that the believers present during these awful times may be so dependent on the Spirit for insight that they are able to properly discern the times. In either case, there is always a need for God's people to address the culture around them with the need for repentance

---

16. The phrase "the word of God and the testimony of Jesus Christ" is taken as two plenary genitives (Wallace, *Greek Grammar*, 119-121).

Conclusion

and coming to Christ in faith or they "too will perish" (Luke 13:3, 5, NIV). In doing so they show love for their enemies and do good to those who harm them (Matt 5:44).

Keep and Obey Jesus'/God's Commands

At several points in the Apocalypse John is commanded to write (Rev 1:11, 19; 2:1, 8, 12, 18; 3:1, 7, 14; 14:13; 19:9; 21:5). In all but three of these occurrences the command comes from Christ. So what one has are instances of Jesus issuing a command and John obeying it. While on earth Jesus issued commands for his disciples to follow (cf. John 13:34), and he is still issuing commands as the exalted Lord.

There is also mention of disciples following "the commandments of God" (Rev 12:17; 14:12). While some argue that these commands refer specifically to the "*ethical* requirements of the Torah,"[17] it is likely broader than this and refers to obeying all of God's word.[18] According to the context of 14:12 the way in which one consistently rejects the enticements of the beast to submit to his worship is by keeping God's word and remaining faithful to Jesus. So for the disciple of Jesus Christ perseverance is linked to obeying God's word, his commands to his people. It is not so much that obeying God's word is the evidence of one's faith in Christ, although it may be, but in 14:12 the emphasis is on the sanctifying effect of Scripture on the individual to remain undefiled and persevere in one's commitment to Christ to the end. This is essentially what Jesus prays for his disciples in John 17:13–19. A similar idea occurs in Eph 5:26, where Christ is said to have given himself up for his church "that he might sanctify her, having cleansed her by the washing of water with the word." For Jesus' disciples to continually be made more like Christ in the way of holiness, there must be a commitment not only to reading and hearing Scripture, but to knowing it well enough through study that one may faithfully be obedient to what it demands of believers.

---

17. Aune, "Following the Lamb," 281. For his entire argument see pages 279–281.
18. Beale, *Revelation*, 766; Mounce, *Revelation*, 242. Koester, *Revelation*, 544, 614.

Witness to "Greater Things"

On at least three occasions (Rev 1:12–16; 2–3; 19:11–16) John is given a vision of the exalted and risen Christ. In 1:12–16 this vision depicts Christ walking amongst his churches. Jesus' symbol-laden appearance identifies him as high priest, the caretaker and intercessor for his people. His appearance is also strikingly white, which denotes his absolute holiness. His eyes ablaze like fire point to his omniscience, his penetrating and exhaustive insight, which enables him to pronounce just judgments (cf. 1:16). His feet of pure bronze walking in the midst of his churches recall the command of God to his people, "You shall be holy, for I am holy" (1 Pet 1:16; cf. Lev 20:26). Jesus' voice is awesome and powerful. It spoke the worlds into existence, commanded the dead to be raised, and as John will soon witness, would announce a revelation of "what [John had] seen, what is now and what will take place later" (Rev 1:19, NIV). What John sees is the glory of Christ, a glory beyond that on display through his death, resurrection, and ascension. This is the exalted and sovereign Lord, in command and in control of all things. It is this vision of Jesus Christ that his followers may hold on to as a source of hope in this fallen world.

The second occurrence takes place in the churches in Asia Minor (2:1, 8, 13, 18; 3:1, 7, 14). To those churches, Christ addresses a deficiency or problem he sees that hinders their effectiveness as his disciples. In doing so, Jesus shows how he is the remedy to what each church needs in its particular situation. Since the churches may be representative of all churches for all time, Christ's particular disclosure of himself to each church continues to speak to churches today. Jesus is still the one to whom his disciples are to look to be effective disciples, for apart from him one can do nothing (John 15:5).

The final occurrence in Rev 19:11–16 is closely connected to the two earlier visions in 1:12–16 and Rev 2–3. Some of these connections are the robe he wore (1:13; 19:16), his eyes that blazed like fire (1:14; 19:12; 2:18), the sword coming out of his mouth (1:16; 19:15; cf. 2:13), and his identification of himself as "holy and true" (3:7) and the "faithful and true witness" (3:14), which are encompassed in the title "Faithful and True" (19:11). These bookends of images remind not only John's audience, but also all disciples of Jesus Christ of his authority over all things and all peoples. To those Christians who may be suffering because of their identification with Christ, the image of Jesus in 19:1–6 should be of great comfort. Their suffering is not in vain. Those who seem to be escaping punishment for their crimes

Conclusion

will one day have to answer to the Lord himself, who will judge and destroy those who have rebelled against him and persecuted his church. Moreover, the image of the warrior Messiah should encourage the persecuted church to continue to follow after Christ, for in the end he will be seen by all to be the King of kings and Lord of lords. Whom they follow is absolutely worth following. They may also be encouraged that he has heard their prayers, as he has the prayers of the saints under the altar (6:10–11), and will one day avenge his holy people. Since he is the one to avenge his people, there is no room for revenge. Vengeance is the Lord's, and he will repay it accordingly (Deut 32:35; Rom 12:19).

Consequences of Following Jesus

In the book of Revelation there are two primary consequences for those who follow Christ. The first is suffering in this present world. John is exiled to Patmos for the gospel (Rev 1:9), believers are promised they will suffer for their faith (2:9–10; 3:10), and the "two witnesses" suffer death for their testimony (11:7). This suffering believers face is at the hand of those in opposition to God (16:6). Those who faithfully follow Christ should expect no less. Such suffering is used to show the genuineness of Christ's disciples (3:10). They will suffer, but the one who remains faithful to the end is promised the "crown of life" (2:10).

However, there is also the promise of the cessation of suffering and persecution. As early as Rev 7, a vision is relayed of the good shepherd caring for his flock, keeping them and protecting them from all harm. Some of the imagery points forward to Rev 21–22, where one finds that the one who perseveres to the end through suffering will experience being with God and Christ forever; the end of suffering, pain, sorrow, and death; and eternal joy with God and all his people, one's brothers and sisters in Christ from every people group. Christ's disciples are called to endure joyfully the suffering and pain associated with living in this fallen world, and that which comes on account of bearing witness to Jesus. The motivation for suffering in this manner is the picture revealed in Rev 21–22. This is similar to what Jesus did and the example he set for his disciples. Hebrews 12:2 notes that Jesus "for the joy that was set before him endured the cross, despising the shame, and is seated at the right hand of the throne of God" (cf. John 13:3). There was something far greater Christ looked forward to that helped him endure suffering. Jesus' disciples need similar motivation and encouragement to carry on faithfully in this world so greatly affected by sin and as targets of the enemy's machinations.

Marks of Discipleship

In the Gospel of John, Jesus states three particular evidences or marks of those who follow him. They are: bearing fruit, loving one another, and keeping Jesus' teaching. All three of these occur in Revelation. At both the beginning and close of the book there is a call to take to heart and keep the words of the prophecy (Rev 1:3; 22:7). The words of the prophecy according to 1:1–2 are those of Jesus Christ, which he is relaying to John through an intermediary, an angel. Thus, what is to be kept and obeyed is none other than the teaching of Jesus Christ concerning those things that are soon to take place, namely, those events that are bound up with the last days. The reason for obeying Christ's words is the nearness of Jesus' second coming. An additional reason may be the blessing one will receive for obeying his teaching. In both instances the blessing is unidentified, but given the mention of Jesus' *parousia*, the blessing is likely the consummation of the disciples' salvation, which includes all of the blessed promises revealed in Rev 21–22 for the one who remains faithful. So not only does keeping Jesus' teaching show evidence of one's salvation, but according to 1:3 and 22:7, the fullness of one's salvation is realized only through continuing to obey Christ's words.

Another instance of this discipleship theme occurs in some of the letters to the seven churches. For instance, both bearing fruit and loving one another are seen in the description of the church in Thyatira. The Lord recognizes that their "latter works exceed the first" (2:19). Jesus' disciples are expected to mature. They are not to remain babes in Christ, but grow up into the head, which is Christ (Eph 4:15). And their growth is to be multifaceted. The particular areas in which they were bearing more fruit were love, faith, service, and patient endurance. The Christian virtue of love likely included their love for God, as well as their love for one another, since both are tightly bound together elsewhere in Scripture (Matt 22:37–39; Mark 12:29–31; Luke 10:27). Jesus clearly taught that Christian love for one another shows evidence of being his disciple. And the standard by which they are to love one another is Christ's own love for them (John 13:34). The emphasis on bearing fruit, loving one another, and being obedient to Christ's teaching is a tall task for any disciple of Jesus, but nevertheless,

CONCLUSION

something he commanded of those who follow after him. Thus, the need for continual dependence on the Holy Spirit to work in one the strength and desire to pursue these things with gusto, for in and of oneself, neither the desire nor the ability will be there.

Distinction between Jesus' Disciples and Non-Disciples

One of the frequently recurring discipleship themes is distinction between Jesus' disciples and non-disciples. Some of these contrasts include the inclusion (cf. Rev 3:5; 21:27) or exclusion (13:8; 17:8; 20:12, 15) of one's name from the book of life; worship of the true Trinity (4:10; 5:14; 7:11; 11:1, 16; 13:15; 14:7; 15:4; 19:4, 10; 20:4; 22:8–9) or worship of a false trinity (9:20; 13:4, 8, 12; 14:9, 11; 16:2; 19:20); having unsoiled, white clothing (7:9, 13, 14; 22:14) or soiled, unclean clothing (22:11, 15), which are indicative of repentance and faith or rebellion and unbelief; being citizens of the city of God (11:2; 22:14) or citizens of the city of Satan (11:8; 22:15); and whether one is sealed by God (7:2, 3, 4, 5, 8; 9:4; 14:1; cf. 22:4) or has the mark of the beast (13:16, 17; 14:9, 11; 16:2; 19:20).

There are several ways in which this theme of discipleship would be of value to Jesus' own. Only a few are mentioned here. First, the distinctions between Jesus' disciples and non-disciples are a constant reminder that Jesus' own are to be different from the culture in which they are located. As noted earlier, they are to be who they are presently in Christ, namely, holy. Jesus instructed his disciples to remain in the world, but not to be like the world (John 17:14–16). They were to be salt and light in their culture (Matt 5:13–16). This continues to be the call for his disciples today. Second, for the disciple of Jesus Christ the picture of being sealed with God's name should offer comfort. Chiefly God's seal is a sign that the Christian is Christ's own. Christians have been purchased with Christ's own blood. They no longer stand condemned and under the wrath to come. The seal also offers assurance, since the seal of God is not so much protection from suffering brought on by persecution or from the ill effects of living in a fallen world, but it is security of one's salvation. The Father has marked all genuine disciples as his own on the basis of his only Son bearing the marks of crucifixion. Finally, the contrasts between Jesus' disciples and non-disciples may be God's way of keeping his own people faithful to him. He may do this by both the promise of blessings and the warnings of judgment. People need different types of motivation, depending on the circumstances.

Jesus' disciples also need different kinds of motivation to stay the course on the narrow road. Both images seem to be among the means God uses to help his people persevere.

Jesus as a Model for His Disciples

There are at least two clear instances of this discipleship theme in the book of Revelation. The first occurs in Rev 2:13, where Antipas is called Jesus' "faithful witness, who was killed" in Pergamum. The phrase "faithful witness" occurs only one other time in 1:5, where Jesus is described as such. Jesus was a "faithful witness" in his testimony about God, which led him to the cross. Likewise, Antipas's faithfulness as a witness to Christ ended in his death. These connections indicate that Antipas followed the "pattern Jesus set" as one who remained a faithful witness even to the point of death.[19] The second occurrence is the "two witnesses" in 11:8–12. Like their Lord they were killed for their testimony, publicly shamed, remained dead for "three and a half days," which may be an allusion to Jesus' own bodily resurrection that transpired "after three days," were resurrected, and ascended into heaven. Jesus serves as an example for his disciples to follow in their mission and the possible consequences associated with it. Believers should expect no less (cf. John 15:18–21). He is also an example of what all believers can expect, a resurrected and glorified existence.

The idea of following Jesus' manner of life and teaching also has implications for holistic education that is common to discipleship, spiritual formation, and Christian education. Not only is one to take in and apply what Jesus teaches, but one is also to examine his way of life, his example. The whole of the Apocalypse is Jesus' way of instructing his disciples about what to expect and how to live in light of the last days. He also provides an example of how to suffer well in the face of persecution for bearing witness to the truth. Antipas is referred to as a "faithful witness" (Rev 2:13) even as Christ is declared a "faithful witness" in the opening chapter of the book (1:5). Antipas followed Jesus' example. But it would also seem that in naming Antipas, John may have intended for him to be an example for others to imitate. Antipas is the only proper name mentioned in the book apart from John and Jesus.[20] Jesus, then, serves as the example *par excellence* of a life lived for God, but Antipas is also someone to whom believers may look to

---

19. Koester, *Revelation*, 288; so also Keener, *Revelation*, 123; Roloff, *Revelation*, 51.

20. Jezebel also occurs, however, the name is used in a figurative sense.

CONCLUSION

pattern a faithful life after. So it is for disciples of Jesus Christ today. They are to live in such a way that they may echo Paul's words, "Be imitators of me, as I am of Christ" (1 Cor 11:1).

RECOMMENDATIONS FOR FUTURE RESEARCH

The following are recommendations for future research using this analysis of the theme of discipleship in the book of Revelation. The following list of suggestions is by no means meant to be exhaustive, but intended to be a starting point for others, to spark interest in the subject of discipleship.

1. This study lays a foundation for a more detailed analysis of discipleship with concentrated attention on any one of the twelve themes of discipleship (i.e., bear witness to Jesus) throughout the NT.
2. The coding frame for this study may also be used to study the themes of discipleship in either the Gospel of John or the Johannine Epistles.
3. One may wish to conduct a study comparing the topic of discipleship as it is developed in the Pauline corpus with the Johannine corpus.
4. Regarding the method appropriated for this study (content analysis), it is possible to do similar analysis of the motif of discipleship on other NT documents.
5. One may wish to research the concept of discipleship in the OT.
6. The topic of discipleship may also be studied with regard to character studies, whether Paul, Timothy, Peter, etc.
7. One may wish to analyze the theme of discipleship with regards to various settings, such as the home or workplace. What does Scripture contribute to each?
8. One may desire to study methods for teaching any one of the aspects of discipleship discussed in this study in various settings, whether in a traditional classroom or in a one-on-one discipling relationship.
9. One may wish to study contemporary approaches and biblical approaches to discipleship in order to evaluate contemporary models.

CONCLUSION

Earlier in this study it was noted that some authors wondered about the value and relevance of Revelation to Christian education, which is essentially the discipling ministry of the local church.[21] This study has shown that the theme of discipleship is not only found in the Apocalypse, but is also relevant for believers today. In many parts of the world Jesus' disciples are facing opposition and persecution for their testimony to Jesus Christ, both in word and deed. Even in North America, where for so long the evangelical community was often respected and at the least tolerated, today it faces increasing hostility from the surrounding culture and government. It would do Christians well to read the book of Revelation once again. As they read it this time through the eyes of the oppressed, the content of the book will prove extremely valuable to aid disciples of Jesus in their efforts to "follow the Lamb wherever he goes" (Rev 14:4), no matter what the cost.

---

21. Gangel, "What Christian Education Is," 28.

Bibliography

Abbott, Edwin A. *Johannine Grammar*. London: Edward and Charles Black, 1906.
Adams, Jay E. *How to Change People*. Grand Rapids: Zondervan, 1986.
Alcorn, Wallace Arthur. "The Biblical Concept of Discipleship as Education for Ministry." PhD diss., New York University, 1974.
Alexander, T. Desmond. *From Eden to the New Jerusalem: An Introduction to Biblical Theology*. Grand Rapids: Kregel, 2008.
Alford, Henry. *The Greek Testament*. Vol. IV. Boston: Lee and Shepherd, 1878.
Andrew of Caesarea. *Commentary on the Apocalypse*. Translated by Eugenia Scarvelis Constantinou. Washington, DC: The Catholic University of America Press, 2011.
Arensen, Allen G. "Making Disciples According to Christ's Plan." *Evangelical Missions Quarterly* 16 (1980) 103–106.
Arnold, Clinton E. *Zondervan Illustrated Bible Backgrounds Commentary: New Testament*. Grand Rapids: Zondervan, 2002.
Atkinson, Michael. "Body and Discipleship." *Theology* 82 (1979) 279–287.
Aune, David E. "Following the Lamb: Discipleship in the Apocalypse." In *Patterns of Discipleship in the New Testament*, edited by Richard N. Longenecker, 269–284. Grand Rapids: Eerdmans, 1996.
———. "A Latinism in Revelation 15:2." *JBL* 11 (1991) 691–692.
———. "The Prophetic Circle of John of Patmos and the Exegesis of Revelation 22:16." *JSNT* 37 (1989) 103–116.
———. *Revelation 1–5, 6–16, 17–22*. Word Biblical Commentary. Vol. 52A–52C. Dallas: Word, 1997–1998.
Badke, William B. "Was Jesus a Disciple of John?" *Evangelical Quarterly* 62 (1990) 195–204.
Baird, J. Arthur. "Content Analysis and the Computer: A Case-Study in the Application of the Scientific Method to Biblical Research." *JBL* 95 (1976) 255–276.
———. "Content Analysis, Computers and the Scientific Method in Biblical Studies." In *Perspectives in Religious Studies* 4 (1977) 109–136.
Barr, David L. "The Apocalypse of John as Oral Enactment." *Interpretation* 40 (1986) 243–256.
Bauckham, Richard. *The Climax of Prophecy: Studies on the Book of Revelation*. Edinburgh: T&T Clark, 1993.
———. "The List of the Tribes in Revelation 7 Again." *JSNT* 42 (1991) 99–115.
———. *The Theology of the Book of Revelation*. New Testament Theology. Edited by James D. G. Dunn. Cambridge: Cambridge University Press, 1993.

Bibliography

Bauder, W. "μιμέομαι." In *NIDNTT* 1:490–492.

———. "ὀπίσω." In *NIDNTT* 1:492–493.

Bauer, Walter. *A Greek-English Lexicon of the New Testament and Other Early Christian Literature*. Revised and edited by Frederick W. Danker, et al. 3rd ed. Chicago: University of Chicago Press, 2000.

Bazar, James L. "Leadership within the Gospels: A Content Analysis an Analysis of the Four Biblical Gospels in Relation to the Full Range Leadership Model." PhD diss., Our Lady of the Lake University, 2007.

Beale, Gregory K. *The Book of Revelation: A Commentary on the Greek Text*. NIGTC. Grand Rapids: Eerdmans, 1999.

———. "Eden, the Temple, and the Church's Mission in the New Creation." *JETS* 48 (2005) 5–31.

Beale, G. K. and Sean M. McDonough. "Revelation." In *Commentary on the New Testament Use of the Old Testament*. Edited by G. K. Beale and D. A. Carson. Grand Rapids: Baker Academic, 2007.

Beasley-Murray, George R. *The Book of Revelation*. New Century Bible Commentary. Grand Rapids: Eerdmans, 1981.

———. *Revelation: Three Viewpoints*. Nashville: Broadman, 1977.

Beck, David R. *The Discipleship Paradigm: Readers and Anonymous Characters in the Fourth Gospel*. Biblical Interpretation Series 27. Leiden; New York: Brill, 1997.

———. "The Narrative Function of Anonymity in Fourth Gospel Characterization." *Semeia* 63 (1993) 143–158.

Beckwith, Isbon Thaddeus. *The Apocalypse of John*. New York: MacMillan, 1919.

Beernaert, P. Mourlon. "Converting to the Gospel." *Lumen Vitae* 42 (1987) 369–379.

Belleville, Linda L. "'Imitate Me, Just as I Imitate Christ': Discipleship in the Corinthian Correspondence." In *Patterns of Discipleship in the New Testament*, edited by Richard N. Longenecker, 120–142. Grand Rapids: Eerdmans, 1996.

Berg, Bruce L. *Qualitative Research Methods for the Social Sciences*. 4th ed. Boston: Allyn & Bacon, 2001.

Bernard, H. Russell. *Research Methods in Anthropology: Qualitative and Quantitative Approaches*. 4th ed. New York: AltaMira, 2006.

———. *Social Research Methods: Qualitative and Quantitative Approaches*. Thousand Oaks, CA: Sage, 2000.

Berry, Bruce L. *Qualitative Research Methods for the Social Sciences*. 4th ed. Boston: Allyn & Bacon, 2001.

Best, Earnest. *Following Jesus: Discipleship in the Gospel of Mark*. JSNTSup 4. Sheffield, England: Sheffield Academic, 1981.

Black, C. Clifton. "Christian Ministry in Johannine Perspective." *Interpretation* 44 (1990) 29–41.

Blauvelt Jr., Livingston. "Does the Bible Teach Lorship Salvation?" *BSac* 143 (1986) 37–45.

Blendinger, C. "ἀκολουθέω." In *NIDNTT* 1:480–483.

Blount, Brian K. *Revelation: A Commentary*. New Testament Library. Louisville: Westminster John Knox, 2009.

Boring, M. Eugene. *Revelation*. Interpretation. Louisville: John Knox, 1989.

———. "The Theology of Revelation: 'The Lord Our God the Almighty Reigns.'" *Interpretation* 40 (1986) 257–269.

Boxall, Ian. *The Revelation of St. John*. Black's New Testament Commentary. Peabody, MA: Hendrickson, 2009.

Bibliography

Boyatzis, Richard E. *Transforming Qualitative Information: Thematic Analysis and Code Development*. Thousand Oaks, CA: Sage 1998.
Boyer, James L. "The Classification of Infinitives: A Statistical Study." *GTJ* 6 (1985) 3–27.
———. "A Classification of Imperatives: A Statistical Study." *GTJ* 8 (1987) 35–54.
Brown, Raymond E. *The Community of the Beloved Disciple: The Life, Loves, and Hates of an Individual Church in New Testament Times*. New York: Paulist, 1979.
Brown, Raymond, E., et al., eds. *Mary in the New Testament: A Collaborative Assessment by Protestant and Roman Catholic Scholars*. New York: Paulist, 1978.
Brown, Schuyler. "'The Hour of Trial' (Rev 3:10)." *JBL* 85 (1966) 308–314.
Brueggemann, Dale. "The Use of the Psalter in John's Apocalypse." PhD diss., Westminster Theological Seminary, 1995.
Bryan, C. Doug. *Relationship Learning: A Primer in Christian Education*. Nashville: Broadman, 1990.
Burke, Trevor J. *The Message of Sonship: At Home in God's Household*. The Bible Speaks Today. Downers Grove: InterVarsity Press, 2011.
Caird, G. B. *A Commentary on the Revelation of St. John the Divine*. Harper's New Testament Commentaries. New York, NY: Harper and Row, 1966.
Calenberg, Richard D. "The New Testament Doctrine of Discipleship." ThD diss., Grace Theological Seminary, 1981.
Callahan, Allen Dwight. "The Language of the Apocalypse." *HTR* 88 (Oct 1995) 453–470.
Carrington, Philip. *The Meaning of the Revelation*. Eugene, OR: Wipf and Stock, 2007.
Carson, D. A. *The Gospel according to John*. Pillar New Testament Commentary. Grand Rapids: Eerdmans, 1991.
———. *How Long, O Lord?: Reflections on Suffering and Evil*. Grand Rapids: Baker, 1990.
———. "Matthew." In *EBC*. Vol. 8. Grand Rapids: Zondervan, 1984.
Carson, D. A., et al. *An Introduction to the New Testament*. Grand Rapids: Zondervan, 1992.
Charles, J. Daryl. "An Apocalyptic Tribute to the Lamb (Rev 5:1–14)." *JETS* 34 (1991) 461–473.
Charles, R. H. *A Critical and Exegetical Commentary on the Revelation of St. John*. International Critical Commentary. 2 Vols. Edinburgh: T&T Clark, 1920.
———. ed. *The Testaments of the Twelve Patriarchs*. London: Adam and Black, 1908.
Chennattu, Rekha M. *Johannine Discipleship as a Covenant Relationship*. Peabody, MA: Hendrickson, 2006.
———. "On Becoming Disciples (John 1:35–51): Insights from the Fourth Gospel." *Salesianum* 63 (2001) 467–498.
Clement of Alexandria. *The Instructor*. In *The Ante-Nicene Fathers*. Vol. 2. Edited by Alexander Roberts and James Donaldson. Grand Rapids: Eerdmans, 1971.
Clouse, Robert G. *The Meaning of the Millennium*. Downers Grove: InterVarsity Press, 1977.
Coenen, L. and A. A. Trites. "παρτυρία." In *NIDNTT* 3:1038–1050.
Coffey, Amanda and Paul Atkinson. *Making Sense of Qualitative Data: Complimentary Research Strategies*. Thousand Oaks, CA: Sage, 1996.
Cohen, Abraham. *Everyman's Talmud*. New York: Dutton, 1949.
Coleman, Lucien. *Why the Church Must Teach*. Nashville: Broadman, 1984.
Collins, Raymond F. "Discipleship in John's Gospel." *Emmanuel* 91 (1985) 248–255.
———. *These Things Have Been Written: Studies on the Fourth Gospel*. Louvain Theological & Pastoral Monographs 2. Grand Rapids: Eerdmans, 1990.

Bibliography

Collinson, Sylvia Wilkey. "Making Disciples and the Christian Faith." *Evangelical Review of Theology* 29 (2005) 240–250.
Cootsona, Greg. "Renewing Minds: Calling and Educating Disciples." *Congregations* 30 (2004) 19–21.
Copan, Victor A. "Μαθητής and Μιμητής: Exploring an Entangled Relationship." *Bulletin for Biblical Research* 17 (2007) 313–323.
Coppes, Leonard J. "הָלַל." In *TWOT* 1:216–217.
Corsini, Eugenio. *The Apocalypse: The Perennial Revelation of Jesus Christ*. Good News Studies 5. Translated by Francis Moloney. Wilmington, DE: Michael Glazier, 1983.
Csino, David M. "'Come, Follow Me': Apprenticeship in Jesus' Approach to Education." *Religious Education* 105 (2010) 45–62.
Culpepper, R. Alan. *Anatomy of the Fourth Gospel: A Study in Literary Design*. Philadelphia: Fortress, 1983.
Dana, H. E. and Julius R. Mantey. *A Manual Grammar of the Greek New Testament*. New York: MacMillan, 1967.
Davids, Peter H. "Controlling the Tongue and the Wallet: Discipleship in James." In *Patterns of Discipleship in the New Testament*, edited by Richard N. Longenecker, 225–247. Grand Rapids: Eerdmans, 1996.
Davis, Dale Ralph. "The Relationship between the Seals, Trumpets, and Bowls in the Book of Revelation." *JETS* 16 (1973) 149–158.
DeBoer, Willis Peter. *The Imitation of Paul*. Kampen: Kok, 1960.
De Jonge, Marinus. *Jesus: Stranger from Heaven and Son of God: Jesus Christ and the Christians in Johannine Perspective*, edited and translated by John E. Steely. Missoula, MT: Scholars, 1977.
DeRidder, Richard R. *Discipling the Nations*. Grand Rapids: Baker, 1975.
Dettoni, John M. "What Is Spiritual Formation." In *The Christian Educator's Handbook on Spiritual Formation*, edited by Kenneth O. Gangel and James C. Wilhoit, 11–20. Grand Rapids: Baker, 1994.
Diodorus Siculus. *Library of History, Volume I: Books 1–2.34*. Translated by C. H. Oldfather. LCL 279. Cambridge, MA: Harvard University Press, 1933.
Dio Chrysostom. *Discourses 37–60*. Translated by H. Lamar Crosby. LCL 376. Cambridge, MA: Harvard University Press, 1946.
Donaldson, James. "Called to Follow: A Twofold Experience of Discipleship in Mark." *Biblical Theology Bulletin* 5 (1975) 67–77.
Draper, J. A. "The Heavenly Feast of Tabernacles: Revelation 7:1–17." *JSNT* 19 (1983) 133–147.
Dunn, James D. G. *Jesus and Discipleship: Understanding Jesus Today*. Edited by Howard Clark Kee. Cambridge: University Press, 1991.
Du Rand, J. A. "Perspectives on Johannine Discipleship According to the Farewell Discourse." *Neotestamentica* 25 (1991) 311–325.
Duvall, J. Scott. *Revelation*. Teach the Text Commentary Series. Grand Rapids: Baker, 2014.
Duvall, J. Scott and J. Daniel Hays. *Grasping God's Word: A Hands-on Approach to Reading, Interpreting, and Applying the Bible*. 2nd ed. Grand Rapids: Zondervan, 2005.
Dyer, Charles H. "The Identity of Babylon in Revelation 17–18." *BSac* 144 (1987) 305–316, 433–449.
Edgar, Thomas R. "Robert H. Gundry and Revelation 3:10." *GTJ* 3 (1982) 19–49.

Bibliography

Eldridge, Daryl. "The Disciple: Called to Learn." In *The Teaching Ministry of the Church: Integrating Biblical Truth with Contemporary Application*, edited by Daryl Eldridge, 75–88. Nashville: Broadman & Holman, 1995.

Elliott, John H. "Backward and Forward 'In His Steps': Following Jesus from Rome to Raymond and Beyond. The Tradition, Redaction, and Reception of 1 Peter 2:18–25." In *Discipleship in the New Testament*, edited by Fernando F. Segovia, 184–209. Philadelphia: Fortress, 1985.

Epstein, Isidore and Maurice Simon, eds. *Hebrew-English Edition of the Babylonian Talmud*. London: Soncino, 1960.

Euripides. *Helen. Phoenician Women. Orestes*. Edited and translated by David Kovacs. LCL 11. Cambridge, MA: Harvard University Press, 2002.

Eusebius. *Ecclesiastical History, Volume II: Books 6–10*. Translated by J. E. L. Oulton. LCL 265. Cambridge, MA: Harvard University Press, 1932.

Fee, Gordon D. *Revelation*. Eugene, OR: Cascade, 2011.

Fekkes, III, Jan. "'His Bride Has Prepared Herself': Revelation 19–21 and Isaian Nuptial Imagery." *JBL* 109 (1990) 269–287.

Ferdinando, Keith. "Jesus, the Theological Educator." *Themelios* 38.3 (2013) 360–374.

Feuillet, André. "The Twenty-Four Elders in the Apocalypse." In *Johannine Studies*, translated by T. E. Crane, 183–214. Staten Island, NY: Alba House, 1964.

Ford, J. Massynberde. *Revelation: A New Translation with Introduction and Commentary*. Anchor Bible. Vol. 38. Garden City, NY: Doubleday, 1975.

Fowl, Stephen E. "Imitation of Paul/of Christ." In *DPL* 428–431.

Freyne, Sean. *The Twelve: Disciples and Apostles: A Study in the Theology of the First Three Gospels*. London: Sheed & Word, 1968.

Friedeman, Matt. *The Master Plan of Teaching*. Wheaton: Victor, 1990.

Furnish, Victor Paul. *Theology and Ethics in Paul*. Nashville: Abingdon, 1968.

Galindo, Israel. "Methods of Christian Education toward Christian Spiritual Formation." *Review and Expositor* 98 (2001) 411–429.

Gangel, Kenneth O. "What Christian Education Is." In *Christian Education: Foundations for the Future*, edited by Robert E. Clark, et al., 13–29. Chicago: Moody, 1991.

Gangel, Kenneth O. and Warren S. Benson. *Christian Education: It's History and Philosophy*. Chicago: Moody, 1983.

Giblin, Charles Homer. "From and before the Throne: Revelation 4:5–6a Integrating the Imagery of Revelation 4–16." *Catholic Biblical Quarterly* 60 (1998) 500–513.

———. *Revelation: The Open Book of Prophecy*. Collegeville, MN: Liturgical, 1991.

Gloer, W. Hulitt. "Come and See: Disciples and Discipleship in the Fourth Gospel." In *Perspectives on John: Methods and Interpretation of the Fourth Gospel*. NABPRSS 11, edited by Robert B. Sloan and Mikeal C. Parsons, 269–301. Lewiston, NY: Edwin Mellen, 1993.

Goldingay, John E. *Daniel*. Word Biblical Commentary. Vol. 30. Dallas: Word, 1989.

González, Catherine and Justo L. González. *Revelation*. Westminster Bible Companion. Louisville: Westminster John Knox, 1997.

Graendorf, Werner C. "The Challenge of Biblical Christian Education." In *Introduction to Biblical Christian Education*, edited by Werner C. Graendorf, 11–24. Chicago: Moody, 1981.

Grbich, Carol. *Qualitative Data Analysis: An Introduction*. Thousand Oaks, CA: Sage, 2007.

Green, Michael P. "The Meaning of Cross-Bearing." *BSac* 140 (1983) 117–133.

Bibliography

Griffin, William Paul. *The God of the Prophets: An Analysis of Divine Action.* JSOTSup 249. Sheffield, England: Sheffield Academic, 1997.

Grudem, Wayne. *Systematic Theology: An Introduction to Biblical Doctrine.* Grand Rapids: Zondervan, 1994.

Gundry, Robert H. *The Church and the Tribulation.* Grand Rapids: Zondervan, 1973.

———. "The New Jerusalem People as Place, Not Place for People." *Novum Testamentum* 29 (1987) 254–264.

Hailey, Homer. *Revelation: An Introduction and Commentary.* Grand Rapids: Baker, 1979.

Happel, Stephen and James J. Walter. *Conversion and Discipleship: A Christian Foundation for Ethics and Doctrine.* Philadelphia: Fortress, 1986.

Harder, Leland. "The Concept of Discipleship in Christian Education." *Religious Education* 58 (1963) 347–358.

Hawthorne, Gerald F. "The Imitation of Christ: Discipleship in Philippians." In *Patterns of Discipleship in the New Testament*, edited by Richard N. Longenecker, 163–179. Grand Rapids: Eerdmans, 1996.

Hays, Richard. *The Moral Vision of the New Testament: Community, Cross, New Creation: A Contemporary Introduction to New Testament Ethics.* New York: HarperOne, 1996.

Helfmeyer, F. J. "הָלַךְ." In *TDOT* 3:388–403.

Helm, Paul. "Disciple." In *BEB* 1:629–631.

Hemer, Colin J. *The Letters to the Seven Churches of Asia in Their Local Setting.* Grand Rapids: Eerdmans: Dove, 2001.

Hendricksen, William. *More Than Conquerors.* Grand Rapids: Baker, 2007.

Hengel, Martin. *The Charismatic Leader and His Followers, Studies of the New Testament and Its World*, edited by John Riches. Translated by James C. G. Grieg. Edinburgh: T&T Clark, 1981.

Hera, Marianus Pale. *Christology and Discipleship in John 17.* WUNT 342. Tübingen: Mohr Siebeck, 2013.

Hernando, James D. "Imitation Language in Paul: Implications for Discipleship and Ministerial Training." Paper Presented at BTH Departmental Lecture, the Assemblies of God Theological Seminary, Springfield, MO.

Herodotus. *The History of Herodotus.* Vol. 1. Translated by G. C. Macaulay. New York: MacMillan, 1890.

Hess, K. "λατρεύω." In *NIDNTT* 3:549–551.

Hesse-Biber, Sharlene Nagy et al. *The Practice of Qualitative Research.* Thousand Oaks, CA: Sage, 2006.

Hillmer, Melvyn R. "The Believed in Him: Discipleship in the Johannine Tradition." In *Patterns of Discipleship in the New Testament*, edited by Richard N. Longenecker, 77–97. Grand Rapids: Eerdmans, 1996.

Hillyer, Norman. "'The Lamb' in the Apocalypse." *EQ* 39 (1967) 228–236.

Hoerber, Robert G. "Mathetes." *Concordia Journal* 6 (1980) 181–182.

Holsti, Ole R. *Content Analysis for the Social Sciences and Humanities.* Menlo Park, CA: Addison-Wesley, 1969.

Homcy, Stephen L. "'To Him Who Overcomes': A Fresh Look at What 'Victory' Means for the Believer according to the Book of Revelation." *JETS* 38 (June 1995) 193–201.

Hood, Jason B. *Imitating God in Christ: Recapturing a Biblical Pattern.* Downers Grove: IVP Academic, 2013.

Bibliography

Hoskins, Paul M. "Deliverance from Death by the True Passover Lamb: A Significant Aspect of the Fulfillment of the Passover Lamb in the Gospel of John." *JETS* 52 (2009) 285–299.

Hudgins, Thomas W. *Luke 6:40 and the Theme of Likeness Education in the New Testament.* Eugene, OR: Wipf & Stock, 2014.

Hurtado, Larry W. "Jesus as Lordly Example in Philippians 2:5–11." In *From Jesus to Paul*, edited by Peter Richardson and John C. Hurd, 113–126. Waterloo, Ontario, Canada: Wilfred Laurier University Press, 1984.

———. "Revelation 4–5 in the Light of Jewish Apocalyptic Analogies." *JSNT* 25 (1985) 105–124.

Irenaeus. *Against Hersies.* In *The Ante-Nicene Fathers.* Vol. 1. Edited by Alexander Roberts and James Donaldson. Grand Rapids: Eerdmans, 1969.

Jauhiainen, Marko. "The OT Background to Armageddon (Rev 16:16 Revised)." *Novum Testamentum* 47 (2005) 381–393.

Jenni, Ernst. "למד." In *TLOT* 2:646–648.

Jervis, L. Ann, "Becoming Like God through Christ: Discipleship in Romans." In *Patterns of Discipleship in the New Testament*, edited by Richard N. Longenecker, 143–162. Grand Rapids: Eerdmans, 1996.

Jiménez, Ramon Moreno. "El Discípulo de Jesucristo, según el evangelio de San Juan." *Estudios Bíblicos* 30 (1971) 269–311.

Johnson, Alan. "Revelation." In *EBC.* Vol. 13. Revised. Grand Rapids: Zondervan, 2006.

Johnson, Luke T. "Friendship with the World/Friendship with God: A Study of Discipleship in James." In *Discipleship in the New Testament*, edited by Fernando F. Segovia, 166–183. Philadelphia: Fortress, 1985.

Josephus. *Jewish Antiquites, Volume III: Books 7–8.* Translated by Ralph Marcus. LCL 281. Cambridge, MA: Harvard University Press, 1934.

Justin Martyr. *Dialogue with Trypho.* In *The Ante-Nicene Fathers.* Vol. 1. Edited by Alexander Roberts and James Donaldson. Grand Rapids: Eerdmans, 1969.

Kaiser, Walter C. "לָמַד." In *TWOT* 1:480.

Kapelrud, A. S. "לָמַד." In *TDOT* 8:4–10.

Keener, Craig S. *Revelation.* NIV Application Commentary. Grand Rapids, MI: Zondervan, 2000.

Kiddle, Martin. *The Revelation of St. John.* Moffat New Testament Commentary. New York: Harper and Brothers, 1940.

Kingsbury, Jack Dean. "On Following Jesus: The 'Eager' Scribe and the 'Reluctant' Disciple (Matthew 8:18–22)." *New Testament Studies* 34 (1988) 45–59.

Kistemaker, Simon J. *Exposition of the Book of Revelation.* New Testament Commentary. Grand Rapids: Baker Academic, 2001.

Kittel, G. "ἀκολουθέω." In *TDNT* 1:210–216.

Kline, Meredith G. "Double Trouble." *JETS* 32 (1989) 171–179.

Knowles, Michael P. "'Christ in You, the Hope of Glory': Discipleship in Colossians." In *Patterns of Discipleship in the New Testament*, edited by Richard N. Longenecker, 180–202. Grand Rapids: Eerdmans, 1996.

Koester, Craig. "Hearing, Seeing, and Believing in the Gospel of John." *Biblica* 70 (1989) 327–348.

———. *Revelation: A New Translation with Introduction and Commentary.* Anchor Yale Bible. Vol. 38A. New Haven, CT: Yale University Press, 2014.

———. *Revelation and the End of All Things.* Grand Rapids: Eerdmans, 2001.

Bibliography

Köstenberger, Andreas J. *John*. BECNT. Grand Rapids: Baker Academic, 2004.

———. *The Mission of Jesus and the Disciples according to the Fourth Gospel: With Implications for the Fourth Gospel's Purpose and the Mission of the Contemporary Church*. Grand Rapids: Eerdmans, 1998.

———. *A Theology of John's Gospel and Letters*. Biblical Theology of the New Testament. Grand Rapids: Zondervan, 2009.

Kowalski, Wojciech. "The Call to Discipleship: A Challenge to Personal Commitment." *African Ecclesial Review* 42 (2000) 120–132.

Krodel, Gerhard A. *Revelation*, Augsburg Commentary on the New Testament. Minneapolis: Augsburg Fortress, 1989.

Kruse, Colin G. *New Testament Models for Ministry: Jesus and Paul*. Nashville: Thomas Nelson, 1985.

Kurz, William S. "Kenotic Imitation of Paul and of Christ in Philippians 2 and 3." In *Discipleship in the New Testament*, edited by Fernando F. Segovia, 103–126. Philadelphia: Fortress, 1985.

Kvalbein, Hans. "Go Therefore and Make Disciples ... The Concept of Discipleship in the New Testament." *Themelios* 13 (1988) 48–53.

Lacocque, André. *The Book of Daniel*. Translated by David Pellauer. Atlanta: John Knox, 1979.

Ladd, George E. *A Commentary on the Revelation of John*. Grand Rapids: Eerdmans, 1972.

Lane, William L. "Standing before the Moral Claim of God: Discipleship in Hebrews." In *Patterns of Discipleship in the New Testament*, edited by Richard N. Longenecker, 203–224. Grand Rapids: Eerdmans, 1996.

Laney, J. Carl. "Abiding Is Believing: The Analogy of the Vine in John 15:1–6." *BSac* 146 (1989) 55–66.

Latz, Andrew Brower. "A Short Note toward a Theology of Abiding in John's Gospel." *Journal of Theological Interpretation* 4.2 (2010) 161–168.

Lauterbach, Jacob Z. *Mekilta de-Rabbi Ishmael: A Critical Edition on the Basis of the Manuscripts and Early Editions with an English Translation, Introduction, and Notes*. Philadelphia: Jewish Publication Society, 1961.

Leedy, Paul D. and Jeanne Ellis Ormrod. *Practical Research: Planning and Design*. 9th ed. Upper Saddle River, NJ: Pearson, 2010.

Lewis, Gordon R. and Bruce A. Demarest. *Integrative Theology*. Grand Rapids: Zondervan, 1996.

Lioy, Dan. *The Decalogue in the Sermon on the Mount*. Studies in Biblical Literature 66. New York: Peter Lang, 2004.

Lohse, E. "ῥαββι." In *TDNT* 6:961–965.

Longenecker, Richard N.. "Introduction." In *Patterns of Discipleship in the New Testament*, edited by Richard N. Longenecker, 1–7. Grand Rapids: Eerdmans, 1996.

———. ed. *Patterns of Discipleship in the New Testament*. Grand Rapids: Eerdmans, 1996.

———. "'Son of Man' Imagery: Some Implications for Discipleship." In *Studies in Hermeneutics, Christology, and Discipleship*, 224–245. New Testament Monographs. Sheffield, England: Sheffield Phoenix, 2004.

———. "Taking Up the Cross Daily: Discipleship in Luke-Acts." In *Patters of Discipleship in the New Testament*, edited by Richard N. Longenecker, 50–76. Grand Rapids: Eerdmans, 1996.

Longman III, Tremper. *Daniel*. NIV Application Commentary. Grand Rapids: Zondervan, 1999.

Bibliography

Luter Jr., A. Boyd. "The New Testament Theology of Discipling." ThD diss., Dallas Theological Seminary, 1985.

———. "Discipleship and the Church." *BSac* 137 (1980) 267–273.

Luz, Ulrich. "The Disciples in the Gospel According to Matthew." In *The Interpretation of Matthew, Issues in Religion and Theology 3*, translated and edited by Graham Stanton, 98–127. London: SPCK, 1983.

Maddix, Mark A. "John Wesley and a Holistic Approach to Christian Education." *Wesleyan Theology Journal* 44 (2009) 76–93.

Magness, Lee. "Teaching and Learning in the Gospels: The Biblical Basis of Christian Education." *Religious Education* 70 (1975) 629–635.

Malina, Bruce J. *On the Genre and Message of Revelation: Star Visions and Sky Journeys*. Peabody, MA: Hendrickson, 1995.

Mangina, Joseph L. *Revelation*. Brazos Theological Commentary on the Bible. Grand Rapids: Brazos, 2010.

Martin, Ralph P. "Salvation and Discipleship in Luke's Gospel." *Interpretation* 30 (1976) 366–380.

Martyn, J. Louis. *The Gospel of John in Christian History: Essays for Interpretation*. New York: Paulist, 1978.

———. *History and Theology* in the Fourth Gospel. 2nd ed. Nashville: Abingdon, 1979.

McBurney, Donald H. *Research Methods*. 5th Edition. Belmont, CA: Wadsworth, 2001.

McComiskey, Thomas Edward. "Alteration of OT Imagery in the Book of Revelation: Its Hermeneutical and Theological Significance." *JETS* 36 (Sept 1993) 307–316.

McIlraith, Donal A. "'For the Fine Linen Is the Righteous Deeds of the Saints': Works and Wife in Revelation 19:8." *Catholic Biblical Quarterly* 61 (1999) 512–529.

Merrill, Eugene H. "הלך." In *NIDOTTE* 2:801–803.

———. "למד." In *NIDOTTE* 2:801–803.

Metzger, Bruce M. *A Textual Commentary on the Greek New Testament*. 2nd ed. New York: UBS, 1994.

Meye, Robert P. "The Imitation of Christ: Means and End of Spiritual Formation." In *The Christian Educator's Handbook on Spiritual Formation*, edited by Kenneth O. Gangel and James C. Wilhoit, 199–212. Grand Rapids: Baker, 1994.

Michaelis, W. "μιμέομαι, μιμητής, συμμιμητής." In *TDNT* 4:659–674.

Michaels, J. Ramsey. "Going to Heaven with Jesus: From 1 Peter to Pilgrim's Progress." In *Patterns of Discipleship in the New Testament*, edited by Richard N. Longenecker, 248–268. Grand Rapids: Eerdmans, 1996.

———. *Interpreting the Book of Revelation*. Guides to New Testament Exegesis. Grand Rapids: Baker, 1992.

———. *Revelation*. IVP New Testament Commentary Series. Downers Grove: InterVarsity Press, 1997.

Miller, Kevin E. "The Nuptial Eschatology of Revelation 19–22." *Catholic Biblical Quarterly* 60 (1998) 301–318.

Miller, Stephen R. *Daniel*. NAC. Vol. 18. Nashville: Broadman & Holman, 1994.

Milligan, William. "The Book of Revelation." In *The Expositor's Bible*. New York: A. C. Armstrong and Son, 1902.

Montefiore, C. G. *Rabbinic Literature and Gospel Teachings*. London: MacMillan, 1930.

Montgomery, James A. *A Critical and Exegetical Commentary on the Book of Daniel*. Edinburgh: T&T Clark, 1927.

Bibliography

Morris, Leon. *The Book of Revelation: An Introduction and Commentary*. Tyndale New Testament Commentaries. Reprint. Grand Rapids: Eerdmans, 2002.

———. *The Gospel according to John*. NICNT. Revised. Grand Rapids: Eerdmans, 1995.

Morrison, Karl F. *The Mimetic Tradition of Reform in the West*. Princeton: Princeton University Press, 1982.

Mounce, Robert H. *The Book of Revelation*. NICNT. Revised. Grand Rapids: Eerdmans, 1997.

Müller, D. "μαθητής." In *NIDNTT* 1:483–490.

Oecumenius. *Commentary on the Apocalypse*. Translated by John N. Suggit. Washington, DC: The Catholic University Press, 2006.

Origen. *De Principiis*. In *The Ante-Nicene Fathers*. Vol. 4. Edited by Alexander Roberts and James Donaldson. Grand Rapids: Eerdmans, 1968.

Osborne, Grant R. *Revelation*. BECNT. Grand Rapids: Baker Academic, 2002.

Ozanne, C. G. "The Language of the Apocalypse." *Tyndale Bulletin* 16 (1965) 3–9.

Palatty, Paul. "Discipleship in the Fourth Gospel." *Bible Bhashyahm* 25 (1999) 285–306.

Park, Sung-Min. "More Than a Regained Eden: The New Jerusalem as the Ultimate Portrayal of Eschatological Blessedness and Its Implication for the Understanding of the Book of Revelation." PhD diss., Trinity Evangelical Divinity School, 1995.

Parrett, Gary A. and S. Steve Kang. *Teaching the Faith, Forming the Faithful: A Biblical Vision for Education in the Church*. Downers Grove: IVP Academic, 2009.

Pate, C. Marvin. *Four Views on the Book of Revelation*. Grand Rapids: Zondervan, 1998.

Pattemore, Stephen. *The People of God in the Apocalypse: Discourse, Structure, and Exegesis*. SNTSMS 128. Cambridge: Cambridge University Press, 2004.

Patterson, Paige. *Revelation*. NAC. Nashville: B&H, 2012.

Pazmiño, Robert. W. "Christian Education Is More Than Formation." *Christian Education Journal* 7 (2010) 356–365.

———. *Foundational Issues in Christian Education: An Introduction in Evangelical Perspective*. 2nd ed. Grand Rapids: Baker, 1997.

———. *Principles and Practices of Christian Education: An Evangelical Perspective*. Grand Rapids: Baker, 1992.

Peterson, David. *Possessed by God: A New Testament Theology of Sanctification and Holiness*. Grand Rapids: Eerdmans, 1995.

Peterson, Eugene H. *A Long Obedience in the Same Direction: Discipleship in an Instant Society*. 2nd ed. Downers Grove: InterVarsity Press, 2000.

Philo. *On Abraham. On Joseph. On Moses*. Translated by F. H. Colson. LCL 289. Cambridge, MA: Harvard University Press, 1935.

———. *On the Cherubim. On the Sacrifices of Abel and Cain. The Worse Attacks the Better. On the Posterity and Exile of Cain. On the Giants*. Translated by F. H. Colson, G. H. Whitaker. LCL 227. Cambridge, MA: Harvard University Press, 1929.

Piper, Otto Alfred. "Unchanging Promises: Exodus in the New Testament." *Interpretation* 11 (1957) 3–22.

Plato. *Cratylus. Parmenides. Greater Hippias. Lesser Hippias*. Translated by Harold North Fowler. LCL 167. Cambridge, MA: Harvard University Press, 1926.

———. *Euthyphro. Apology. Crito. Phaedo. Phaedrus*. Translated by Harold North Fowler. LCL 36. Cambridge, MA: Harvard University Press, 1914.

———. *Laches. Protagoras. Meno. Euthydemus*. Translated by W. R. M. Lamb. LCL 165. Cambridge, MA: Harvard University Press, 1924.

Bibliography

———. *Lysis. Symposium. Gorgias.* Translated by W. R. M. Lamb. LCL 166. Cambridge, MA: Harvard University Press, 1925.

———. *Republic, Volume I: Books 1–5.* Edited and translated by Christopher Emlyn-Jones, William Preddy. LCL 237. Cambridge, MA: Harvard University Press, 2013.

Plummer, Robert L. "Imitation of Paul and the Church's Missionary Role." *JETS* 44 (2001) 219–235.

Porteous, Norman W. *Daniel: A Commentary.* Philadelphia: Westminster, 1965.

Proudfoot, C. Merrill. "Imitation of Realistic Participation?: A Study of Paul's Concept of 'Suffering with Christ.'" *Interpretation* 17 (1963) 140–160.

Ramsay, William M. *The Letters to the Seven Churches of Asia and Their Place in the Plan of the Apocalypse.* Grand Rapids: Baker, 1979.

Randall, John. *Book of Revelation: What Does It Really Say?* Locust Valley, NY: Living Flame, 1976.

Ray, Daniel Lee. "A Content Analysis of Jesus' Teaching Method in Comparison with Current Differentiated Teaching." EdD diss., Southeastern Baptist Theological Seminary, 2010.

Richards, Lawrence O. *Christian Education: Seeking to Become Like Jesus Christ.* Grand Rapids: Zondervan, 1975.

Ridderbos, Herman. *The Gospel according to John: A Theological Commentary.* Translated by John Vriend. Grand Rapids: Eerdmans, 1997.

Rengstorf, K. H. "διδάσκω, διδάσκαλος." In *TDNT* 2:135–165.

———. "μαθητής." In *TDNT* 4:415–461.

Reynolds, Edwin. "The Feast of Tabernacles and the Book of Revelation." *Andrews University Seminary Studies* 38 (2000) 245–268.

Rissi, Mathias. "The Kerygma of the Revelation to John." *Interpretation* 22 (1968) 3–17.

Robertson, A. T. *A Grammar of the Greek New Testament in the Light of Historical Research.* Nashville: Broadman, 1934.

———. *Word Pictures in the New Testament.* Vol. 6. Nashville: Broadman, 1933.

Roloff, Jürgen. *Revelation: A Continental Commentary.* Translated by John E. Alsup. Minneapolis: Fortress, 1993.

Rosscup, James E. "The Overcomer of the Apocalypse." *GTJ* 3 (1982) 261–286.

Ryan, Gery W. and H. Russell Bernard. "Data Management and Analysis Methods." In *Handbook of Qualitative Research.* 2nd ed., edited by Norman K. Denzin and Yvonna S. Lincoln, 769–802. Thousand Oaks, CA: Sage, 2000.

Samra, James G. "A Biblical View of Discipleship." *BSac* 160 (2003) 219–234.

Sanders, Boykin. "Imitating Paul: 1 Cor. 4:16." *HTR* 74 (1981) 353–363.

Sauer, G. "הלך." In *TLOT* 2:365–370.

Sawicki, M. "How to Teach Christ's Disciples: John 1:19–37 and Matthew 11:2–15." *Lexington Theological Quarterly* 21 (1986) 14–26.

Schnackenburg, Rudolf. "Excursus 17: The Disciples, the Community and the Church in the Gospel of John." In *The Gospel According to St. John.* Vol. 3, translated by C. Hastings, 203–217. New York: Herder and Herder, 1987.

Schreier, Margrit. *Qualitative Content Analysis in Practice.* Thousand Oaks, CA: Sage, 2012.

Schüssler Fiorenza, Elisabeth. *The Book of Revelation: Justice and Judgment.* 2nd ed. Minneapolis: Augsburg Fortress, 1998.

Bibliography

———. "The Followers of the Lamb: Visionary Rhetoric and Social-Political Situation." In *Discipleship in the New Testament*, edited by Fernando F. Segovia, 144–165. Philadelphia: Fortress, 1985.

———. *Revelation: Vision of a Just World*. Proclamation Commentaries. Minneapolis: Augsburg, 1991.

Schweizer, Eduard. *Lordship and Discipleship*. Studies in Biblical Theology. London: SCM, 1960.

Segovia, Fernando F., ed. *Discipleship in the New Testament*. Philadelphia: Fortress, 1985.

———. "Introduction." In *Discipleship in the New Testament*, edited by Fernando F. Segovia, 1–23. Philadelphia: Fortress, 1985.

———. "'Peace I Leave with You; My Peace I Give to You:' Discipleship in the Fourth Gospel." In *Discipleship in the New Testament*, edited by F. F. Segovia, 76–102. Philadelphia: Fortress, 1985.

Seift, Fletcher Harper. *Education in Ancient Israel from Earliest Times to 70 AD*. Chicago: Open Court, 1919.

Seneca. *Epistles, Volume I: Epistles 1–65*. Translated by Richard M. Gummere. LCL 75. Cambridge, MA: Harvard University Press, 1917.

Shirley, Chris. "It Takes a Church to Make a Disciples: An Integrative Model of Discipleship for the Local Church." *Southwestern Journal of Theology* 50 (Spring 2008) 207–224.

Siew, Antoninus King Wai. *The War Between the Two Beasts and the Two Witnesses: A Chiastic Reading of Revelation 11:1—14:5*. Library of New Testament Studies 283. London: T&T Clark, 2005.

Siker-Gieseler, Jeffrey S. "Disciples and Discipleship in the Fourth Gospel: A Canonical Approach." *Studia Biblica et Theologica* 10 (1980) 199–227.

Slotki, Israel Wolf. *Isaiah*. Soncino Books of the Bible. London: Soncino, 1949.

Smalley, Stephen S. *The Revelation to John: A Commentary on the Greek Text of the Apocalypse*. Downers Grove: InterVarsity Press, 2006.

Smith, Christopher R. "The Portrayal of the Church as the New Israel in the Names and Order of the Tribes in Revelation 7:5–8." *JSNT* 39 (1990) 111–118.

———. "The Tribes of Revelation 7 and the Literary Competence of John the Seer." *JETS* 38 (1995) 213–218.

Spicq, Ceslas. "δοῦλος, οἰκέτης, οἰκεῖος, μίσθιος, μισθωτός." In *TLNT* 1:380–386.

———. "ὑπόδειγμα." In *TLNT* 3:403–405.

Stanley, D. M. "Become Imitators of Me." *Biblica* 40 (1959) 859–877.

Steibel, Sophia R. G. "Christian Education and Spiritual Formation: One and the Same?" *Christian Education Journal* 7 (2010) 340–355.

Strack, Hermann L. and Paul Billerbeck. *Commentary on the New Testament from the Talmud and Midrash: English and German*. Bellingham, WA: Lexham, 2013.

Strathmann, H. "μάρτυς, μαρτυρέω, μαρτυρία, μαρτύριον." In *TDNT* 4:474–514.

Stuckenbruck, Loren T. "Revelation: Historical Setting and John's Call to Discipleship." *Leaven* 8 (2000) 1–5.

Sweet, J. M. P. *Revelation*. Westminster Pelican Commentaries. Philadelphia: Westminster, 1979.

Sweetland, Dennis M. *Our Journey with Jesus: Discipleship According to Luke-Acts*. Good News Studies 23. Wilmington, DE: Michael Glazier, 1990.

Swete, Henry Barclay. *Revelation*. 3rd ed. London: Macmillan, 1911; Reprint: Grand Rapids: Kregel, 1977.

Bibliography

Tannehill, Robert C. "The Disciples in Mark: The Function of a Narrative Role." In *The Interpretation of Mark. Issues in Religion and Theology* 7, edited by William Telford, 134–157. London: SPCK, 1985.
Tertullian. *Against Marcion*. In *The Ante-Nicene Fathers*. Vol. 3. Edited by Alexander Roberts and James Donaldson. Grand Rapids: Eerdmans, 1968.
Thomas, Robert L. *Revelation 1–7, 8–22: An Exegetical Commentary*. Chicago: Moody, 1992, 1995.
Thompson, Leonard. "Hymns in Early Christian Worship." *Anglican Theological Review* 55 (1973) 458–472.
Townsend, Jeffrey L. "The Rapture in Revelation 3:10." *BSac* 137 (1980) 252–266.
Trakatellis, Demetrios. "'*Akoloutheō moi*/Follow me' (Mark 2:14) Discipleship and Priesthood." *Greek Orthodox Theological Review* 30 (1985) 271–285.
Trebilco, Paul. "What Shall We Call Each Other? Part Two: The Issue of Self-designation in the Johannine Letters and Revelation." *Tyndale Bulletin* 54 (2003) 51–73.
Tuente, R. "δοῦλος." In *NIDNTT* 3:589–598.
Vanni, Ugo. "Commitment and Discipleship in the New Testament." In *Biblical Themes in Religious Education*, edited by Joseph S. Marino, 156–162. Birmingham: Religious Education, 1983.
Vellanickal, Mathew. "'Discipleship' According to the Gospel of John." *Jeevadhara: A Journal of Christian Interpretation* 10 (1980) 131–147.
Vincent, John J. *Disciple and Lord: The Historical and Theological Significance of Discipleship in the Synoptic Gospels*. Sheffield, England: Sheffield Academic, 1976.
Vos, Louis A. *The Synoptic Traditions in the Apocalypse*. Kampen: Kok, 1965.
Wagner, C. Peter. "What Is 'Making Disciples'?." *Evangelical Missions Quarterly* 9 (1973) 285–293.
Wall, Robert. *Revelation*. NIBCNT. Peabody, MA: Hendrickson, 1991.
Wallace, Daniel B. *Greek Grammar Beyond the Basics: An Exegetical Syntax of the New Testament*. Grand Rapids: Zondervan, 1996.
Wallen, Norman E. and Jack R. Fraenkel. *Educational Research: A Guide to the Process*. 2nd ed. Mahwah, NJ: Lawrence Erlbaum, 2001.
Walvoord, John F. *The Revelation of Jesus Christ*. Chicago: Moody, 1966.
Weaver, Jason G. "Paul's Call to Imitation: The Rhetorical Function of the Theme of Imitation in its Epistolary Context." PhD diss., The Catholic University of America, 2013.
Westerhoff, John. "Formation, Education, Instruction." *Religious Education* 82 (1987) 578–591.
Whitters, Mark F. "Discipleship in the Fourth Gospel: Four Profiles." *Word & World* 18 (1998) 422–427.
Wilcock, Michael. *The Message of Revelation: I Saw Heaven Opened*. Bible Speaks Today. Downers Grove: Inter-Varsity Press, 1984.
Wild, Robert A. "'Be Imitators of God': Discipleship in the Letter to the Ephesians." In *Discipleship in the New Testament*, edited by Fernando F. Segovia, 127–143. Philadelphia: Fortress, 1985.
Wilhoit, James C. *Spiritual Formation as if the Church Mattered: Growing in Christ through Community*. Grand Rapids: Baker Academic, 2008.
Willard, Dallas. *Renovation of the Heart: Putting on the Character of Christ*. Colorado Springs: NavPress, 2002.

Bibliography

Wilkins, Michael J. *The Concept of Disciple in Matthew's Gospel: As Reflected in the Use of the Term* μαθητής. Supplement to Novum Testamentum 59. Leiden: Brill, 1988.

———. "Discipleship." In *DJG* 176–182.

———. *Following the Master: Discipleship in the Steps of Jesus.* Grand Rapids: Zondervan, 1992.

Wilson, Mark. *Charts on the Book of Revelation: Literary, Historical, and Theological Perspectives.* Grand Rapids: Kregel, 2007.

———. *The Victor Sayings in the Book of Revelation.* Eugene, OR: Wipf & Stock, 2007.

Winberry, Carlton L. "Abiding in Christ: The Concept of Discipleship in John." *The Theological Educator* 38 (1988) 104–120.

Xenophon. *Memorabilia. Oeconomicus. Symposium. Apology.* Translated by E. C. Marchant, O. J. Todd. Revised by Jeffrey Henderson. LCL 168. Cambridge, MA: Harvard University Press, 2013.

Yarbro Collins, Adela. *The Apocalypse.* New Testament Message 22. Wilmington, DE: Michael Glazier, 1979.

———. *The Combat Myth in the Book of Revelation.* Eugene, OR: Wipf and Stock, 2001.

———. *Crisis and Catharsis: The Power of the Apocalypse.* Philadelphia: Westminster, 1984.

———. "The History-of-Religions Approach to Apocalypticism and the 'Angel of the Waters' (Rev 16:4–7)." *CQB* 39 (1977) 367–381.

———. *Jewish and Christian Apocalypticism.* Supplements to the Journal for the Study of Judaism. Vol. 50. Leiden: Brill, 1996.

Young, Edward J. *The Book of Isaiah.* Grand Rapids: Eerdmans, 1965.

Young, Rick A "The Goal of Christian Teaching: Christlikeness." In *The Teaching Ministry of the Church: Integrating Biblical Truth with Contemporary Application*, edited by Daryl Eldridge, 141–169. Nashville: Broadman & Holman, 1995.

———. "Jesus, the Master Teacher." In *The Teaching Ministry of the Church: Integrating Biblical Truth with Contemporary Application*, edited by Daryl Eldridge, 21–42. Nashville: Broadman & Holman, 1995.

———. "A Theology of Christian Education." In *The Teaching Ministry of the Church*. 2nd ed., edited by Rick Yount, 3–15. Nashville: B&H, 2008.

Author Index

Abbott, Edwin A., 105
Atkinson, Paul, 15
Aune, David E., 2, 3, 4, 79, 81, 82, 85,
    93, 97, 98, 109, 111, 126, 127, 130,
    138, 140, 144, 146, 150, 153, 156,
    157, 158, 160, 161, 162, 163, 166,
    171, 174, 176, 178, 179, 183, 184,
    185, 192, 193, 194, 197, 200, 203,
    207, 208, 209, 212, 217, 231

Bauckham, Richard, 80, 82, 89, 90, 105,
    125, 127, 128, 130, 150, 157, 160,
    168, 171, 173, 174, 183, 187, 203
Bazar, James L., 14
Beale, Gregory K., 81, 83, 86, 92, 94,
    95, 96, 97, 101, 104, 106, 107, 110,
    112, 114, 116, 117, 122, 124, 126,
    128, 129, 130, 133, 134, 135, 138,
    139, 140, 141, 146, 148, 149, 150,
    153, 155, 156, 157, 159, 161, 163,
    165, 168, 169, 170, 171, 172, 173,
    174, 176, 177, 182, 184, 191, 192,
    193, 194, 195, 199, 200, 201, 203,
    206, 210, 213, 216, 220, 229
Beasley-Murray, George R., 96, 113,
    115, 137, 158, 160, 173, 195, 203,
    206
Beck, David R., 59, 64, 76
Beckwith, Isbon Thaddeus, 113, 157
Berg, Bruce L., 13, 14
Bernard, H. Russell, 14
Billerbeck, Paul, 23
Blendinger, C., 33
Blount, Brian K., 109, 129, 137–138
Boring, M. Eugene, 108, 158, 187, 228

Boxall, Ian, 196
Boyatzis, Richard E., 14
Boyer, James L., 216
Brown, Raymond E., 57, 58, 156
Brueggemann, Dale, 159
Bryan, C. Doug, 7

Caird, G. B., 92, 137, 196, 203
Calenberg, Richard D., 26, 28
Carson, D. A., 64, 78, 137
Charles, R. H., 10, 11, 80, 97, 102, 104,
    106, 114, 119, 128, 135, 138, 139,
    141, 142, 150, 153, 158, 172, 175,
    176, 184, 189, 200
Chennattu, Rekha M., 67, 68–70, 73, 76
Clement of Alexandria, 11
Clouse, Robert G., 9
Coffey, Amanda, 15
Coleman, Lucien, 7
Collins, Raymond F., 51, 58, 59–60, 76
Corsini, Eugenio, 152
Culpepper, R. Alan, 47, 51, 56–57, 73,
    76

Davids, Peter H., 43
DeBoer, Willis Peter, 40
De Jonge, Marinus, 48, 50–51, 73
Demarest, Bruce A., 9
Donaldson, James, 32, 33
Draper, J. A., 137
Du Rand, J. A., 58, 60–61, 76
Duvall, J. Scott, 132

Elliott, John H., 42
Euripedes, 21

253

Author Index

Fekkes, III, Jan, 186, 192
Feuillet, André, 122
Ford, J. Massynberde, 115, 122, 137, 153, 173, 174, 203
Fraenkel, Jack R., 12
Freyne, Sean, 31–32, 37
Furnish, Victor Paul, 40

Gangel, Kenneth O., 4, 7
Giblin, Charles Homer, 147, 150
Gloer, W. Hulitt, 59, 61–62, 73, 76
González, Catherine, 152
González, Justo L., 152
Graendorf, Werner C., 5
Grbich, Carol, 12
Green, Michael P. 37
Griffin, William Paul, 13
Grudem, Wayne, 9
Gundry, Robert H., 133, 191

Hailey, Homer, 160
Hawthorne, Gerald F., 41–42
Hays, J. Daniel, 132
Hays, Richard, 40
Helm, Paul, 2
Hemer, Colin J., 96, 101, 114, 115
Hendricksen, William, 215
Hengel, Martin, 28, 35, 37
Hera, Marianus Pale, 67, 70–73, 76
Hernando, James D., 39
Herodotus, 18
Hesse-Biber, Sharlene Nagy, 12
Hillmer, Melvyn R., 63
Hillyer, Norman, 127
Hoerber, Robert G., 7
Holsti, Ole R., 13, 15
Hood, Jason B., 44
Hudgins, Thomas W., 14, 41

Irenaeus, 11

Jervis, L. Ann, 43
Jiménez, Ramon Moreno, 48–49
Johnson, Alan, 88, 96, 110, 113, 123, 127, 137, 145, 146, 147, 151, 153, 158, 162, 171, 173, 206, 216
Josephus, 24, 28
Justin Martyr, 11

Kapelrud, A. S., 26
Keener, Craig S., 83, 109, 132, 137, 150, 153, 161
Kiddle, Martin, 156, 157, 158
Kistemaker, Simon J., 95, 96, 101, 103, 137
Kittel, G., 32, 33
Knowles, Michael P., 43
Koester, Craig, 83, 96, 97, 102, 105, 111, 112, 114, 125, 126, 128, 134, 135, 136, 138, 141, 142, 145, 146, 150, 151, 153, 156, 157, 158, 160, 161, 162, 163, 164, 166, 171, 172, 173, 176, 177, 180, 182, 183, 187, 194, 195, 196, 203, 204, 207, 215
Köstenberger, Andreas J., 59, 64, 65–66, 76
Kurz, William S., 42

Ladd, George E., 101, 123, 126, 141, 150, 158, 176, 216
Lane, William L., 42
Leavy, Patricia L., 12
Leedy, Paul D., 12
Lewis, Gordon R., 9
Lioy, Dan, 14
Longenecker, Richard N., 30, 37, 39

Malina, Bruce J., 97
Martyn, J. Louis, 58
McDonough, Sean M., 140
Merrill, Eugene H., 26
Metzger, Bruce M., 64, 96, 194
Michaelis, W., 40, 42
Michaels, J. Ramsey, 216
Miller, Kevin E., 191, 197
Miller, Stephen R., 96
Montefiore, C. G., 34–35
Morris, Leon, 53, 64, 78, 157
Moo, Douglas J., 78
Mounce, Robert H., 78, 79, 96, 103, 106, 116, 118, 125, 137, 141, 145, 146, 152, 156, 158, 171, 173, 174, 176, 180, 184, 192, 193, 199, 203, 209, 216, 229
Müller, D., 30, 31

Oecumenius, 160

Author Index

Origen, 11
Ormrod, Jeanne Ellis, 12
Osborne, Grant R., 9, 11, 81, 83, 84,
    89, 98, 101, 102, 104, 109, 111,
    113, 114, 118, 122, 125, 127, 129,
    137–138, 141, 143, 146, 149, 150,
    153, 154, 156, 157, 159, 164, 168,
    169, 170, 171, 173, 174, 176, 177,
    178, 184, 187, 192, 196, 197, 199,
    203, 206, 208, 209, 214, 217, 220

Palatty, Paul, 59, 66–67, 76
Pate, C. Marvin, 8
Patterson, Paige, 79, 96, 158
Pazmiño, Robert W., 5
Peterson, David, 225
Peterson, Eugene H., 7
Philo, 24
Plato, 18, 19, 20, 21
Porteous, Norman W., 96

Randall, John, 152
Ray, Daniel Lee, 14
Ridderbos, Herman, 64
Rengstorf, K. H., 18, 21, 22, 23, 25–26,
    28, 29, 30
Reynolds, Edwin, 137
Rissi, Mathias, 152
Robertson, A. T., 83, 109, 177
Roloff, Jürgen, 156, 176, 203

Samra, James G., 6–7
Sauer, G., 27
Schnackenburg, Rudolf, 48, 49–50, 76
Schreier, Margrit, 12, 13, 14, 15
Schüssler Fiorenza, Elisabeth, 2–3, 4,
    173
Schweizer, Eduard, 38
Segovia, Fernando F., 6, 17, 38, 39, 47,
    51, 57–58
Seift, Fletcher Harper, 27
Seneca, 21

Siker-Gieseler, Jeffrey S., 51, 53–56
Slotki, Israel Wolf, 26
Smalley, Stephen S., 103, 108, 116,
    118, 126, 129, 138, 139, 141, 142,
    156, 157, 159, 161, 162, 163, 170,
    171, 173, 175, 176, 179, 183, 184,
    185, 191, 192, 194, 200, 201, 204,
    207–208, 209, 216, 229
Spicq, Ceslas, 41, 85
Stanley, D. M., 40
Steibel, Sophia R. G., 6
Strack, Hermann L., 23
Stuckenbruck, Loren T., 2, 4

Tertullian, 11
Thomas, Robert L., 83, 92, 94, 96, 98,
    101, 104, 110, 111, 117, 119, 125,
    126, 127, 128, 132, 133, 137, 141,
    145, 147, 153, 156, 157, 158, 168,
    169, 171, 172, 173, 174, 175, 176,
    178, 180, 184, 188, 190, 197, 203,
    205, 206, 207, 226
Thompson, Leonard, 173

Vellanickal, Mathew, 51–53, 76
Vos, Louis A., 85

Wall, Robert, 138, 203
Wallace, Daniel B., 53, 80, 83, 86, 114,
    125, 126, 138, 162, 170, 171, 173,
    179, 188, 197, 200, 215, 230
Wallen, Norman E., 12
Walvoord, John F., 158, 169, 172, 190
Whitters, Mark F., 56
Wild, Robert A., 42
Wilkins, Michael J., 1, 2, 6, 22, 23, 26,
    29, 30, 31, 37, 38, 39, 80

Xenophon, 18, 21

Yarbro Collins, Adela, 97, 155, 157
Young, Edward J., 26–27

Scripture Index

OLD TESTAMENT

Genesis

1–3	203, 217
1:7	170
2–3	109
2:25	179
3:3	179
3:22–24	217
4:15	136
5:22	118
5:24	118
9:20–25	179
12:4	27
13:5	27
13:16	137
14:24	27
15:2	27
15:5	137
17:1–22	
17:7	208
22:17–18	137
26:3–4	137
26:19	207
32:28	116, 229
33:12	27
48:15	139
49:9–10	125
49:9	125
49:10	125
49:24	139

Exodus

3:14	89
7–12	170
7:20–25	145
9:22–25	145
10:12–15	145
10:21–23	145
12	126
12:6	129
12:7	136
12:13	136
12:22–28	136
14:13–14	183
14:29	27
15	173, 174
15:1–18	173
19:6	130
22:15	218
25:8	69
25:9	204, 226
28:36–38	135, 136, 147
26:36	136
29:45–46	69
29:45	204
32:1	27
33:7–11	204, 226
34:6	104

Leviticus

11:25	216
13:6	216
14:6	207
14:8	216

Leviticus (continued)

14:13	129
14:25	129
16:11	129
16:15	129
19:32	96
20:26	100, 232
21:16–24	165
22:21	165
26:11–12	204

Numbers

3:13	127
8:21	216
24:17	214
31:24	216

Deuteronomy

5:1	26
5:2	26
10:17	197
17:6	84
23:17–18	218
26:17	27
28:9	27
32	173
32:35	198, 233
33:17	128

Joshua

3:10	90
8:35	27
14:10	27
22:5	27
23:14	27
24:3	27
24:19–20	69
24:25–28	69

Judges

3:31	26
5:31	98
11:16	27
11:18	27

1 Samuel

12:2	27
15:33	129

2 Samuel

5:6–9	159
7:7	139
7:12	214
7:14	208, 209
22:35	26

1 Kings

7:23–26	170
10:19–20	125
19:21	28, 29, 35

2 Kings

19:32–35	183
25:7	129

1 Chronicles

5:18	26
25:8	26

2 Chronicles

17:7	26
17:9	26
20	183

Ezra

6:20	129

Job

10:16	125
21:22	26

Scripture Index

Psalms

2	158
2:6	159
9:11	159
16:10	103
18:2	128
22:16	218
22:20	218
23:1	139
23:3	139
28:4	213
33:3	129
40:3	129
42:2	90
46:4	205
60	26
62:12	213
68:7–10	139
76:2	159
80:1	139
86:15	104
96:1	129
112:9	128
132:13	159
136:2–3	197

Proverbs

16:31	96
19:12	125
24:12	213

Isaiah

1:4	103
2:4	26
4:2–6	159
6:9–10	107
8:16	26, 27, 28, 45
11	214
11:1–5	125, 214
11:1	125
11:4	125, 214
20:1–6	179
24:23	122, 159
25:6	188
25:8	125
31:4	125, 159
37:23	103
37:33–36	183
40:11	139
40:25	103
41:4	90, 213
42:10	129
44:6	90, 213
44:28	139
48:12	90, 213
49:10	139, 140, 142
49:18	186
53	126
53:4	126
53:5	126
53:7	126, 129
53:9	165
53:12	126
54:5	186, 188
54:11–12	186–187, 192
55:1	207
60	203
61:10	186–187, 188, 192
62:2	116, 229
62:5	186
63	196
63:1–3	193, 195, 196
65	203
65:6	199
65:15	116, 229
65:16	104

Jeremiah

2	165
2:2–3	165
3:15	139
5:23	27
7:23	205
17:10	213
23:18	80
30:22	205
31:1	205
31:32	186, 188
31:33	205
32:33	26
32:38	205
50:19	139

Scripture Index

Jeremiah (continued)

50:44	125

Ezekiel

1:13	96
1:24	97
1:27	96
8:2	96
9	135–136
9:4	135, 147
11:20	205
16:8	188
16:36	179
18:23	219
18:32	219
23:29	179
33:11	219
34:23–24	139
36:28	205
37:23	205
37:27	204
39:17–20	190
40–48	203
40:41–42	129
43:2	97

Daniel

1:12–15	112
2	81
2:28–29	81
2:37	197
2:45	81
2:47	197
7	88, 95, 152
7:9	95
7:10	199
7:13–14	88
7:13	87, 94
7:25	151
8:25	197
9	150
10:6	96, 98
10:11	96
10:19	96
11:36	197
12:1–2	199
12:1	137
12:7	151

Hosea

1:10	90
2	188
5:14	125
10:1	26

Joel

1–2	146
2:32	159
3:11b	183

Amos

3:7	80, 150
3:8	125

Micah

4:3	26
4:7	159
5:4	139

Nahum

3:4–5	179
3:18	139

Habakkuk

3:3	103

Zechariah

2:10–11	205
3:9	128
4:1–14	102
4:1–6	151
4:2	94, 128
4:10–14	151
4:10	94, 128
6:9–15	127
6:12–13	127

Scripture Index

8:8	205
12:10	87–88
14	137
14:5b	183

Malachi

3:16	199

NEW TESTAMENT

Matthew

1:1	125
1:6	125
1:20	188
3:12	200
4:15	151
5	85
5:13–16	235
5:44	231
8:11–12	188
8:19	164
8:21	35
9:13	190
10:5	151
10:38	32
13:41	196
15:24	139
16:21	153
16:27	196, 213
17:2	98
18:16	84
19:15	188
22:37–39	106, 234
23:31	175
23:37	175, 219
24	137
24:9	151
24:21	137
24:30	87, 88
24:33	110
25:31	196
25:32	139
25:41	193
26:29	188
26:31–32	139
27:63	153
28:18	221, 228
28:19–20	38, 221, 228, 230

Mark

1:17	33
1:24	103
2:19–20	188
4:10–12	107
8:31	153
9:31	153
9:34	200
10:42–45	80
10:43	153
10:47	125
12:29–31	106, 234
13:26	88, 95
13:29	110
14:25	188
14:27–28	139
14:62	88
15:29–32	153

Luke

1:35	103
2:4	125
2:32	151
3:17	200
3:31	125
4:34	103
5:1	93
5:34–35	188
6	85
6:13	31
6:17	31
6:40	14
8:11	93
8:21	93
8:31	152
9:59	35
10:20	116
10:27	106, 234
11:28	85, 93
12:36	110
13:1–5	230

Luke (continued)

13:3	231
13:5	231
13:28–29	188
13:34	219
16:23	91
19:10	139
22:18	188
22:24–27	80
24:45–48	84
24:47	38

John

1–12	54, 55, 71, 72
1–3	57
1	68, 126
1:1	196
1:3	105
1:10–13	76
1:10–11	71
1:12	72
1:13	72
1:14	196, 210, 226
1:29	59, 127
1:35—2:11	62
1:35–51	50, 62, 68, 69, 73, 75
1:35–50	67
1:35–42	51
1:35–39	51, 59
1:35–37	71
1:35	56, 59, 127
1:37–43	66
1:37	54, 56, 66
1:38	54, 58
1:39	54, 74
1:40–41	69, 75
1:40	56, 66
1:41–46	54
1:41	74, 75
1:42–43	54
1:42	69, 74
1:43	66, 74, 75
1:45–46	75
1:45	69, 74, 75
1:47	74
1:49–50	69, 74
1:49	54, 69, 74
1:50–51	69
1:50	94
1:51	75, 94
2:1–5	64
2:11	54, 71, 75
2:17	54
2:19–21	151
2:22	54
3:5	140
3:16–17	74
3:39	188
4–12	57
4	208
4:3	66
4:4–42	64
4:4–16	208
4:7–45	75
4:7–30	55
4:10	140
4:13–14	140
4:14	143
4:33	54
4:38	65
4:46–54	55
4:46–53	64
5:2–16	64
5:22	213
5:24	128
5:30	66, 128
5:38	66
6	62
6:1–71	62
6:7–9	54
6:10–12	75
6:19	54
6:35	74, 89, 140, 143
6:56–57	76
6:56	74
6:60	54
6:66	118
6:68	54
6:69	54, 103
6:70	54, 74
7:17–18	140
7:24	98
7:37	143
7:38–39	140

Scripture Index

Reference	Pages	Reference	Pages
7:53—8:11	64	13:20	66
8:12	61, 66, 74, 89	13:23–26	67
8:17	82	13:25	54
8:31–47	112	13:31	75
8:31–32	53, 75, 105	13:33	70
8:31	48, 53, 56, 74	13:34–35	57, 75, 105
8:33	54	13:34	75, 231, 234
8:42	128	13:35	48, 50, 61
9:1–41	55, 64	13:37	54
9:38	71	14:6	89
10	66	14:10	52
10:1–30	140	14:15	75
10:4–5	74, 120, 227	14:16–17	99
10:4	54, 74	14:21	75
10:7	89	14:23	75
10:11	89, 139	14:26	99, 128
10:14–15	71, 76	14:28	70
10:15	74	15–17	57, 69, 70
10:27	54, 74	15	65
10:28	55	15:1–17	68, 69–70, 74
11:1–44	55	15:1–6	117
11:4	75	15:1	65, 89
11:25–26	101	15:4–7	52
11:25	89	15:4	75
11:40	75	15:5	70, 232
11:42	128	15:8	48, 56, 75, 101
12:4	54	15:9–17	70
12:7	75	15:9	75
12:16	53, 54	15:10	75
12:23–24	75	15:15	66, 80
12:24–26	65, 74, 75	15:16	65, 69
12:25	53	15:18—16:24	69
12:26	53, 66, 74	15:18–25	221
12:44	66	15:18–21	236
12:45	66	15:18–20	69
13–21	54, 55	15:20	74, 75, 80, 186
13:21—21:25	62	15:21–25	71
13–17	50, 60, 68, 69	15:26–27	69
13–14	57	15:26	128
13:1–15	74, 75	15:27	65, 75
13:1b–3	57	16:2	69
13:1	55	16:4–24	69
13:3	233	16:4	54
13:6	54, 80	16:7	128
13:12–20	57	16:20	176
13:12–17	66	16:21	54
13:14	54	16:25–33	69
13:16	186	16:33	125, 137

Scripture Index

John *(continued)*

17	70–71, 72
17:1	72
17:2	73
17:3	74
17:4	72
17:6–8	70
17:6	54
17:7	54, 66
17:8	54, 66
17:12	72
17:13–19	231
17:14–16	235
17:15–16	76
17:17	76
17:18	66
17:20–23	70
17:20–21	75
17:21–23	191
17:23	55
17:25–26	70
17:25	54, 66
17:26	55
18–20	58
18:15	54
19:14	127
19:25–27	64, 67
19:26	55
19:31–36	127
19:34	140
19:37	87
20–21	68, 70
20	50
20:2–10	67
20:3	54
20:21	66, 128
20:23	65, 70
20:25	54
20:29–31	55
20:30–31	50
20:31	71, 74
21	57
21:1–6	70
21:7	54, 67
21:9	54
21:15–23	66
21:15–19	101
21:15–17	140
21:15	158
21:19	74
21:22	74
21:24	67

Acts

1:9–11	153
2:18	80
3:14	103
4:27	103
4:29	80
4:30	103
4:31	93
5:41	92
6:2	93
6:7	93
7:52	175
7:56	95
8:14	93
8:25	93
9:1	112
9:5	112
10:42	213
11:1	93
12:24	93
13:5	93
13:33	102
13:44	93
13:48–49	93
13:50	112
14:2	112
14:5	112
14:15	90
14:19	112
14:22	137
15:35–36	93
17:5	112
17:13	93
18:11	93
19:10	93
19:20	93

Romans

1:1	81
1:3	102, 125

Scripture Index

1:5	151	4:5	41
1:6	183	4:10	41
1:17	43	6:16	117, 151, 205
2:6	213	8:1–5	41
2:16	213	8:9	41
5:3	137	10:1	41
6:4	205	11:2	188
6:17	81	13:4	41
6:22	81	13:5	113
8:17	205		
8:30	190	### Galatians	
9:24	190		
9:26	90	1:10	81
10:3	43	2:20	205
11:3	175	3:13	81
12:1	138	4:4–5	81
12:11	81	4:26	158
12:19	198, 233		
16:5	165	### Ephesians	
		1:3–14	120
### 1 Corinthians		2:5	205
1:9	190	2:8–10	189
1:24	183	2:19–22	117
3:16–17	117, 192	2:21	151
3:16	151	3:4	85
5:1	151	4:15	234
6:19	151	5:22–33	188
6:20	81	5:26	231
7:23	81	6:9	81
11:1	43, 237		
12–14	3	### Philippians	
12:2	151		
12:7	225	1:1	81
12:12–30	43	1:11	42
14:3	225	1:19	42
14:31	225	2:5–11	42, 44
14:36	93	2:8–11	129
15:4	153	2:9–11	174
15:54	125	2:12b–13	42
16:15	165	3:2	218
		3:17	40
### 2 Corinthians		4:3	116
1:5	41	### Colossians	
1:24	41		
2:17	93	1:13	102
4:2	93	1:15–17	105

Scripture Index

Colossians (continued)

1:18	105
2:20	205
3:1	205
3:24	81
4:16	85

1 Thessalonians

1:8	93
1:9–10	102
2:15	175
3:13	196
4:5	151
4:15	93
4:16–17	153
4:17	88
5:27	85

2 Thessalonians

1:7–11	213
1:7–8	193
1:7	196
1:9–10	194
2:3	137
2:14	190

1 Timothy

1:15	190
3:1	190
4:9	190
6:15	197

2 Timothy

2:11	190

Titus

3:8	190

Hebrews

1:1–3	99
1:5	102
5:5	102
6:4–6	117
10:26–31	117
10:33–34	113
11	41
11:2	122
11:15	113
11:35–37	175
12:1	41
12:2	153, 233
12:22–24	158
12:23	116
13:20	139

James

1:12	113
1:22	86
5:9	110

1 Peter

1:16	100, 232
2:9	183
2:12	151
2:18–25	42
2:21	40
2:25	139
4:12	137, 171
5:4	139

2 Peter

2:20–22	117
3:9	219
3:11–14	213
4:4	152

1 John

2:20	103
3:12	129
5:4–5	120
5:4	109
5:9	82

Scripture Index

3 John

7	151
12	82

Jude

6	152
14	196

Revelation

1	89, 99, 111, 143
1:1–20	78, 79–100, 157, 212
1:1–3	212
1:1–2	214, 234
1:1	10, 79–80, 81, 83, 86, 128, 212, 225
1:2	82, 83, 230
1:2b	85
1:3	84, 85, 86, 93, 178, 212, 214, 216, 234
1:3a	85
1:3b	85, 86
1:3c	86
1:4	10, 102
1:4a–5a	84
1:5–6	139
1:5	97, 99, 104, 105, 108, 114, 120, 183, 230, 236
1:5a	92, 103
1:5b–8	84
1:6	92, 136, 151, 212
1:7	87–88, 99, 158, 212, 227
1:8	89, 206, 212, 213
1:9	82, 83, 84, 99, 111, 137, 142, 152, 188, 230, 233
1:9a	91, 92
1:9b	92, 93
1:10	94
1:11	81, 93, 94, 231
1:12–20	94, 100, 103, 104, 119
1:12–16	81, 89, 94, 98, 100, 198, 232
1:12	97
1:12b	94
1:13–15	95
1:13	94, 95, 101, 198, 232
1:14	103, 194, 198, 232
1:14a	95
1:14b	96, 101
1:15	94, 96
1:15a	96, 101, 103
1:15b	97
1:16	97, 101, 193, 198, 232
1:16a	97, 101
1:16b	97, 100, 102, 103
1:16c	98
1:17	99
1:17a	89, 94
1:17b–18	94
1:17b	89–90, 101
1:18	87, 89, 95, 99, 127, 158, 212, 227
1:18a	90
1:18b	90, 101, 103
1:18c	90
1:19–20	94
1:19	81, 93, 99, 100, 231, 232
1:20	97
2–3	81, 88, 94, 209, 224, 227, 228, 232
2:1—3:22	78, 100–121, 119
2:1	93, 107, 108, 198, 231, 232
2:1b	101
2:2–3	92, 188
2:2	105
2:3	101
2:4	101, 106
2:5	88, 101, 117, 177, 181
2:7	87, 107, 109, 119, 124, 171, 180, 204, 227, 228
2:7b	109
2:8	93, 107, 108, 198, 231, 232
2:8b	101
2:9–10	152, 233
2:9	111, 120, 137, 142
2:9b	112
2:10–11	124
2:10	108, 109, 112, 113, 120, 123, 137, 142, 183, 188, 209, 233
2:10c	113
2:10d	101

267

Scripture Index

Revelation (continued)

2:11	87, 107, 109, 119, 124, 171, 180, 200, 227, 228
2:12	93, 107, 108, 198, 231
2:12b	102
2:13	84, 99, 102, 107, 108, 109, 113, 114, 120, 152, 183, 188, 198, 228, 230, 232, 236
2:13b	102
2:13c	114
2:15–16	193
2:16	88, 177, 181, 212
2:17	87, 107, 109, 115–116, 117, 121, 124, 135, 171, 180, 227, 228–229
2:18	93, 94, 96, 107, 193, 194, 198, 231, 232
2:18b	102
2:19	105, 106, 108, 109–110, 188, 209, 228, 234
2:20–23	102
2:20	79, 80, 118, 121, 177, 212, 225
2:22	181
2:23	213
2:25–26	107
2:26–28	109, 171, 228
2:26–27	159
2:26	124, 180, 204
2:27	139
2:29	87, 107, 119, 227
3:1	93, 105, 107, 108, 117, 198, 231, 232
3:1a	102
3:3	86, 93, 107, 177, 178, 181, 200
3:4–5	179, 197, 225
3:4	95, 117, 118, 121, 179, 183, 202, 209
3:5	96, 109, 116, 117, 123, 124, 134, 171, 180, 199, 228, 229, 235
3:6	87, 107, 108, 119, 227
3:7	93, 104, 107, 198, 231, 232
3:7b	103
3:8	86, 93, 105, 107, 209
3:9–10	92
3:9a	104
3:10	86, 93, 104, 107, 113–114, 120, 146, 188, 209, 233
3:11	88, 103, 212
3:12	109, 115–117, 121, 124, 135, 151, 171, 180, 191, 204, 228
3:13	87, 107, 119, 227
3:14–22	120
3:14	93, 99, 104, 107, 108, 114, 194, 198, 230, 231, 232
3:14b	104
3:17–18	120
3:17	104, 112, 200, 229
3:18	95, 105, 171, 179, 225
3:19	110, 177, 181
3:20	87, 110–111, 158, 212, 227
3:21	109, 123, 124, 127, 171, 180, 209, 228
3:22	87, 107, 119, 227
4–22	81
4–5	122, 224
4:1—5:14	78, 121–131, 130
4	122
4:1–14	102
4:1–2	121, 154
4:3—5:14	121
4:3	94
4:4	95, 122, 197
4:4a	122–123
4:4b	122–123
4:5	102
4:6	94, 170
4:7	94
4:8	121
4:9	90
4:10–11	121, 122, 123
4:10	90, 122, 134, 147, 235
4:11	130
5	122
5:5–14	124
5:5–13	200
5:5–10	159
5:5–6	158, 166

Scripture Index

5:5	87, 122, 123, 124, 158, 193, 200, 212, 214, 227	7:1–8	132, 133, 136, 146
5:5b	124, 125	7:1	132
5:5c	126	7:2–3	132
5:6–14	158	7:2	115, 132, 134, 188, 235
5:6–10	185	7:3–8	160, 167
5:6	102, 122, 124, 125, 126, 127, 128, 227	7:3	79, 80, 115, 132, 134, 135, 136, 212, 225, 235
5:6a	126, 127	7:4–9	160
5:6b	127	7:4	115, 134, 135, 235
5:7–8a	129	7:5	115, 134, 235
5:8–14	121, 122, 123, 227	7:8	115, 134, 235
5:8	122, 123, 130–131	7:9–17	132, 133, 141, 142, 158
5:9–14	127	7:9–10	118, 137
5:9–12	130	7:9	96, 119, 132, 134, 139, 143, 144, 197, 205, 235
5:9–10	129, 139, 162, 167, 173	7:11–12	138
5:9	81, 124, 125, 126, 128, 129, 131, 139, 162, 163, 165, 205, 227	7:11	134, 147, 235
		7:13–17	141
		7:13–14	119, 123, 138, 197
5:10	123, 130, 131, 136, 151	7:13	134, 164, 235
5:11–14	121	7:14	134, 137–138, 141–142, 144, 164, 189, 202, 217, 235
5:11	122		
5:12–13	129, 130		
5:12	124, 125, 129, 227	7:15–17	203, 225
5:13–14	130	7:15	136, 138, 139, 141, 142, 205
5:13	130		
5:14	122, 129, 134, 147, 235	7:16	140, 142–143
6–8	132	7:17	127, 139, 140–141, 142, 144, 166, 183, 225
6:1—8:5	78, 131–144, 143		
6:1–14	132	7:17a	139
6:2	96, 188	7:17b	139, 142
6:4	188, 200	8–10	224
6:8	188	8:1–5	132
6:9–11	90, 123, 131	8:2	188
6:9–10	176	8:3–5	176
6:9	83, 93, 99, 115, 131, 152, 176, 188, 230	8:3–4	123, 131, 144
		8:3	123, 188
6:10–11	131, 144, 198, 233	8:4	123
6:10	103, 104, 146, 176, 207	8:6—11:19	78, 144–155, 145, 154
6:11	119, 188, 197	8:6—9:21	144
6:12–16	132	8:7–12	148
6:15–17	132	8:7	145
6:15	79, 159	8:8–11	145
6:17	132	8:12	145
7	131, 132, 134, 136–137, 143–144, 151, 160, 167, 183, 233	8:13	146
		9	147
		9:1–11	145
7:1–17	131, 141, 144	9:1	91, 146, 188

269

Revelation *(continued)*

9:2–4	146
9:3	188
9:4	115, 134, 154, 235
9:5	146, 188
9:7–19	145
9:7–11	146
9:7	152
9:9	152
9:10	94
9:11	91, 146
9:13	176
9:15	148
9:19–21	135
9:19	94
9:20–21	147, 154, 230
9:20	134, 147, 148, 235
10:1—11:14	144, 149
10:1–2	149
10:3–4	149
10:4	200
10:5–7	149
10:5	171
10:6	90
10:7	79, 80, 147, 150, 154, 225
10:8	171
10:9	200
11	147
11:1–13	145, 147, 150
11:1	94, 134, 147, 150, 188, 235
11:2	147, 150, 151, 154, 189, 230, 235
11:3–12	154
11:3–10	115
11:3	84, 99, 151
11:4–6	151
11:4	151, 163
11:6	151, 163
11:7	84, 91, 99, 146, 152, 154, 230, 233
11:8–12	236
11:8	147, 153, 154, 235
11:10	146, 163
11:11	153
11:12	153–154, 204
11:13	148, 176
11:13b	148
11:15–19	132, 144
11:15	159
11:16–18	123
11:16	134, 147, 150, 154, 235
11:18	79, 80, 123, 150, 151, 154, 159, 225
12:1—15:4	155
12:1—14:20	78, 155–168, 156, 166, 169
12:1—13:18	156, 167
12	137, 152, 224
12:1–17	138
12:1–6	156
12:1	137, 155, 169, 170
12:3	128, 155, 169, 170, 194
12:4	148
12:5–6	150
12:5	139, 159
12:7	86, 93, 152
12:10	204
12:11	99, 115, 171, 188, 196, 230
12:11a	156
12:11b	156
12:12	146
12:13–17	156, 178
12:14	189
12:17	82, 84, 99, 152, 156, 188, 230, 231
13	152, 156
13:1–10	171, 172
13:1–2	146
13:1	128, 152, 155, 194
13:2	94, 183
13:4	94, 134, 147, 157, 235
13:5–6	180
13:5	189
13:6	151
13:7	123, 156, 157, 172, 189
13:8–10	135
13:8	116, 117, 134, 146, 147, 157, 199, 200, 202, 229, 235
13:9	178
13:10	92, 108, 123, 156, 188
13:11	94, 127, 128, 155

Scripture Index

13:12	134, 146, 147, 157, 180, 235	14:10	156
13:13–14	170, 171	14:11	134, 147, 157, 235
13:14	146, 189	14:12	86, 92, 93, 108, 123, 156, 178, 188, 231
13:15	134, 147, 157, 178, 189, 235	14:13	85, 93, 178, 214, 231
13:16–18	160, 167	14:14–20	157, 168
13:16	79, 134, 235	14:14–16	156, 157, 165
13:17	134, 135, 158, 235	14:14	87, 94, 123, 155, 157, 158, 166, 193, 212, 227
13:18	160, 161	14:17–20	156, 157, 158, 166, 193, 195, 197
14:1—15:4	168	14:18	176
14	156, 160, 165, 183, 196	15–16	170, 171, 224
14:1–5	2, 3, 139, 156, 157, 158, 161, 162, 166, 168, 172, 178, 187	15:1—16:21	78, 168–181, 169, 180
		15	168, 174
14:1	87, 115, 134, 135, 136, 139, 155, 157, 158–159, 160, 193, 212, 227, 235	15:1–8	168
		15:1	155, 168, 169, 170
		15:2–4	168, 172
14:1a	158, 166	15:2	171–172, 178, 228
14:1b	160, 167	15:2a	170
14:1c	160, 167	15:2b–3a	172
14:2–3	158, 187	15:3–4	170, 172, 173, 181
14:2	162	15:3	79, 104, 170, 207, 225
14:2a	161, 162	15:3b–4	173
14:2b	161, 162	15:4	134, 147, 155, 235
14:3–4	129, 159, 162, 163, 165	15:4c	174
14:3	81, 139, 162	15:5–8	168, 174
14:3a	162	15:5	168, 170
14:3b	162, 163, 167	15:6	170, 197
14:4–5	226	15:7	174
14:4	3, 32, 118, 139, 158, 159, 160, 162, 163, 165, 166, 183, 197, 225, 238	15:8	168, 170
		16–17	184
		16	168, 169, 177, 179
14:4a–5	166	16:1–21	168, 174
14:4a	163, 167	16:1	204
14:4b	164, 167	16:2–4	175
14:4c	164, 165, 166, 167	16:2	134, 147, 173, 180, 181, 235
14:5	165–166, 167		
14:6–13	156, 168	16:4–11	130
14:6–11	168	16:5–7	174
14:6	146, 155, 205	16:5–6	175
14:7–11	130	16:5	176
14:7	134, 147, 157, 235	16:5a	175
14:8–11	161	16:5b	175
14:8	151	16:6	123, 175, 176, 180, 233
14:9–11	135, 161, 167	16:6a	175
14:9	134, 147, 157, 235	16:6b	175
14:10–11	200, 210	16:7	104, 176

271

Revelation (continued)

16:8–9	177	18:1–24	181
16:8	189	18:1–3	184
16:9–11	175	18:2	202
16:9	170, 176–177, 181, 230	18:4–8	184
16:11	176–177, 181, 230	18:4	182
16:12	178, 181	18:6	184
16:14	152, 170, 178	18:9–19	184
16:15	85, 178, 183, 212, 214, 225, 227	18:9–10	184
		18:9	88
16:15a	178, 181	18:10	147, 153
16:15b	178–179, 181	18:11–17a	184
16:16	178	18:16	147, 153, 192
16:17	204	18:17b–19	184
16:17a	180	18:18–19	147, 153
16:17b–21a	180	18:18	94
16:19	147, 153	18:20	123, 182, 184, 185, 186
16:21	130, 177, 230	18:21–24	184
16:21b	180	18:21	147, 153
17:1—20:15	78	18:22	161
17:1—19:8	190	18:24	123, 182, 186
17:1—19:5	78, 181–186	19–22	132, 191
17–18	169	19–21	192
17	152	19–20	191
17:1–18	181	19	195, 198, 201
17:1–3	182	19:1–10	154
17:2	146	19:1–6	198, 232
17:3	128	19:1–5	181, 185
17:4–6	182	19:1–3	185
17:4	225	19:1	185
17:5	195	19:2	79, 80, 104, 182, 185, 186, 212, 225
17:6	82, 84, 99, 115, 152, 182, 186, 230	19:4	123, 134, 147, 185, 202, 235
17:7–14	182	19:5	79, 80, 182, 185, 186, 204, 212, 225
17:7	128		
17:8	91, 116, 117, 134, 146, 199, 229, 235	19:5c	197
		19:6—20:15	79, 186–202, 201
17:12–14	182	19:6–9	186, 201
17:12	128, 183	19:6–8	186
17:13	163, 183	19:6	187
17:14	108, 163, 183, 186, 188, 190, 192, 193, 196, 197, 229	19:7–9	186–187, 189, 190, 191, 192
		19:7–8	189
17:15–18	184	19:7	187, 225
17:16	128, 183	19:7b	187–188, 193
17:17	83	19:8–9	179, 225
17:18	147, 153	19:8	119, 123, 193, 197, 199, 202

Scripture Index

Reference	Pages
19:8a	188
19:8b	189
19:9–10	186
19:9	85, 93, 104, 163, 178, 189–191, 201, 214, 231
19:9a	189, 190, 193
19:10	82, 99, 134, 147, 201, 202, 212, 215, 225, 230, 235
19:10a	190, 193
19:10b	190
19:10c	193
19:11–21	183, 187
19:11–16	193–194, 202, 232
19:11	87, 96, 104, 108, 180, 193, 198, 212, 227, 232
19:11b	194
19:12	115, 198, 232
19:12a	194
19:12b	194
19:13	196
19:13a	195
19:13b	196
19:14	32, 95, 196
19:15	139, 151, 159, 197, 232
19:15a	196, 197
19:15b	197
19:15c	197
19:16	159, 197–198
19:16b	195, 196
19:17–21	195
19:17–18	190
19:17	186, 191, 201
19:18	79, 199
19:19	83, 152
19:20	91, 134, 147, 170, 202, 235
19:21	188
20:1–10	187
20:1–3	91
20:1	146
20:3	151, 188
20:4	82, 83, 99, 134, 147, 152, 188, 189, 202, 230, 235
20:5	163
20:6	85, 151, 178, 200, 202, 214, 216
20:7	187
20:8	152
20:9	123, 151, 201
20:10	91, 138, 200, 210
20:11–15	170, 187
20:11–14	213
20:11	198
20:12–13	198, 200
20:12	116, 134, 200, 202, 229, 235
20:12a	198
20:12b	199
20:12c	199
20:13–14	90, 91, 199
20:13	199–200
20:14–15	91
20:14	163, 200
20:15	116, 117, 134, 199, 200, 202, 217, 229, 235
21–22	224, 233, 234
21:1—22:5	79, 92, 141, 203–211, 210
21	203, 212
21:1–6	209, 211
21:1–5	207
21:1–4	211
21:1	203, 206
21:2–3	191, 192
21:2	151, 186, 191, 192, 201, 203, 204
21:3–8	203, 204, 210
21:3	87, 182, 203, 204, 205, 210, 212, 224, 226, 227
21:3a	204
21:3b	205
21:4–5	226
21:4	203, 209
21:4a	206
21:4b	206
21:5–8	206
21:5	87, 93, 104, 108, 163, 204, 206–207, 210, 211, 212, 227, 231
21:5a	207
21:5b	206
21:6–7	140, 225
21:6	89, 140, 203, 206, 213, 228
21:6b	207, 213
21:6c	207, 208
21:7–8	117, 192, 211

Revelation *(continued)*

21:7	140, 192, 203, 210, 211, 229
21:7a	209
21:7b	208
21:8	91, 200, 203, 209, 210, 211, 217, 218
21:9–27	203, 204
21:9–14	192
21:9–11	203
21:9	186, 191, 201, 212
21:10	151
21:11	94
21:12–14	122, 193
21:15	212
21:18–21	186, 192
21:18	94
21:22	141, 203, 210
21:24–26	192
21:24	151, 192
21:26	151, 192, 203
21:27	116, 134, 199, 200, 202, 210, 211, 218, 229, 235
22:1–5	203
22:1	140, 207, 212, 225
22:2	151, 203, 204, 207
22:3–4	135
22:3	79, 80, 203, 210, 212, 217, 225
22:4	115, 134, 136, 203, 210, 235
22:5	304
22:6–21	79, 211–221, 212
22:6–7	211, 212
22:6	79, 80, 104, 108, 128, 163, 207, 212, 225
22:7	85, 86, 87, 93, 178, 212–213, 214, 220, 221, 227, 234
22:7b	214
22:8–11	211
22:8–9	134, 147, 235
22:8	10
22:8a	215
22:8b–9	215
22:9	86, 93, 212, 214, 215, 221, 225
22:10–12	213
22:10–11	176
22:10	86, 212, 215
22:11	134, 212, 215–216, 217, 235
22:12–20	211
22:12–19	212
22:12	87, 212–213, 217, 220, 227
22:13	89, 90, 212, 221, 228
22:14–15	216, 221
22:14	85, 134, 178, 189, 200, 202, 212, 214, 216–218, 235
22:14a	216
22:14b	217
22:15	134, 217–218, 235
22:16	125, 219
22:16b	214, 220
22:17–18	117
22:17	186, 201, 212, 218, 228
22:17a	220
22:17b	219, 221
22:18–19	82, 214, 219
22:18	82, 220
22:19	151, 220
22:20	99, 212, 219, 230
22:20a	220
22:20b	220
22:21	211, 220

www.ingramcontent.com/pod-product-compliance
Lightning Source LLC
Chambersburg PA
CBHW070237230426
43664CB00014B/2336